Legal Method

Cavendish
Publishing
Limited

London • Sydney

First published in Great Britain 1999 by Cavendish Publishing Limited, The Glass House, Wharton Street, London WC1X 9PX, United Kingdom

Telephone: +44 (0) 171 278 8000   Facsimile: +44 (0) 171 278 8080

e-mail: info@cavendishpublishing.com

Visit our Home Page on http://www.cavendishpublishing.com

© Hanson, S 1999

Reprinted 2001

Hanson, Sharon

Legal Method
1. Law – England 2. Law – Wales
I. Title

349.4′2

ISBN 1 85941 424 9

ınd bound in Great Britain

Legal Method

Sharon Hanson, LLB, MA
Director of the Certificate in Legal Method
Birkbeck College, University of London

Cavendish
Publishing
Limited

London • Sydney

TABLE OF CONTENTS

HOW TO USE THIS TEXT

Successful legal study depends upon holding the following skills in tension:

(a) excellent language skills;

(b) thorough knowledge of the relevant area of law;

(c) highly competent argument identification, construction and evaluation skills.

The primary focus of this legal method book will be the legal text. Texts *of* the law (statutes, law reports) and texts *about* the law (textbooks, journals, articles) will be the objects of analysis. They will be studied in order to understand the construction of legal rules, to acquire skills of argument construction, analysis and critique, to appreciate links in the texts, and to use this knowledge to solve practical and theoretical legal problems.

Too often, students are not clearly informed at the beginning of studies of the full extent of the skills required. Even when they are informed, students seem to forget. They are too busy memorising the obviously relevant to waste time trying to understand as well! Frequently, memorising becomes a comfortable tranquilliser protecting the student from the productive pain of fighting with incomprehension to reach a place of partial understanding. Sadly, within the discipline of law, successful memorising often merely ensures failure as the student knows it all and yet understands nothing.

The majority of books on the market that deal with method, that is, the way in which legal rules are used to resolve certain types of disputes, do so in the context of legal process. Inevitably many of these books tend to be weighted in favour of explicating the English legal system, its processes, personnel and doctrines. They do not give an appreciation of how to break into texts, often tending to veer between English legal system and legal theory, with some study skills and library usage information.

Although this text acknowledges the complexities of legal rules and the construction of arguments, it also attempts, in a user friendly manner, to make interrelationships clear and to allow the commencement of the task of seeing arguments and using them.

Essentially, it is a book about thinking and the acquisition of skills and, as such, relies on reader reflection.

My objective in producing this book was to provide a usable manual: the text draws a map to enable students to reach a place of understanding where they can recall relevant memorised knowledge and apply it, or interpret it confidently with a clear comprehension of the interrelationships between rules, arguments, and language, in the search for plausible solutions to real or imaginary problems.

This text is not a philosophical enquiry that asks why English law prefers the methods of reasoning it has adopted. Although such texts are of the utmost importance, they will mean more to the student who has first acquired a thorough competency in a narrow field of legal method and practical reason. Then, a philosophical argument will be appreciated, considered, evaluated and either accepted or rejected. Nor is this a book that critiques itself, or engages in a post-modern reminder that what we know and see is only a chosen, constructed fragment of what may be the truth. Although self-critique is a valid enterprise, a fragmentary understanding of 'the whole' is all that can ever be grasped.

This is a 'how to do' text; a practical manual. As such, it will concern itself primarily with the issues of

How to ...

(a) develop awareness of the importance of understanding the influence and power of language;

(b) read and understand texts talking *about* the law;

(c) read and understand texts *of* law (law cases; legislation (in the form of primary legislation or secondary, statutory instruments, bye laws, etc), European legislation (in the form of regulations, directives, opinions, etc));

(d) identify, construct and evaluate arguments;

(e) use texts about the law and texts of the law and the ability to construct arguments to produce plausible solutions to problems (real or hypothetical, in the form of essays, case studies, questions, practical problems);

(f) make comprehensible the interrelationships between cases and statutes, disputes and legal rules, primary and secondary texts;

(g) search for intertextual pathways to lay bare the first steps in argument identification;

(h) identifying the relationship of the text being read to those texts produced before or after it.

The chapters are intended to be read, initially, in order as material in earlier chapters will be used to reinforce points made later. Indeed, all the chapters are leading to the final section which concentrates on piecing together a range of skills and begins to offer solutions to legal problems. There is often more than one solution to a legal problem. Judges make choices when attempting to apply the law. *The study of law is about critiquing the choices made, as well as critiquing the rules themselves.*

However, individual chapters can also be looked at in isolation by readers seeking to understand specific issues such as how to read a law report, or how to begin to construct an argument.

The text as a whole will introduce students to the value of alternatives to purely textual explanations. An ability to comprehend diagrammatic explanations will be encouraged. Diagrams present another way of seeing, and the sheer novelty value of seeing the interconnections in a diagram can sometimes be enough to change confusion into comprehension.

The numerous diagrams used here are integral to the successful understanding of legal method as presented in this text.

They have been specifically designed to:

(a) provide a way of taking students to deeper levels of understanding;

(b) give a basic description or blueprint for an area;

(c) demonstrate interconnections between seemingly disconnected areas/texts/skills.

To emphasis the value of diagrams, Figure 1, below, illustrates the layout of this legal method text.

The text is divided into four parts.

Part I: language skills

Part II: handling primary legal texts

Part III: handling secondary texts, information generally

Part IV: putting it all together   –   the mechanics of argument construction

– using legal rules to construct arguments to solve legal problems

– using knowledge of legal rules and secondary texts to deal with theoretical and practical questions.

Where specific materials are required to be read, these will be found in Part V, Appendices 1–6.

Patient study will be rewarded by clear progress in substantive law areas.

If students work through the text methodically, they *will* reach a place of understanding, where they know how to competently present arguments. They can then develop these skills during the course of their studies.

> **Legal study and intellectual discipline come with a cost. It is an often costly struggle to reach a place of understanding. However, to demonstrate a good level of competency in legal study is within the grasp of everyone.**

Figure 1: the layout of this legal method text

LAYOUT OF TEXT

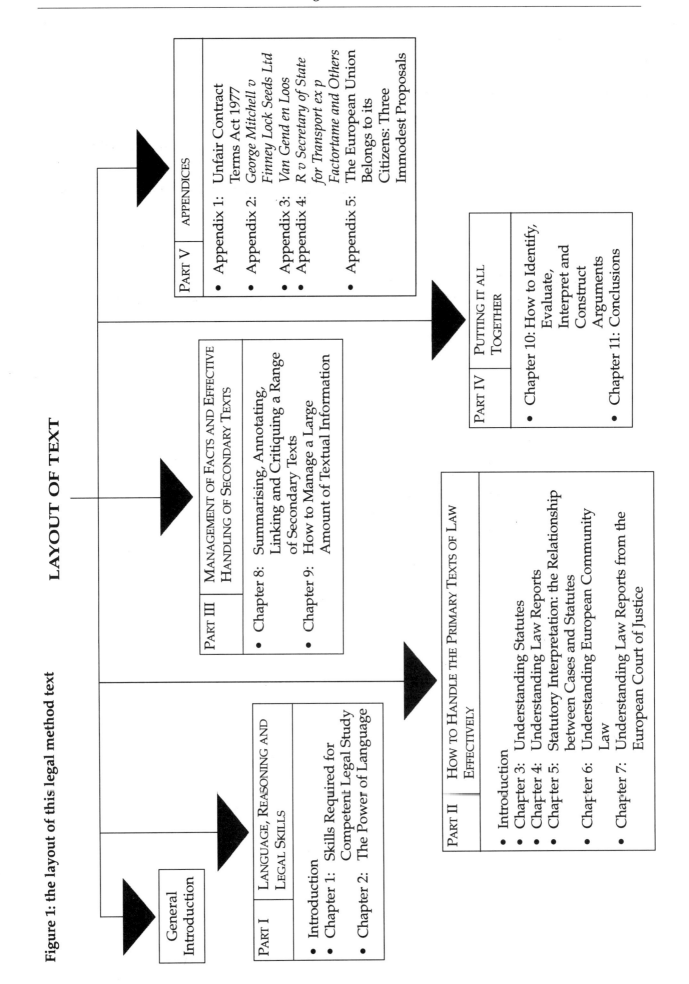

General Introduction

PART I — LANGUAGE, REASONING AND LEGAL SKILLS
- Introduction
- Chapter 1: Skills Required for Competent Legal Study
- Chapter 2: The Power of Language

PART II — HOW TO HANDLE THE PRIMARY TEXTS OF LAW EFFECTIVELY
- Introduction
- Chapter 3: Understanding Statutes
- Chapter 4: Understanding Law Reports
- Chapter 5: Statutory Interpretation: the Relationship between Cases and Statutes
- Chapter 6: Understanding European Community Law
- Chapter 7: Understanding Law Reports from the European Court of Justice

PART III — MANAGEMENT OF FACTS AND EFFECTIVE HANDLING OF SECONDARY TEXTS
- Chapter 8: Summarising, Annotating, Linking and Critiquing a Range of Secondary Texts
- Chapter 9: How to Manage a Large Amount of Textual Information

PART IV — PUTTING IT ALL TOGETHER
- Chapter 10: How to Identify, Evaluate, Interpret and Construct Arguments
- Chapter 11: Conclusions

PART V — APPENDICES
- Appendix 1: Unfair Contract Terms Act 1977
- Appendix 2: George Mitchell v Finney Lock Seeds Ltd
- Appendix 3: Van Gend en Loos
- Appendix 4: R v Secretary of State for Transport ex p Factortame and Others
- Appendix 5: The European Union Belongs to its Citizens: Three Immodest Proposals

PART I

THE RELATIONSHIP BETWEEN LANGUAGE, REASONING SKILLS AND LEGAL STUDIES

PART I

THE RELATIONSHIP BETWEEN LANGUAGE, REASONING SKILLS AND LEGAL STUDIES

INTRODUCTION: THE AIM OF PART I

Part I highlights the importance of appreciating language, in terms of the power that it exerts, its potential for interpretation and, therefore, its flexibility. Acquiring an appreciation of the range of skills that need to be competently demonstrated is vital in order to engage in successful legal study and this range will be looked at here.

As will be repeatedly demonstrated in this text, students of law have to be competent:

(a) users of language (both oral and written);

(b) researchers of legal rules (found in texts *of* law and texts *about* the law);

(c) deconstructors of arguments (taking arguments apart and breaking them into their constituent parts);

(d) constructors of arguments (they must be able to put arguments together).

Competency, as a law student, involves a balance between all of the above skills: language usage (reading, writing and speaking); research; argument evaluation and interpretation; and argument construction.

Chapter 1 briefly describes approaches to ways of thinking and seeing the world and discusses, in more detail, the range of skills involved in legal study and their interrelationships. Time is also spent discussing the range of texts that students will encounter in legal study. The major argument of Chapter 1 is that the combination of critical thinking and excellence in a range of skills is necessary for successful legal study.

Chapter 2 takes time to consider the power that users of language can exert through language and the residual power that language has, by virtue of its existence over time. We are born into a community of language users. Language imposes, often unconsciously, pre-determined ways of seeing and thinking about the world. These are 'taken-for-granted' assumptions. They are not questioned; they have 'always been there', therefore, they are 'true', 'right', the 'way of doing or thinking about things'. It is assumed, by their very familiarity, that these assumptions reflect reality without distortion.

The main argument of Chapter 2 is that language is never neutral, perhaps especially when its users say that it is! A number of examples are taken from religious, political and legal texts to illustrate this argument.

CHAPTER 1

SKILLS REQUIRED FOR COMPETENT LEGAL STUDY

INTRODUCTION

Studying is about learning: learning about self, academic subject areas and how to learn. New information about subjects, ideas, ways of seeing, arguing and thinking have to be understood, evaluated and used.

The *Shorter Oxford English Dictionary* refers to 'learning' as the obtaining of knowledge about a skill or an art, through study, experience or teaching. Study is defined in several ways. Perhaps the definition that sums up the view of many students is as follows:

... a state of mental perplexity or anxious thought.

A more standard definition is also given as:

... mental application for the acquisition of some kind of learning.

Studying is also referred to as an act or as action.

SO –

**studying is not a passive thing,
it is dynamic and interactive.**

Many students see studying as passive, as a process of soaking up and memorising what is, hopefully, just handed out by the teacher. It is, therefore, not seen as an engaged active process of searching for other ideas, weighing up possibilities and alternatives, criticising and evaluating.

Developing critical thinking

Everyday, all the time, information is received, processed, evaluated, ignored or acted upon by the human brain. This information is received via all the senses: hearing; seeing; touching; smelling. It is processed in microseconds, often without conscious awareness of the process of:

(a) receiving information;

(b) evaluating information;

(c) taking action based on evaluation:

- doing nothing;
- doing something;
- storing information for later use.

If the information is not received, evaluated and acted upon in some way, even if the receiver just decides to ignore it, it would not be possible for the human organism to function.

Sometimes, the action taken is, in part, based on guesswork; for example:

(a) the saucepan handle has been left hanging over a heated hot plate;

(b) the handle on that saucepan is hot;

(c) is it too hot to hold for a few moments to move it?;

(d) it has not been over the heat for too long;

(e) therefore, it is probably not too hot;

(f) I will lift it.

      OUCH!!

(Well, you can't always guess correctly!)

Given that everyday life is a process of receipt of information, evaluation and action, it is obvious that learning an academic subject is no exception to the normal rhythms of life (receipt, evaluation, action).

One important characteristic of highly competent people is that, in many areas of their lives, they have developed a critical approach to what they do, see and think: they are *critical thinkers*.

Not critical in the sense of 'fault finding' but critical in the sense of:

> **... exercising careful judgements based upon careful observation, investigation and consideration of issues relevant to the matter about which a judgment is to be made.**

Such people are always searching for the hidden assumptions behind what others just call common sense or everyday accepted ways of acting or thinking. They are aware of diversity in values and behaviour. They locate underlying assumptions and ask whether these fit in with current notions of social reality. These assumptions are then carefully dissected and their accuracy, as well as their validity, questioned.

Critical thinkers take nothing for granted. Once they have located underlying assumptions, these competent individuals consider alternative ways of acting and alternative assumptions to back these new ways of acting. For critical thinkers, nothing is closed, fixed, certain. Everything is potentially flexible, open and possible. They are always asking: what is it that lies behind the ideas, beliefs, actions that people hold or take?

This is not to say that critical thinkers hold no strong views or cannot believe in anything because they are of the view that everything is essentially open to question. It is possible to hold the strongest convictions that something is right, while accepting that there can be alternative views. These people can always imagine another plausible story or explanation or value. They are not going to believe in universal truths without thorough investigation and, indeed, will probably always remain healthily sceptical of universal views, truths and explanations.

Consider, for a moment, what happens when a law case goes to trial. There are two sides, both strenuously arguing that they are right. The court decides in favour of one party, but there is still the alternative view of the party that 'lost'. In all court cases, two explanations of what happened compete for acceptance as the official version. The official view is an interpretation of 'what really happened'. In law, as in other areas, there are always other stories. The official view, however, has the institutional authority and power to enforce that view and close the possibility of the other view being acceptable (unless issues are re-opened on appeal).

Considering all possibilities, carefully making judgments, looking for underlying assumptions – this is what it is to think critically. Critical thinking is a *process* over time. Its core is the constant identification and challenging of the accepted. It involves the evaluation of values, beliefs, competing truth explanations and, of course, texts. It involves both rationality/objectivity and emotions/subjectivity.

Some commentators have described the progress towards critical thinking as like the process of waking up, of seeing things differently. Certainly, many students will poetically describe their arrival at understanding as achieving the ability 'to see'.

In academic studies, critical thinking, and a healthy scepticism of universality, are demonstrated by approaches to reasoning. Critical thinkers are, for example, aware that often arguments contain contradictions and these contradictions have to be looked for. They are also able to distinguish between differing types of statement. For example, they can understand the difference between a statement of fact and a statement of opinion. This naturally affects the expertise of their reasoning processes. It makes a great deal of difference whether an argument is based on opinions or facts.

It is essential for students to utilise a critical approach to studies, because this ensures that they:

(a) search for hidden assumptions;

(b) justify assumptions;

(c) judge the rationality of those assumptions;

(d) test the accuracy of those assumptions.

In this way, students ensure proper coverage for each area of their study.

Range of skills required for legal studies and their interrelationships

That a wide range of skills is needed for the study of law should by now be quite clear.

The required skills can be generically grouped into:

(a) general study skills;

(b) language skills;

(c) methodology skills;

(d) substantive legal knowledge skills,

and then subdivided into specifics –this is the best way of discussing them.

General study skills

This text is **not** concerned with the detail of general study skills; there are excellent books on the market that cover them, and these can be found in the bibliography.

However, it is vital to be alerted to the core need for highly competent study skills. Skills under this heading would include:

(a) how study time is managed, 'pre-planning the week';

(b) knowledge of course organisation;

(c) knowledge of the lecture role, small groups timetable;

(d) the development of powers of concentration.

Some students find it physically or emotionally impossible to sit down for two hours or even less and read in a useful, meaningful manner. Concentration is a skill acquired over time; it is a process;

(e) organising a *place* to study;

(f) setting up filing systems for:

- handouts;
- notes made of books, articles, lectures;
- subject specific problem questions, essay questions and past examination papers;

(g) learning to be a highly competent user of the library facilities;

(h) developing computing skills;

(i) developing writing and reading skills (also comes under language and legal method skills);

(j) developing the ability to answer questions (also comes under language and legal method skills).

Language usage skills

Students need to be competent language users. This involves demonstrating a competency in the following areas:

(a) English grammar;

(b) punctuation;

(c) spelling;

(d) vocabulary;

(e) reading;

(f) writing (notes, summaries and extended academic writing);

(g) interpretation of arguments by the analysis of the language in which they are presented.

Again these areas are **not** specifically dealt with in this text but the bibliography makes useful suggestions for further reading.

Legal method skills

These are skills concerning formal ways of understanding and analysing issues relating to the law. Much of this book is concerned with a **few** aspects of legal method; there are many more.

Legal method skills would include:

(a) handling, application and interpretation of law reports;

(b) handling, application and interpretation of UK legislation and delegated legislation;

(c) handling, application and interpretation of European Community legislation and delegated legislation;

(d) argument construction and deconstruction;

(e) answering legal questions, both problem and essays

(f) legal reading and writing skills.

Substantive legal knowledge skills (for example, criminal law, tort)

There is a range of skills to be held in tension and these are set out in diagrammatic form in Figure 1.1 to give another way of seeing the interrelationships between the range of skills. It is possible to divide sub-skills into even smaller constituent parts and the diagram does this merely to illustrate the complex nature of the undertaking of such studies.

This complexity is not peculiar to the law either. If the course being undertaken was life sciences, again one would need similar generic skills:

(a) general study;

(b) language usage skills (and perhaps foreign language skills);

(c) scientific method skills;

(d) understanding of substantive science subjects.

Students who think that it is enough to memorise chunks of their substantive law subjects are unsuccessful. They do not understand the skills required in each of the other three main headings of general study skills, English language skills and method skills and the balance of expertise required among them.

All of these skills need to be identified; students need to know which skills they have a basic competency in, which skills they are deficient in and which skills they are good at. Then, each skill needs to be developed to the student's highest possible competency.

Figure 1.1: diagrammatic representation of skills involved in the study of law

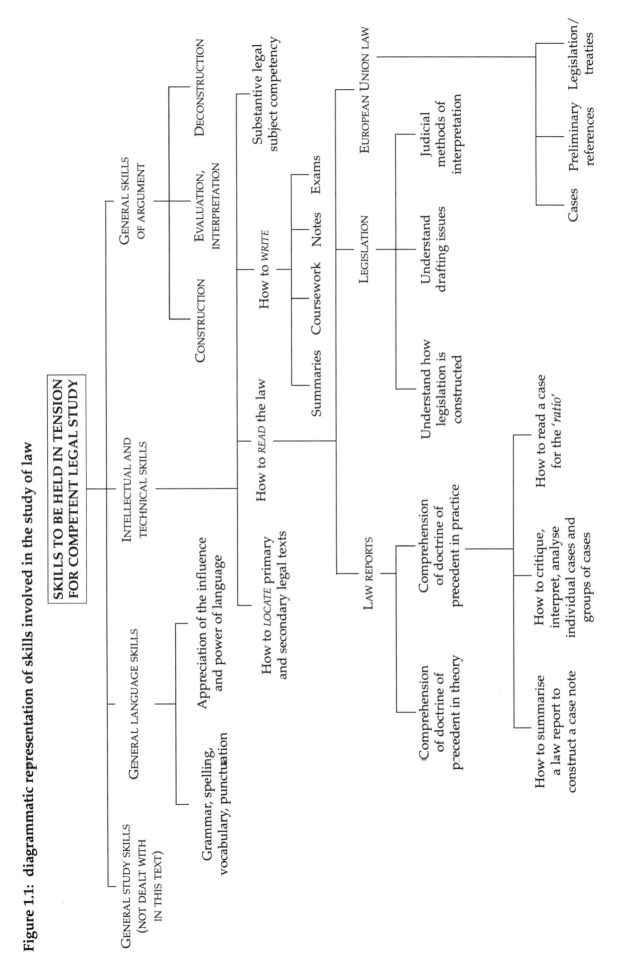

CHAPTER 2

THE POWER OF LANGUAGE

INTRODUCTION

Language, like the air we breathe, surrounds us, and, also like the air we breathe, rarely do we question it. However, at the outset of legal studies it is vital to take an opportunity to consider the potential language has for both the exertion of power and the shaping of ideas. It is important to realise that language is the mediating and shaping structure of law, which is in turn mediated and shaped by users and interpreters of the law.

Desire, goals, experience, raw emotions, pain, happiness, fear, pleasure are all internally processed through language and outwardly communicated through language. Language is a key vehicle through which a person internalises life experiences, thinks about them, tries out alternatives, conceptualises a future and strives towards future goals.

Often people agree that they 'come to know themselves' through language. Through language someone can succinctly put into words the feelings of another. That other relates to that description and takes it for his or her own, usually increasing regard for the speaker. People can be explained through language. A person, using language, can make what is not present seem present. The past described today.

THE RELATIONSHIP BETWEEN LANGUAGE, LAW AND RELIGION

Religion, politics and, of course, law find power in the written and spoken word. Many aspects of English law remain influenced by Christianity. The two books making up the Christian sacred text, the Bible, are the Old Testament and the New Testament. Both have much to say concerning the power that human beings exert through their monopoly of language.

The Old Testament tells the story of the creator, God, giving power to Adam, the first male created by God, to name and possess all that he saw. Similarly, the story of the Tower of Babel, when God removed a unitary language and people could not understand each other, illustrates both the uniting and the dividing power of language in its story of the destruction of common purpose by the removal of linguistic competence.

In the New Testament, a disciple of Christ, called John, announces in the opening words of his text 'The Gospel of John' (meaning, 'God speak', of John) that 'In the beginning was the Word and the Word was God'.

Knowledge of Christian belief would inform a reader that 'Word' in this context stands for the awaited world saviour, the Christ called Jesus Christ, Son of God. So, in stating the above, John is saying more than the superficial message of the words. He is saying Christ, born into the story of the New Testament was present prior to the creation of the world described in the Old Testament. This sentence then testifies to the mystery of all time, as one time, that Christ was the Word and, by implication, God from time immemorial to time unknown, a seamless fabric of eternity caught in each present moment. The emotive power of language begins to exert its influence.

The language of English law, steeped in the language of Christianity, speaks of the 'immemorial' aspects of English law – although the law artificially sets 1189 as the date for 'immemoriality'!

For religion, particularly for religions very much reliant upon written sacred texts, language is a vehicle of immense importance. The Christian story built into the foundation of English law is about the mysterious way in which the 'Word' of God became human, stepping out of eternity into human time and history, to became social action and to become the means of the salvation of the world. The emphasis is on the 'Word' of God becoming human, and the truth of the sacred written texts. Language is of core importance.

What is fascinating is to see how this mystery is replicated in the relationship between law and political authority in Europe and, particularly, in England. Theories of law describe the word of the Sovereign as law. That what is spoken is authority and power, actively creating law; just as God spoke Christ into creation.

Since the 16th century, when Henry VIII's well known dispute with the Holy Catholic Church caused England to move away from an acceptance of the religious and political authority of the Pope, English monarchs have been charged with the role of 'Defender of the Faith'. As an acknowledgment of modern pluralist society, there have recently been suggestions that the Prince of Wales, if he becomes King, should perhaps consider being 'Defender of Faith', leaving it open *which* faith; although the role is tied at present to Anglicanism, that Christian denomination 'established by law'.

English law recognises the Sovereign as the fountain of justice, exercising mercy traceable back to powers given by the Christian God. Indeed, this aspect of the monarch's power, delegated to the Lord Chancellor gave rise to a stream of English law known as equity, that area of law which rectifies the cruelties and injustices of the common law. An area of law where would be litigants must prove their moral worth prior to the hearing of the case.

It can be seen that it is the body of the sovereign that tacitly unites religion, law and politics. It is, of course, the Government that has acquired these powers in reality; the monarch is merely the symbol of their existence.

The English system of secular justice, in terms of personnel, processes and rules is steeped in the Judaeo-Christian justice as interpreted, and mediated through English translations of the Greek translations of the Hebrew and Aramaic of the Bible. A Greek language whose vocabulary is shot through with the philosophy of dualism – light/dark, good/bad, good/evil, male/female, slave/free, gods/humans – a dualism not that apparent in Hebrew and Aramaic. This dualism has entered the law through language.

So language is powerful, it enables the manifestation of the past in the present and the projection of the future into the present. Language thus facilitates easy discussion of complexities like time.

Religious leaders of all persuasions, whose belief is centred on written texts would maintain that it is essential that the words carrying their message are not misunderstood.

Lawyers too, in a similar manner, have tried to prove that the integrity of the judge and/or legislator is carried in the words. A key problem in relation to the integrity of law is the maintenance of certainty *despite* the variability of language.

Some legal doctrines relating to the interpretation of law deny that language has a flexibility, fearing that this would be a sign of its weakness and lack of certainty. Others acknowledge the flexibility of language and look to the legislators intention. This, too, is a search for the mythical as legislation is changed for a variety of reasons during its drafting and creation stages.

The root problem here is the language, not the law, yet the two are intimately connected, for the law is *carried* by the language; so is it not true that the law is the language?

The following illustration of linguistic difficulties that concern translation, interpretation and application initially draws quite deliberately from religion to attempt to break preconceptions about language, and to illustrate the problems arising from the necessarily close relationship between language and law. There will be a return to law shortly.

The Christian religion, rather than any other religion, is being considered because it is the religion that remains today at the core of English law. This is one reason why English law can have, or has had, difficulty with concepts from differing religious traditions that have presented themselves before the courts demanding acceptance and equality.

SACRED TEXTS AND THE PROBLEM OF LANGUAGE

The sacred texts of the Old Testament and the New Testament collected in the Bible have been translated into numerous languages. Many misunderstandings of texts can be caused by mistranslations.

English translations of the Bible are translations of translations. The Aramaic of the original speakers of the Christian message was written in Greek during the first century and from there translated into other languages. The historical Jesus did not, so far as we know, speak to people in Greek; he most likely spoke Aramaic. A few fragments were written in Aramaic. Yet the English translations are made from the 'original' Greek!

The Old Testament was written in Hebrew, yet, again, it is from an 'original Greek translation' of the Hebrew that English translations are prepared.

To suggest why the source of translation might matter is also to illustrate the importance of other readings, other interpretations. Other readings and other interpretations are core issues for lawyers. What do these words mean for this situation rather than what do these words mean for ever.

To illustrate this point within religion the first phrase in the first sentence from a Christian prayer known as the 'Our Father' or 'The Lord's Prayer' will be considered. The English translation found in the 'King James Version' from the 'original' Greek will be compared to an English translation from an Aramaic version dating from 200 AD.

The King James Version of the Bible was developed after much bloodshed in the 17th century, and the Aramaic comparison is derived from Douglas Koltz who tried a reconstitution of the Aramaic from the Greek. This latter translation is, therefore, a little suspect as Aramaic is far more open textured than Greek (or indeed English) as will be discovered. However, the exercise provides a useful illustration of the flexibility of language, as well as the manipulation of language users!

The King James translation from the Greek is as follows:

Our Father which art in heaven. [The Gospel of Matthew, Chapter 6, verse 9.]

The translation from the Aramaic into English is startlingly different:

O Birther! Father-Mother of the Universe.

Suddenly, potential nuances inherent in the words of the suggested original source language, Aramaic, become apparent.

The power of translators to choose words is often not thought of or not seen. Those who rely on translations often do not realise the enormous power they entrust to others to mediate language for them. Even less do readers realise the power entrusted to those who interpret texts. In Aramaic, the sex of God is opened out into male/female, in Greek and hence English the choice is made, male, Father.

Koltz has an agenda which is outside the present discussion. However, the potential paradigm shift involved in considering an English translation from the Aramaic is tremendous and shows the power of language, and the importance of understanding its cultural situation.

The mundane English concept of Father, as God **in** heaven, in the translation from Greek, opens out in the Aramaic translation into 'Birther', potentially, 'Mother/Father.' One of the greatest conflicts of interpretation concerns the relationship between male and female.

The concept 'Heaven', chosen for the Greek and hence the English translation, is taken to be that particular place of God. In Aramaic, it opens out into 'Universe' a cosmology of infinite size and one in which we and the universe are in an osmotic relationship with all that is created and all that is the creator God.

For a person who has a religious belief, the idea of Gods or deities, the concept of the will of God and of situation and place in the universe are largely formulated by both word and experience.

Experience is inevitably communicated to others by *word* as well as by action, and the concept of 'word' (as has already been noted) is incorporated into the notion of the Christian God in the reference to John's Gospel 'In the beginning was the word' and this is itself a reference back to the beginning of Genesis, the first book in the Old Testament – 'In the beginning was the word' – the two sacred texts are thereby linked together, they are hermeneutically sealed.

The following diagram, Figure 2.1, demonstrates the openness of Aramaic to suggest fuller meanings that may possibly be attributed to this single, ordinary English sentence as translated from the Greek. It soon becomes apparent that the English does not capture the full sense.

Figure 2.1: diagrammatic representation of the shades of meaning attributed to 'Our father who art in heaven' in the Aramaic rendering of Abwoon d'bwashmaya

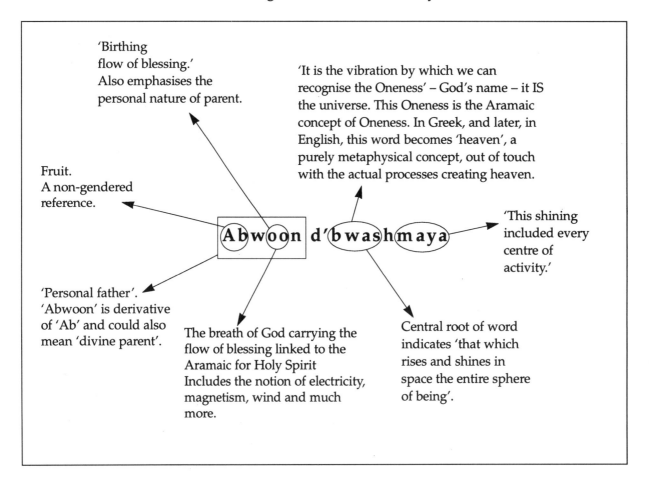

The impoverishment of the English text is shocking by comparison and even the latest version of the New Testament, 'The message' (1996) from the Greek reads:

Father, reveal who you are. Set the world right.

Lawyers and legal theorists, like priests and theologians put interpretations upon the meaning of words and phrases. Both professions engage in a creativity that is unimaginable in the traditional explanations of what they are doing.

LANGUAGE AND WORLD CONSTRUCTION

Both law and religion share a striking similarity. Both contain rules in verbal form which are formal, authoritative, to be obeyed and of the highest authority. Both deal in rules and stories which shape world views, which construct cosmologies. Law finds its sources in legal cases decided by the judges over time, in Acts of a Parliament that has inherited its power from the monarch, and in the body of the monarch itself which contains the promises of both God and people. Today, law also finds its sources in the legislative acts of the European Community.

All our understanding is reducible to the ability to comprehend the expansiveness and limits of our language and the cultural boundedness of our language. It was Edward Sapir who most poignantly maintained that the limits of our language are the limits of our world. Within a religious world view and non-religious world view, there are constant conflicts of language interpretation. For example, between a God-centred and a human-centred cosmos; between God's laws and man's laws.

Over the years of socialisation, 'ways of seeing' are developed that are socially constructed by the limits of a particular language. Yet, as language is all around, there is a temptation to see it as a neutral tool, a mirror that tells it 'like it is'.

All language does is to give someone else's interpretation of *their* belief, or *their* experience. It is no more, and no less, than a guide to social reality. What is seen as, or believed to be, the real world may be no more than the language habits of the group.

Languages also have their limits, if language does not have a word for something or some concept then that 'something' will not be seen nor that 'concept' thought. All language is, however, responsive to what linguists call the 'felt needs' of its speakers. Indeed, it is more likely that not only are thoughts expressed *in* words but that thoughts themselves are *shaped* by language.

An example from the vocabulary of weather provides a good illustration of this point. Although the English are often said to enjoy talking of the weather, for many decades our essentially mild climate has provided us with the need for only one word for 'snow' (that word is 'snow'!). In English there are several words for cold, but only one word for ice.

By contrast, the Aztecs, living in the tropics had only one word to cover 'snow', 'ice', 'cold' as separate words were unlikely to be used. As English speakers, it is impossible to state that 'cold' is synonymous with snow. Coldness is a characteristic of snow, but there can be 'cold' without 'snow'.

However, Inuits have many different words for 'snow'. Words describe it falling, lying, drifting, packing, as well as the language containing many words for wind, ice, cold.

The above is one small illustration of the relationship between seeing, naming, language and thought. Language habits predispose certain choices of word. Words we use daily reflect our cultural understanding and at the same time transmit it to others, even to the next generation. Words by themselves are not oppressive or pejorative, but they acquire a morality or subliminal meaning of their own .

For example, when parents or teachers tell a boy not to cry because it is not manly, or praise a girl for her feminine way of dressing, they are using the words for manly and feminine to reinforce attitudes and categories that English culture has assigned to males and females. Innocent repetition of such language as 'everyday, taken-for-granted' knowledge reinforces sexism in language and in society. Language, as a means of communication, becomes not only the expression of culture but a part of it. The feminine, masculine vocabulary is rarely questioned yet its usage creates expectations, that determine male as the norm, female as the secondary. Verbal descriptions of sex and gender *construct*, not merely describe.

When defining 'manly' *Webster's Dictionary* says:

... having qualities appropriate to a man:

>   open in conduct
>
>   bold
>
>   resolute
>
>   not effeminate or timorous
>
>   gallant
>
>   brave
>
>   undaunted
>
>   drinks beer. [Give me a break!!!]

For 'womanly' one finds:

... marked by qualities characteristic of a woman, belonging to attitudes of a woman not a man.

Female is defined by the negative of the other, of the male.

Sexist language pervades a range of sacred texts and legal texts and processes. Religion can be one of the most powerful ideologies operating within society, and many religions and religious groupings are hierarchically male oriented. The law maintains that the male term encompasses the female. Many religions maintain that man is made in the image of God, woman in the image of man. The female is once removed.

Even in the 19th century, English law continued to maintain that the Christian cleaving of male and female meant the subjugation of the female and the loss of her property and identity to the male.

Both law and Christianity reflect a dualism in Western society. The power of language is illustrated here. A pervasive sexism is made possible and manifest through language.

DOES ACCENT MATTER?

So far, the discussion has centred on the construction of the world by, and through, language as word. There are different ways of speaking and writing. People use the modes experience and education notes as the most appropriate.

But language exerts power, too, through a hierarchy given to 'ways of speaking'; through a hierarchy based on accent as well as choice of, or access to, vocabulary.

People often change the way they speak, their accent and/or vocabulary. Such change may be from the informal of family communication to the formal of work. It may be to 'fit in'. The artificial playing with 'upper class', 'middle class', 'working class', 'northern', or 'Irish' accent. Sometimes presentation to a person perceived by the speaker as important may occasion an accent and even a vocabulary change. Speakers wish to be thought well of. Therefore, they address the other in the way it is thought they wish or expect to be addressed.

It has been said that Britain in the 1940s and 1950s was the only place in the world a person's social status could be noted within seconds by accent alone. Oral communication and vocabulary was status laden. Accent revealed education, economic position and class. Today, particularly in certain professions, including law regional accents can often be a source of discrimination. Such discrimination is not spoken of to those whose speech habits are different; only to those whose speech habits are acceptable.

Given the variety of oral communication, accent, tone, vocabulary it is clear that it is not just the language that is important but how it is communicated, the attitude of the speaker. Does it include or exclude?

Written expressions of language are used to judge the ultimate worth of academic work but also it is used to judge job applicants. Letters of complaint that are well presented are far more likely to be dealt with positively.

So – language is extremely powerful.

Rightly or wrongly, it is used to label one as worthy or unworthy, educated or uneducated, rich or poor, rational or non-rational. Language can be used to invest aspects of character about which it cannot really speak. An aristocratic well spoken English accent with a rich vocabulary leads to the assumption that the speaker is well educated, of noble birth and character and is rich. A superficial rationale for nobleness, education and wealth is quite often found to be baseless.

LANGUAGE AND THE LAW

Lawyers work with language all the time. They have been described as wordsmiths, people whose craft, trade, is the highly competent use of both oral and written language.

Lawyers work with legal rules that are analysed in their written format. Such rules come in two major forms – legislation and European Community law (where it is said that the legal rule is in a 'fixed verbal form'), or common law. At common law the judgment of the judges contain the rules of law but these rules have to be extracted from the personal communication of the rule given by the judge. Although written, as the judgment is always taken down verbatim by the court stenographer, it is therefore said that such rules are *not* in a 'fixed verbal form'. Both forms give a certain latitude to interpreters.

Lawyers when dealing with rules:

(a) determine their likely application to facts;

(b) predict;

(c) interpret the language of rules.

In order to give to the law:

(a) credibility;

(b) respectability;

(c) intelligibility.

The major functions of the lawyer are therefore:

(a) analysis;

(b) critique;

(c) interpretation.

The language of the law is not only intertwined with religion it is also entwined with history. Often, the justification of a rule can be by history, by age, alone.

Coke, a lawyer of much influence in the 17th century gave the following explanation for the importance of history in relation to law:

> We are but of yesterday ... our days upon the earth are but as a shadow in respect of the old ancient days and times past, wherein the laws have been the wisdom of the most excellent men, in many successions of age, by long and continued experience, (the trial of light and truth) fined and refined.
>
> **Coke, *Calvin's Case*, 7 Cokes Reports.**

Precedent

Our common law is said to be the collective wisdom of the ages. This is powerful *myth*, not a powerful *truth*!

A key doctrine of English common law is the doctrine of precedent. This is the doctrine that states when deciding cases in court judges must have regard to whether the same issue has come before the courts in the past. If it has then the same decision must be reached. This doctrine is of immense importance because it determines the development of the law.

Not only is precedent important to the language of the law, defining the relevant and the irrelevant, but the language of the law defines appropriate argument strategies and vocabulary.

It is often said that law has its own language; it does not, but the language of law does have its distinctive characteristics.

For example, those social actors engaged in creating law tend to use linguistic terms dealing with generalisations and categories that have to be applied to individual specific circumstances.

It is necessary to begin to understand the processes involved in reasoning, and particularly to begin to understand how lawyers are taught to think. English law deals in terms of broad principles, rules and standards. The guardians, enforcers, creators, and interpreters of the law will state that the law is objective, that these legal rules and standards are objective. Yet they had their origins in the subjective analysis of one or more judges or other social actor.

Other characteristics of legal language are formality, precision and the existence of a technical vocabulary. Often everyday words are used, but given a different, specialised meaning. Figure 2.2 gives a fuller indication of the characteristics of legal language.

Figure 2.2: the characteristics of legal language

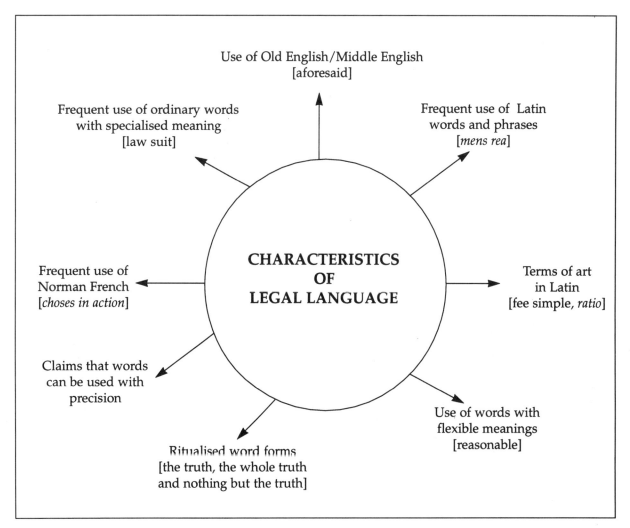

Many characteristics of legal language have their roots in the historical origins of legal procedure and it is now difficult to provide rational justification for them. They have become fossils, indicators of historical development. Other characteristics remain as justifiable attempts to reach precision in language usage.

Lawyers want to be able to use a distinctive language that is precise, brief, intelligible and durable, but of course, they fail. Failure is inevitable. Lawyers are particularly reliant on being able to persuade by argument. Argumentation will be considered in Part IV. It is useful now, however, to spend a little time considering language as used for the purposes of persuasion.

LEGAL RHETORIC

Rhetoric was defined by Aristotle as the universal art of persuasion and, before him, Plato called it in typically sexist form:

... winning men's minds by words.

A specialised form of rhetoric was identified by Aristotle as belonging to the law, and this was forensic rhetoric. In English law the principle persuasive device is the appeal to legal authority, to previous decisions of the court or of a higher court pointing to similar situations and reasoning connected to those situations.

This chapter has been concerned with presenting students with the view that language is in itself powerful and enables the world to be constructed, interpreted and organised. Language gives structure and meaning to an otherwise disorganised mass of experiences.

It is instructive to consider the potential for persuasive power that exists in the use of poetic language or, more appropriately, figurative language. Therefore, three extracts from two different types of oral communication that have been noted verbatim will be considered in order to explore poetic language, its function and its existence. The first extract is from a speech by a political activist in America in 1966, the second and third extracts are from the summing up in an English libel case in 1983.

Extract 1: 'I have a dream', Dr Martin Luther King on the steps of the Lincoln Memorial in Washington DC, 28 August 1963

(Each line of the extract has been numbered for ease of reference.)

1 Five score years ago, a great American, in whose symbolic
2 shadow we stand signed the Emancipation Proclamation. This
3 momentous decree came as a great beacon light of hope to
4 millions of Negro slaves who had been seared in the flames
5 of withering injustice. It came as a joyous daybreak to end
6 the long night of captivity.
7 But one hundred years later, we must face the tragic fact
8 that the Negro is still not free. One hundred years later,
9 the life of the Negro is still sadly crippled by the
10 manacles of segregation and the chains of discrimination.
11 One hundred years later, the Negro lives on a lonely island
12 of poverty in a vast ocean of material prosperity. One
13 hundred years later, the Negro is still languishing in the
14 corners of American society and finds himself an exile in
15 his own land. So we have come here today to dramatise an
16 appalling condition.
17 In a sense we have come to our nation's capital to cash a
18 check. When the architects of our republic wrote the
19 magnificent words of the constitution and the Declaration
20 of Independence, they were signing a promissory note to
21 which every American was to fall heir. The note was a
22 promise that all men would be guaranteed the inalienable

23 rights of life, liberty, and the pursuit of happiness.
24 It is obvious today that America has defaulted on this
25 promissory note insofar as her citizens of colour are
26 concerned. Instead of honouring this sacred obligation,
27 America has given the Negro people a bad check which has
28 come back marked 'insufficient funds'. But we refuse to
29 believe that the bank of justice is bankrupt. We refuse to
30 believe that there are insufficient funds in the great
31 vaults of opportunity of this nation. So we have come to
32 cash this check — a check that will give us upon demand the
33 riches of freedom and the security of justice. We have come
34 to this hallowed spot to remind America of the fierce
35 urgency now. This is no time to engage in the luxury of
36 cooling off or take the tranquillising drug of gradualism.
37 Now is the time to rise from the dark and desolate valley
38 of segregation to the sunlit path of racial justice. Now is
39 the time to open the doors of opportunity to all of God's
40 children. Now is the time to lift our nation from the
41 quicksand of racial injustice to the solid rock of
42 brotherhood.

This is a political speech, using religious imagery, poetic and emotional language to construct an argument challenging the American Government, calling upon it to honour the promises made in the Declaration of Independence.

Many students may not properly take in the importance of the place where the speech is made. It is made at the Lincoln memorial. This is the memorial to Abraham Lincoln who went to war on the issue of slavery, won and secured the freedom of slaves in the emancipation declaration.

So, the opening sentence grandly draws attention to Lincoln:

Five score years ago, a great American, in whose symbolic shadow we stand signed the emancipation declaration.

The raw poetic quality of this speech comes from its original orality. A range of images is used to communicate to the listener, and later the reader, the feelings of the speaker. For example:

Light:

'great beacon light of hope'	Line 3
'joyous daybreak'	Line 5
'the sunlit path of racial justice'	Line 38

Fire

'seared in the flames of withering injustice'	Lines 4–5

Darkness

'the long night of captivity'	Line 6
'the dark and desolate valley of segregation'	Lines 37–38

Captivity

'the negro is still not free'	Line 8
'manacles of segregation'	Line 10
'chains of discrimination'	Line 10
'an exile in his own land'	Lines 14–15

Money

'cash a check'	Lines 17–18
'promissory note'	Line 25
'insufficient funds'	Line 28
'bank of justice'	Line 29
'great vaults of opportunity'	Lines 30–31

Drugs

'the tranquillising drug of gradualism'	Line 36

Geology

'quicksand of racial injustice'	Line 41
'solid rock of brotherhood'	Lines 41–42

Geography

'lonely island of poverty'	Lines 11–12
'vast ocean of material prosperity'	Line 12

Religion

'to all of God's children'	Lines 39–40
'this hallowed spot'	Line 34
'honouring this sacred obligation'	Line 26

Building

'architects of our republic'	Line 18

Infirmity/sickness

'crippled by the manacles of segregation'	Line 9
'languishing in the corners of American society ...'	Lines 13–40

This extract is full of poetic, emotional language. Feelings and conditions are described by reference to a range of metaphors and similes. Figure 2.3 demonstrates the imagery in diagrammatic format.

The major figurative vehicles are the likening of the Declaration of Independence to a promissory note to all Americans, and the concept of the Negro coming to cash a check (cheque) which they feel has been returned marked 'insufficient funds' and have come incredulous to cash it again refusing to believe that 'there are insufficient funds in the great vaults of opportunity'– (lines 30–31). The hearer would easily recall these major similes, and be able to classify the honouring behaviour of a government keeping promises and contrasting it to a dishonouring government. They also remain vivid to the reader.

The argument links follow from the setting up of these images of cheques to be cashed and the dishonouring of checks which consequentially require re-presenting. In the third and fourth paragraphs, the argument is set up as follows:

Third paragraph

'... to cash a check'
'... the architects of our Republic'
'... were signing a promissory note'
'... every American was to fall heir'
'... a promise that all men would be'
'... guaranteed the inalienable rights of life, liberty, and the pursuit of happiness.'

> **NOTE: non-poetic summary**
>
> When the Declaration of Independence was signed, all Americans were promised inalienable rights.

Fourth paragraph

'... America has defaulted on this promissory note ... Instead of honouring'

'... America has given the Negro people a bad check'

'... which has come back marked insufficient funds'

'... we refuse to believe that there are insufficient funds'

'... we have come to cash this check'

'... give us upon demand the riches of freedom and the security of justice.'

> **NOTE: non-poetic summary**
>
> But America has not kept this promise, but we refuse to believe it has not kept its promise.

A particular rhetorical device utilised in the text is repetition, which tends to add emphasis, to thicken the impact, aid the memory in recalling the argument or illustration, yet nothing is added except momentum which is poetic. Repetition which concerns calls for justice is also given a momentum that is emotionally charged, for example, in the fourth paragraph the following clusters of repetition occur:

1. '... we refuse to believe'
   '... we refuse to believe'
2. '... we have come'
   '... we have come'
3. '... now is the time' [to rise from ...]
   '... now is the time' [to open the door of opportunity]
   '... now is the time' [to move from the quicksand.]

Another device is particular to the Greek dualism of the West, that of a range of illustrations based on opposites:

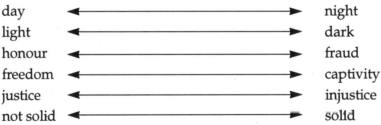

day	night
light	dark
honour	fraud
freedom	captivity
justice	injustice
not solid	solid

What carries the message of this speech is:

(a) the emotive, poetic language;

(b) the imagery of the opposites;

(c) the image of the cheque and the fraud.

What is the core argument? That the emancipation agreement and the Declaration of Independence assured all Americans, and negroes are Americans, that they had rights that could never be taken away. Negroes had asked for those rights and had not been given them. America had unjustifiably denied these rights.

Figure 2.3: imagery used in Extract 1

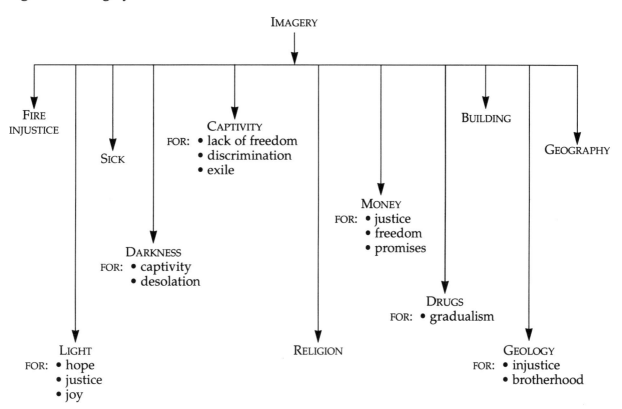

This is a forceful argument made far more immediately forceful and poignant by the use of the poetic and emotive, passionate language. People may acknowledge the logic of an argument without agreeing to concede to demands. Persuasion can therefore be an essential device to encourage people to move from concept to action.

That such language is used in politics is not surprising. Politicians seek to persuade by all means possible and, as Aristotle remarked, persuasive language is used to effect by the introduction of figurative language. Such language is only one aspect of rhetoric, but, as this extract demonstrates, it is a powerful aspect.

Emotional and poetic language, it is said, has no place in the courtroom, in the language of law. Poetic and emotional language can exercise much power and in matters of innocence and guilt it is surely more just to rely on rationality not emotion.

This view can be particularly traced back to the insistence by Francis Bacon who, in the 17th century, insisted that law must be seen to have an objective, scientific, rational methodology. However it is *im*possible for there to be a pure science of law given its reliance on language, and the imprecision of language.

Figurative language is often used in the courtroom despite the view that it is inappropriate, as extracts two and three illustrate.

Extract 2: Lord Justice Comyn summing up in *Orme v Associated Daily Newspapers* (1981)

This is not a battle between the freedom of religion and the freedom of the press; two freedoms which we treasure greatly. This is rather a battle of right and wrong. Has the *Daily Mail* infringed the plaintiff's right to a good, clean reputation, or has the plaintiff Mr Orme in all the circumstances no right to any reputation at all in this case because of what he and his organisation have done and do? Was the *Daily Mail* wrong about its allegations in its article? Was it wrong about its allegations during this case? Or was the plaintiff wrong; was the plaintiff giving a false picture? That is what it is, members of the jury, not a battle between freedom of the press and freedom of religion, but a battle of right and wrong.

This extract is useful as an illustration of language techniques, repetition, figurative language (particularly, metaphor) in action; as well providing the basis for a necessarily limited discussion of what the function of these techniques may be.

It is set out again below, with certain phrases and sentences numbered for discussion purposes.

1   This is not a battle between the freedom of religion

2   and the freedom of the press;

3   two freedoms which we treasure greatly.

4   This is rather a battle of right and wrong.

5   Has the *Daily Mail* infringed the plaintiff's right to a good, clean reputation,

6   or has the plaintiff Mr Orme in all the circumstances no right to any reputation at all in this case because of what he and his organisation have done and do?

7   Was the *Daily Mail* wrong about its allegations in its article?

8   Was it wrong about its allegations during this case?

9   Or was the plaintiff wrong;

10 was the plaintiff giving a false picture?

11 That is what it is, members of the jury, not a battle between freedom of the press and freedom of religion,

12 but a battle of right and wrong.

The first and last sentences of the extract (lines 1, 2, 11 and 12), form a 'sandwich' comprising repetition of the main assertion that the case is not a battle between freedom of the press and freedom of religion.

It is as if he is saying that the argument is so because 'I say so, twice!'.

Another example of repetition is found in the structure of the run of three rhetorical questions, both in terms of length and the use of amplification through alliteration 'Was it wrong?' in lines 7, 8 and 12.

The structure of the extract also demonstrates that the judge has the authority to impose that reading of events. For he says, in line 11, 'This is what it is, members of the jury'.

Who is the 'we' found in line 11?

(a) Is it the royal 'We', symbolising the ultimate authority of the court?

(b) Is it merely the judge?

(c) Does it include judge and jury?

'We' is undeniably an inclusive term. It is suggested that, in this instance, the judge is talking in relation to the court and the law, as an official spokesman of the law.

The choice of the word 'battle', as part of what turns out to be a continuing war metaphor which runs throughout the entire summing up, as a major organising theme that argument is war, is interesting. The word 'fight' or 'skirmish' is not chosen, but 'battle'. The reference to battle puts the case 'high up' in a hierarchy of modes of physical fighting – for example skirmish, scrap, fight, battle'. Battle denotes that opposing armies gather together with their greatest degree of strength to fight for as long as it takes for a clear victor.

Of course, it is not unusual to find 'fighting' metaphors used to describe English trials. Because of their accusatorial nature ('He did it judge.' 'No, he did it judge.'). Early in the history of English dispute resolution, trial by battle (a physical fight) was used to determine guilt and innocence as a perfectly acceptable *alternative* to trial by law.

There were also other alternatives such as blood feud (speaks for itself) and trial by ordeal. At the latter, the Church was in attendance to oversee a range of tests that, to an observer, would look like the infliction of punishment after guilt had been determined. If the test was successfully passed – and it could only be 'won' if the Christian God intervened – the person taking the test was innocent. For example, the person claiming innocence would plunge a hand into boiling water. If there was no blistering after a few days (highly unlikely, it was believed at the time, without supernatural intervention), the person was judged to be innocent.

For those who feel adventurous, trial by battle remains on the statute books. Relief may be felt that trial by ordeal is no longer an option.

Gradually, royal justice as trial by law took over through a combination of efficiency and threat by the crown. Later in this extract, Comyn J refers to the battle as a 'Battle Royal'. This connection could be taken as a reminder that the majority of battles from the 16th century onwards involving the monarch were indeed battles concerning religious differences. A serious event about right and wrong. The notion of 'right' suggesting ideas of 'Good' and the notion of wrong suggesting ideas of 'evil'.

The Christian Bible speaks of the battle between 'Good' and 'Evil' which resulted in the fall of the archangel Lucifer. A shadowing here of the religious is clear. 'Right' and 'Wrong' are also suggestive of the moral dimensions of the case.

Whilst the English adversarial system lends itself to the use of such war imagery, the judge reserves the right to say what the battle is about and he clearly rules out the possibility that it is a battle between individual freedoms of expression (religious freedom and the freedom of the press). A classic example of setting boundaries by stating what is *not* legitimately involved.

No rationale is given for the boundaries and exclusion. Indeed the elaborate explanations given for exclusion could be evidence that strongly suggest that insofar as the judge is concerned the dispute before him *is* indeed a battle concerning religious freedom.

Comyn J defines the area of dispute. He draws its boundaries without the slightest recognition of another interpretation of events. For the court has the power to draw boundaries without explanation in this way. It is part of its exercise of power.

Extract 3: *Orme v Associated Daily Newspapers Ltd* (1981)

The following 16 examples are drawn from the totality of the summing up which ran to over 200 pages. They give the flavour of the summing up but have been chosen particularly to illustrate the use of repetition and alliteration.

1 'Are the **m**oonies a **m**alevolent **m**enace?'

2 'has the *Daily Mail* behaved **dis**honestly and **dis**gracefully?'

3 'that **poor** man, his **poor** wife, his **poor** son'

4 '**searching**, perhaps more than we did, **searching searching searching** for the truth and for reason'

5 'Decide it **fairly, squarely,** and **truly**'

6 '**m**ean, **m**erciless, **m**aterialistic and **m**oney-grabbing'

7 '**bad** press, **bad** deal, **bad** treatment'

8 '**m**atching, **m**atching and **m**ating'

9 '**r**amp and **r**acket'

10 '**devious** and **deceitful**'

11 '**chanting, cheering** and **g**iggling'

12 'A **f**raud, a **f**ake , a hoax'

13 'Is this a **m**ad **m**an or a bad **man ... or** a megalomaniac'

14 '**human** and **humane** people'

15 '**inherent** badness, **inherent** greed'

16 '*Is he* an old **h**umbug, *is he* a **h**ypocrite or *is he* a decent **h**onourable man standing up manfully for an **h**onourable *bona fide* religion?'

Even from the disconnected statements above, it can be gathered that the dispute revolves around the character of a man or group and it is noticeable that there are more references to 'bad' qualities than to 'good' in relation to the qualities of this man or group – a characteristic feature of the entire summing up. It is clear that some authority needs to decide whether the individual or group is, therefore, good or bad.

The above 15 examples illustrate quite clearly Comyns J's preference for alliteration and repetition. In addition, examples 12 and 13 are framed according to a classic argument within Christian theology concerning the claims of Jesus Christ to be the son of God. 'Is he mad, or bad or who he says he is?' However the two examples cited only allow for pejorative choices. Example 15 instills a sense of balance in that the third choice is 'an honourable' choice and, in that sense, correctly mirrors the theological argument referred to above.

The text in its entirety contains in excess of 162 metaphors. In many instances, there are several to a page, often repeated up to 50 pages later and expanded to become organising thematic metaphors for the text, the predominant themes relating to nature or war. Elaborate metaphors are repeated much later in the text in shorter format. However. the immediate effect is to recall the vividness of the original format.

These three examples of figurative language interwoven with persuasion give an illustration of poetic language in action:

(a) enhancing argument;

(b) thickening it without adding substance;

(c) adding effect;

(d) carrying substantive argument;

(e) making weak arguments appear strong.

Later, when the mechanics of argument construction have been identified, it will be useful to return to these extracts and read them again with an eye on argument connected to figurative language. This chapter has considered a range of issues:

(a) religion and language;

(b) law and language;

(c) the power of language to limit, express and shape the world;

(d) law and figurative language.

Law is carried by words: excellent English language skills are the beginning of basic competency in handling legal rules that are either derived from the common law, statutory activity or the European Community. Sophisticated language skills, coupled with meticulous attention to detail and a thorough understanding of the substantive field of law, ensures appropriate levels of analysis; for the skills of handling complex legal rules, communicated through language, constitute the major practical and intellectual skill of the lawyer.

> **The important message to be taken from this chapter is that, as the rules of law are learned, and the methods of making law discerned, it is essential to be aware of the power of language in order not only to analyse the rules themselves but to ascertain in what way, if any, language is exerting a powerful influence on the constructors, applicators and interpreters of the law.**

PART II

HOW TO HANDLE PRIMARY TEXTS EFFECTIVELY

HOW TO HANDLE PRIMARY TEXTS EFFECTIVELY

INTRODUCTION

The study of law is really the study of how ideas become words of authority, for as explained previously the *law* is *words*.

There are three major sources of English law that need to be understood immediately. Common Law, legislation and European Community law. There are other sources and classifications but for the purposes of this text these three will be concentrated upon and are set out in Figure II.i below.

Figure II.i: the three major sources of English law

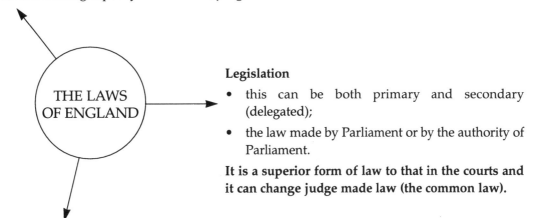

The common law
- the law found in law reports;
- the law making capacity of the courts, judge made law.

THE LAWS OF ENGLAND

Legislation
- this can be both primary and secondary (delegated);
- the law made by Parliament or by the authority of Parliament.

It is a superior form of law to that in the courts and it can change judge made law (the common law).

The law of the European Community

By virtue of our accession to the European Economic Community in 1971 and the subsequent enactment of the European Communities Act 1972, the law of the European Community can be directly incorporated into English law. Some laws will need the 'domestic' (English) government to enact them. This whole issue raises many questions about **parliamentary supremacy** and **autonomy.**

One factor which may seem difficult at first is getting to grips with these various legal rules. To competently handle such primary texts of law there is need to:

(a) locate the various sources of the rules;

(b) learn how they can be used to provide a resolution to disputes of a legal nature;

(c) learn how to engage in applying and interpreting the rules;

(d) understand the interconnections between the main sources of English law.

In order to give a context for the reading and analysing techniques that enable primary texts of law to be properly understood, it is necessary to describe briefly each of the main three sources of law.

THE COMMON LAW

The phrase 'common law' has several meanings which vary according to context but as used in this text it means no more and no less than:

all the laws
made by judges
relating to
the whole of
the United Kingdom

There has been, and continues to be, much argument among legal philosophers as to whether judges actually make/create law out of nothing, or merely declare what the law has always been. Many judges state that they do not make the law they discover it and thus **declare** what it has always been. This latter viewpoint is referred to as the *declaratory theory* of law making.

This is a practical book about *how to* analyse the *existing* common law as recorded in the law reports. It is, therefore for the reader to come to a conclusion about who is right over the issue of declaring or creating.

What is clear is that an English judge when deciding a case must refer to similar prior decisions of the higher courts and keep to the reasoning in those cases. If a previous case has dealt with similar facts and the same rules, then the present case has to be decided in the same way. This process is known as the doctrine of precedent.

The doctrine is usually referred to by the use of a shorthand Latin phrase:

Stare decisis = **let the decision stand**

Often, the whole doctrine *and* the specific legal rule created in the case is referred to by an even more abbreviated Latin term, *ratio*.

- No *legal rule* exists to demand such adherence to previous cases.
- However, the senior judiciary enforce it rigidly.

When is a court bound by a previous case?

- Everything depends upon the court's position in the hierarchy of courts.
- The English legal system is unique among ALL others because of the manner in which courts keep to the doctrine of precedent.

Advantages of the doctrine

- It gives certainty to the law.
- It is a curb on arbitrary decisions.
- It is based on a notion of justice which maintains equality.
- It provides a rational base for decision making.

Disadvantages of the doctrine

- It makes the law inflexible.
- Change is slow and convoluted.
- It encourages a tedious hairsplitting tendency in legal argument.

The importance of accurate reporting of legal cases

- The importance of cases *and* the extent of the legal rule developed *only* become apparent *after* the case.
- If you cannot trust the reporting, then you cannot trust the law.

LEGISLATION

Legislation is the law made by Parliament or by groups acting on parliamentary authority. The technically correct term for a piece of legislation is 'legislative Act'.

In addition to creating legislation, Parliament can delegate, to another person or group, by an Act of Parliament, the power to create a limited range of laws for others. For example, powers can be delegated to:

(a) a local authority;

(b) a Government minister;

(c) a professional body.

When this occurs the legislation that *is created* is referred to as:

a statutory instrument

OR

delegated legislation

OR

secondary legislation
(for it is once removed from parliamentary power)

The legislation giving the power to make such secondary or delegated legislation is referred to as the *primary legislation,* or the *parent act.*

Consideration of statutes and delegated legislation by the courts

Quite often, the law created by Parliament, as well as that created by delegated parliamentary authority, is considered by judges in courts. Most commonly, judges will be called upon to decide the precise meaning of a phrase or a word. Given the discussion above concerning the flexibility of language and the problems of interpretation, the difficulties that such consideration can cause are obvious.

Issues of tremendous importance can be raised when a problem about the meaning of a statutory provision goes before a court. How do judges interpret statutes? The ability to have the final say in this manner gives judges, an undemocratic body, unprecedented power.

Judges have to:

(a) apply legislative rules to various fact situations;

(b) decide the meaning of words and phrases used in the statute (and of course words can mean many things, and can change over time);

(c) deal with judicial disagreement over the meaning of words.

A range of purported rules of interpretation has been developed over time for use by judges:

(a) there are three *known* rules of statutory interpretation, set out in Figure II.ii;

(b) there are probably *many unknown* rules. For example, the '*gut-feeling rule*'.

Figure II.ii: the three main rules of statutory interpretation

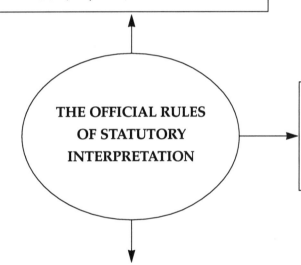

Literal rule

All words have a literal meaning which is discoverable by the judge (consulting dictionaries, etc).

THE OFFICIAL RULES OF STATUTORY INTERPRETATION

Golden rule

Of course, sometimes literal interpretations are absurd and this rule says that judges do not have to use the literal rule in such circumstances. There is no direction as to what to do instead!

Mischief/purposive rule

Look at the reason for the enactment of the legislation.

When using the mischief or purposive rule sometimes judges look outside the statute to try to find the intention of Parliament in the speeches in the *Houses of Parliament*.

This can be problematic but, in some circumstances, has been endorsed by the courts. See *Pepper v Hart* (1993).

Which rule do judges use first?

Invariably, the literal! Although, on rare occasions, there are those who go directly to the mischief/purpose rule.

NO LEGAL RULES EXIST WHICH STATE WHICH RULES OF INTERPRETATION CAN BE USED AND THE RULES OF INTERPRETATION THAT HAVE BEEN IDENTIFIED ARE NOT, THEMSELVES, LEGAL RULES.

THE LAW OF THE EUROPEAN COMMUNITY

The third major source of English law is the law of the European Community.

In 1973, the UK joined the European Community. At the time legislation was enacted which said quite clearly that European Community law, created in the areas covered by the treaties signed by the UK Government, would have superiority over any conflicting UK legislation. So, in areas within the competence of the European Community, if there is a clash between national law and European Community law, European Community law must prevail.

Furthermore, the UK Government promised to legislate where necessary to ensure that Community law was observed in the UK.

There are several different types of law in the European Community with differing effects. Some European Community law is immediately incorporated in the body of English law, some has to be specially enacted by Act of Parliament.

Because of the initial complexities of the background, sources and classification of European Community law, these issues will be discussed in greater detail in Chapter 7.

Figure II.iii sets out the various areas that need to be understood and interlinked to handle European Community law and relate it to the English legal system.

Figure II.iii: areas of European Community law which must be understood

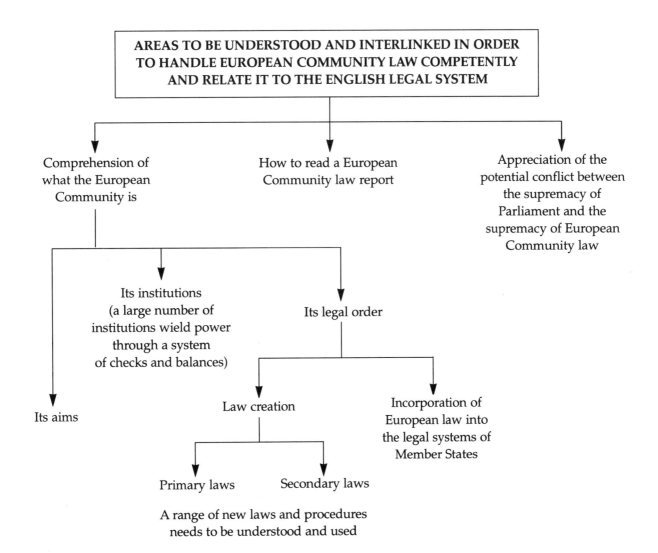

Having briefly outlined the three main types of English law that this text is primarily concerned with, it is also now possible to offer the following, more detailed diagram of the *sources* of English law.

Figure II.iv: sources of law

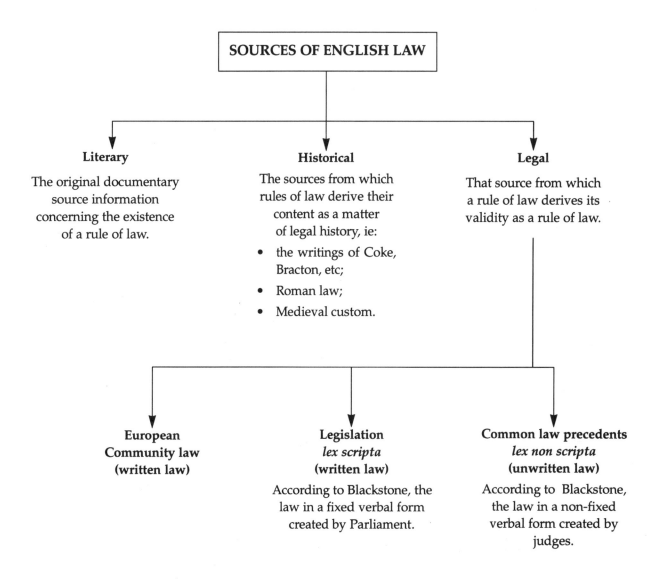

CONCLUSION

The successful comprehension of the historical and political sources and differences between the three major sources of English law will give the student a firm grasp of how to use these primary texts. Such understanding is an indispensable foundation for competent legal studies.

It is now appropriate, after this brief overview of the three main types of law, to look at each area in detail. Chapters 3 to 8 consider the nature of the three areas of law and strategies for reading and understanding them.

CHAPTER 3

UNDERSTANDING STATUTES

Section 3 of the Unfair Contract Terms Act 1977

3 (1) This section applies as between contracting parties where one of them deals as consumer or on the other's written standard terms of business.

(2) As against that party, the other cannot by reference to any contract term:

(a) when himself in breach of contract, exclude or restrict any liability of his in respect of the breach; or

(b) claim to be entitled:

(i) to render a contractual performance substantially different from that which was reasonably expected of him, or

(ii) in respect of the whole or any part of his contractual obligation, to render no performance at all,

except in so far as (in any of the cases mentioned above in this subsection) the contract term satisfies the requirement of reasonableness.

INTRODUCTION

Having spent time:

(a) discussing the power of language;

(b) considering issues of meaning;

(c) becoming alerted to the influence of figurative language,

the importance of excellent language skills for the study of law should be clear.

In its statutory format, the language of the law will be found to be:

(a) potentially confusing;

(b) tediously literal;

(c) exhibiting scant punctuation;

(d) liberally peppered with alphabetical and numerical dividers.

Interpreters of legal texts strive to ascertain what is being suggested at all levels of the text. Some interpret from a biased position, for example, the prosecution or defence. Others interpret from an open position, merely asking: what does this provide for? How might these legal rules apply to this fact situation?

It can be argued that an interpreter is creating something which is new by their act of interpretation: an interpretation which is triggered by the text but which, in reality, bears no resemblance to the writers' intention. This concept may be the basis of the school of art criticism which says: do not confuse the intellect of the artist with the beauty of the work created; do not expect the artist to know the meaning of the work!

Interpreters of legal texts have to adapt their methods according to the type of document they are dealing with, the myth of ascertaining the real meaning of words always being held out as an attainable and sensible goal.

This chapter will demonstrate the importance of various techniques for breaking into texts containing statutory legal rules, using a range of skills and methods in preparation for evaluating, analysing and critiquing them. All these skills require constant practice and reflection, and each type of legal text may require different methods of analysis. Practice steadily increases intellectual awareness, language appreciation, skills of prediction concerning interpretation difficulties and the ability to evaluate.

(a) skills of language analysis:

- sophisticated comprehension skills;
- vocabulary skills;
- grammar skills;
- excellent reading and writing skills;

(b) diagrammatic methods for organising texts:

- tree diagrams;
- flow charts;
- algorithms;
- Venn diagrams;

(c) textual methods for organising texts:

- tables;
- paragraph analysis, linking and summarising:

(d) identification of interrelationships.

Many people do not know how to listen or read for an argument. They hear or see words and do not know how to capture the potential meanings, arguments, truths and errors that they carry. Every skill that is necessary for the competent study of law is interconnected and most problems, whether purely theoretical (what is law?) or practical (what does this law mean for the defendant?) require the competent handling of interconnected skills of language use, legal rules and facts.

Figure 3.1 demonstrates some of the complexities and interrelationships referred to in this introduction: it is important to internalise these issues.

Those who grasp these interconnections and become competent handlers of rules and facts are successful interpreters of rules, assessors of situations and excellent problem solvers. They are, by definition, excellent lawyers.

Figure 3.1: skills required for competent legal rule analysis

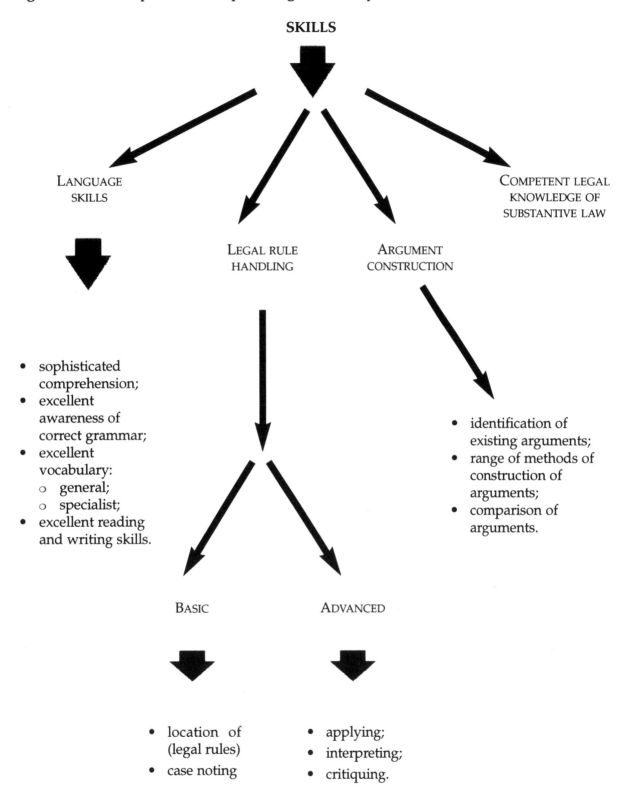

STATUTORY RULES: UNDERSTANDING THE STRUCTURE OF LEGAL RULES CREATED BY PARLIAMENT'S DIRECT OR INDIRECT AUTHORITY

Introduction

Parliament authorises the creation of a range of differing types of legal rule, as set out below in Figure 3.2. They are all united by the fact that they are created in a fixed verbal form. Only those words were agreed by Parliament as containing the legal rule, not other words.

A characteristic of such rules is that they rarely come as single units – they are usually a collection of rules. They also come with attached definitions, defences, modes of interpretation and guidelines for operation.

Sometimes statutes are a reasonably well considered responses to a particular issue such as:

(a) consumer protection;

(b) public order;

(c) European Community obligations;

(d) family law.

Sometimes, legislation is a knee jerk reaction by parliament to a crisis or public outcry or a one off situation. Of course, in reality, it is the Government of the day that determines what issues are put into the parliamentary law making machinery. Figure 3.3 illustrates the major procedure for the creation of legislation.

However, this text concentrates on the techniques for *understanding* such rules and the processes of *interpretation* that the courts, officials, ordinary people and law students follow in order to apply these rules.

Although each statute responds to particular issues, the finer details of the situations that the rules will have to be applied to will vary enormously. Therefore, another characteristic of statutes is that they are drafted in a general way, in order, it is hoped, to be applicable to the widest possible range of situations.

This often presents a major challenge to those drafting the legislation and to those who are subsequently called upon to interpret it.

Another factor that must be borne in mind when considering the meaning and application of legislation is that it may have been changed in some way since enactment. For example, it may have been changed:

(a) by parliamentary authority, by statutory amendment (added to or subtracted from), or by repeal (abolished);

(b) by the House of Lords or the Court of Appeal determining the meaning of words and phrases used to make up the legal rule;

(c) by European Community legal obligations directly entering English law and conflicting with the legal rule.

Figure 3.2: diagram indicating the range of direct and indirect legal rules created by Parliament

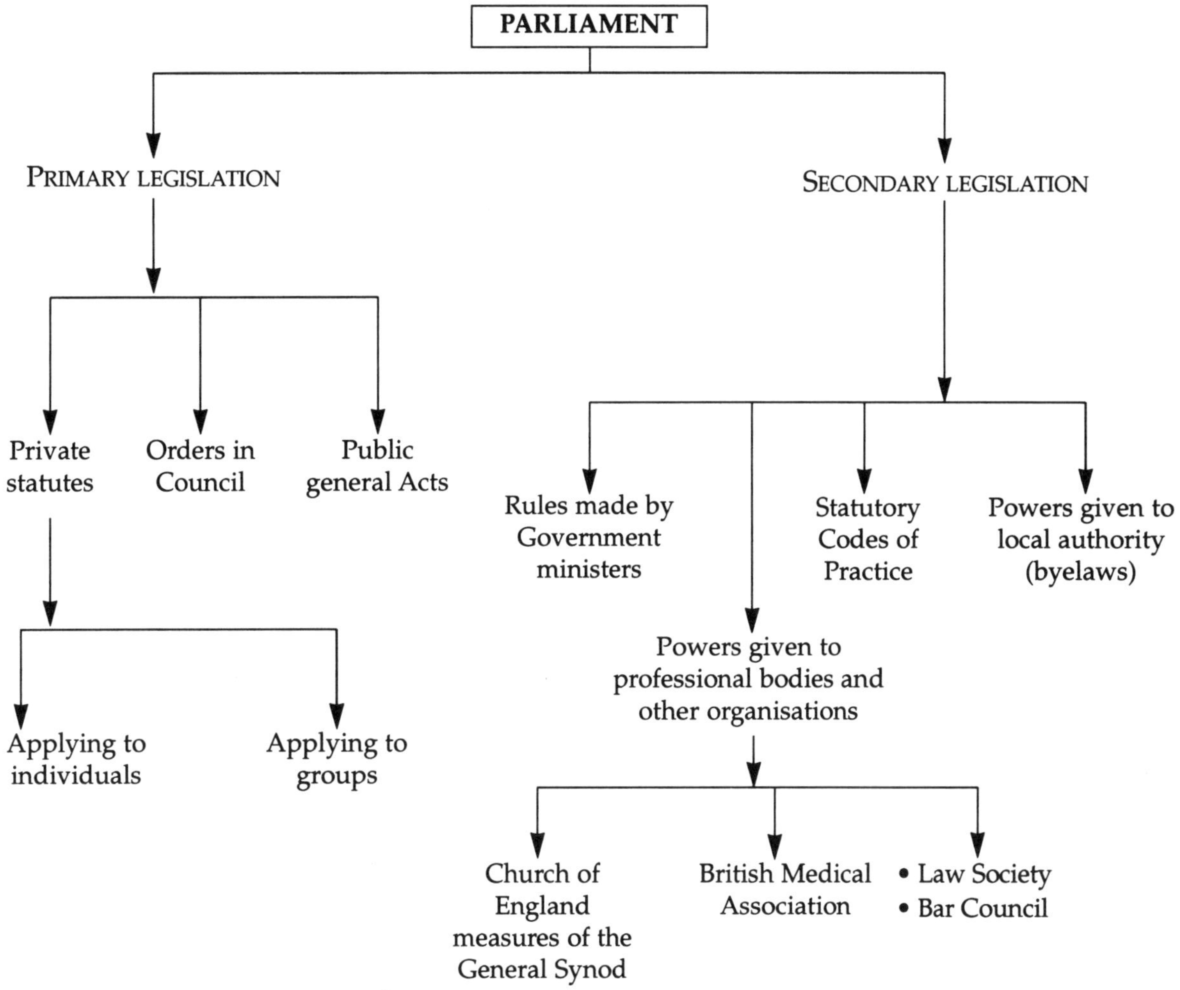

```
                           ┌──────────────┐
                           │  PARLIAMENT  │
                           └──────────────┘
              ┌───────────────────┴────────────────────┐
              ▼                                          ▼
      PRIMARY LEGISLATION                        SECONDARY LEGISLATION
```

PRIMARY LEGISLATION

- Private statutes
- Orders in Council
- Public general Acts

Private statutes:
- Applying to individuals
- Applying to groups

SECONDARY LEGISLATION

- Rules made by Government ministers
- Statutory Codes of Practice
- Powers given to local authority (byelaws)

Powers given to professional bodies and other organisations:
- Church of England measures of the General Synod
- British Medical Association
- • Law Society
  • Bar Council

Synonyms for primary legislation	
• Act of Parliament; • legislation (plural: still 'legislation'); • statute (plural: statutes) meaning 'decree'.	You might think that the terminology is confusing ... **IT IS!**
Synonyms for secondary legislation • delegated legislation; • Statutory Instrument; • subordinate legislation.	

NOTE: the legislation currently in force has been created by Parliament over the past 700 years. Most legislation, however, has been created since 1850. There are surviving parchment rolls of legislation dating from about 1299. Statutes began to be printed towards the end of the 15th century.

Figure 3.3: procedure for the creation of legislation

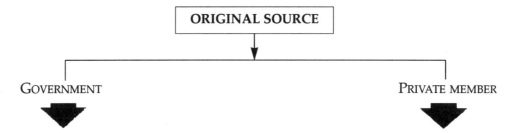

ORIGINAL SOURCE

GOVERNMENT

PRIVATE MEMBER

- make election promises and react to current need for new law;
- consider how to translate promises or current need into legal action;
- Treasury considers financial implications;
- civil servants in PM's office (parliamentary counsel) prepare a draft legislation (called 'a Bill');
- after final Government perusal, draft Bill is timetabled for the parliamentary law creation procedure.

Parliamentary time given by a ballot. Individual lobby groups will often try to get an MP to adopt their cause and introduce a draft Bill.

- FIRST READING

Private MP introduces Bill. If it is successful, the government *may* take it over if MP agrees, *or* MP may proceed.

FIRST READING

Government minister introduces 'the Bill' by reading out the title. A date is given for second reading. Bills are usually introduced in the House of Commons.

The government may take it over

SECOND READING

- full debate;
- yes/no vote.

Successful Bills go to a committee for fuller debate and are timetabled for third reading.

Private member continues to take it through the parliamentary process through a SECOND and THIRD READING.

THIRD READING

- debate;
- yes/no vote.

If successful, Bill goes to House of Lords to go through the same three procedures. If successful, it receives the Royal Assent.

Very few Private Members' Bills are ultimately successful if they are not taken over by the Government.

ROYAL ASSENT

PUBLICATION by HMSO

Q: When does an ACT OF PARLIAMENT become law?

THE INTERNAL LAYOUT OF A STATUTE

There is a standard method of laying out statutes which, when recognised and understood, becomes a great help for analysis or evaluation.

Most large statutes will be divided into parts for ease of reference. Each part will deal with different aspects of the overall collection of rules and their meanings. Each part contains sections which give more details in each area.

Sections can be further divided with the use of arabic numerals into sub-sections. Sub-sections are capable of further division, with the use of roman numerals, into paragraphs. Paragraphs can be further divided with alphabetical ordering into sub-paragraphs.

At the end of the statute, there will often be schedules and these are numerically divided as well. These deal further with matters raised in the various parts. Schedules can only relate to previous sections in the Act. They cannot create anything new without an anchoring in the main body of the statute. All statutes also contain marginal notes, headings and sub-headings. These organising devices, however, are said not to form part of the law.

Correct understanding of the relationship between parts, sections, sub-sections, paragraphs, sub-paragraphs, marginal notes, headings and schedules enables the general layout of the Act to be ascertained. Assistance is also obtained from the 'long title' of the Act, which looks more like a long sentence about what the statute is about!

Central to the analysis of statutes is the ability to understand these intratextual relationships. Figure 3.4 sets out the general layout of statutes and Figure 3.5 is an annotated first page of an imaginary statute.

Figure 3.4: the general layout of statutes

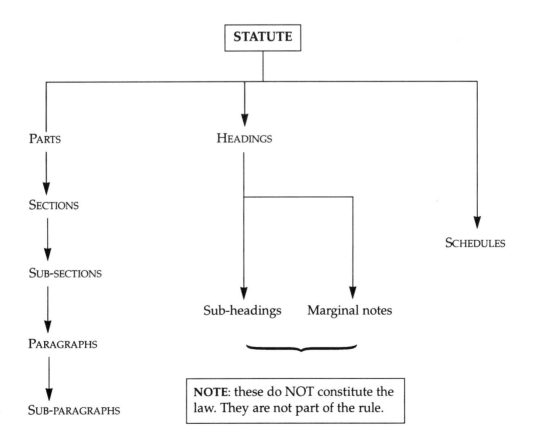

Figure 3.5: annotated first page of an imaginary statute

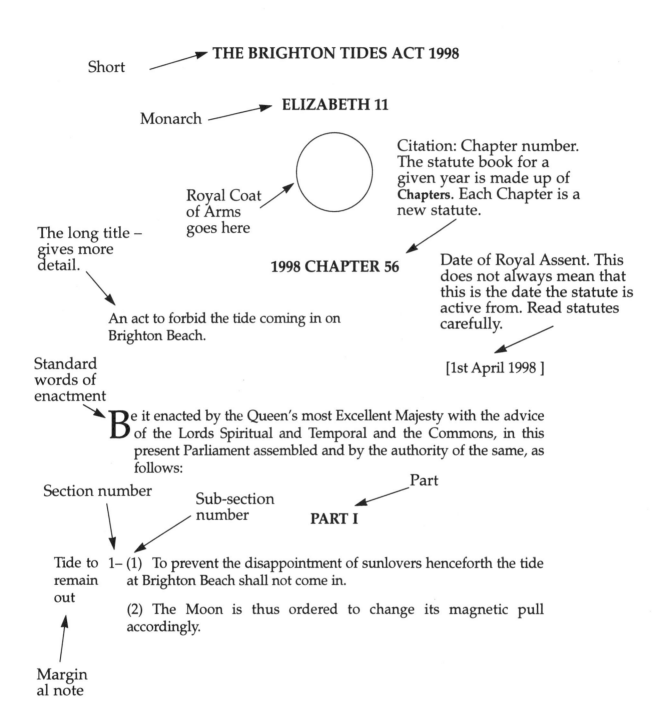

A STATUTE IS DIVIDED INTO:

- sections;
- sub-sections;
- paragraphs;
- sub-paragraphs;
- Parts;
- Schedules (at the end).

VOCABULARY

REPEAL – abolition of all or part of a previous statute.

AMEND – changing part of a previous statute.

Parliament can enact laws about anything – but a law may prove impossible to enforce. Legend records that a particular English king, Canute, was humbled when he attempted to demonstrate his sovereign power by seating his throne on the beach and ordering the tide not to come in! For come in it did, much to his embarrassment.

When approaching a statute as a new law student the most difficult task is understanding, at a basic macro (wide) level, what the statute as a whole is striving to do and at the micro (narrow) level what each section is saying.

As proficiency is gained in handling statutory rules it will be found that it is not usually necessary to deal with the entire statute. The overall statue can be briefly contextualised and only relevant sections need to be extracted for detailed consideration, analysis, or application. However, 'sections', those micro elements of statutes, will be all the more confidently analysed because, at any given moment, it is known how to relate any aspect of the statute to its general layout.

Often, initial understanding eludes the law student. Doubts concerning the meaning of parts of the statute do not occur at the level of sophisticated analysis. They occur at the basic level of combining English language skills and legal skills to obtain foundational understanding. If doubts remain at this level there can be no possibility of attaining sophisticated analysis!

To explore methods of breaking into statutes and understanding statutes at the macro and micro level the rest of this chapter will deal with a real statute, the Unfair Contract Terms Act 1977 (UCTA).

Figure 3.6 builds on the abstract general layout of Figure 3.4 by customising it to fit the Unfair Contract Terms Act 1977. This statute will continue to be used for demonstration purposes for the rest of the chapter. The full text of the statute can be found in Appendix 1.

Study Figure 3.6 carefully. Note which parts are linked and which are not by following the lines and arrows. Reading the summarised headings constructs a basic overview of what the statute is about.

Before considering how to break into statutory language in such a way as to be able to confidently précis whole sections for the purposes of such a layout, it is important to study the layout until it is familiar and comprehensible. There are no shortcuts. This takes time.

Figure 3.6: the general layout of the Unfair Contract Terms Act 1977

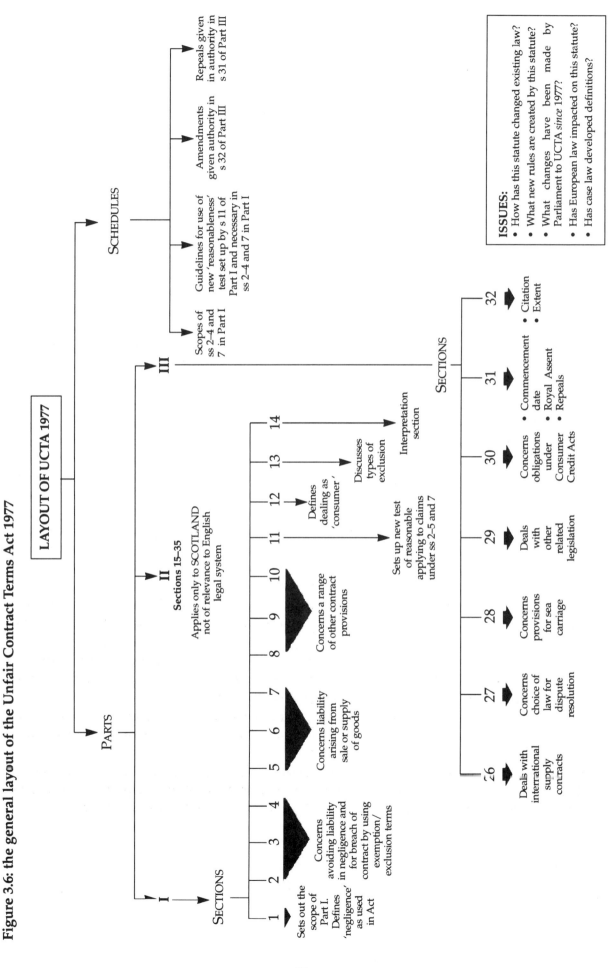

To test your comprehension, answer the following questions by recourse only to Figure 3.6:

(1) What areas of the statute need to be considered to find out if the exclusion terms in a contract is reasonable?

(2) What areas of the statute need to be considered to ascertain the repeals and amendments made by the statute?

(3) Where can the definition of dealing as a consumer be found?

(4) If a contract is dated 27 October 1977, how can I find out if it is covered by the statute? This question in fact can be definitively answered from the layout.

(5) If I want to bring an action under s 4 in Part I of the statute, what other sections may be relevant and would, therefore, need to be considered?

This should have been a reasonably simple exercise and should also demonstrate both the use of such a layout and the importance of understanding how an entire piece of legislation fits together.

ANALYSING STATUTES

The next stage in building up expertise in the basics of handling statutes is to turn to the minute detail and consider how to break into the text as a piece of comprehension. Let us, therefore, consider s 3 of the Unfair Contract Terms Act 1977:

> 3 – (1) This section applies as between contracting parties where one of them deals as consumer or on the other's written standard terms of business.
>
>   (2) As against that party, the other cannot by reference to any contract term:
>
>   (a) when himself in breach of contract, exclude or restrict any liability of his in respect of the breach; or
>
>   (b) claim to be entitled:
>
>   (i) to render a contractual performance substantially different from that which was reasonably expected of him, or
>
>   (ii) in respect of the whole or any part of his contractual obligation, to render no performance at all,
>
>   except in so far as (in any of the cases mentioned above in this sub-section) the contract term satisfies the requirement of reasonableness.

A glance back at the general layout of UCTA in Figure 3.6 will reveal that s 3 can be found in Part 1 of the statute and is one of three sections that are concerned with avoiding liability for breach of contract subject to the condition of reasonableness.

Using the language and grammar of s 3

An initial clue as to the relationship between the various parts of this section can be gathered from a consideration of:

(a) connectors; connectors are words such as:

- 'or';
- 'and';
- 'on';
- 'but';
- 'if';
- 'for';

(b) punctuation;

(c) sentences;

(d) specialist vocabulary.

Connector consideration

Section 3 contains two subsections. Sub-sections are grouped together because they are intimately connected. Therefore, the first task is to look for connectors, those words that indicate what that intimate connection is.

Punctuation consideration

The second task is to consider the punctuation which although sparse is another clue as to which phrases belong together.

Similarly paragraphs and sub-paragraphs within sub-sections are intimately connected.

A diagram (Figure 3.7) can be constructed which gives relational indicators between s 3 and its sub-sections, paragraphs and sub-paragraphs. It can be seen to hang together like a two dimensional mobile. The value of such a diagram is that the links are immediately apparent.

Figure 3.7: relational diagram of s 3

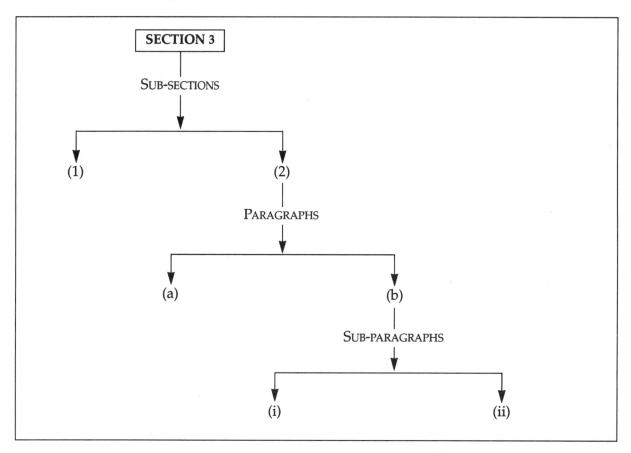

There are only two sentences in s 3. Sub-section (1) and sub-s (2) are both a sentence each. However the sentence making up sub-s (2) is *96 words long*!

The semi-colon in s 3(2)(a) suggests an appropriate end to a sentence but for the fact that the drafter presumably felt it that it would be misleading as the intimate idea-link desired with the rest of s 3(2) might not be made.

Subject search of sentences

Sentence 1: s 3(1)

The subject of the sentence is the 'contracting parties' to whom the '*section*' (that is, s 3 of UCTA) '*applies*'.

When does *the section* apply to contracting parties? In two situations:

(a) *'where one of them deals as a consumer';*

or

(b) *'on the other's written standard terms of business'.*

The important connector word 'or' connects the word 'on' to the previous phrase 'when one of them deals.'

If the word 'or' is replaced by 'and', a different link would be made. Both situations (a) and (b) would need to occur together for s 3(1) to apply. The word, 'or', clarifies that in *either* situation, s 3(1) applies.

So, s 3 applies when one of the parties to a contract is entering the contract as a consumer or agrees to contract on the other party's pre-prepared written standard terms.

Getting this far does not solve any difficulties but merely begins to limit the area covered by the section. It is now possible to exclude classes of contract which are not included in s 3.

All contracts that are *not* consumer contracts or are not on the other party's written standard terms of business are excluded from s 3. Students often fail to notice the negative.

Looking at the original s 3(1), there are still phrases that may need explanation, for example, what do the following phrases mean:

(a) 'deals as a consumer'?

(b) 'written standard terms'?

(c) 'applies'?

The answer to the meaning of (a) and (b) lies in definitional sections in other parts of the statute.

(The answer to (c) lies in reading on!)

Sentence 2: s 3(2)

This section fleshes out the impact of s 3(1) in describing *what* it *is* that *applies*! The ordering is unusual to a first time reader. Surely it might be thought, one should first be told the rule and then told categories that need to comply with it?

Remember that sub-sections within a section are intimately linked so that just as sub-s (1) appears to refer forward by use of the phrase 'This section applies', then a reader of sub-s (2) may need to refer back to sub-s (1) – it may not stand alone.

This cross-referencing takes place immediately in the first words of sub-s (2), '*As against that party, the other'.*

Q: (a) What *'party'* might that be?;

       (b) and who is the *'other'*?

A: (a) The party is the *'one'* who is *'dealing as a consumer or on the others standard terms of business'* in s 3(1).

       (b) Therefore, by process of elimination, the *'other'* is the one who is ***not*** *'dealing as a consumer or on the others standard terms of business'.*

Q: How do I know this?

A: Because 'other' is *specifically referred to* in the first few words of sub-s (2). This other is:

       (a) first, the hidden 'other' referred to by implication in sub-s 3(1) (that is, the one who is *not* dealing as a consumer);

       (b) *secondly*, there is the 'other' party who actually writes the *'standard terms of business'.*

Another implication can be drawn from the wording of this phrase that this 'other' is probably not contracting with a consumer and is more likely to be contracting with a business.

There are, therefore, two categories of 'other'.

Q: So what is the subject of sub-s (2)?

A: It is the *other*.

Q: How do we know this?

A: Because the person or company referred to as *that party* has already been:

(a) identified; and

(b) defined in sub-s 1.

Sub-section 2, therefore, is concerned with what that *other* can and *cannot* do. That is outlined in paras (a) and (b).

It has taken a time textually to explain the interconnections between sub-s (1) and the first seven words of sub-s (2) at a basic level. The full complexities of sub-s (2), paras (a) and (b) have not been touched. Luckily once alerted to the types of issues to look out for, our minds are powerful tools and all of the foregoing discussion, questions, connectors, will begin to be answered and noticed purely mentally whilst reading. A point will be reached when only a few points would actually be noted down.

It is useful, at this stage, to turn again to the words of s 3 so far considered and annotate them.

Figure 3.8: annotation of s 3

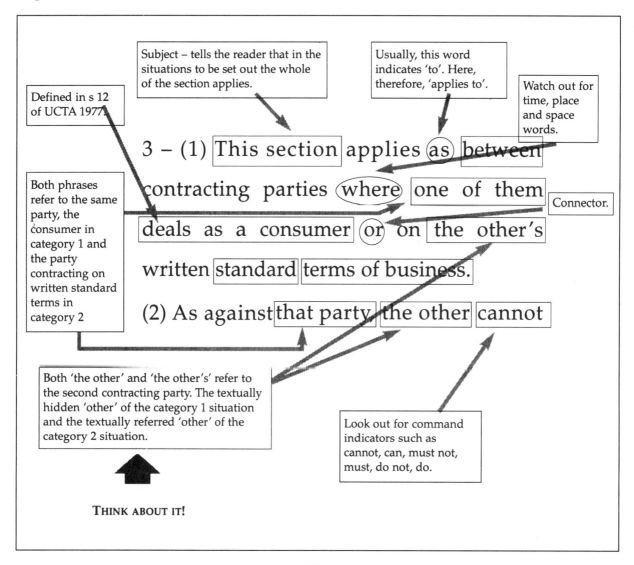

The discussion of 'breaking into' the text has been tedious because it is necessary to set out in minute detail what the experienced reader and analyst scans in seconds, virtually instantaneously, so that the *process* can be examined.

Figure 3.9 sets out s 3 in full; study it carefully and be sure that textual intraconnections are understood.

Note that, as in Figure 3.8, certain words have been outlined. This is to highlight the fact that the key to understanding statutory language and structure is to pay strict attention to grammatical clues as already indicated. In addition, it is vital consistently to look for the prepositional links. Words such as:

(a) to;

   or;

   and;

   if;

   so;

   but;

   therefore,

as these connect the words in the statute together like cement connects bricks in a building.

In addition consider the time and place words, such as:

(b) where;

   when;

   were,

as well as the command style words such as:

(c) cannot;

   may not;

   should not;

   shall,

and beware of subject words which can also be overlooked:

(d) it;

   other;

   one;

   part.

These little words in lists (a)–(d) are the very words that are often overlooked by the hasty reader. Reading in haste is a perilous thing for a lawyer to do.

Now try another difficult section: s 11 of UCTA 1977 (which sets up what has come to be called the *reasonableness test*). Figure 3.10 sets out s 11. Also included in Figure 3.10 are the guidelines for the application of the *reasonableness test* as set out in Schedule 2 of the Act.

Figure 3.10 is a complicated diagram and, as expertise develops in the reading of statutory material, much analysis is done mentally and summarised notes taken. Confidence can result in the ability to paraphrase main provisions in order to catch intratextual references alone.

Figure 3.11 is such a summarised version of s 11 together with Schedule 2 of UCTA 1977. Or, to put it another way, Figure 3.11 is a summarised version of Figure 3.10.

Given the relationship between law cases and statutes, it would also be useful to add, initially in list form only, to a 'section tree diagram' any cases dealing with aspects of the section – cases which may define the meaning of words or phrases or which apply aspects of the section. Figure 3.12 merely adds one case, the case that will be the subject of consideration in Chapter 4.

Figure 3.9: full text of s 3 set out as a tree diagram showing the internal connections

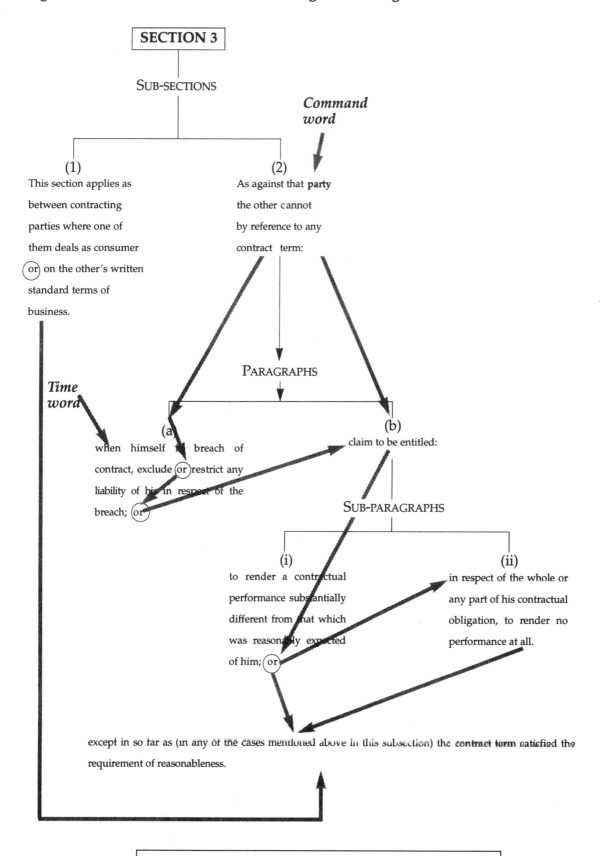

NOTE: follow the grey arrows for linking comprehension
– to understand the intra-textual relationship.

Figure 3.10: layout of s 11 including Schedule 2 of UCTA 1977

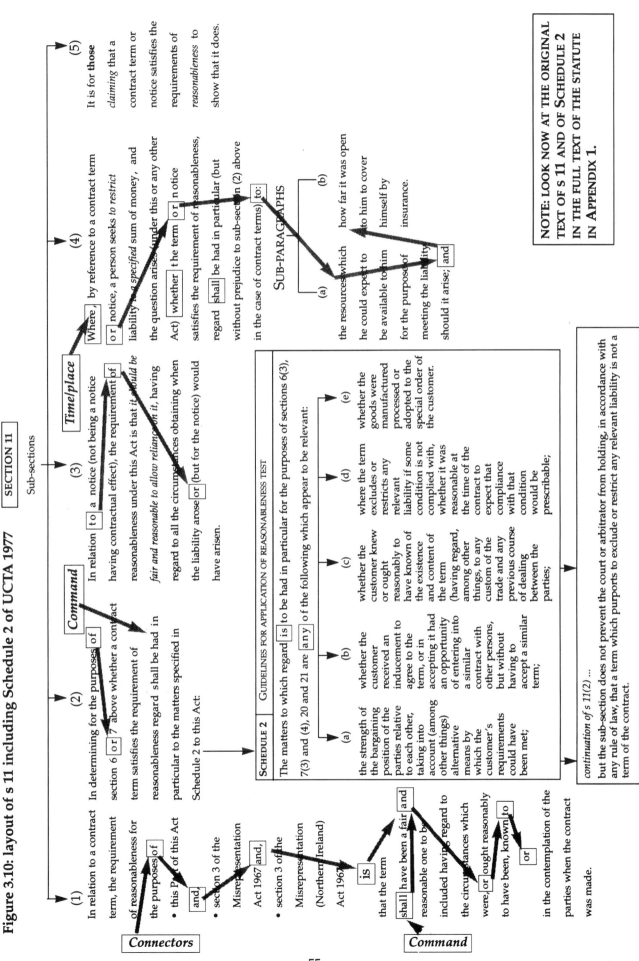

NOTE: LOOK NOW AT THE ORIGINAL TEXT OF s 11 AND OF SCHEDULE 2 IN THE FULL TEXT OF THE STATUTE IN APPENDIX 1.

Figure 3.11: s 11 of UCTA 1977

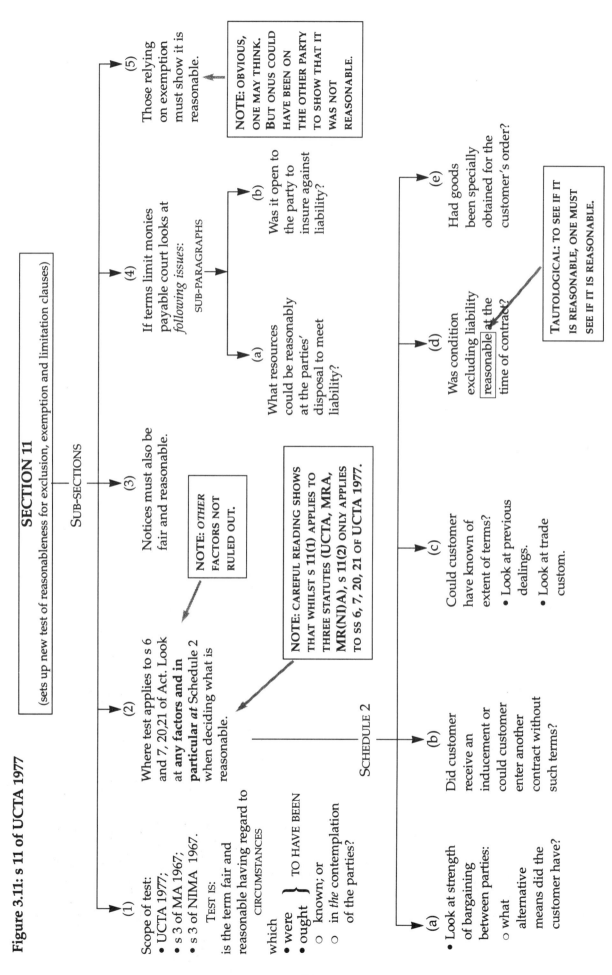

Figure 3.12: s 11 of UCTA 1977

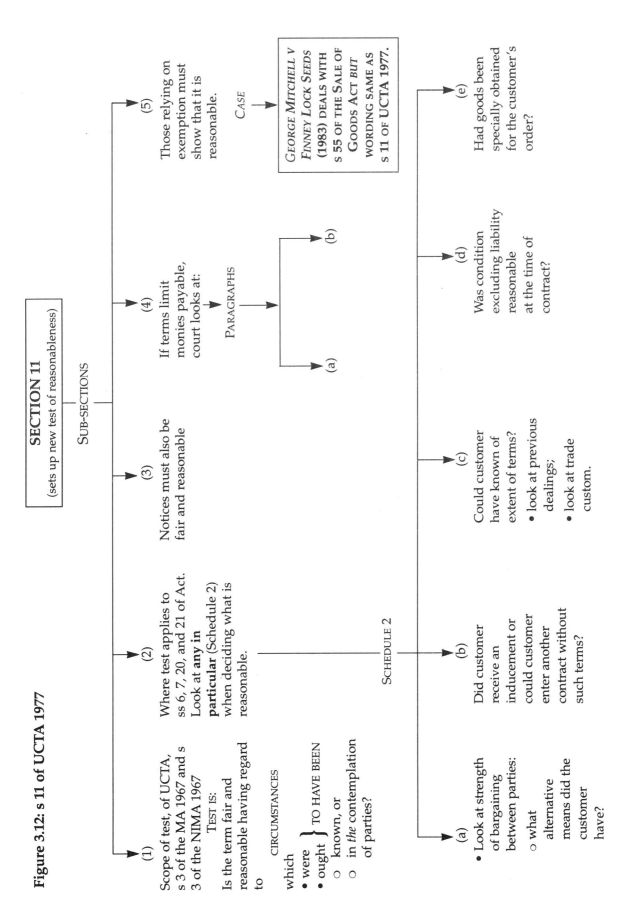

CHAPTER 4

UNDERSTANDING LAW REPORTS

INTRODUCTION

The few legal disputes that cannot be resolved by negotiation between lawyers or last minute settlements outside the court are determined by the judges in the trial courts, and in even fewer cases, decided in the appellate courts by the senior judiciary.

The word, 'few', must be stressed because a law student surrounded by law reports may think that the entire English legal system is composed of nothing but law reports. This is not the case, only about 4% of all formally commenced disputes reach a hearing in court.

The decisions of judges are delivered orally in court and at the time of delivery they are also recorded verbatim by the court stenographer. In addition, official law reporters, as well as unofficial, are in court taking shorthand notes.

Usually, judges in the civil courts and appellate courts (both criminal and civil) will reflect upon the case before reaching a final decision; they therefore hold back (reserve) judgment until a later date. In criminal cases after the jury has reached a verdict in the trial court, the judge may sentence immediately or call for reports and sentence at a later date.

What judges say in their judgments is of immense importance, not only for the litigants, but for the development of the law.

The English legal system is unique in its public insistence that cases must be decided in keeping with the reasoning process used by judges reaching decisions in similar previous cases of the same court or higher. This process of deciding in accordance with past judicial reasoning in similar cases is reasoning in accordance with the *doctrine of precedent*.

The concept of keeping to past decisions is also tied to rules concerning the hierarchy of English courts. Trial courts (or courts of first instance) are at the bottom of the hierarchy and appeal courts at the top.

The House of Lords, as the highest court of appeal, is often referred to as the 'apex' of the court hierarchy. The further up the hierarchy one goes, the fewer cases the court deals with and the longer cases will last. This hierarchical relationship in relation to precedent is set out in Figure 4.1.

Many legal systems throughout the world have a rule of thumb adherence to the doctrine of precedent. However, few keep to the concept of binding precedent as rigidly as the English legal system. Indeed, it has been said that it is more difficult to get rid of an awkward decision in England than it is anywhere else in the world.

Figure 4.1: the hierarchical relationship of the courts

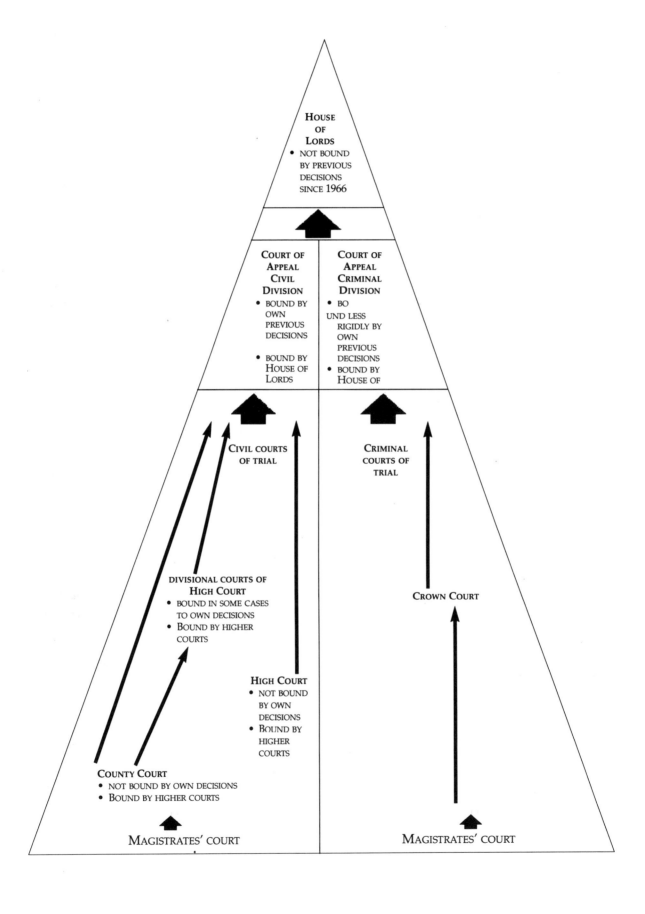

THE RELATIONSHIP BETWEEN LAW REPORTING
AND THE DOCTRINE OF PRECEDENT

The only way of being able to keep successfully to the doctrine of binding precedent is to have a reliable system of law reporting. The competent production of volumes of reports of past cases is indispensable to the operation of the doctrine. Reliable law reports have only been available in England since 1865 although there is a range of law reports going back to the 12th century. However, the accuracy of reports pre-dating the setting up of the Incorporated Council of Law Reporting in 1865 cannot be guaranteed.

Surprisingly, there are no *official*, authoritative series of law reports in England to equate with the *Queen's Printers* copy of an Act of Parliament. Her Majesty's Stationery Office (HMSO) is responsible for publishing revenue, immigration and social security law cases. However, traditionally, law reports remain in the hands of private publishers. Today, there are numerous, often competitive, private publishers.

Although there are no official series of law reports, the courts do respect some reports more than others. A long established, conventional rule is that a law report, if it is to be accepted by the relevant court as an authority, must be prepared by and published under the name of a fully qualified barrister.

Reports existing in the *Yearbooks* cover the period from the late 12th century to the early 16th century. However, it is not always possible to discover if the report is of an actual case or a moot (an argument contest between lawyers). This makes them an unreliable source. Also, the detail that was given and the quality of the reports varies considerably. Some reports record outcome, but not facts, others record facts and outcome, but give no reasoning process. Reports also exist in the Nominate (named) reports dating from the late 15th century to 1865. By the 19th century, a court authorised reporter was attached to all higher courts and their reports were published in collected volumes again by name of reporter.

By 1865, there were 16 reporters compiling and publishing authorised reports. They were amalgamated into the Incorporated Council of Law Reporting and the reports were published in volumes known as the Law Reports. These reports are checked by the judges of the relevant case prior to publication and a rule of citation has developed that if a case is reported in a range of publications, only that version printed in the Law Reports is cited in court. The greater accuracy of modern reporting, and the vetting by judges, necessitates longer delays before the cases are published. Also, the Law Reports only cover 7% of the cases in the higher courts in any given year. Interesting issues are:

(a) Who selects which cases to report?

(b) How are they selected?

Editors select the cases for inclusion for the publishers. These are highly trained lawyers, well acquainted with precedent and the likely importance of cases. During the past 100 years publishers of law reports have been generalists or specialists. Some law reports are annotated, particularly for the use of practitioners, others left without annotations, introductions, etc. In addition to reported cases, the Supreme Court Library contains thousands of files of unreported cases. In 1940, the Lord Chancellor's Department prepared a report: *The Report of the Law Reporting Committee*. The Committee considered that, after editors had made their choices, 'What remains is less likely to be a treasure house than a rubbish heap in which a jewel will rarely, if ever, be discovered' (p 20). (Note the poetic language that forcefully carries the point.)

Of course, today, there is a vast range of electronic retrieval systems, which contain thousands of details of unreported cases. This has caused its own problems and there was a legitimate concern that courts would be inundated with cases that did not really contain any new law, but which had been retrieved from electronic sources. In the case of *Roberts Petroleum Ltd v Bernard Kenny Ltd*

(1983), the House of Lords took the step of forbidding the citation of unreported cases of the civil division of the Court of Appeal without special leave. The rule remains, however, that to be an accepted version that can be quoted in court the report must have been prepared and published by a barrister.

When law students read law reports they must ask:

(a) is this report the most authoritative version available?;

(b) are there fuller versions?;

(c) if unreported, does this case add to the law?

Figure 4.2 sets out the types of reports available for the law student to consult.

THE THEORETICAL DIMENSIONS OF THE DOCTRINE OF PRECEDENT

Many theorists and practitioners have attempted, over the years, to give precise definitions of the English doctrine of precedent, unfortunately for law students, there are no simple shortcuts to understanding the practical everyday working of the doctrine of precedent.

However, a few theoretical ground rules can be established, which at least place its operation within a context:

(a) judges in the higher courts must follow previous decisions of their own court or that of a higher court if the case was similar;

(b) since a Practice Statement by the Lord Chancellor in 1966, judges in the House of Lords have the freedom to decline to follow their own previous decisions.

Much depends on the definition of similar. How similar must a previous case be before it becomes a precedent to be followed in a current case? Notice, again, how everything turns on language and the meaning of words.

The facts of cases usually vary in some way. Law is about life and life rarely replicates itself.

(a) Must the law be similar now as then?

(b) What happens if there are small differences?

(c) What if there are a range of small differences is the case sufficiently similar?

There are no definitions of similar for the purposes of the doctrine and this is where the judge can bring subjective influences into the decision making processes.

In addition, how can the reason for the case be extracted? Similar cases must be decided in accordance with the same reasoning process.

The actual doctrine as it has developed refers to keeping to the reasons for deciding past cases. How does one find the reasoning?

Wambaugh, a theorist working in America in the late 19th century, suggests that one way of ascertaining the reason for the decision (*ratio decidendi*) is to look for a general rule of law in the judgments and test whether it is foundational for deciding the case by translating it into the negative form and seeing if the case would then have been decided differently.

In other words, he suggests locating the *ratio* by using a negative method as illustrated by the flow chart in Figure 4.3. Wambaugh emphasises the *search* for a rule.

Figure 4.2: the range of available law reports

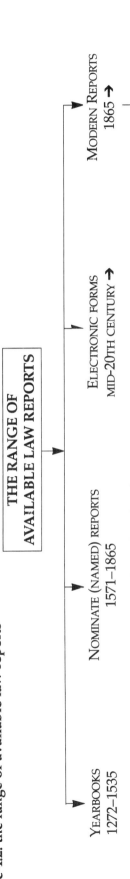

THE RANGE OF
AVAILABLE LAW REPORTS

YEARBOOKS
1272–1535

Anonymously compiled for, it is thought, the personal use of lawyers.

They were:
- handwritten;
- language: legal French;
- a few printed from 15th century onwards;
- concentrated on the pleadings;
- often no judgment recorded.

They are rarely cited today.

Modern reprints include a series by the Selsdon Society.

NOMINATE (NAMED) REPORTS
1571–1865

Begins with Edmund Plowden's *Commentaries* and ends with the founding of the law reports in 1865.

The earliest reports were never meant to be published. There was little attempt to systematise the reports until the mid-18th century.

Then, in the 18th century, Burrow, Cowper and Douglas began to standardise the layout.

In the late 18th century, judges began to review reports of their judgments or make written versions available to reporters. They also got involved in the appointment of reporters to courts.

Reports began to be published more quickly.

ELECTRONIC FORMS
MID-20TH CENTURY →

MODERN REPORTS
1865 →

Generalist

Specialist

Advance edited

Full version

Edited

Full version

NOTES:
- Weekly Law Reports (WLR) take five months to be published;
- the Law Reports (LR) take 10–14 months to be published;
- cases in Appellate Courts appear on *LEXIS*, an electronic data base, within days;
- there are about 500 different publishers;
- English Reports 1771–1865 most comprehensive;
- Revised Reports 1785–1865;
- All England Reports (All ER). A selection between 1558–1993.

Figure 4.3: Wambaugh's method for locating the *ratio*

EXTRACT A PROPOSITION OF LAW.

CHANGE ITS FORMULATION TO THE NEGATIVE.

APPLY THE NEGATIVE FORMULATION TO THE CASE.

IF OUTCOME IS THE SAME: THE IDENTIFIED PROPOSITION OF LAW *is not* THE *RATIO* OF THE CASE.

IF OUTCOME IS NOT THE SAME: THE IDENTIFIED PROPOSITION OF LAW *IS* THE *RATIO* OF THE CASE.

> **PROBLEM: this method is designed to work only with one proposition of law. Cases can have more than one proposition.**

Another famous legal theorist, Goodhart, wrote an influential essay 'Determining the *ratio* of a case' which refers far more to the *'principle'* in the case than the *'ratio'*. He emphasises facts:

(a) What are the material facts as found by the judge?

(b) What is the judge's decision?

(c) Unless there is a new material fact (or there are some missing material facts) a future court depending upon its place in the court hierarchy and, thus, its obligations under the doctrine of precedent, must follow it.

Goodhart does consider the rule, or what he calls the principle of the case. He gives a thorough discussion of finding the principle of a case, which revolves around the tension between a range of issues. He also appears clearer about where he considers the principle *cannot* be found.

A major problem with Goodhart's suggested method, an aspect of which is set out in Figure 4.5, is that he places rather a lot of emphasis upon the facts.

Although it can be said that reading a judgment in the light of the facts of the case is a core requirement of the doctrine, there also needs to be attention given to the way that the case was:

(a) argued;

(b) pleaded; and

(c) reasoned,

in relation to other precedents. Every judgment has to be read in the light of previous and, if relevant, subsequent cases.

Even taking these two methods together, problems remain:

(a) what should an interpreter do when there is a decision without reasons? Can the *ratio* be inferred?;

(b) what can be done with the diversity of forms of judgments?

While it is true to say that the *ratio decidendi* of a previous case comes from the language of a judge, the interpreter (as seen from Chapter 2) can bring new meanings.

WHAT HAPPENS WHEN THERE IS MORE THAN ONE JUDGMENT?

In the appellate courts, depending upon the importance of the case, three, five or seven judges can sit. Each can give judgment, although often a judge says 'I concur with my learned colleague, Lord Bridge' or some such similar phrase. At times there may be one or more judgments disagreeing with the majority view that a certain litigant should win the case.

In such cases, there is no doubt that *each reasoned judgment* has a *ratio*. But can it be said that there is a *ratio of the court*?

There is, of course, no problem where it is clear that the majority agree with the same statements of the application of the law. But what if the different judges *agree* on outcome and *disagree* on reasons for the outcome? This can happen.

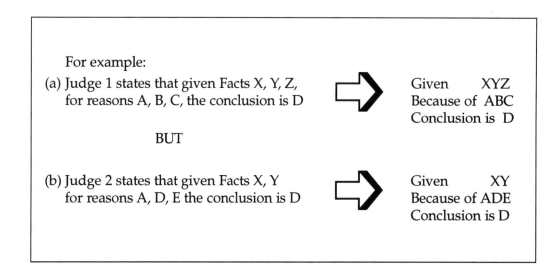

How can these differences be reconciled?

There are therefore a range of situations which complicate statements about the bindingness or strength of a given precedent. Lack of agreement among judges in relation to the reasoning process can weaken the precedential value of the case, because judgments in cases can result in different scenarios:

For example:

(a) the majority of judges agree to dismiss/allow the appeal on one ground.

A minority of judges agree with the majority as to *outcome*, but base their decision on a *different* ground.

In this situation, the *ratio* of the majority is binding and strong. The *ratio* of the minority is entitled to weighty consideration in a future case;

(b) the majority agree to dismiss/allow the appeal but there is no common ground as to why the appeal has been dismissed or allowed.

In this situation, there is no clear majority in favour of any *ratio*. The case, therefore, lacks authority for the narrowest interpretation of the *ratio*. But it is impossible to state clearly how such a case is viewed other than to treat it as a weak authority.

When there is a strong original *ratio* that is wide, there is most scope for later interpretation to mould the law. What seems clear is that at the time of the case the *ratio* for which the decision is binding is to be found in the actual opinion of the judge. However, in later cases, seeking to interpret and apply the earlier case, the judge seeking the ration can interpret that earlier case in the light of the facts and subsequent cases.

Figure 4.5: Goodhart's method of locating the *ratio*

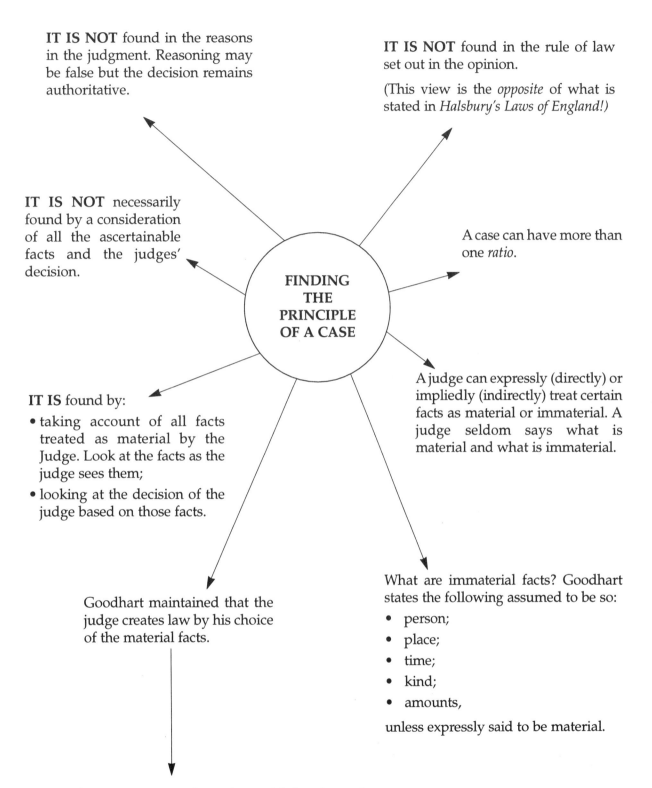

IT IS NOT found in the reasons in the judgment. Reasoning may be false but the decision remains authoritative.

IT IS NOT found in the rule of law set out in the opinion.

(This view is the *opposite* of what is stated in *Halsbury's Laws of England!*)

IT IS NOT necessarily found by a consideration of all the ascertainable facts and the judges' decision.

A case can have more than one *ratio*.

FINDING THE PRINCIPLE OF A CASE

A judge can expressly (directly) or impliedly (indirectly) treat certain facts as material or immaterial. A judge seldom says what is material and what is immaterial.

IT IS found by:
- taking account of all facts treated as material by the Judge. Look at the facts as the judge sees them;
- looking at the decision of the judge based on those facts.

Goodhart maintained that the judge creates law by his choice of the material facts.

What are immaterial facts? Goodhart states the following assumed to be so:
- person;
- place;
- time;
- kind;
- amounts,

unless expressly said to be material.

NOTE: however, Rupert Cross has said that it can be impossible to formulate the ratio by reference to the facts regarded as material. You may need to know what legal rules the court was thinking of and also know why certain facts were seen as material.

What seems to happen is that, when a judge is considering Case E currently before the court:

(a) the judge states what is considered to be the *ratio* in the earlier Case A;

(b) the judge then considers that *ratio* in the light of the facts in Case A;

(c) the judge also considers the observations made by judges in later Cases B, C and D concerning Case A.

(d) ultimately, the judge formulates a rule of law based on a number of cases, the original Case A and Cases B, C and D and applies this composite reasoning to Case E before the court.

However, before previous cases can be considered as potential *ratios* they need to be located according to whether or not they are similar to the present case.

Sometimes, counsel for the litigants will strenuously argue that previous cases are not precedents because they can be distinguished on their facts. In other words, they are not similar. The court may agree out of persuasion or policy. In this way extremely subtle 'differences' are found between two cases.

It is difficult if not impossible to come up with a clear formula that will always work for ascertaining the *ratio* of a case. But a reasonable idea of the *difficulties* in ascertaining the *ratio* is a necessary and revealing step for any interpreter engaged in the search for a *ratio*.

Appreciation of the difficulties prevents simplistic case analysis which will ultimately lead to simplistic and inadequate construction of legal arguments. If an argument is being made on strong, weak, tenuous or stretched grounds, it is better to know than be ignorant as to the basis of the case one is constructing.

One of the major difficulties involved concerns the different types of information and skills that have to be utilised in deciding whether a case is a precedent. To provide some light relief, work through the questions in the chart in Figure 4.6. It is an over simplistic chart asking some of the necessary questions to decide if a previous case constitutes a precedent to be followed in a current case.

As mentioned above, the law tends to work through generalised rules which have to be applied to specific circumstances. This is why lawyers spend so much time comparing, contrasting and differentiating situations, for they are constructing arguments based upon similarity and difference. Legal rules are, by convention and necessity, expressed as general rules. Lawyers have to reason from the generality of the rule to the specificity of the situation.

At times, lawyers have to research previous cases meticulously to assist in prediction of the outcome of the current case. After all, there is no point in going to court if the exact point the client wishes to make has already come before a court and been determined.

Part of the lawyer's particular expertise is knowing how to look quickly through past cases to find relevant decisions either supporting or opposing a client's case. The location of materials is relatively easy given the range of on-line databases available.

Unfortunately students often do not have unlimited access to training in how to use such databases. So, there is a need to rely on one of the citators to locate relevant cases.

Searches can be made, first, to pinpoint cases dealing with specific legal rules; secondly, a range of cases with similar facts can be located through analysing the first trawl of data.

These cases then need to be carefully read and analysed in the law library. The lawyer has to construct an argument and predict the opponent's arguments. This is done by, initially, checking relevant cases.

It must be evident by now that the ability to locate and subsequently analyse law reports are extremely important skills.

After careful reading, the lawyer has to construct detailed arguments concerning similarities with other cases that help the client's position, and arguments need to be constructed demolishing the potential precedent value of cases not helping the client. This latter skill is called *distinguishing*.

Figure 4.6: chart for assistance in deciding whether a given case constitutes a binding precedent

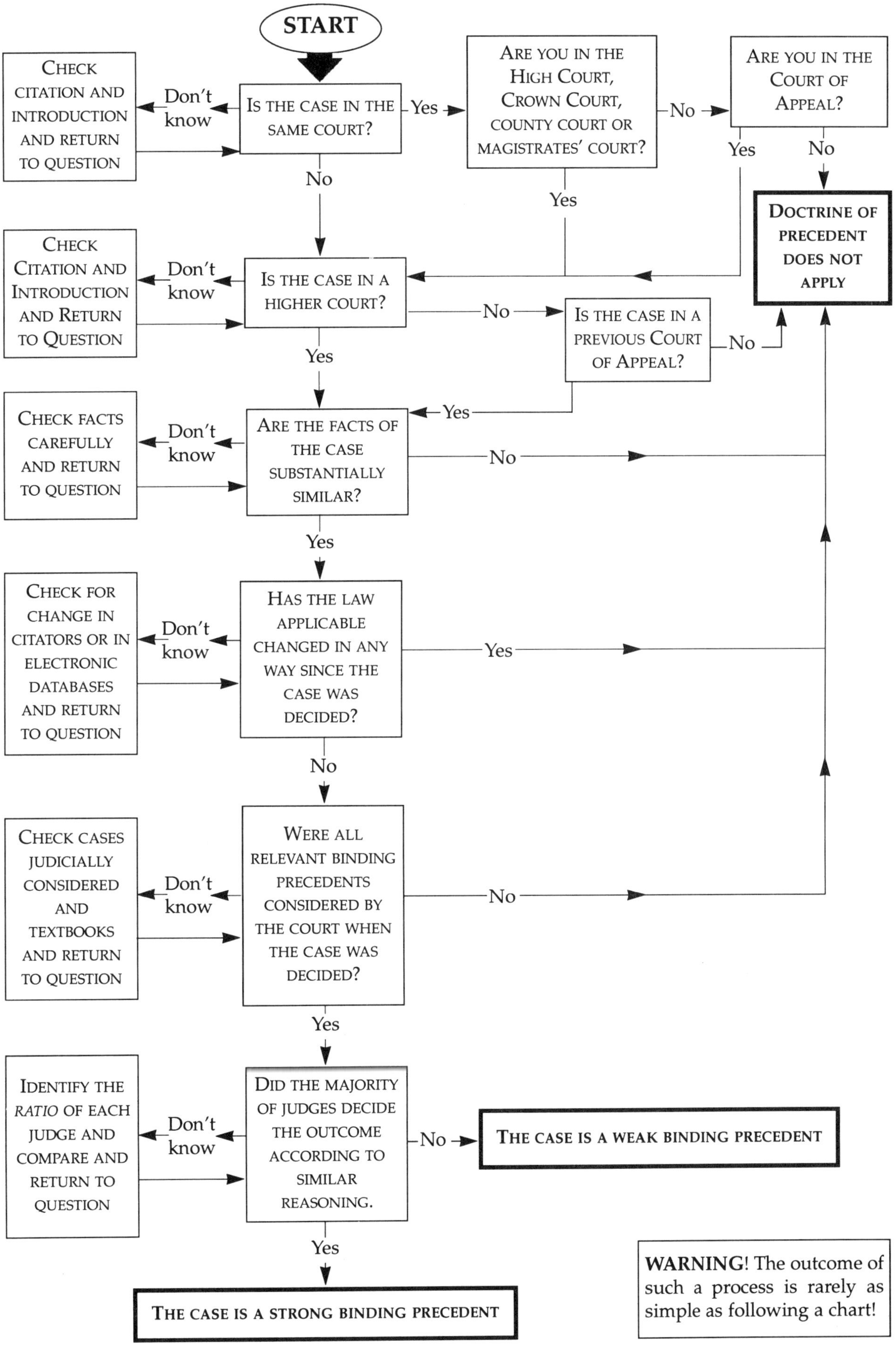

WARNING! The outcome of such a process is rarely as simple as following a chart!

This is a particularly important skill for those who wish to ensure that a precedent is not followed.

A lawyer may need to argue convincingly that the part of the previous judgment that is being relied on by an opponent is not part of the reasoning process leading to judgment; that it was an 'aside' comment, based on a hypothetical situation.

On the other hand, perhaps the only argument a lawyer has to support client's position is an aside comment (technically referred to as *obiter dictum*). If the comment was made by a senior judge in the Court of Appeal or the House of Lords, and it is a relevant comment on the exact circumstances of the present case, then it could be argued that this is an important indicator of what that court would do if such a case came before it.

Cases in the higher appellate courts, the Court of Appeal and the House of Lords, contain more than one judgment. Usually, there are three in the Court of Appeal and five in the House of Lords, but there can be more in an important case. Here, the lawyers' task in ascertaining the strength of a precedent in a previous case may be more difficult.

Often, there will be a dissenting judgment. This judgment can eventually, through a range of other cases, come to represent the majority view of an area of law. If the judge who is dissenting has a particular reputation for excellence, then the judgment will be seriously considered by those coming to read the case for the precedential value of the majority judgments. In time, the argument presented by the dissenting judge, the minority view, may be accepted as the more appropriate way forward.

English law, as created, developed and refined in the courts, does not resemble a straight line of development; rather, it is a winding road of distinctions; consideration of majority and minority views; determinations according to similarity; more judgments; then more distinctions. Change is slow but law remains flexible, as illustrated in Figure 4.7.

Figure 4.7: slow but sure?

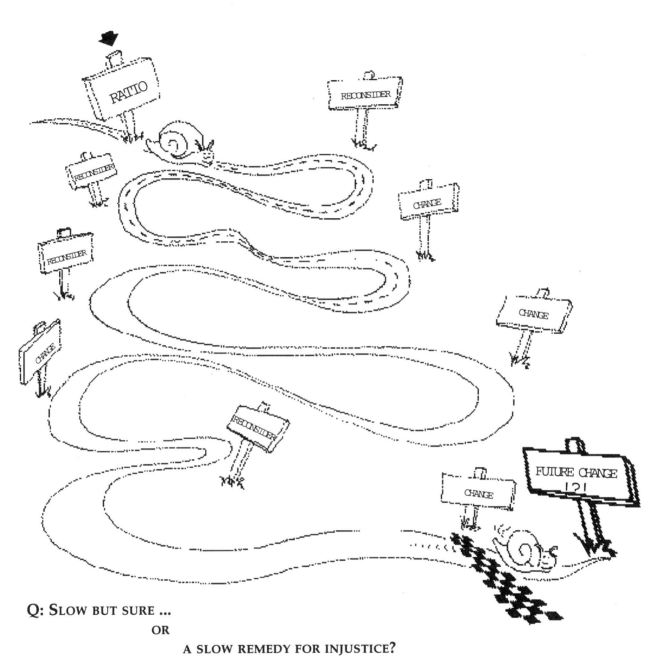

Q: Slow but sure ...
        OR
    A slow remedy for injustice?

THE DOCTRINE OF PRECEDENT IN PRACTICE

When law cases in any area are considered, it is important that the reader knows and holds in tension several things about the case for future usage. These are set out in Figure 4.8.

Figure 4.8: issues that must be understood to apply a case

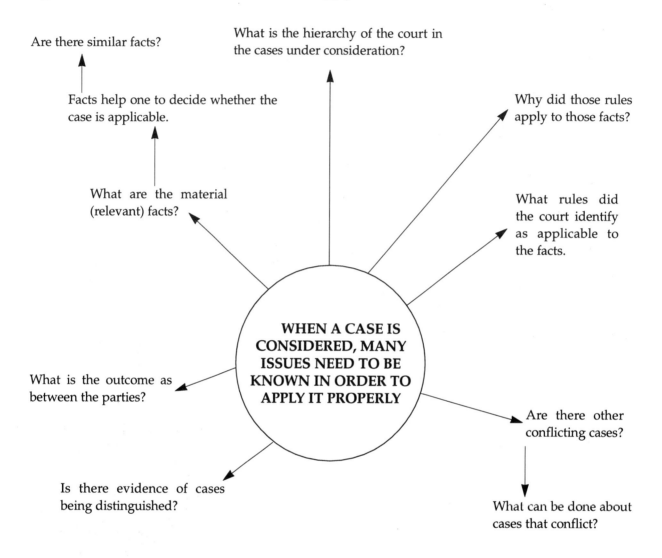

What happens if a judge does not like a precedent?

Some judges are better than others at 'dodging' precedent:

> If a judge of reasonable strength of mind thought a particular precedent was wrong he must be a great fool if he couldn't get round it.
>
> [Lord Radcliffe (House of Lords) in an interview with Alan Patterson (1984).]

Yet, contrast this with the following quotation:

> I am unable to adduce any reason to show that the decision which I am about to pronounce is right – but I am bound by authority which of course it is my duty to follow.
>
> [*Per* Buckley LJ, *Olympia Oil and Cake Co Ltd v Produce Brokers Ltd* (1915).]

> **It is all a matter of interpretation! Perhaps the difficulties of this area are beginning to become apparent.**

Figure 4.9: a typical English law report with its constituent parts labelled

Figure 4.10: the anatomy of a law report

As revealed by Figure 4.9, each law report is made up of a range of parts each doing different things which are as follows:

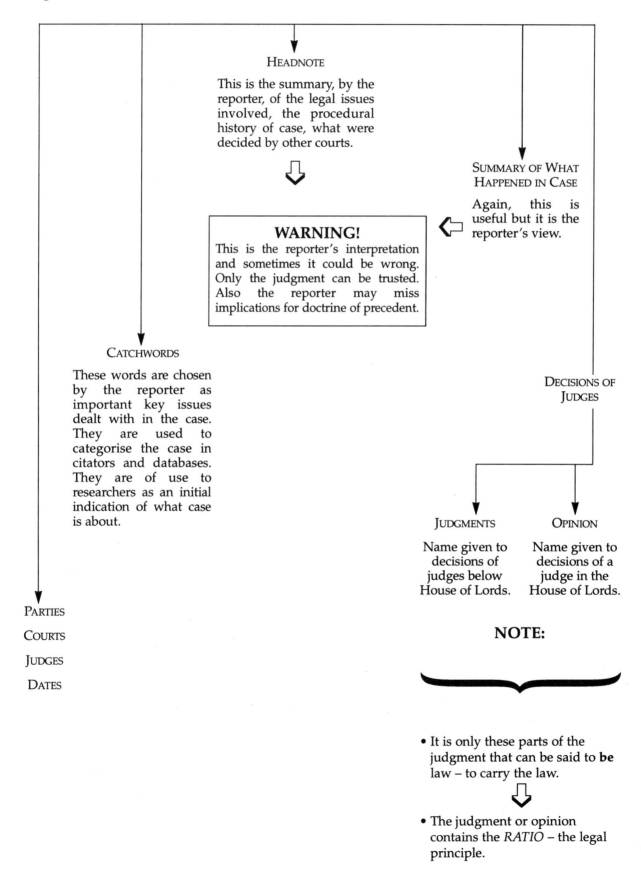

In the same way that religious texts can be said to be literature in terms of both prose and poetry, so the law report can also be considered as a literary text.

The illustrations and aside comments made by judges in their judgments may be complex, relating to politics, history, art, religion, literature and so on. Quotations may be given in different languages and reports can sometimes be liberally peppered with Latin legal maxims (see Figure 4.11 for some of the most common). Law reports are complex pieces of written English and, therefore, of double difficulty to students in terms of their legal content and, generally, in terms of their sophisticated English usage.

All judges have different ways of expressing themselves but they all share seniority within the English legal system. Unlike other jurisdictions there is no such concept as the career judge. Promotion to the 'bench' occurs as recognition of years of proven ability, usually, as a barrister. However, lower ranks of the judiciary are now appointed from successful solicitors.

Therefore, although law students are very new to the enterprise of law, they are called upon to engage in sophisticated evaluation of the highly competent analysis of the English legal system's most senior judges, who combine years of successful practice with excellent skills in language usage and technical substantive law ability. These judges may discuss several complex issues simultaneously, applying and interpreting the law to the facts of specific disputes.

The student is, therefore, confronted by excellent and sophisticated written texts and needs:

- a good grasp of the relevant area of substantive law;
- an appreciation of issues relating to language usage;
- an understanding of the doctrine of precedent in practice;
- a familiarity with statute;
- a sound foundation in the mechanics of argument construction to make initial sense of the text.

Judges are social actors with their own preferences who attempt to act fairly in judgment despite themselves and their natural inclinations. However, at root a judgment is a subjective text and a student's or a lawyer's interpretation of that text is also subjective. It should be tested against the text and evaluated to see if it is a plausible reading. As noted already in Chapter 2, the language of the law tries to be injected with scientific objectivity, but flounders because of the imprecision of language.

One law report will now be considered in depth in order to demonstrate one method of reading, note taking, evaluating and using a case to construct arguments.

It will, initially, be approached as a sophisticated English comprehension exercise. This will demonstrate how far one can get by meticulous reading in the absence of detailed knowledge of a particular area of law, (in this case, the law of contract). No assumptions will be made concerning the reader's knowledge of the law of contract.

It is, of course, useful if a student *does* understand the legal context of a dispute. For this reason, the basic framework of the law of contract is set out in Figure 4.12. The events which occur in *George Mitchell* are signalled by the square.

Figure 4.11: some common Latin phrases used by judges in reports

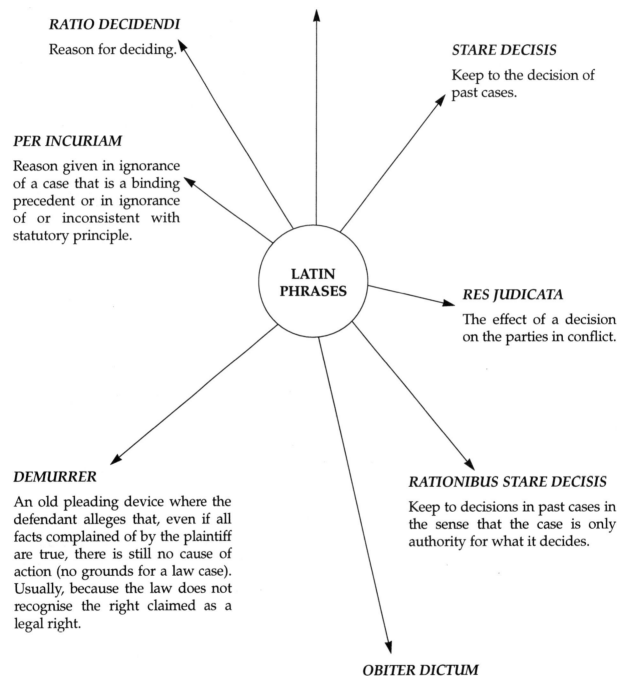

CESSANTE RATIONE CESAT IPSA LEX

When the reason of the rule ceases then the rule ceases too.

RATIO DECIDENDI

Reason for deciding.

STARE DECISIS

Keep to the decision of past cases.

PER INCURIAM

Reason given in ignorance of a case that is a binding precedent or in ignorance of or inconsistent with statutory principle.

LATIN PHRASES

RES JUDICATA

The effect of a decision on the parties in conflict.

DEMURRER

An old pleading device where the defendant alleges that, even if all facts complained of by the plaintiff are true, there is still no cause of action (no grounds for a law case). Usually, because the law does not recognise the right claimed as a legal right.

RATIONIBUS STARE DECISIS

Keep to decisions in past cases in the sense that the case is only authority for what it decides.

OBITER DICTUM

A judicial opinion that is not necessary for the decision in the case. It can be a proposition of law that is not the *ratio*. It can be a conclusion based on a fact the existence of which has not been determined. It can be a conclusion based on hypothetical facts.

Figure 4.12: diagrammatic representation of the law of contract

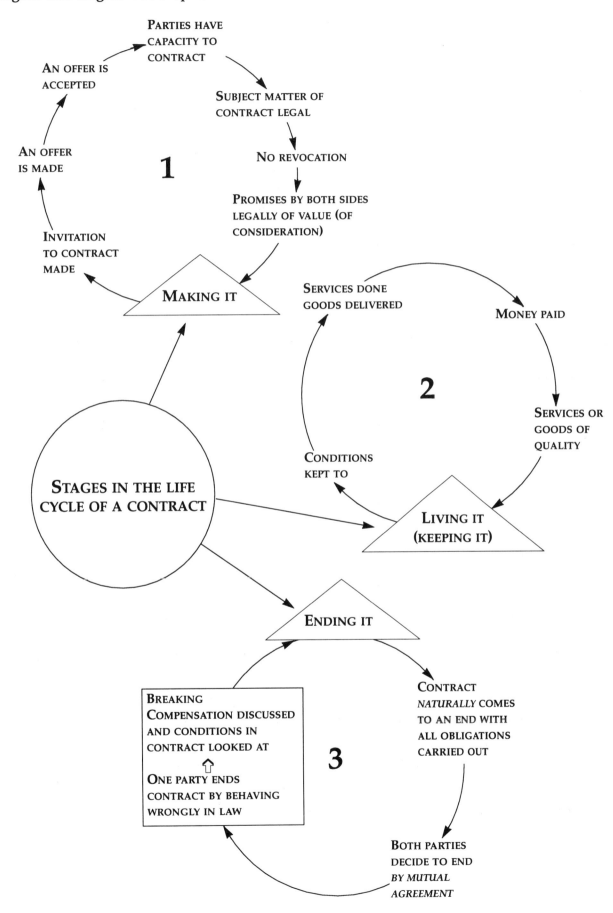

The case of *George Mitchell v Finney Lock Seeds*

Of the three main areas of the law of contract identified in Figure 4.12:

- making it;
- living it (keeping it);
- ending it,

the case under consideration concerns 'ending it' (breaking it by wrongdoing).

In other words, it is concerned with what should happen under the contract to compensate the plaintiff. (The plaintiff is the person or company complaining and bringing a case in the civil courts.) Usually, contracts contain provisions that lay down the compensation payable to one party if the other party breaks the contract by not doing what he or she says will be done. The contract in *George Mitchell (Chesterhall) Ltd v Finney Lock Seeds* is no exception.

However, to ascertain properly what the main issues are in the case it has to be broken into with some determination. This case has been specifically chosen for several reasons:

(a) it is short;

(b) there is only one main, agreed judgment;

(c) the issues discussed are highly complex;

(d) the case involves consideration of both common law rules and statutory rules operating side by side;

(e) it links into the work already discussed in Chapter 3;

(f) it links into Chapter 6.

Any student successfully breaking into this case and comprehending the methodology will be able to use it to break into other cases.

STOP NOW!

(a) Turn to Appendix 2.

(b) Read the case of *George Mitchell v Finney Lock Seeds* as quickly as you can. If this takes you more than 60 minutes you need to work on your reading strategies generally.

(c) As you read, note how paragraphs begin and end, as these are often indicators of the progression of discussion or argument.

(d) Carefully register differences in language as you move from the information packed first pages through to the different judgments:

- be aware of the use of any technical language;
- look up non-technical words you do not understand in a good dictionary.

After this initial skim, it should be possible to have a view as to what this case is about:

(a) remember that the section of the law report that contains the law is the judgment;

(b) *remember that the binding aspect of the judgment is the* ratio decidendi ...

> **the** reason for deciding
>> the **reason** for deciding
>>> the reason **for** deciding
>>>> the reason for **deciding;**

(c) knowledge of facts alone does not give you a clue as to the precedent;

(d) knowledge of the applicable rules alone does not give you the precedent;

(e) knowledge of rules and facts does not give you the precedent. Only the **reasons *why those* rules applied to *those* facts gives you an understanding of the precedent created**.

Intellectual Health Warning!

Do not proceed with this chapter until you have quickly read the case.

What is the case about?

Many students pick up that it is about a buyer of seeds wanting compensation because he was sold the wrong seeds. Furthermore, the buyer made it clear which seeds he wanted. However, this is far too general a description of the issues in the case. On a first reading, with the help of the headnote it may have been apparent that the buyer won this case which, incidentally, was on appeal in the House of Lords.

But knowing that a supplier of seeds has to pay compensation to a buyer if the wrong seeds are delivered will not give you any useful information for future use. It certainly does not give the precedent of the case.

So look again.

(a) What are the facts in this case? Make a note.

(b) Are any of the facts disputed by the parties or are they agreed? Write your answer.

(c) What are the specific issues in this case? State them in list form.

(d) What is the procedural history of the case? What other courts has this case been in and what did the previous courts decide?

Answering questions (a)–(d) properly enables you to follow the development of arguments.

Go back and carefully read and make notes on:

(e) the headnote;

(f) the procedural history;

(g) the judgment of Lord Bridge;

(h) list words and phrases that you do not know, check them out in a dictionary or in the text for sense.

DO NOT CONTINUE OVER UNTIL YOU HAVE COMPLETED (a)–(h). WHEN YOU HAVE FINISHED, CONTINUE BELOW ...

Figure 4.13: *George Mitchell v Finney Lock Seeds (1983): facts, issues and procedural history*

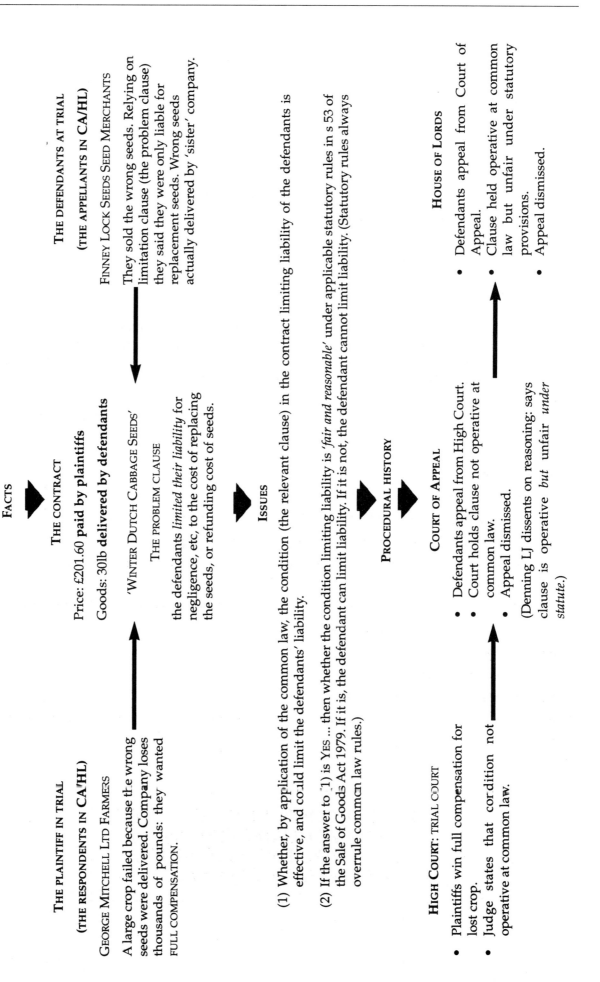

FACTS

THE PLAINTIFF IN TRIAL

(THE RESPONDENTS IN **CA/HL**)

GEORGE MITCHELL LTD FARMERS

A large crop failed because the wrong seeds were delivered. Company loses thousands of pounds: they wanted FULL COMPENSATION.

THE DEFENDANTS AT TRIAL

(THE APPELLANTS IN **CA/HL**)

FINNEY LOCK SEEDS SEED MERCHANTS

They sold the wrong seeds. Relying on limitation clause (the problem clause) they said they were only liable for replacement seeds. Wrong seeds actually delivered by 'sister' company.

THE CONTRACT

Price: £201.60 paid by plaintiffs

Goods: 30lb delivered by defendants

'WINTER DUTCH CABBAGE SEEDS'

THE PROBLEM CLAUSE

the defendants *limited their liability* for negligence, etc, to the cost of replacing the seeds, or refunding cost of seeds.

ISSUES

(1) Whether, by application of the common law, the condition (the relevant clause) in the contract limiting liability of the defendants is effective, and could limit the defendants' liability.

(2) If the answer to '1) is YES ... then whether the condition limiting liability is *'fair and reasonable'* under applicable statutory rules in s 53 of the Sale of Goods Act 1979. If it is, the defendant can limit liability. If it is not, the defendant cannot limit liability. (Statutory rules always overrule common law rules.)

PROCEDURAL HISTORY

HIGH COURT: TRIAL COURT

- Plaintiffs win full compensation for lost crop.
- Judge states that condition not operative at common law.

COURT OF APPEAL

- Defendants appeal from High Court.
- Court holds clause not operative at common law.
- Appeal dismissed.

(Denning LJ dissents on reasoning: says clause is operative *but* unfair *under statute.*)

HOUSE OF LORDS

- Defendants appeal from Court of Appeal.
- Clause held operative at common law but unfair under statutory provisions.
- Appeal dismissed.

(i) Did you find all the facts, and issues?

(j) Did you correctly ascertain the procedural history?

Check yourself against the diagram in Figure 4.13. This diagram was constructed by a careful reading of the headnote together with the introductory summaries made by the law reporter of the decisions in the earlier courts and in the court deciding the actual report being read. These explanations are the reporter's summaries and do not form part of the law.

**Do not forget that the only part
of the law report containing the law
is the judgment of each judge.**

Finding and beginning to understand the issues in the case

It is necessary to look in detail at the issues because these may seem extremely complicated on a first reading. Did you find all the issues? The issues, according to Lord Bridge, are as follows:

(1) The first issue is whether the relevant condition, on its true construction in the context of the contract as a whole , is effective to limit the appellant's liability to a refund of ... the price of the seeds (the common law issue).

(2) The second issue is whether, if the common law issue is decided in the appellant's favour, they should nevertheless be precluded from reliance on this limitation of liability pursuant to the provisions of the modified s55 of the Sale of Goods Act 1979 which is set out in para 11 of Schedule 1 to the Act and which applies to contracts made between 18 May 1973 and 1 February 1978 (the statutory issue).

[Lord Bridge, see Appendix 2, p 238, para 4, below.]

Figure 4.13 states the issues, although finding and understanding what these issues are as a matter of basic comprehension is not easy. The identification of the correct sentences because the judge has stated these are the issues does not necessarily lead to an understanding of what the issues are and what is meant by them.

So how can one begin to understand these issues. The immediate problems are:

(a) unfamiliar vocabulary;

(b) unfamiliar legal references;

(c) complex grammatical structure.

The first task is to annotate the above text to reveal the areas of lack of understanding and the areas of interconnection. This is similar in method to the annotation of s 3 of UCTA 1977 in Chapter 3. This is done in Figure 4.14.

Figure 4.14: the *two* issues as set out by Lord Bridge

Issue (1)

What is 'the relevant condition'? It is the one mentioned by Lord Bridge on p 238. It is his label for the contentious clause that is the subject of case. On p 238, he divides the condition into three clauses. See Figure 4.15.

The first issue is whether the relevant condition, on its true construction in the context of the contract as a whole, is effective to limit the appellant's liability to a refund of ... the price of the seeds (the common law issue). [Lord Bridge, p 740, para (d).]

This relates to the law made through precedent in the courts. Contract is a creature of precedent not Parliament. But over the years, Parliament has intervened to protect parties.

This is crucial. The condition agreed by the buyers is that *if* there is a problem they can only claim back the cost of the seeds. But here the loss of the buyers is in the region of £60,000. The seeds cost a mere £201.60.

Issue (2)

The second issue is only live if the answer to 1 is 'yes' if at common law it is a valid condition *then* the court looks at the protective role of the statute.

The common law condition limits the liability of the seller to replacement cost of seeds.

The second issue is whether, if the common law issue is decided in the appellant's favour, they should nevertheless be precluded from reliance on this limitation of liability pursuant to the provisions of the modified s 55 of the Sale of Goods Act 1979 which is set out in para 11 of Sched 1 to the Act and which applies to contracts made between 18 May 1973 and 1 February 1978 (the statutory issue). [Lord Bridge, p 740, para (d).]

The appellants are the sellers. See Figure 4.12.

This is a section found in Schedule 1, para 11 of Sale of Goods Act 1979.

The Sale of Goods Act 1979.

This is the second issue. The decision is whether the statute applies, hence the statutory issue. It concerns the judicial interpretation of the legislation.

As can be seen, a number of matters needing to be clarified arise from the mere identification of these issues. However, students often read and re-read without appreciating how to move from lack of understanding towards understanding. They do not notice how words can be clarified by an appreciation of the intertextual links and which words or phrases could be clarified by recourse to text books in the area.

It is useful here to ensure that the procedural history of this case is understood. This will enable the student to obtain an appreciation of the differences in opinion by the various judges who have considered the case before its arrival in the House of Lords. Lord Bridge discusses the procedural history and it is set out in the headnote.

The case was won by the plaintiffs (the buyers) in the trial court (the High Court) and the defendants (the sellers) appealed to the Court of Appeal, where they are called the appellants, and again lost. They then appealed to the House of Lords , where they also lost. There was a lot of money at stake: the difference between the £201.60 that the seeds cost as awarded by the Court of Appeal or the £90,000+ that the trial judge awarded.

Consider, for a moment, what you have read and what you know so far. Does it seem fair to you that George Mitchell won? If so, why? If not, why not?

Summary of information so far known

(a) Procedural history.

(b) Facts.

(c) A general idea of the operative rules of law should be emerging:

- it is known that both common law rules and statutory rules are relevant to the case;
- further it is known that if the common law rules are found to apply in the seller's favour he still has to jump the hurdle presented by the statutory rules;
- recall, if there is a clash between common law rules and statutory rules, the statutory rules prevail.

(d) A verbatim account of the two issues in the case. (However, these are probably not fully comprehended yet, despite Figure 4.14!):

- it is clear that Lord Bridge will argue through each of the issues;
- if the appellants succeed in issue (1) they may still fail overall if they fail over issue (2);
- logically, one would expect Lord Bridge to commence with the arguments over issue (1), the common law issue as this is the gateway to an argument over the issue (2) which will only take place if issue (1) is decided in the appellant's favour (and this is what he does).

Now take time to consolidate the information we have so far and return to the judgment of Lord Bridge, concentrating on his arguments concerning issue (1) (p 238, para 3).

Lord Bridge's arguments concerning issue (1), the common law issue

The arguments in this case are quite complex and the initial method of breaking into the text for understanding is to look at each paragraph.

Paragraphs are intended to convey a new idea. So each paragraph represents an idea or a cluster of ideas. Careful ordering of paragraphs is essential in a piece of writing if a sense of progression is to be maintained.

When reading for understanding a précis of each paragraph begins the process of understanding.

Paragraphs must not be skipped over, as the task in hand is to ensure that *each* paragraph *is understood*. Each paragraph is a stepping stone, leading the reader to the end of the text and the conclusion of the argument.

As paragraphs relate to each other, any points not understood in a paragraph should be cleared up in earlier or later paragraphs, unless they contain information *assumed* known to the reader. So if you find references you do not understand cast your eyes back to see if this has already been clarified.

One of the most important connections in a text is the relationship between paragraphs. The paragraphs in the text of Lord Bridge's speech will be numbered and summarised. As expertise is acquired, such summaries will normally take place in the head of the student with only a few paragraphs noted in rough.

LORD BRIDGE'S SPEECH

START

PARA 1

- Facts.

PARA 2

- Issues arise from three sentences in the conditions of sale.
- These are set out and identified.
- States he will call the contentious limitation clause, the relevant condition, and will refer to each sentence as a clause, so clause 1, 2, 3 (see p 238) (see Figure 4.15).

PARA 3

- Sets out the two issues as the common law and the statutory issues.
- Gives details of relevant legislation.

PARA 4

- Discusses the finding of the trial judge that under the common law the 'relevant condition' could not be relied upon by the sellers. The reason being the seed delivered was 'wholly different'. (As we have already noted Question 2, the statutory issue, need only be dealt with if Question 1 is decided in favour of the sellers.)

PARA 5

- Discusses the finding of Lord Denning in the Court of Appeal. Here, the common law issue decided in favour of the sellers. He said that the wording of the condition was sufficient to cover the situation. Kerr and Oliver LJJ decided the common law issue against the sellers.
- Kerr LJ's reasoning was that the condition would only cover them for *defects* in the *'correct'* named seeds. Not for delivery of the wrong seeds.
- Oliver LJ's reasoning was that condition did not cover the breach because it only happened through the negligence of the seller.

PARA 6

- The Court of Appeal, however, was unanimous in deciding the statutory issue against the sellers.

PARA 7

- Lord Bridge discusses the way that Lord Denning traced the history of the court's approach to such conditions. The conditions being ones that 'limit' or totally 'exclude' a contractual party's liability for any damage caused.
- Lord Bridge picks out two relevant cases (*Photo Production* (1980) and *Ailsa Craig* (1983)) and uses these to explore the common law issue.

PARA 8

- Lord Bridge brings up an unknown phrase 'fundamental breach'. Depending on the positioning of the student in a contract course, this phrase will be known or unknown. The word 'fundamental' suggests an important, core, foundation breach/break of the contract. The essence of the points made are:
  - the *Photo Production* case made it clear that, even if there is a finding of fundamental breach of contract by one party, like the seller here, this finding does not stop a party, the seller, relying on limiting or excluding conditions in the contract;
  - the *Ailsa Craig* case drew distinctions between:
    limiting clauses;
    exclusion clauses.

Basically, limitation clauses should not be judged according to the strict principles applied to exclusion clauses, although they remain to be construed *contra proferentem* against the party claiming their protection).

PARA 9

- Lord Bridge criticises the trial judge, Parker J, and the Court of Appeal judge, Oliver LJ, for trying to go back to the position:
  - before the *Photo Production* case, Lord Bridge said a fundamental breach DOES NOT stop a party relying on exclusions/limitation clauses.

PARA 10

- Lord Bridge points out that the condition applies to seeds sold and indeed seeds were sold!
- Lord Bridge says that the condition unambiguously applies to the present situation.

PARA 11

- Lord Bridge says that Kerr LJ (in Court of Appeal) in finding for the seller had in fact misinterpreted what Lord Fraser had said in the *Canada* case (1952)!
- This is an excellent paragraph for demonstrating the way in which judges argue about other cases.
- Lord Bridge decides the common law point in favour of the sellers in agreement with Lord Denning in the Court of Appeal.

PARA 12

- Lord Bridge turns to discuss the statutory issue.
- We now begin to understand the reference to 'the Act' in issue (2) as set out by Lord Bridge on p 238 at para 3.
- The modified s 55 of the Sale of Goods Act 1979 is set out.
- The Sale of Goods Act 1979 was a pure exercise in consolidation. (This means that it merely collected together the existing law and put it in one place.)
- Modified s 55 preserves the law between 18 May 1973 (the date that the Supply of Goods (Implied Terms) Act came into force)

  AND

  1 February 1977 (the date that the Unfair Contract Terms Act 1977 came into force).

PARA 13

- Section 55, sub-ss (1), (4), (5) and (9) is set out. (Students need to study this carefully to ensure that they understand what it is providing for and that they can follow the discussion of it by Lord Bridge.)

So, let us stop here for a moment ...

STATUTORY DIVERSION

This is an appropriate moment to return to s 55 of the Sale of Goods Act 1979 as set out and to experiment with ways of breaking in. To understand properly the development of the reasoning of the court on the statutory issue, it is vital to spend time understanding the basic layout, interconnections and effect of the provisions. Often, students do not pay sufficient attention to such matters and then wonder why they cannot understand discussions!

The purely textual explanation is complicated and needs to be read in conjunction with the statutory provision.

Two diagrams will follow, the first (Figure 4.16) sets out s 55 in its entirety according to the method used in Chapter 3 for s 11 of UCTA. This enables the parts to be seen as a whole and the interconnections are apparent. It will be similarly annotated. Can you notice any similarities between s 11 of UCTA and s 55 of the Sale of Goods Act?

The second diagram Figure 4.17 is a précis version of s 55, identifying the most relevant sections according to the facts of the case.

Putting personal comprehension time in before the judge's deliberation enables readers to check out their view against that of the judge and begins the process of evaluation.

Often, students continue reading text when it is clear to them that they do not understand what they are reading. The sensible thing to do is to return to that point in the text when understanding was last achieved and re-read, not continue past the part of the text that is not understood.

In texts discussing complex issues, tiny connectors, if missed, rob the reader of understanding. A paragraph by paragraph reconsideration will often restore comprehension.

> **Ensure that you carefully consider these diagrams before moving on.**

Figure 4.16: text of s 55 in diagrammatic format

Circled = connectors
Boxed = key phrases

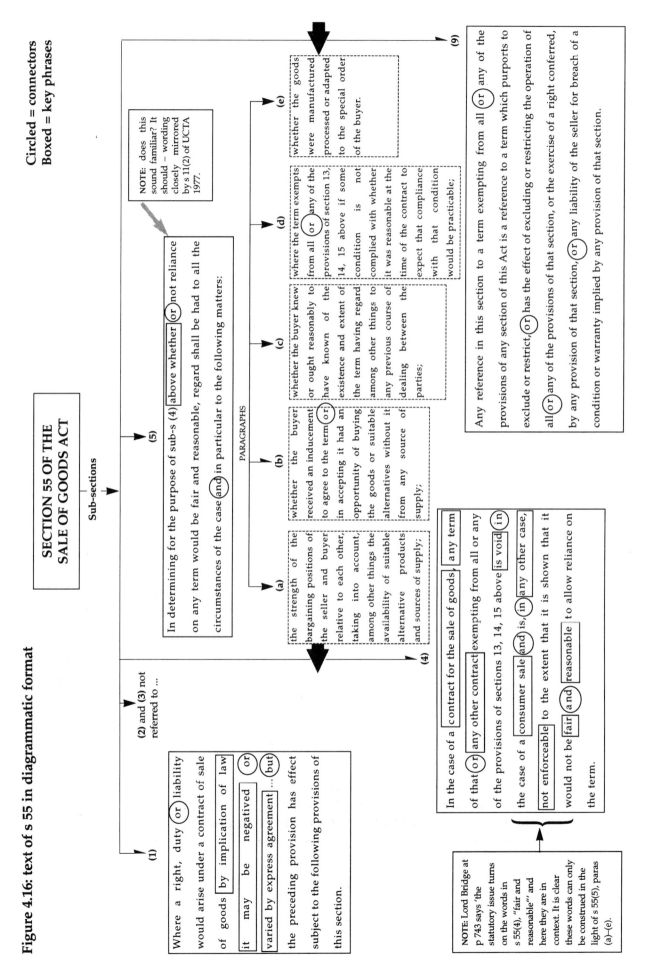

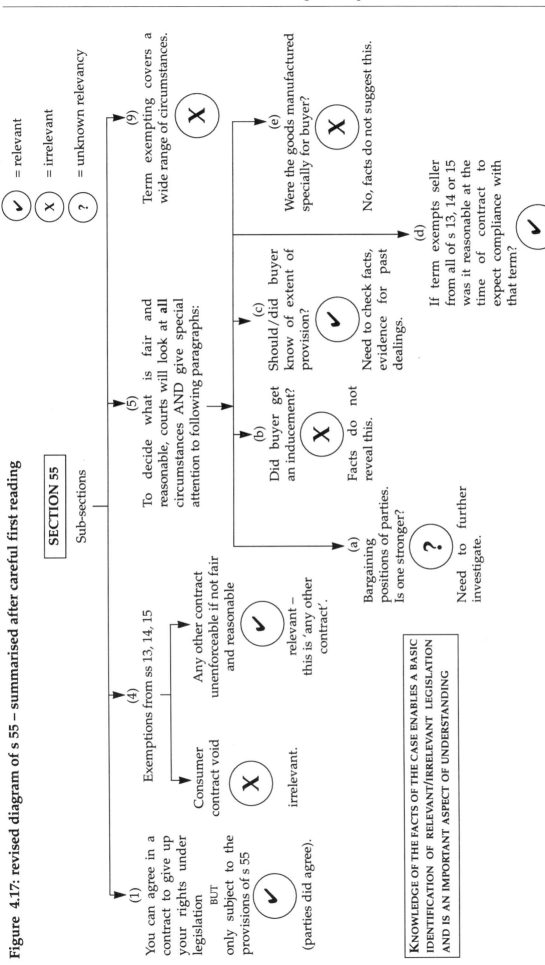

Figure 4.17: revised diagram of s 55 – summarised after careful first reading

Q: What do ss 13, 14, 15, say? If you were studying contract you would already know. However, from a comprehension perspective, Bridge does discuss them – you can work it out as a matter of comprehension. At p 241, para 14, he says, ' ... cl 3 of the relevant provision is to exclude, *inter alia*, the terms implied by ss 13, 14, 15. Statute law, while accepting that all common law parties can agree to any legal contract, provides that, in some areas, "protective" terms will be "read into" [implied into] the contract even if, in reality, they have not been written in or spoken'.

Now, the paragraph by paragraph consideration will recommence.

PARA 14

- Lord Bridge observes that the contract in question is not a consumer contract but 'any other contract':
  - this information is obtained by a careful reading of s 55(4) plus knowledge of what a consumer sale is;
  - look back at Figure 4.16 *and* re-read s 55(4);
  - as for consumer contract recall the phrase as it was referred to in Chapter 3 when the UCTA 1977 was dissected;
  - this contract is commercial not consumer and therefore falls under the second heading in s 55(4).
- Lord Bridge further observes that cl 3 of the relevant condition exempts the seller from liability for breach of ss 13 and 14 of the Sale of Goods Act:
  - this is a good example of the need to have an active dialogue with the text. Clause 3 is the third sentence of the relevant condition and the relevant condition is the condition limiting liability;
  - how is this known? Because on p 238 Lord Bridge states (para 2 (see précis above)): issues arise from three sentences in the conditions of sale. These are set out and identified. States he will call this the relevant condition, and will call each sentence a clause, so cl 1, 2, 3. See, also, Figure 4.19.
- Lord Bridge goes on to say that ss 13 and 14 refer to:
  - seeds sold by description should correspond to the description;
  - seeds sold should be of merchantable quality,

  and that cll 1 and 2 substitute for the full protection of the legislation the limited obligation to replace seeds or refund price of seeds.
- Bridge sums up that the statutory issue depends on whether cll 1 and 2 are 'fair and reasonable' as set out in s 55(4)(5).

PARA 15

- Lord Bridge gives some general guidelines about how the judiciary should respond to the powers given to it in s 55.
- Students may be tempted to skip over this paragraph, but valuable information is given concerning judicial interpretation of statutes.
- For the first time, the House of Lords is being asked to consider a modern statutory provision that gives the court power to decide to override contractual provisions limiting or excluding liability that have been agreed between the parties at common law. This is a far reaching power to interfere with the freedom of individuals to contract. The court can say 'NO'. you cannot freely agree this, because, in our opinion, it is not fair and reasonable.
- The actual decision regarding s 55 is of limited importance (as it is protecting the contracts made between 18 May 1973 and 1 February 1978) and, as such, will soon outlive its usefulness.
- *However*, the wording of s 55 is substantially replicated in s 11 and Schedule 2 of UCTA, which will be of increasing importance.

- He discusses the fact that the exercise of any power to decide what is fair or reasonable will involve legitimate judicial differences and that the courts should refrain from interfering with the decision of the previous court unless they feel that there was a clearly wrong decision or that the case was decided on some clearly erroneous principle.

PARA 16

- Lord Bridge turns to a question of construction, of the meaning of words used in the statute.
- The onus is on the respondents to show that it would not be fair or reasonable to allow the appellant to rely on the relevant condition.
- Appellants said the court must look at the situation at the date of the contract, but Lord Bridge said that the true meaning of the phrase in s 55(5) 'regard shall be had to all the circumstances of the case' must mean that the situation at the time of breach *and* after breach must be taken into account.

PARA 17

- Lord Bridge discusses another issue of the meaning of words used in the statute. The meaning of the words 'to the extent' in s 55(4).
- Lord Bridge asks: 'Is it fair and reasonable to allow partial reliance on a limitation clause, to decide ... that the respondents should recover say, half their consequential damage?'
- Lord Bridge goes on to say that he considers that the meaning of the phrase 'to the extent ' is ' in so far as or in circumstances in which'.
- He suggests that the phrase does not 'permit the kind of judgment of Solomon illustrated by the example':
  - ○ the reference to Solomon is typical of the literary / religious referencing that one often finds in cases;
  - ○ Solomon was an old testament king accredited with much wisdom in his judging. When confronted with a baby claimed by two mothers he suggested cutting it in half so each could have half. The false mother agreed, the real mother said no, the other mother could have the baby. Thus, he located the real mother.

PARA 18

- He then goes on to say that his answer in relation to the question is not necessary for the outcome of this case and declines to answer one way or the other!
- It is interesting to note that if he *had* categorically answered the question, yes or no, it would be a clear example of an *obiter dictum* statement in a strong case by a senior judge and may well have been used in argument in a later case where this issue is at the core of the case.

PARA 19

- Eventually, Lord Bridge turns to the 'application of the statutory language' to the case.
- He states that only s 55(5)(a) and (c) are relevant. (**This is the moment to re-read s 55(5)(a)–(c) if you do not remember the provisions. Otherwise, one loses sight of the argument!**)
- As to s 55(5)(c), he says of course the correspondent knew of condition as it was standard throughout the trade.

PARA 20

- As to s 55(5)(a), he states that there was evidence that similar limitations had never been negotiated with representative bodies.
- Witnesses for the appellant said that it had always been their practice in genuine justified claims to settle above the price of the seeds but that, in this case, settlement had not been possible. Lord Bridge said 'this evidence indicated a clear recognition ... that reliance on the limitation of liability imposed by the relevant condition would not be fair or reasonable'.

PARA 21

- Lord Bridge concluded, therefore, that wrong seed was supplied by negligence of applicant's sister company. Seedsmen could insure against the risk of crop failure caused by the wrong supply without materially increasing the cost of seeds.

PARA 22

- Lord Bridge felt no doubts about decision of the Court of Appeal over statute.
- Lord Bridge refers to an earlier point in para 15 that its wise to 'refrain from interference' in matters of legitimate judicial difference (see p 251, para 15).

PARA 23

If I were making the original decision, I should conclude without hesitation that it would not be fair or reasonable to allow the appellants to rely on the contractual limitation of their liability.

PARA 24

- Appeal dismissed.

A quick review of the paragraphs begins to show the patterns of argument delivery. Re-reading the paragraphs looking at the statutory diagrams (Figures 4.16 and 4.17) allows the argument to be reviewed whilst looking at the entire provision.

The paragraph approach has also allowed the common law issue and the statutory issue to be isolated. Reviewing Figure 4.13 dealing with the facts, issues and procedural history enables the appreciation of the differences between the reasoning in the Court of Appeal and the House of Lords, although both courts reached the same decision.

It should be possible at this stage to identify the precise rationale behind the courts' view of the common law issue and the statutory issue. In relation to the statutory issue, it should be possible to pinpoint precisely the statutory areas of relevance and how the court dealt with the issue. A summary of this information has been put into diagrammatic form in Figure 4.18.

As proficiency is developed, it is possible to read carefully and move straight away to a diagrammatic representation, although, ultimately, a conventional textual note should be made to supplement the diagram.

Figure 4.18: issues in *George Mitchell v Finney Lock Seeds* and their resolution
(References to 'paras' are to paragraphs in Lord Bridge's judgment.)

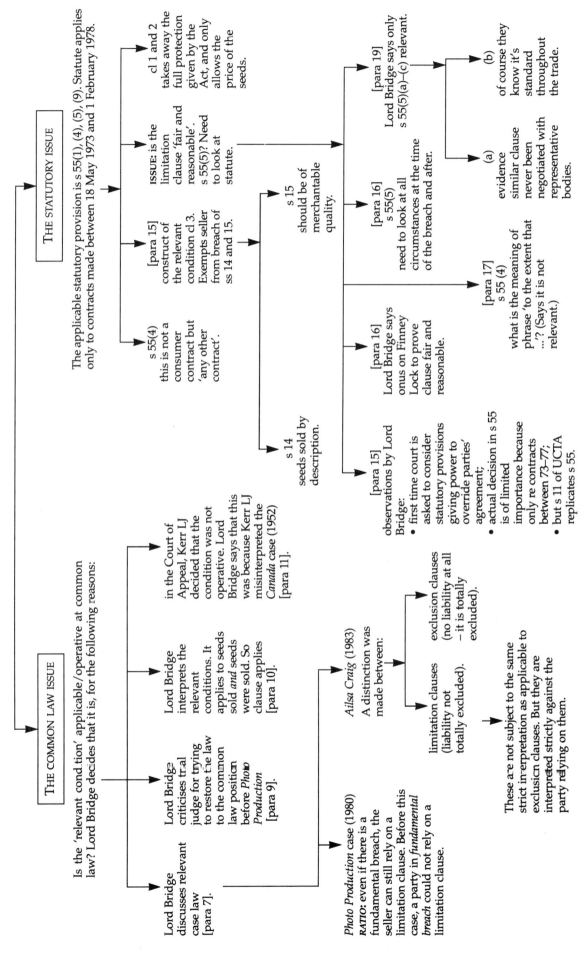

Figure 4.19: diagrammatic text of the relevant condition

At p 238, Lord Bridge says he will call the *condition* in the *contract* that limits liability the 'relevant condition'.

In the same paragraph, stated that the condition was composed of three sentences, numbered 1, 2, 3. He states he will call each sentence a clause. The condition is set out below according to the structure imposed by judge.

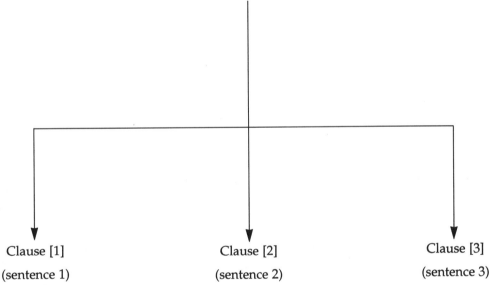

'I will refer to the whole as "the relevant condition" and to the parts as "clauses [1], [2] and [3]" of the relevant condition' (Lord Bridge, p 238, para 2).

Clause [1]

(sentence 1)

'In the event of any seeds or plants sold or agreed to be sold by us not complying with the express terms of the contract of sale ... or any seeds or plants proving defective in variety or purity we will, at our option, replace the defective seeds or plants, free of charge to the buyer or will refund all payments made to us by the buyer in respect of the defective seeds or plants and this shall be the limit of our obligation.'

Clause [2]

(sentence 2)

'We hereby exclude all liability for any loss or damage arising from the use of any seeds or plants supplied by us and for any consequential loss or damage arising out of such use or any failure in the performance of or any defect in any seeds or plants supplied by us or for any other loss or damage whatsoever save for, at our option, liability for any such replacement or refund as aforesaid.'

Clause [3]

(sentence 3)

'In accordance with the established custom of the seed trade any express or implied condition, statement or warranty, statutory or otherwise, not located in these conditions is hereby excluded.'

CASENOTING

It is at this point that a casenote can be made. The casenote has to contain all of the information that enables the case to be used. One of the most important tasks of a law student or, indeed, a legal professional is the ability to read a case and make a usable record of it.

The cases that are reported are invariably important as non-important cases remain as court transcripts. The casenote must note all of the important issues for the application of precedent, such as:

(a) date of court and formal citation;

(b) hierarchy of court, judges;

(c) facts;

(d) issues before the trial court;

(e) identification of applicable legal rules;

(f) issues, if different before appellate court(s);

(g) procedural history of the case (in what other courts has the matter been heard);

(h) judicial reasoning as to:

> **why those** rules applied
>
> to **those** facts
>
> in **that** way.

A casenote cannot be used if it only records the facts and not the rationale for the outcome as everything in law depends upon the legal reasoning. A case can only be properly used in legal argument when the reasoning of the court is both known and understood.

Many students misunderstand the purpose of casenoting and think that it is sufficient to have the facts of the case and know the rules concerned. This is a little like having the ingredients for a cake and knowing that, when heated, something changes, but not knowing what to do with the ingredients.

It is often not even necessary to rehearse the facts of a case in an argument in which the case is used. What is important is to know points of similarity and difference in facts so that adjustments can be made to the reasoning processes in applying the earlier case to the later situation.

If strenuous efforts have been made to understand a law report thoroughly, the following benefits will be achieved:

(a) the casenote will contain all the ingredients to enable it to be competently applied to any problem question or incorporated into any relevant essay;

(b) understanding of the topic and arguing techniques will be increased.

CASENOTE   *George Mitchell Ltd v Finney Lock Seeds*

[1983] 2 All ER 737–44

COURT   HOUSE OF LORDS

JUDGES   Lords Diplock, Scarman, Roskill, Bridge of Harlow, Brightman

DATE   23, 24 May and 30 June 1983

FACTS

The respondents purchased 30lb seeds from the appellants for £201.60 in December 1973. The invoice contained a standard limitation clause stating that the only liability of the appellants was replacement of the seeds or a refund of the cost of the seeds. All other liability was excluded. The respondent's crop failed. The wrong seed and seed of an inferior quality had been delivered due to the negligence of the appellant's sister company.

ARGUMENT

The respondents argued that the limitation clause did not apply:

(1) at common law, because the wrong seed was delivered and it was not of merchantable quality;

(2) under statutory provisions, because the clause was not fair and reasonable under s 55 of the Sale of Goods Act 1979; the limitation clause in the contract was unenforceable at law according to s 55(4).

PROCEDURAL HISTORY

Trial

Parker J: The limitation clause was not operative at common law because of the negligence in delivering the wrong seed.

Court of Appeal

On appeal by Finney Lock Seeds: Denning, Kerr, Oliver LJJ

Kerr and Oliver LJJ held the limitation clause could not be relied upon because:

(1) on its true construction the condition did not apply at common law because loss due to the negligence of sister company and the seed was wholly different than delivery of the wrong seed (Kerr and Oliver LJJ);

(2) also, applying s 55 it would not be fair and reasonable

(NOTE: comment by drafter of casenote: Having said the clause did not apply at common law to negligence there was of course no relevance in dealing with the statutory issue which is only operative if the clause is deemed to apply at common law!);

(3) Denning LJ held, in the minority, that the limitation clause could apply at common law. However it was not a fair and reasonable clause under s 55 Sale of Goods Act 1979.

DECISION IN CASE

House of Lords

All judges agreed with the opinion of Lord Bridge:

(1) The common law issue

That the limitation clause was operative and could effectively limit liability. The wording of the condition was unambiguous in this regard. Limitation clauses do not have to adhere to the strict principles laid down for complete exclusion clauses (see *Ailsa Craig* (1983)), although they must be clearly expressed and must be strictly interpreted against the party relying on them (*contra proferentem*).

Decision partly supported by the following precedents

Photo Production Ltd (1980)

Even in cases of fundamental breach, (core) limitation clauses are available to be relied upon by one party.

Ailsa Craig (1983)

There is a difference of approach appropriate between limitation and exclusion clauses. Limitation clauses do not have to be so strictly interpreted.

(2) The statutory issue

Even though the clause was enforceable at common law, after considering s 55(4)(5)(a) and (c), Bridge decided that the common law provision was overridden by the statutory obligation in s 55(4) for such clauses to be fair and reasonable otherwise. The clause was therefore unenforceable.

The grounds for deciding clause unfair and unreasonable were that:

(a) in applying s 55(5)(a), it was clear that in the past appellants had sought to negotiate a settlement that was higher than the price and had not relied on the limitation clause;

(b) supply of seed was due to the negligence of appellants sister company;

(c) appellant could easily have insured against loss.

Obiter dicta

(a) The phrase 'to the extent that' discussed and said to mean 'in so far as' or 'in the circumstances which'. s 54(4). Although this is not relevant to this case it is possibly an important *obiter dictum*.

(b) There may be some mileage in discussion concerning whether there can be partial reliance on limitation clauses again. Although this is not relevant to this case, possible important *obiter dicta*.

(c) The phrase 'in all the circumstances' in s 55(5) means one should take account of circumstances at and after time of the breach.

(d) Appellate courts in a case like this, where there is room for legitimate judicial difference, should refrain from interfering unless it is considered that the decision reached was based on the application of wrong principles or the case is clearly wrongly decided.

Decision of court

Appeal dismissed.

CHAPTER 5

STATUTORY INTERPRETATION:
THE RELATIONSHIP BETWEEN CASES AND STATUTES

The discussion of *George Mitchell v Finney Lock Seeds* (1985) has indicated what happens when a problem about the meaning of a statutory provision goes before a court. In this section, attention will be given to this issue in particular, the issue of statutory interpretation .

The courts and tribunals have, as one of their most important tasks, the application of legislative rules to various fact situations. They must decide whether these legislative rules apply to given situations.

Despite the supposed certainty of statutory rules, rules in 'fixed verbal form', already, in this text, there have been several illustrations of words not meaning what they appear to mean. Words can change over time, and courts will disagree over the meaning of words. Choices of meaning, not perceived by the drafters, may lie latent in the words and are drawn out in a manner defeating intention, narrowing, extending or making meaningless the ambit of the rule.

Many people need to apply statutory rules, often this application will be purely routine but sometimes doubts will arise. Such doubts may, or may not, reach court. How do judges set about deciding the meaning of words? Reference has already been made to the three rules of statutory interpretation. The literal, the mischief and the golden rules (see Figure II.i in the introduction to Part II). These rules it should be remembered are rules of practice not rules of law.

Do judges really use the rules of statutory interpretation? If so, which rule do they use first? Judges rarely, if ever, volunteer the information that they are now applying a certain rule of interpretation. Often, judges look to see if there can be a literal meaning to the words used in the disputed statutory rule. However, there is no rule that states that they must use the literal rule first.

Holland and Webb (1994) quite correctly assert that interpretation is more a question of judicial style than the use of interpretational rules. Indeed, should a student attempt to use the rules of statutory interpretation as a guide in the interpretation of a statutory word or phrase, the uselessness of the rules as an interpretational tool becomes immediately apparent.

However, as a justificatory label they may have a function. As students gain experience in reading judgments they notice vast differences in judicial styles. Some judgments seem to be based on a blow by blow analysis of precedents and earlier usage of words, others seem based on tenuous common sense rationales.

Decisions based on the external context of the statute will be identified. This covers situations where judicial decision making appears to be based on issues of public policy, a particularly favoured device in the 1960s and 1970s. Reliance on public policy rationale can be referred to as the 'grand style' or the 'teleological' approach.

Cases may also turn on the *form of* the statute itself, that is, its *internal* context. Much of the analysis engaged in here is at the level of the internal. However, never forget the external world context. Judges who rigidly adopt the internal approach are often referred to as *formalists*. Such judges say that they do not create law they find it. They find it by following the pathways of the rules of statutory interpretation.

A closer consideration of the simplest definitions of the rules of statutory interpretation enables the classification of the literal rule as the *formalist* approach and the mischief rule as the *teleological* approach. The golden rule, of course, allows one to ignore the formalist approach of the literal rule. It is most likely to result in a teleological approach as the judge, through the golden rule, is released from formalism! (See Figure II.i.)

TASK

Read the extract from the judgment of Lord Fraser in the case of *Mandla v Dowell Lee* (1983) in Appendix 6 and then read and reflect on the following discussion based upon the reading of the judgment as giving examples of formalism and a teleological approach.

The case of *Mandla v Dowell Lee* involved the interpretation of legislative provisions in the Race Relations Act 1976 and went through both appellate courts (the Court of Appeal and the House of Lords) in the middle of much publicity. The crux of the case concerned whether Sikhs constituted an ethnic group and could claim the protection of the Race Relations Act 1976. The Court of Appeal decided that Sikhs did not constitute a racial group and could not claim the protection of the Race Relations Act.

It was an unpopular decision, taken two days before Lord Denning MR's retirement as Master of the Rolls (the senior judge in the Court of Appeal) and caused rioting in the streets before a quick reversal of the Court of Appeal's decision by the House of Lords.

The particular legislative provisions were ss 1 and 3 of the Race Relations Act 1976. Section 3 was the gateway provision. If this section gave Sikhs protection, then the Act applied and the claim under s 1 could be made.

More particularly, the entire case revolved around the interpretation of three words. The meaning of the word 'ethnic' in s 3 and the meaning of the words 'can' and 'justifiable' in s 1.

The case is a good example of the movement from theoretical rules to their interpretation and application in reality; a movement from rules in books, to the legal construction of reality.

The facts of the case were that Mr Mandla, a Sikh, wanted his son to go to a certain private school. The child was given a place which was subsequently taken away when the father informed the school that the child would not remove his turban as school rules required. The headmaster stated that the rules concerning uniform were rigid and that other Sikh pupils removed turbans during school hours. Mr Mandla reported the matter to the Commission for Racial Equality (CRE) who took up the case.

The CRE alleged that the son had been unlawfully discriminated against, either directly or indirectly, on racial grounds, in that he had been denied a place at the school because of his custom of wearing a turban.

The meaning of the word 'ethnic' in s 3 of the Race Relations Act 1976

The case raised a number of issues. The first issue which was of tremendous importance to Sikhs was whether the Race Relations Act was the relevant statute to take action under. To bring an action, it had to be proved that Sikhs were a racial group.

In s 3 of the Act, racial grounds was defined as:

... a group of persons defined by reference to colour, race, nationality or ethnic or national origins.

The main argument centred around whether Sikhs fitted into the word 'ethnic'. It was accepted that they did not fit into any of the other descriptions.

The trial court found that Sikhs were not a racial group and the appellant appealed to the Court of Appeal and came before Lord Denning.

The Court of Appeal had two choices. It could take the teleological approach – looking at the wider context – considering the history behind the legislation, the mischief that it was designed to rectify; or it could choose a formalist approach, considering the text, the word or words, and their possible meanings in a more literal sense.

Lord Denning had always, in essence, taken a teleological approach. He had, for much of his legal career as a senior judge, fought against blind literalism. He had always fought for the right to 'fill in the gaps' left in legislation. Indeed, his career was often based on the right to take the broad view, when, days before his retirement, a case concerning conflicting liberties came before him.

Surprisingly, he chose, in this case, to take the formalist approach, to stand by the literal meaning of the words. He discussed the history of the word 'ethnic.' Certainly, the etymology of the word is fascinating; however, why did the legislators put in the word 'ethnic'? Did they do so after scanning its etymology? Of course, it is not known. Yet, an interpretation based on the history of a word obviously presumes that, yes, the legislators did consider the etymology of the word. Otherwise, there is no point in the court doing so.

When constructing legal rules in fixed verbal form, language is of the utmost importance. Thought is given to the best words to be used to 'fix' or 'stick' the rule, so that contrary interpretations cannot be reached by courts; and so that the mischief to be tackled is tackled. However, as noted in Chapter 2, the flexibility of language will not allow it to be permanently fixed.

The choice of words is often determined by a:

(a) desire to make it impossible for judges to change the meaning;

(b) desire to make a major policy change as uncontentious as possible;

(c) desire to compromise, or a need to compromise, to ensure that major aspects of the draft statute get through the legislative process, and are not blocked by the opposition within, or external to, the government.

In the Court of Appeal, in *Mandla v Dowell Lee*, Lord Denning looked at the history of the word 'ethnic', charting its meaning and usage through three editions of the *Oxford English Dictionary* (1890, 1934, 1972). He used the classic dictionary approach argument: when in doubt, use the dictionary. However, he always argued that words do not and cannot have a literal meaning and yet, here, in a highly contentious case, he traced the history of words.

He noted that, in its original Greek form, 'ethnic' meant 'heathen' and was used by the translators of the Old Testament from Hebrew to Greek to mean non-Israelite, or gentile. Earlier in this text, in Chapter 2, we considered the issue of the use of the phrase 'the original Greek'. He identified the first use of 'ethnic' in English as describing people who were not Christian or Jewish.

Lord Denning referred to the 1890 edition of the *Oxford English Dictionary* to confirm this etymology. He then referred to the 1934 edition, stating that its meaning had, by then, changed to denote 'race, ethnological'. This is hardly surprising as the great anthropological expeditions of the 1920s and 1930s introduced the idea of ethnography as the descriptions of unknown groupings of people. His Lordship stated that the 1934 version indicated that 'ethnic' meant 'divisions of races' and, as far as he was concerned, this was right.

This is, of course, a highly subjective viewpoint. But a judge has the power, via language analysis, to make a choice between what is and what is not right. Indeed, this is his task. The court has to decide.

Finally, he referred to the 1972 version of the dictionary, which gave a wider definition of 'ethnic'. It was this definition that was relied upon by the plaintiff's counsel. Here, 'ethnic' was defined as relating to:

> ... common racial, cultural, religious, or linguistic characteristics, especially designating a racial or other group within a larger system.

Lord Denning then turned to discuss 'origins' for, as used in s 3 of the Race Relations Act, 'ethnic' appears in a small phrase including the word 'origins' ('or ethnic or national origins'). He then discussed 'origins' and turned again to the dictionary, noting its usage with parentage and deciding that it meant, as in previous case law, 'a connection arising at birth'.

'Origin', he said, therefore meant a group with a common racial characteristic. His Lordship reconsidered the entire phrase as used in s 3:

> ... a group of persons defined ... by reference to ... ethnic ... origins.

and concluded that the group must be distinguishable from another by a definable characteristic. Re-reading his judgment in the Court of Appeal, it is noticeable that he constantly used the words he is supposed to be defining in the definitions. He arbitrarily decided that, when Parliament added the phrase 'ethnic origin' in 1976, it had in mind the Jews, anti-semitism must not be allowed.

Yet, Lord Denning's normally preferred technique was the teleological, the mischief or the purposive rule. He may have reasoned in a manner more in keeping with the Race Relations Act if he had used his favourite technique of the purposive approach.

Having defined ethnic origin, the next task was to apply that definition to Sikhs to consider whether they could be said to be a 'people defined ... by reference to ... ethnic origins'.

Lord Denning launched into a potted and largely inaccurate history of the word 'Sikh' and the people who follow the teaching of Guru Nanak. Again, in a subjective and arbitrary manner, Denning decided:

(a) that Sikhs can only be distinguished by religion, *and therefore*

(b) they are not defined by 'ethnic origins', *and therefore*

(c) they are not a racial group, *and therefore*

(d) it is not illegal to discriminate against Sikhs.

Lord Denning's entire reasoning process rests on dictionary definitions and homespun inaccurate conclusions. He went on to criticise the CRE for bringing the case, stating that schools should not be interfered with when they properly manage their affairs.

Oliver LJ in the same court said that the dictionary shows 'ethnic' to be a vague word and he doubts whether only the most general assistance can be obtained from dictionaries. Can one discern a community in a loose sense among Sikhs, he asked rhetorically? Without providing evidence, he says no, customs among Sikhs are so disparate they cannot be said to be members of an ethnic group.

However, the essence of the discrimination legislation is that the 'man in the street' is the one to discriminate.

The court concluded that Sikhs were not an ethnic group. The CRE appealed to the House of Lords.

The House reversed the decision of the Court of Appeal, allowing the appeal. The House found that, to be an ethnic group, a group must be regarded by itself and others as a distinct community with, for instance, a shared culture, history, language, common descent or geography, customs, religion. Not all of these factors need be present.

The main judgment given was by Lord Fraser. He discussed the views of Lord Denning and Oliver LJ in the Court of Appeal. He dispensed with the dictionary arguments and the suggestion that ethnic denotes race by saying, in favour of a teleological approach:

> My Lords, I recognise that 'ethnic' conveys a flavour of race but it cannot, in my opinion, have been used in the Act of 1976 in a strictly racial or biological sense. For one thing, it would be absurd to suppose that Parliament can have intended that membership of a particular racial group should depend upon scientific proof of biological characteristics (if possible to prove). It is clear that Parliament must have used the word in a more popular sense. 'Racial' isn't a term of art, either legal or scientific. No, ethnic today has a wide popularist meaning denoting common factors of shared history, etc. It would include converts, etc. So by birth or adherence one can have an ethnic origin.

He finds support for his views in a line of New Zealand cases which maintain that it is important how a group regards itself, and is regarded by others. He says that, not only does he like this definition, but:

> ... it is important that courts in English speaking countries should, if possible, construe the words which we are considering in the same way where they occur in the same context.

He concludes that, applying his broader definition of ethnic origin, Sikhs are a racial group on ethnic grounds.

This opens the gateway for the court to consider if indeed the boy had been unfairly discriminated against by the school which had refused to admit him unless he removed his turban.

The answer to this issue revolves around the meaning of two words in s 1(1)(b) of the Race Relations Act 1976. These words are 'can' in s 1(1)(b)(i) and 'justifiable' in s 1(1)(b)(iii).

Section 1(1)(b) is a potentially difficult section and is set out for consideration below:

1   (1) A person discriminates against another in any circumstances relevant for the purposes or any provision of this Act if:

(a) ...

(b) he applies to that other a requirement or condition which he applies or would equally apply to persons not of the same racial group as that other but:

   (i) which is such that the proportion of persons of the same racial group as that other who can comply with it is considerably smaller than the proportion of persons not of that racial group who can comply with it; and

   (ii) which he cannot show to be justifiable irrespective of the colour, race, nationality or ethnic or national origins of the person to whom it is applied; and

   (iii) which is to the detriment of that other because he cannot comply with it.

Let us leave Lord Fraser for a moment and consider s 1(1)(b).

An immediate 'mobile' tree diagram indicates the connections between the section and its sub-section. See Figure 5.1.

Figure 5.1: s 1 of the Race Relations Act 1976

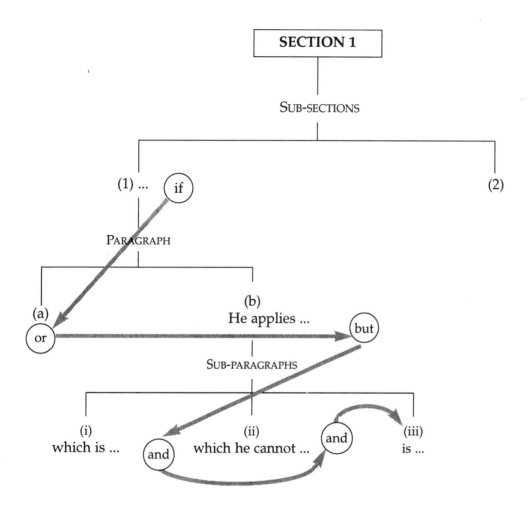

The first task is to break into this section and to search for connectors to see what sub-sections and paragraphs or sub-paragraphs are connected and which ones, if any, are not connected. This section again illustrates the fundamental importance of *connectors* to ascertain meaning of statutory phrases.

The connectors between the sections, sub-sections, paragraphs and sub-paragraphs reveal the type and function of the connection. For example, if the connector is 'or' it is clear that the connector is indicating that *two* things are in the *alternative*.

If the connector is '**and**', it is equally clear that the connector is indicating that two things *both* have to be present.

There is a major difference between saying

- (i) **or** (ii); and saying
- (i) **and** (ii).

However, as has been mentioned above, students often do not read the connectors **'and'**, **'if'**, **'but'**.

Now consider the connectors between sections, sub-sections, paragraphs and sub-paragraphs in Figure 5.1 above. The following pattern is obtained:

s1 (1) ... if

    (a) ... or

    (b) ... but

        (i) ... and

        (ii) ... and

        (iii) is ...

What can be ascertained from this seemingly abstract pattern?

(a) Something in s 1(1) will be the case **if** something in para (a) **or** (b) is the case.

(b) Paragraph (b) is tied to sub-paras (i), (ii), and (iii) by the connector **'but'**.

(c) Sub-paragraphs (i), (ii) and (iii) are all tied together by the two connectors **'and'** which occur at the end of sub-paras (i) and (ii).

After the study of s 1, both in terms of connectors and substance, it is appropriate to return to the discussion of the meaning of the words 'can' and 'justifiable', which were the subject of deliberations in the House of Lords. Recall, we have only been considering the judgment of Lord Fraser. These matters were also discussed in the Court of Appeal.

Consideration of the word 'can' in s 1(1)(b)(i)

One argument suggested was that 'can' simply meant that someone could do something physically. So, of course, it is always physically possible to remove a turban. However, the religious, conscientious, cultural, psychological dimensions of behaviour are thereby ignored. If the Race Relations Act is to have any impact, it cannot be the object of such simplistic interpretation.

Lord Fraser stated that 'can' does not merely mean 'can physically comply'. 'Can' means 'can comply' in practice, given the constraints of ethnic origin.

If restrictive interpretations were to be placed on a word as seemingly innocent as 'can', it would be possible to undermine the entire purpose of the Act.

Herein lies the power of the interpreter of language which, at root, will always remain flexible.

Consideration of the word 'justifiable' in s 1(1)(b)(ii)

Sub-paragraph (ii) of s 1 maintains that a condition is discriminatory if it cannot be justified on grounds other than race.

The school argued that it wanted total equality in all areas including dress. Therefore, the 'no turban rule' was a necessary aspect of uniform, discipline and equality. The school insisted that it was non-sectarian yet the headmaster also maintained that the school wished to project a 'a Christian image'. Therefore, the turban was also said to be a challenge to the Christian faith. The headmaster also objected because it was a manifestation of the appellant's ethnic origins.

Lord Fraser found that the school could not justify the condition on grounds other than on ethnic origin and that this was illegal under the Act.

In addition, Lord Fraser stated that Lord Denning's criticism of the CRE was completely unjustified.

This brief discussion of one case through two courts reveals vastly different approaches to statutory interpretation. Context and perhaps judicial attitudes dictate rules used. Rules of interpretations are not referred to. Perhaps the best indicator of what is going on is a careful consideration of what is being said and what 'styles' of interpretation seem represented by the tone of the judgment. Each judge does indeed have a personal style.

Interpretational problems can never be solved by the neat application of interpretational rules, even worse perhaps the rules do little or nothing to solve problems. At the risk of heresy, perhaps all that purported interpretational rules do is simply to justify solutions. As mentioned above, there is rarely one right answer, only a range of more plausible and less plausible outcomes, varying according to interpretational styles.

Judges use their creativity in working out a solution according to criteria which must be rational either in reality or in argument. They invariably go beyond the text when constructing answers. Lord Denning, for example, moved from dictionary definitions to subjective assertion. Often, judges say no more than 'this is the answer because I say so'.

Judges, as previously noted, can be classified as formalists or contextualists. It is possible to begin to guess as to which rules the judges think they are using. It is good also to accept that it is not always possible to understand what they are arguing, and to realise that, at times, judges themselves are wrong and not themselves too sure of the appropriate outcome. This is what makes comprehension of the methods of statutory interpretation, and the use of precedents, so difficult. It is essential to realise the limits of a supposed scientific approach and the limitless possibilities that open up when the illogical bridges from one set of rationale to the next are located and the power of language appreciated.

CHAPTER 6

UNDERSTANDING EUROPEAN COMMUNITY LAW

INTRODUCTION

From the perspective of legal method, several issues arise.

A range of differing types of legal rule originate in the European Community. These are created by different institutions or combinations of institutions with differing effects and jurisdictions. By virtue of the European Community Act 1972, European law is now a direct source of English law and legal rules created in the Community can automatically become part of UK legal systems, including the English legal system; others need to be ratified by Parliament; and yet others need Parliament to choose how to implement the intention of the Community.

European Community law impinges in several ways on our reading of English law. It is expected, for example, that in certain situations an English court, in common with the courts of other Member States, when considering an important point of European Community law, will refer to the European Court for a preliminary ruling as to the correct interpretation of European law and rights of the parties. In other situations, an English court *may* refer, but does not *have* to. Under Art 177 of the Treaty of Rome, courts from which there are no recognised national appeal have to ask for a preliminary ruling from the European Court of Justice. Other courts, where there is an appeal, may choose whether to ask for a preliminary ruling.

A BRIEF GUIDE TO THE CONSTITUTIONAL AND LEGAL FORMATION OF THE EUROPEAN COMMUNITY AND THE EUROPEAN UNION

In 1957, some European nations, as part of the rebuilding process after the Second World War, agreed by the Treaty of Rome to come together to create an economic market.

This has been described as a peaceful revolution of a socio-economic nature felt necessary after the Second World War, itself the result of failures during the inter-war period 1919–39. A majority of victorious nations in a shocked Europe were determined to ensure the development of a strong Western European bloc interdependent, united in defence, not reliant on America and protected from a growing perceived threat from the new alliances and power flowing from the Soviet bloc.

In September 1946, speaking in Zurich, Winston Churchill forcefully spoke of the need for a new, 'United States of Europe'. This famous speech became known as 'the United States of Europe Speech'. This was a vision that he soon stepped back from but which was carried forward by two leading French politicians, Jean Monet (responsible for economic planning) and Robert Schumann (responsible for foreign affairs).

In 1957, six founding states (France, West Germany, Netherlands, Belgium, Luxembourg and Italy) signed the Treaty of Rome establishing the European Economic Community (EEC).

The preamble to this treaty states the main goal of the Community as the maintenance of economic and social progress and that the principles of this new community are:

(a) laying the foundations of an ever closer union among the peoples of Europe;

(b) common action to ensure economic and social progress;

(c) the constant improvement of living conditions;

(d) the removal of existing obstacles to joint action to ensure expansion and trade;

(e) the strengthening of economies and ensuring their harmonious development;

(f) a desire to contribute, through a common commercial policy, to the progressive abolition of international restrictions on trade;

(g) confirmation of European solidarity in accordance with the United Nations (UN) Charter;

(h) the pooling of resources to strengthen peace and liberty.

The preamble to the Treaty of Rome invited other European States to join the founding six and today there are 15 Nation States in the Community.

From its origins, the desire of some national politicians had been for closer social ties beyond the purely economic, and the Maastricht Treaty 1995, as amended by the Treaty of Amsterdam 1997 (a rather clumsy attempt to tidy up problems on the Maastricht Treaty), creates the political and social phenomenon of the European Union which attempts to:

(a) bind the European Communities together in ever closer working relationships as a prelude to monetary union;

(b) to make provision for greater co-operation between Member States in relation to security and justice.

The switch in name from European Economic Community to European Community was effected by Maastricht. The formal name of the Maastricht Treaty is the Treaty on European Union and it begins to structure a much looser entity, the European Union. This is a *political* and *social* concept which is much broader than the European Community.

The Union created by Maastricht is based on three foundational principles:

(a) common security and foreign policy;

(b) the three communities (European Coal and Steel Community (ECSC) 1957; European Atomic Energy Community (EURATOM) 1957; the European Community (EC));

(c) co-operation in justice and home affairs.

Although it may seem that the phrases European Community and European Union are used interchangeably, they are *not* the same, as the simple diagram in Figure 6.1 illustrates.

Figure 6.1: the European Community and the European Union in context

EUROPEAN COMMUNITY

EUROPEAN UNION
The European Union is a broad agreement between the Member States of the European Community to pledge to ever closer unity

The European Community is difficult to comprehend:

- it is a market place that cannot be seen;
- a community that cannot be visited;
- a people that are united in their diversity.

> **Although the European Community is not a specific place, but a way of trading and relating financially, legally, politically, socially and culturally, it does have a specific supra-national legal and political order.**

The United Kingdom's membership of the European Community made the UK part of a steadily increasing economic, political and social networking of nation States, States committed to working together in a range of spheres for the mutual advantage of all members.

Before and after entry in the 1970s, a common worry had been: 'has the UK Parliament given away some of its political power, its sovereignty?' And the simple answer is 'yes' and 'no'. Yes, because if you give someone else the ability to make decisions for you, you have given away some of your autonomy of action. No, because it can always, theoretically at least, be taken back.

The three treaties setting up the communities are referred to as the 'founding treaties' of the European Community and, initially, shared some institutions but also retained their own institutions and executives. The institutions and executives were merged in 1965 by the Merger Treaty.

The first major amendment to the three founding treaties was the Single European Act 1986, this was followed by two treaties on European Union: the Maastricht (1993) and Amsterdam Treaties (1997). These:

(a) extended the competence of the European Economic Community to allow it to legislate for the whole Community on a wide range of areas as shown in Figure 6.2;

(b) set a target for the creation of a single market by removing all remaining legal, technical and physical obstacles to the free movement of goods, persons, capital, and services.

Figure 6.3 indicates the important aspects of changes in the Maastricht Treaty and notes important name changes and power changes.

Figure 6.2: the areas in which the European Community has legislative competence (can make law)

Achieved through Articles in:

- the European Community Treaty   1957   (Rome)
- the Single European Act   1986
- the Treaty on European Union   1993   (Maastricht)
- the Treaty on European Union   1997   (Amsterdam)

Figure 6.3: the most important changes instituted by the Treaty on European Union 1993

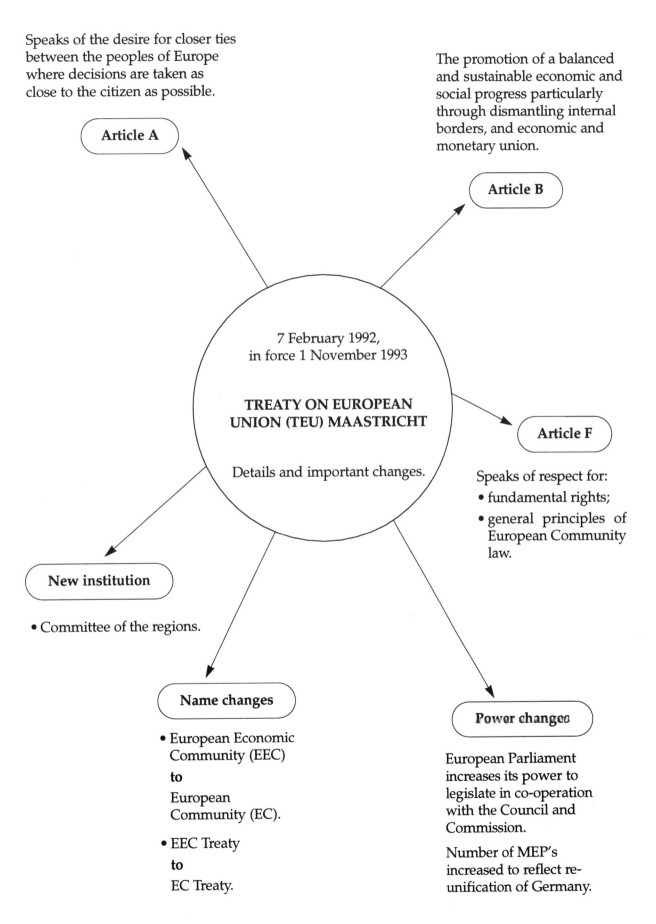

Speaks of the desire for closer ties between the peoples of Europe where decisions are taken as close to the citizen as possible.

Article A

The promotion of a balanced and sustainable economic and social progress particularly through dismantling internal borders, and economic and monetary union.

Article B

7 February 1992, in force 1 November 1993

TREATY ON EUROPEAN UNION (TEU) MAASTRICHT

Details and important changes.

Article F

Speaks of respect for:
- fundamental rights;
- general principles of European Community law.

New institution

- Committee of the regions.

Name changes

- European Economic Community (EEC)

  to

  European Community (EC).

- EEC Treaty

  to

  EC Treaty.

Power changes

European Parliament increases its power to legislate in co-operation with the Council and Commission.

Number of MEP's increased to reflect re-unification of Germany.

SUPREMACY OF COMMUNITY LAW

The Community was created through the three founding Treaties (Treaty of Paris 1951 and the two treaties of Rome 1957) as amended by the Treaties of Maastricht and Amsterdam, the Single European Act and small amendments made in some of the accession treaties and founding treaties. Community law is, therefore, ultimately derived from the Treaties. Its constitution is contained in the founding Treaties as amended.

Of most importance for an understanding of how European Community law affects the English legal system is Art 5 of the European Community Treaty, as the Treaty of Rome 1957 has now been renamed.

By Art 5 Member states are said to be bound:

> ... to take all appropriate measures, whether general or particular to ensure fulfilment of the obligations arising out of this treaty or resulting from action taken by the institutions of the Community. They shall facilitate the achievement of the Community's tasks.

Failure to comply with Art 5 can result in an action being brought in the European Court of Justice by any other Member State or by the European Commission. It was quickly established in early cases brought before the European Court of Justice that a new legal order had been created by the Community and that individual Member States were bound by this legal order in areas covered by the treaties.

A case in 1964 was to become a landmark case: *Costa v ENEL* (Case 6/64). The European Court of Justice held in that case that the Treaty of Rome:

> ... has created it own legal system which, on entry into force of the treaty, became an integral part of the legal systems of the Member States and which their courts are bound to apply.

The outcome of the case has come to be known as the *Costa* principle.

By 1977, the European Court of Justice had, in the case of *Commission v Italy*, declared that a national law was incompatible with the European Community and that all Italian bodies were to automatically and immediately cease to implement that national law.

For the avoidance of doubt, in the *Simmenthal* case in 1977 the European Court said that, once a national law has been declared incompatible with European Community law, then even national courts must cease to recognise it.

Through such decisions, the supremacy of European Community was law established with two angles:

(a) that European Community law itself, in its sphere of competency, is supreme over all national law;

(b) that Member States must have processes whereby the individual can claim the protection of European Community law, through the courts of their own Member States.

The second point was most clearly demonstrated within the English legal system in the series of cases concerning the *Secretary of State for Transport ex p Factortame* (Case 213/89), when the European Court of Justice ruled that limited national remedies cannot be allowed to restrict access to legal rights in European Community law.

Most surprisingly, when the *Factortame* case first came before the English High Court, the High Court itself took the view that an English statute in conflict with European Community law should be disapplied pending the final outcome in the case, although, within English constitutional law, no English court has the right to question the validity of a statute that has correctly gone through all of the processes necessary for legal enactment.

According to the European Community, European Community law has supremacy over national law. In addition, national remedies must also be adapted to allow for the effective delivery of community law rights. The European Court of Justice has correctly been described as the guarantor of the rights conferred by Community law.

The Court has stated that one could consider the founding treaties together with appropriate changes in the related treaties as a 'constitution'. They represent the supreme internal primary creative source of law. By analogy, one could say that they are like Acts of the UK Parliament, primary sources of law.

Many Articles in the EC Treaties give legal rights to individual citizens of Member States which can be enforced in the courts of Member States. It is said that these laws have direct effect. A well known example here is Art 119 of the EC Treaty which provides for equal pay for equal work.

Often, law making in the EC creates legal obligations with legal effect immediately and automatically in all Member States, or some, depending on the type of law. Here, such laws are said to be directly applicable. At other times, law making in the European Community results in an obligation imposed on Member States to implement their own procedures to achieve the desired outcome within a specified time.

Article 5 has caused difficulties within the legal systems of the United Kingdom. According to UK constitutional law, an international treaty only operates at the level of international law and cannot automatically become part of English law. If any government desires a treaty to have legal effect within the legal systems making up the United Kingdom, this must be done through an Act of Parliament. The treaties making up the Community were no exception and legislation, the European Communities Act 1972, was enacted to incorporate them into UK law.

The European Communities Act 1972

(See especially s 2(1), (2) and (4).)

Section 2(1) is the key section, and provides that, where Community treaties give rise to rights, powers, liabilities, obligations, these shall be recognised in UK courts along with any remedies and procedures provided by the treaties.

Section 2(2) provides for the Queen by an order in council or a minister by regulation to make provisions for implementing Community obligations. No power, however, is given in the area of taxation, delegated legislation, creation of new criminal offences with certain punishments, or retrospectivity. In these cases Parliament must act.

In order to understand how EC law affects the English legal system and impacts on legal method, it is vital to appreciate:

- the treaties setting up the Community and forming its constitution and primary laws;
- the institutions of the Community created by the treaties;
- the differing types of law making provided for under the Treaties and their differing effects;
- the place of the accession treaties.

Carefully consider the following four diagrams (Figures 6.4–6.7), before moving on. (All references to Articles are to Articles of the Treaty of Rome unless otherwise stated.)

Figure 6.4: treaties constituting the European Community

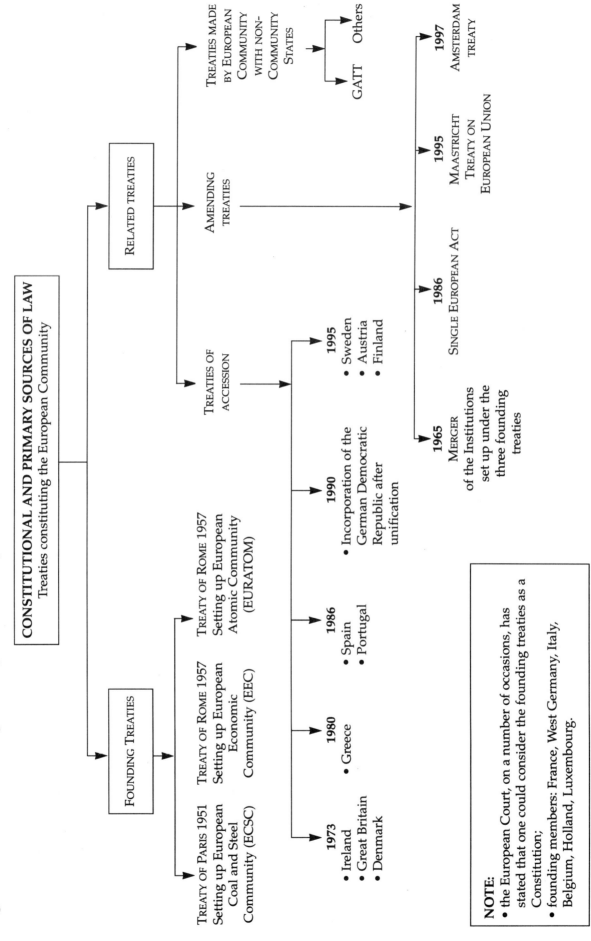

Figure 6.5: the institutions of the European Community

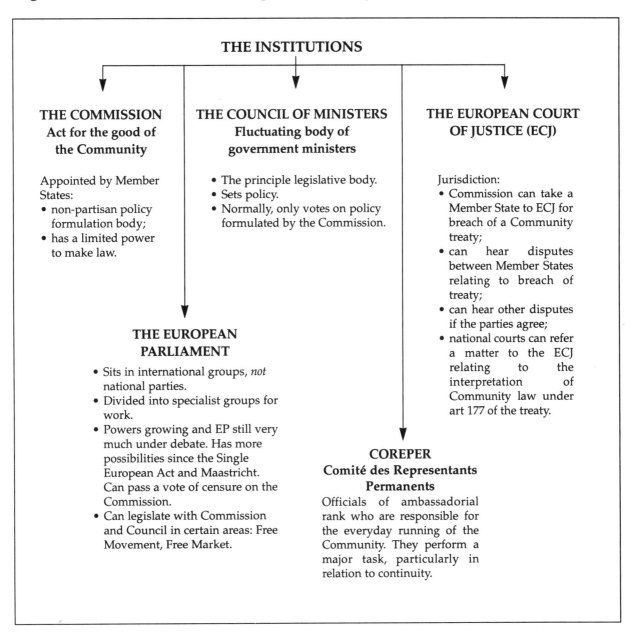

Whilst the treaties can be described as primary sources of law, law making by the institutions is referred to as secondary sources, secondary Acts of law. By analogy they are like the United Kingdom's concept of delegated or secondary legislation. Such secondary legislation is briefly described in Art 189 of the EC Treaty, where it is said to be of three main types:

- Regulations;
- Directives;
- Decisions.

Regulations, Directives and **Decisions** adopted under Art 189 must be signed by the President of the European Parliament and by the President of the Council of Ministers and published in the Official Journal of the Community.

There are also further enactments which need to be mentioned for the sake of completeness:

* making recommendations, delivering opinions.

Each of these secondary types of law have:

* **different effects;**
* **different geographical boundaries.**

Fig.6.6: types of secondary law created by the institutions of the EC

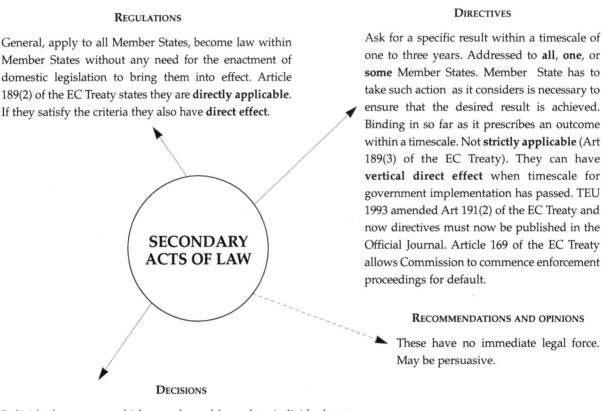

REGULATIONS

General, apply to all Member States, become law within Member States without any need for the enactment of domestic legislation to bring them into effect. Article 189(2) of the EC Treaty states they are **directly applicable**. If they satisfy the criteria they also have **direct effect**.

DIRECTIVES

Ask for a specific result within a timescale of one to three years. Addressed to **all**, **one**, or **some** Member States. Member State has to take such action as it considers is necessary to ensure that the desired result is achieved. Binding in so far as it prescribes an outcome within a timescale. Not **strictly applicable** (Art 189(3) of the EC Treaty). They can have **vertical direct effect** when timescale for government implementation has passed. TEU 1993 amended Art 191(2) of the EC Treaty and now directives must now be published in the Official Journal. Article 169 of the EC Treaty allows Commission to commence enforcement proceedings for default.

SECONDARY ACTS OF LAW

RECOMMENDATIONS AND OPINIONS

These have no immediate legal force. May be persuasive.

DECISIONS

Individual measures which are often addressed to individual states and/or individuals themselves. Binding in its entirety, immediate in effect and not requiring any other action by Member States to be law: Art 189(4). They are **directly applicable**.

Interpretation of the treaties and secondary legislation by the ECJ

Cases in the ECJ are becoming increasingly important and this court has developed some general principles to guide it when interpreting the law of the Community.

Rules of interpretation are based on principles of international law, European legal systems and concepts derived from the European Court of Human Rights. For example, concepts such as:

* natural justice;

    knowing case to get a fair hearing through known processes.

Figure 6.7 sets out the commonly agreed principles upon which the legal rules of the Community are judged and which are held in high esteem by the European Court of Justice.

Figure 6.7: commonly agreed principles for evaluating Community law

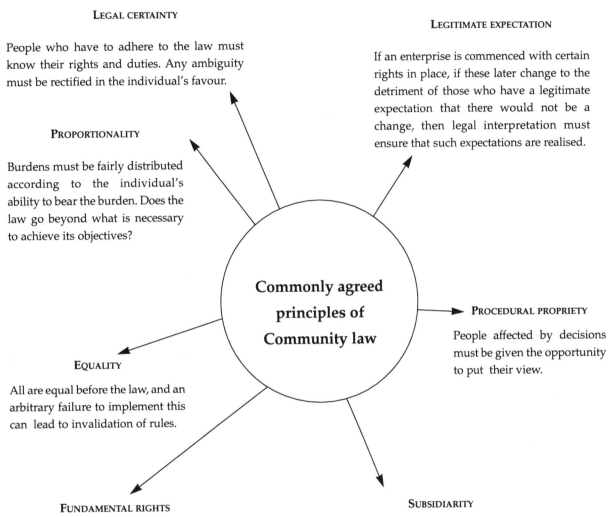

LEGAL CERTAINTY

People who have to adhere to the law must know their rights and duties. Any ambiguity must be rectified in the individual's favour.

LEGITIMATE EXPECTATION

If an enterprise is commenced with certain rights in place, if these later change to the detriment of those who have a legitimate expectation that there would not be a change, then legal interpretation must ensure that such expectations are realised.

PROPORTIONALITY

Burdens must be fairly distributed according to the individual's ability to bear the burden. Does the law go beyond what is necessary to achieve its objectives?

Commonly agreed principles of Community law

PROCEDURAL PROPRIETY

People affected by decisions must be given the opportunity to put their view.

EQUALITY

All are equal before the law, and an arbitrary failure to implement this can lead to invalidation of rules.

FUNDAMENTAL RIGHTS

All law making institutions of the Community have declared that the utmost importance is given to fundamental rights in the European Convention of Human Rights and the Court has always stated that it operates to protect fundamental rights.

SUBSIDIARITY

If action is to be taken it must be taken legally as near to those to be affected as possible. Hence the Community should only act if Member States cannot achieve the goals and in the circumstances community action would be most appropriate.

Intellectual Health Warning!
EC not sure what it means by subsidiarity!

THE METHODS BY WHICH EUROPEAN COMMUNITY LAW BECOMES PART OF NATIONAL LEGAL SYSTEMS

> **Law in the European Community is either primary, contained in treaties concluded by the governments of Member States, or secondary, law enacted by one of the institutions of the European Community.**

Primary law is of only one type, an Article in a treaty.

Secondary law is of three types and can become part of the law of a Member State in one of the two following methods:

(a) automatic incorporation: the technical expression used is that such law is *directly applicable*.

Article 189 states the types of secondary law automatically incorporated into the legal systems of Member States:

- Regulations;

(b) action required by the national law making bodies.

Article 189 states the types of secondary law which required some action by the national law making bodies:

- Directives;
- Decisions.

Again, a diagrammatic representation is helpful.

Figure 6.8: the methods by which European law enters the English legal system

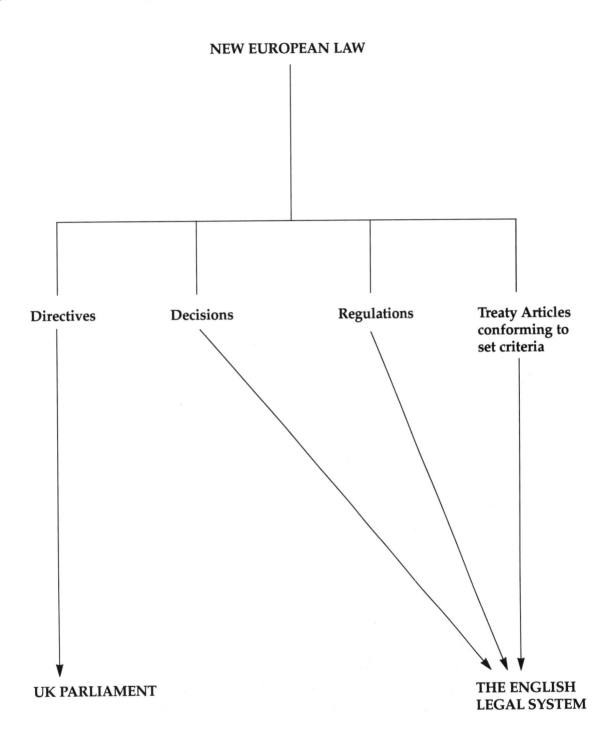

THE METHODS BY WHICH EUROPEAN COMMUNITY LAW IS ENFORCEABLE BY INDIVIDUAL CITIZENS OF MEMBER STATES IN THEIR OWN DOMESTIC COURTS

It is possible for Community law to be incorporated into the legal system of a Member State without being enforceable by individual citizens in the domestic courts of Member States.

Promises made between Member States and the Community, laws detailing certain action that only governments can control, cannot legitimately form the basis of individual rights of action.

When a provision of Community law *does* create a legal right for individual citizens of Member States to enforce in their own domestic courts, it is said that such Community law has direct effect. So, the concept of direct effect refers to the enforceability of Community law once it has been received into the domestic legal system.

The European Court of Justice has made it clear that it considers direct effect to be the norm and any deviation from it needs to be argued. It must be argued that, in a specific circumstance, direct effect is not possible.

If a provision of Community law has direct effect, individuals can either have the power to take:

- the Member State to its own domestic courts

   (vertical direct effect);

or

- another member of the Member State to the domestic court

   (horizontal direct effect).

Over the course of the last 20 years, the Court has developed conditions that must exist for a primary or a secondary Community law to have *direct effect*.

The relevant community legal provision:

- must be **clear;**
- must be **precise;**
- must be **self contained** (in the sense that its implementation must not depend on the exercise of discretion by the public authorities of Member States).

> **These qualities of clearness, precision and self containment could be referred to as the *criteria* for direct effect to take place.**

CHAPTER 7

UNDERSTANDING LAW REPORTS FROM
THE EUROPEAN COURT OF JUSTICE

The European Court of Justice (ECJ) sprang to life out of the joining together of a number of Nation States creating a new limited political and legal order. With the exception of the United Kingdom, the legal system of all the Member States is a code deriving its structure from Roman law and referred to as civil law or the civil code.

It is a deeply embedded proposition in any civil law system that what the court says is merely *evidence* of what the law is. So, a number of cases supporting a law constitutes a body of evidence of the law. Courts *do not* and *cannot* make law.

The ECJ, not surprisingly, when setting up legal principles that were to apply across the Community, drew upon the legal experience of all Nation States.

Whereas in the English common law system arguments are presented to the court referring to other cases as precedents, in the ECJ arguments are presented referring to principles of Community law. These were set out above in Figure 6.7 and could really be likened to doctrines, such as, for example, there must be equality before the law:

> ... if a ruling can be shown to be derived from a principle of sufficient generality as to command common assent, a firm legal foundation for the judgment will be provided.
>
> [Hartley, 1994, p 129.]

It should have been apparent from the discussion on precedent in English law that, despite its theoretically rigid binding nature, it is a flexible doctrine in the mouths of the judges.

Equally paradoxical is the *lack* of precedent in the ECJ and in the Court's determination to carefully develop and keep legal principles which give a great deal of consistency and coherence to Community law. Commentators have noted that it has now become normal and accepted for courts to refer to earlier cases and use these earlier cases as the rationale for decisions. However, even given these suggestions of openness to the concept of precedent, there is no suggestion that the ECJ would ever reach a decision that it did not want to purely because of other cases deciding matters differently.

The reports of cases before the ECJ are characterised by short sentences detailing facts, arguments and final conclusions. The language appears formal and characterless in contrast to English judgments which take on the linguistic style of the judge.

There are no judgments disagreeing that correspond to the English concept of the dissenting judgment. Indeed, these are forbidden and judges have to swear to secrecy in such matters as dissent. There is only one judgment given reflecting the opinion of the court.

English judges will often support conclusions to arguments by arguing the alternative. What would be the result if the outcome was not as suggested? So, a potential solution to a problem is tested by asking what would happen if this solution was not adopted? The ECJ does not use this format of reasoning.

Instead of reading a judgment that constructs an argument to provide a rationale for the outcome, often, the judgment contains conclusions that read like assertions and are certainly not backed by reasons, for the reasoning processes are not recorded.

In this chapter, the task is to read a European Community report.

The case chosen is *Van Gend en Loos* (Case 26/62), an older case, predating the United Kingdom accession, but a case which is still of immense importance within the development of the European Community. It can be found in Appendix 3. The layout of the case is similar to the layout of many European Community cases and is quite different from that found in the English legal system. Although, as the case is relatively old, some of the headings are different in newer cases.

Basic layout of a European Court report

Text

Sets out, in simple paragraphs, the procedural background and the questions before the European Court of Justice.

Judgment

Issues of fact and law are set out:

- facts of the case: the Court sets out the facts;
- arguments and observations: here the Court gives a précis of the arguments presented by all involved parties;
- grounds of judgment: the court begins its determination;
- costs;
- formal finding of the Court.

TASK

As with *George Mitchell v Finney Lock Seeds* (1983), this is the moment to turn to the case and skim read it quickly, experiencing the difficulties and differences of style and content. This will constitute a difficult piece of text to read despite the development, by now, of a certain expertise in reading legal documents. This initial reading is to obtain a first grasp of the facts and the issues.

**DO NOT CONTINUE UNTIL YOU
HAVE SKIM READ THE CASE!**

Initial observations after skim reading

One thing that should have been noticed is that the language of the law report is very different in style – at times hardly making sense which, of course, may be the fault of the translation. (The working language of the Community is French, not English, although all languages have equal status within the Community.) What is being read in English is a translation. The problems of translation were briefly referred to in Figure 2.1 in Chapter 2.

The text reads as a series of descriptions and assertions, devoid of the reasoned, illustrative argumentative techniques that are familiar to the common law lawyer.

The layout is also different from that of an English report as indicated in Figure 7.1. Part of the initial difficulties in reading a Community law report is the necessity to hold a number of pieces of information in tension as illustrated in Figure 7.2.

The reading that will be given will continue in the micro-reading method, utilising an initial paragraph by paragraph approach. This time, however, a table method will be used to demonstrate another way of organising information. Here, the *nature* of the paragraph is additionally classified as argument, description and so on.

Figure 7.1: skills and issues necessary for an understanding the text of a European Community law report

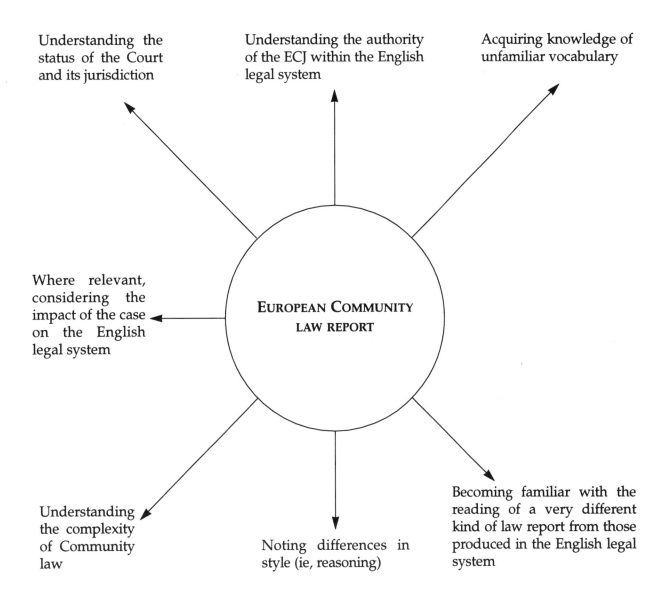

Understanding the status of the Court and its jurisdiction

Understanding the authority of the ECJ within the English legal system

Acquiring knowledge of unfamiliar vocabulary

Where relevant, considering the impact of the case on the English legal system

EUROPEAN COMMUNITY LAW REPORT

Understanding the complexity of Community law

Noting differences in style (ie, reasoning)

Becoming familiar with the reading of a very different kind of law report from those produced in the English legal system

NOTE: a leading case in any field of law yields treasure far beyond the dispute and any narrow summary by a student. Constantly searching the text, its connectors and references will enable ever deeper levels of analysis to be achieved. Again, no more than a sophisticated comprehension exercise is being engaged in using this paragraph by paragraph approach.

Figure 7.2: an overview of the issues to be understood when dealing with European Community Law

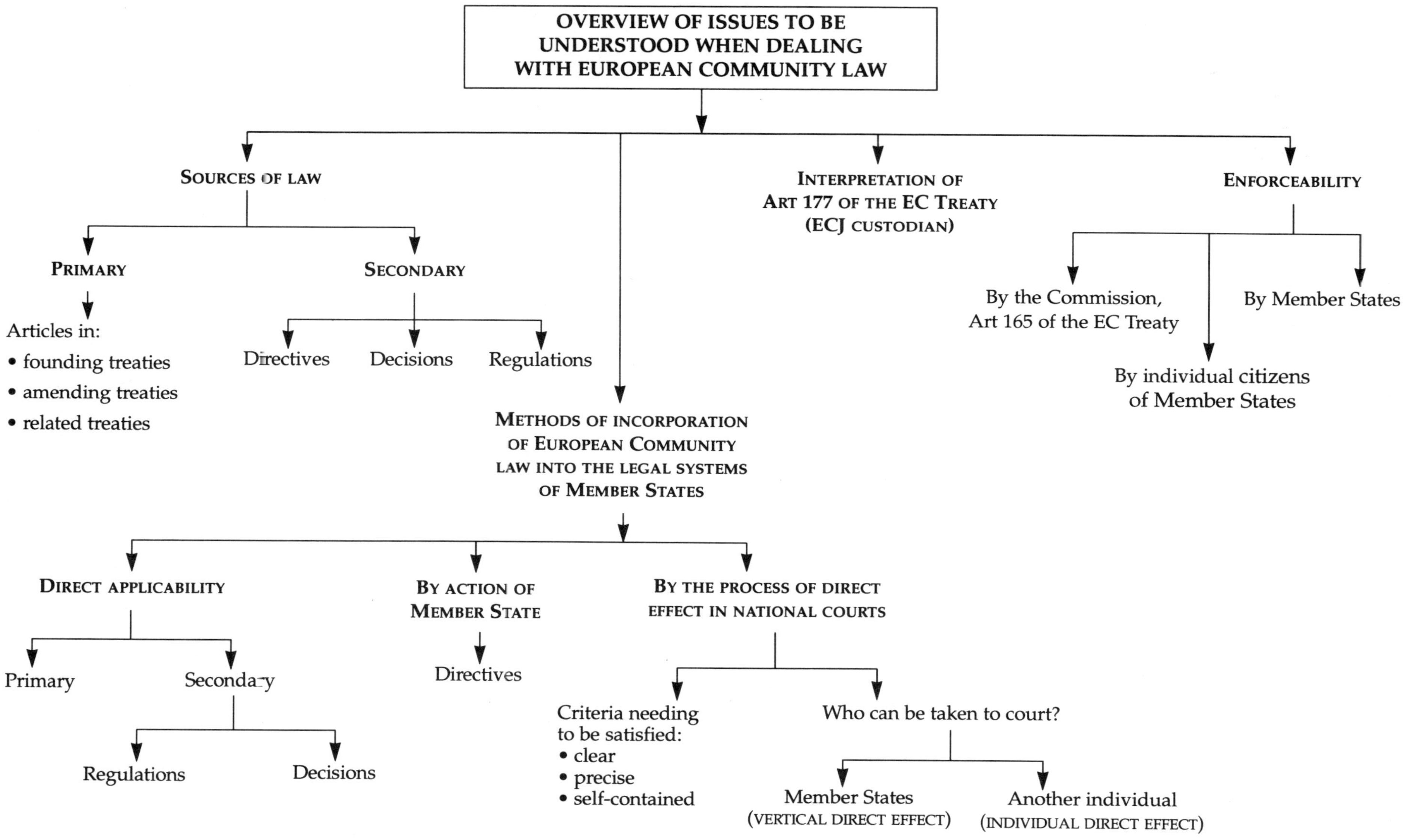

Tabulated micro-analysis of *Van Gend en Loos*

Recall that the attempt is being made to understand each paragraph before moving on. Understanding is assisted by looking at preceding and subsequent paragraphs and, if necessary, a dictionary.

It may be necessary, for example, to keep re-checking the law, as a characteristic of European Community law reports is that they do not replicate in the text the full text of the relevant primary or secondary law. English reports, by contrast, fully replicate the texts of relevant law.

The case itself has been numbered by the reporter for the purposes of organisation and subsequent ease of cross reference.

The paragraphs have not only been numbered as before (when we considered the case of *George Mitchell*) but, also, headed and classified according to the following functions:

(a) stating a point in an argument;

(b) inference;

(c) evidence;

(d) descriptive (of facts, rules, procedural history);

(e) concluding point in an argument;

(f) illustration of a point;

(g) stating the law itself.

Compiling the information in the tables represents much labour prior to summarising. It may also be necessary to set out the law in detail elsewhere in note form and to construct diagrams of issues raised in the case as a supplement to the tables.

The table set out here is supported by texts of relevant laws and diagrams which will be indicated in the table. Where useful, a **note** will be placed in the relevant section of the table giving additional information.

Remember the only function of these tables, diagrams, texts of laws is to enable an ultimately firm foundation for analysis.

> NOTE: **it is important to realise that critique is only as good as the initial comprehension of the issues, rules, facts and arguments.**

Tabulated micro-analysis of *Van Gend en Loos*

Headings	Paragraph nos	Précis of paragraph	Classification of paragraph
Text	2–3	Reference for a preliminary ruling, ruling, under Art 177, para 1(a) and para 3 of the EEC Treaty from the Tariefcommissie, the final court of jurisdiction in revenue cases in the Netherlands, (Art 177 set out in full at p 260) **NOTE:** the EEC Treaty refers to the Treaty of Rome 1957 setting up the European Community. Since the Treaty of Maastricht 1995, this Treaty is now referred to as the EC Treaty.	Descriptive: states the legal basis of the case in the European Court of Justice.
	4–6	States questions for preliminary ruling: (1) Is Article 12 of the EEC Treaty directly applicable and can individuals make a claim in their own domestic courts under Art 12? (2) If the answer to question (1) is 'yes'. was the application of an import duty in breach of Art 12 or was it a reasonable alteration as allowed by Art 12?	Descriptive: states issues to be determined by the ECJ.
The Court **Note how sentences flow into and out of headings.**	5	President Presidents of Chambers (2) Rapporteurs (2) Judges (2) Advocate General Registrar **NOTE:** the Advocate General is always asked to give an opinion in major cases. He operates as the *conscience* of the Court but does not have to be listened too. However, his opinion is published and can, on occasion, be seen as a type of dissenting opinion.	Descriptive: Court personnel.

Headings	Paragraph nos	Précis of paragraph	Classification of paragraph
Judgment, Facts and procedure	6	9 September 1960 Van Gend en Loos imported urea-formaldehyde into the Netherlands from the Federal Republic of Germany describing it as 'Harnstoffharz (UF resin) 70, Aqueous emulsion of ureaformal-dehyde'. Customs declaration 8 September 1960.	Description: the facts.
	7	The Tariefbesluit in force since 1 March 1960 classified the product under 39.01-a-1, headed according to a protocol between Belgium and the Netherlands of 25 July 1958 and ratified in law, in the Netherlands, 16 December 1959.	Description: facts continued.
	8	Specifies the duty for emulsion at 8%.	Description: facts continued.
	9	8% charged.	Description: facts continued.
	10	20 September 1960 Van Gend en Loos lodges an objection with Inspector of Customs and Excise against application of the duty.	Description: procedure.
	11	Van Gend en Loos argues that on 1 January 1958 the date in force of the EEC Treaty the classification was 279-a-2 in the Tariefbesluit of 1947 and the duty 3%. The Tariefbesluit of 1 March 1960 heading 279-a-2 replaced by heading 39-01-a-1.	Point in argument to inspector.
	12	The tariefbesluit created a sub-division in what was 279-a-2 for amino-plasts in aqueous emulsions of 8%. The rest were charged at 3%. So all is not the same.	Continuation of point to inspector.
	13	By increasing the import duty after the EEC Treaty in force the Dutch Government had infringed Art 12 which says that Member States cannot between themselves introduce any new customs duties or increase those already in existence.	Conclusion of argument to inspector.

Headings	Paragraph nos	Précis of paragraph	Classification of paragraph
	14	6 March 1961: objection of Van Gend en Loos dismissed by the inspector on grounds of inadmissibility. It was complaining not about *how* tariff *applied* but *how* it was *set*.	Point in argument and conclusion to inspector.
	15	4 April 1961: Van Gend appeals to the Tariefcommissie.	Procedure.
	16	Van Gend presents same arguments as in paras 11–13 above to Tariefcommissie. Netherland's argument was that when the EEC Treaty came into force, the product concerned was not under 279-a-2 but 332 and that was now charged at 10%, so there was no increase.	Argument of Van Gend en Loos. Argument of Netherlands.
	17	Tariefcommissie did not formally decide if product within 279-a-2 or 332 of the 1947 list. They said parties raised issues concerning the interpretation of the EEC Treaty and proceedings were suspended and the matter referred to the ECJ on 16 August 1962 under Art 177.	Procedure of Tariefcommissie in asking for a preliminary ruling.
	18	23 August 1962: decision of the Tariefcommissie given to the parties, the Member States and Commission of EEC.	Procedure: notification of interested and affected parties.
	19	Written observations were submitted by: • *parties to the main action;* • *Belgium Government;* • *German Government;* • *Commission of EEC;* • *Government of the Netherlands.* **NOTE:** any interested Member State can submit written observations.	Procedure.
	20	29 November 1962: oral submission of Van Gend en Loos heard and views of EEC Commission heard. Questions put to them by Court and written replies given.	Procedure in ECJ.

Headings	Paragraph nos	Précis of paragraph	Classification of paragraph
	21	12 December 1962: Advocate General gives his reasoned oral opinion, stating that the ECJ can only answer question 1 put to it by the Tariefcommissie and hold that Art 12 imposes a duty only on Member States. **NOTE:** see paras 4–6 above.	Procedure: opinion of Advocate General in ECJ.
Eleven arguments and obser-vation	22	Refers to the arguments in para 19 above and says summarised.	Information.
The first question: admis-sibility	23	The Government of the Netherlands and tax authority are in agreement and confirmed that the main complaint was that they had infringed Art 12.	Argument: agreement on the point in issue.
	24	The Government of the Netherlands states that an individual cannot have the right to bring an action concerning infringement of the treaty. Only Member States *or* the Commission can do this under Arts 169–70 and that individual cannot seek a preliminary ruling.	Point in argument of Netherlands.
	25	Dutch Government says ECJ cannot decide this issue because it is not about interpretation, but application.	Point in argument of Netherlands Government.
	26	Belgium Government says first question is a reference to the Court of a problem of constitutional law and therefore falls exclusively within the jurisdiction of Netherlands courts.	Point in argument of Belgium Government.
	27	The Court states that it has two international treaties both part of national law. It needs to decide under national law which treaty prevails if they conflict. Does the earlier prevail?	Point in argument of Belgium Government.

Headings	Paragraph nos	Précis of paragraph	Classification of paragraph
	28	Question is a typical question of national constitutional law within the exclusive jurisdiction of national law and has nothing to do with interpretation of the EEC Treaty.	Point in argument of Belgium Government.
	29	Decision on first question unnecessary for Tariefcommissie to give judgment but cannot have any influence on the solution to the problem.	Point in argument of Belgium Government.
	30	Whatever the ECJ says the Tarief-commissie has the same problem to solve. Can it ignore the law of 16 December 1959 ratifying protocol because it conflicts with the law of 5 December 1957 ratifying the EEC Treaty?	Point in argument of Belgium Government.
	31	So, question raised is not appropriate for a preliminary ruling because the answer cannot enable the Tariefcommissie to make a final decision.	Conclusion of argument of Belgium Government.
	32	EEC Commission observed that it is not up to the national court to determine the effect of the EEC Treaty. The problem is indeed one of interpretation.	Point in argument of EEC Commission.
	33	EEC Commission says if there is a finding of inadmissible then individuals would not be protected from infringement by Member States.	Point in argument of EEC Commission.
On the substance	34	Van Gend en Loos argues that Art 12 has direct applicability. It also has direct effect without the need for national law to give the right. Infringement of Art 12 affects fundamental principles of Community and individual also needs protection. Article 12 is well suited for direct application and national court must set aside custom duties in breach of it.	Argument and conclusion of Van Gend en Loos before the ECJ.

Headings	Paragraph nos	Précis of paragraph	Classification of paragraph
	35	EEC Commission says answer to question (1) is important and will affect interpretation and effect of Art 12 in the legal systems of other Member States and other clear articles regarding the principle of direct applicability.	Point in argument of Commission before ECJ.
	36	EEC Commission states that an analysis of the treaty shows that there was an intention by Member States to create a legal system of Community law and that it should apply in national courts.	Point in argument of EEC Commission.
	37	Community law must be effectively and uniformly applied throughout the whole of the Community.	Point in argument of EEC Commission.
	38	Internal effect of Community law cannot be decided internally. Only Commission can do this and Community law must prevail.	Point in argument by EEC Commission.
	39	Just because Community law is directed to the State it does not mean that an individual with an interest cannot apply to the Court.	Point in argument by EEC Commission.
	40	Commission believes that Art 12 contains a rule of law capable of being the subject of an effective application to a national court.	Point in argument by EEC Commission.
	41	Provisions are clear – they create a specific, unambiguous obligation not affected by other articles. It is self-sufficient and does not require any Community action to make the obligation clear.	Point in argument by EEC Commission.
	42	Dutch Government draws a distinction between (1) internal effect (**note:** what we now refer to as direct applicability) and (2) direct effect, Says (1) is a pre-requisite for (2).	Point in argument of Netherlands Government.

Headings	Paragraph nos	Précis of paragraph	Classification of paragraph
	43	Can only have internal effect. (that is, direct applicability) if it is the intention of the contracting parties and terms and conditions allow it.	Point in argument of Netherlands Government.
	44	Wording only puts obligation on Member States who are free to decide how they intend to fulfil obligations.	Point in argument of Netherlands Government.
	45	It does not have internal effect it can have direct effect.	Point in argument of Netherlands Government.
	46	Even if it did have internal effect it cannot have direct effect.	Point in argument of Netherlands Government.
	47	Alternatively, treaty does not differ from a standard international treaty. The conclusive factors remain intention of the parties and provisions of the treaty.	Point in argument of Netherlands Government.
	48	Whether Art 12 is directly applicable is one of interpretation of Netherlands law and not in the jurisdiction of the ECJ.	Point in argument of Netherlands Government.
	49	If it was held that Art 12 applied internally and had direct effect it would upset the system created by treaty – creating uncertainty in law and the responsibility of States could be put in issue by means of a procedure that was never intended.	Point in argument of Netherlands Government.
	50	Article 12 is not an exception and does not having direct internal effect.	Conclusion of argument of Belgium Government.
	51	Article 12 is not a rule of law of general applicability saying that any new duty is without effect. It says members should refrain from imposing new duties.	Point in argument of Belgium Government.

Headings	Paragraph nos	Précis of paragraph	Classification of paragraph
	52	Article 12 does not create directly applicable rights for individuals. Government asked to obtain a goal. National courts cannot be asked to enforce it.	Point in argument of Belgium Government.
	53	Article 12 is not directly applicable. It imposes international obligations which need to be nationally implemented.	Point in argument of German Government.
	54	Customs duties only come from Nation States not EEC Treaty.	Point in argument of German Government.
	55	Obligation only applies to other contracting Member States.	Point in argument of German Government.
	56	In German law, a provision contrary to Art 12 would be valid.	Point in argument of German Government.
	57	Only measures taken by the institutions protect nationals which are of direct or individual concern to nationals.	Point in argument of German Government.
The second question: admissibility	58	Netherlands and Belgium Governments say second question is inadmissible.	Conclusion of argument of Belgium and Netherlands Governments.
	59	Article 177 procedure inappropriate to explain issues raised in questions.	Argument of Belgium and Netherlands Governments.
	60	If a State can be brought before the ECJ outside Arts 169/170, the legal protection of States would be diminished.	Point in argument of Netherlands Government.
	61	Article only created state obligation so ECJ under Art 177 cannot decide issues of conflict.	Point in argument of German Government.
	62	Van Gend en Loos says that the direct form of question (2) needs an examination of facts for which the Court has no jurisdiction under Art 177.	Conclusion of argument of Van Gend en Loos.

Headings	Paragraph nos	Précis of paragraph	Classification of paragraph
	63	The real question should be 'can it be said moving from rules before 1 March 1960 that it is not an increase even though it is an arithmetical increase'.	Point in argument of Van Gend en Loos.
Grounds of judgment Procedure	64	Tariefcommissie did not make objection to reference. And there are no grounds for the ECJ to do so.	Procedure: comment by ECJ.
The first question: jurisdiction of the court	65	Discuss argument of Belgium and Netherlands Governments challenging the jurisdiction of ECJ to determine whether EEC Treaty prevails over Netherlands legislation. Only national courts can be subjected to application in accordance with Arts 169–70	Point in argument of ECJ dealing with issues raised by Belgium and Netherlands Governments.
	66	ECJ is not asked to decide on applicability of treaty according to national law. It is interpreting the scope of Art 12 within the context of community law in conformity with Art 177. So the argument put forward by the two governments has no foundation.	Conclusion of argument of ECJ to point raised on jurisdiction by Belgium and Netherlands Governments.
	67	Belgium states that ECJ has no jurisdiction because no answer by ECJ would have a bearing on Tariefcommissie answer to the issues before it.	ECJ notes point in argument of Belgium Government.
	68	Belgium further argues that to get jurisdiction the question raised has to be clearly interpretational. ECJ cannot review why question asked in certain ways.	Point in argument of ECJ in response to issues raised by Belgium Government.
	69	Wording relates to the treaty, therefore, there is jurisdiction. The argument concerning lack of jurisdiction is unfounded.	Conclusion of argument of ECJ.
On the substance of the case	70	The Court restates question (1). Has Art 12 direct applicability in national law in the sense that nationals may lay claim?	Information: restatement of first issue.

Headings	Paragraph nos	Précis of paragraph	Classification of paragraph
	71	Considers the spirit, schema and wording of the Article to find the answer.	Point in argument of ECJ.
	72	Objective of treaty is a Common Market which implies treaty is more than an agreement of mutual obligations. Preamble to the treaty speaks of government and peoples. Institutions established who affect nationals.	Point in argument of ECJ.
	73	Article 177 confirms that States have acknowledged that Community law can be invoked by nationals in national courts.	Point in argument of ECJ.
	74	Community constitutes a new legal order. States have limited sovereignty in certain areas and nationals, independently of the legislation of Member States, have rights/obligations granted by the treaty.	Conclusion of point argued by ECJ.
	75	Article 9 bases community on a customs union, prohibits custom duties. It is at the beginning of defining the Community and is applied and explained by Art 12.	Description of relationship between Art 9 and Art 12.
	76	Wording of Art 12 creates a clear and unconditional negative obligation. Nothing for States to do. Article is ideal for direct effect in relationship between Member States and their subjects.	Point in the argument of ECJ.
	77	Article 12 does not require any legislation by Member States. Nationals can benefit from a negative obligation.	Point in argument of ECJ.
	78	Argument put forward on Arts 169–70 by the governments giving observations was misconceived. Just because power is given for the Commission and Member States to raise issues before the ECJ it does not mean such issues *cannot* be raised in national courts in appropriate circumstances.	Point in argument of ECJ.

Headings	Paragraph nos	Précis of paragraph	Classification of paragraph
	79	If action under Art 12 were restricted to Arts 169–70 actions, this would deny direct legal protection of nationals. Also, Arts 169–70 action may be ineffective after national changes.	Point in argument of ECJ.
	80	Nationals having rights increases effectiveness of supervision in addition to Arts 169–70	Point in argument of ECJ.
	81	According to the spirit, general scheme and wording of treaty, Art 12 must be interpreted as having direct effect creating individual rights.	Conclusion of argument of ECJ.
The second question: the juris-diction of the court	82	Belgium and Netherlands Governments say look at classification of product. Van Gend en Loos and inspectors have different ideas.	Description.
	83	The Court has no jurisdiction to consider the reference made by the Tariefcommissie.	Conclusion of argument by ECJ.
	84	But the real meaning of the question by the Tariefcommissie is whether in law an effective increase in duties charged due to a new classification contravenes the prohibition in Art 12.	Point in argument by ECJ.
	85	This question does involve the interpretation of the treaty and the meaning to be given to the concept of duties.	Point in the argument of the ECJ.
	86	Therefore, we do have jurisdiction.	Conclusion of point made by ECJ.
	87	Wording of Art 12 makes it clear that one must look at duties and charges applied at date of entry into force of treaty.	Point in argument of ECJ.

Headings	Paragraph nos	Précis of paragraph	Classification of paragraph
	88	With regard to prohibition an illegal increase may arise by rearrangement and re-classification under a higher percentage duty.	Point in argument of ECJ.
	89	It does not matter how increase achieved, the fact of the increase is the important matter.	Point in the argument of the ECJ.
	90	Application of Art 12 with interpretation given above is within the jurisdiction of the national court. The courts must ask if product charged at a higher rate than on 1 January 1958.	Conclusion to second question.
	91	ECJ has no jurisdiction to check the validity of conflicting views, this is for national courts.	Conclusion by ECJ.
The costs	92	Costs by EEC and Member States not recoverable. This ruling is part of the case before the Tariefcommissie so decisions as to costs for them.	Decision regarding costs.
	93	On those grounds, after pleadings, reports, parties, opinions of Advocate General and with regard to Arts 9, 12, 14, 169, 170 and 177 of the treaty.	Grounds.
The court rules *that*	94	*In* answer to the question: (1) Art 12 has direct effect and creates rights for nationals to be protected in national courts; (2) to determine whether there is an increase look at charges before and after 1 January 1958; (3) decision as to costs for the Tariefcommissie.	End.

Having persevered with the reading of the case and the notations, the differences between this Community case and common law reports is stark. The judges in the ECJ do not use analogy, poetic language, asides, stories, counter arguments.

There is a veneer of scientific detachment in the language of the Court. The style is unadorned description, technical language without explanation, assertion, the summarising without comment of a wide range of arguments by the parties, the Advocate General, and the governments wishing to make observations. When the ECJ turns to the decisions it will make, it dismisses arguments without explanation with phrases such as, 'this is misconceived', 'No, this is not right' and states 'this is the case' without giving reasons why.

The Court argues deductively without making any attempts to refer to policy. Yet, it must surely be aware of the policy dimensions of its decisions. If it had decided against Van Gend en Loos then the power of the fledgling Community would have been severely diminished. In the view of the Advocate General, companies would follow the national customs tariffs and not be guided by the provisions of the treaty. The ECJ may well have been taking the opportunity to assert the power of the Community over the individual Member State. This is conjecture in the absence of any comment on policy from the Court itself.

Potentially powerful and persuasive arguments were put forward that the ECJ did not have the jurisdiction to hear the case. The Court merely replied that they did have jurisdiction. This was based on the grounds that the meaning behind the question raised an issue of interpretation within its jurisdiction.

The Court's simplistic decision following from this that any arithmetical change, even if it resulted from a re-classification within the existing order rather than a deliberate increase, would constitute an infringement of the treaty – is severe and open to question. In the face of arguments that would concentrate upon the intention of Member States concerning infringement, the ECJ says any arithmetical increase constitutes an infringement irrespective of intention.

Indeed, much policy has to be read into all judgments of the ECJ and this judgment is no exception. Perhaps given the tensions between Member States and their creation, the European Community, this is a wise and deliberate policy. The Member States gave birth to something that, in many respects, is more powerful and can dictate terms to an individual Member State.

There is little usage of what may be described as the forensic skill of the English judge. The major part of the report concerns summaries of the arguments put forward by both parties, the Advocate General, other interested Member States, and the governments of affected Member States.

Given the detail of the summarised arguments, and the range of arguments presented, it is interesting to note that it is acceptable for the Court to dismiss arguments without reasons. Theoretically, of course, an English judge could do the same, but the entrenched method of reasoning by analogy based on precedent makes such a course of action unlikely.

PART III

MANAGEMENT OF SECONDARY TEXTS
AND A RANGE OF DIFFERING FACTUAL INFORMATION

MANAGEMENT OF SECONDARY TEXTS AND A RANGE OF DIFFERING FACTUAL INFORMATION

INTRODUCTION: THE AIM OF PART III

The two chapters in Part III are designed to consider dealing with books about law (secondary texts) and also with how to organise a mass of variable information. Students need to be able to find strategies for analysing law itself, but they also need strategies for reading a large amount of secondary data and for organising factual information (fact management).

The competent location, notation and use of secondary texts is an integral aspect of legal studies. Secondary texts provide commentaries on the law, theorise concerning its cultural and or institutional context, expanding on concepts developed in the cases.

Fact management will obviously be seen to be necessary at the vocational stage and during the professional career, but doubts are often expressed concerning its use at the undergraduate stage of academic training. However, it further develops essential skills of identification, classification and analysis. Also, students are continuously dealing with textual accounts of the facts and it is important that, despite these being presented as neat stories, students have an appreciation of their 'raw' state. It is the lawyers for both parties who first deal with raw facts and weave the story. The court decides which story it will follow. The lawyer first translates the story into a grievance for the legal system to adjudicate. The judge re-translates it into the story of facts and rules leading to judgment.

CHAPTER 8

SUMMARISING, ANNOTATING, LINKING AND CRITIQUING A RANGE OF DIFFERING SECONDARY TEXTS

The core of legal studies is, or should be, the primary legal text. However, it is also necessary to competently handle secondary legal texts – textbooks, journal articles, newspaper articles.

Books about law are consulted, in panic or at leisure, for a range of reasons:

- **to obtain a general grasp of an area of law;**
- **to obtain a description of a topic;**
- **to obtain a range of different views about the same case/statute/area/theory/method;**
- **to obtain a sophisticated analysis of a topic or case, and so on.**

Usually, this information is being sought to provide the raw material for use in answering an essay question, writing a project, or answering a problem question.

The ultimate piece of writing will only be as good as the student's ability to:

- **competently undertake the research required;**
- **identify the arguments in the material read;**
- **understand the arguments in the material read;**
- **evaluate the arguments in the material read;**
- **compare the arguments in the material read;**
- **differentiate between information, description and argument.**

It is absolutely essential from the outset to have a plan for reading. Reading in the context of studying always implies reading for the purposes of solving a problem. The parameters of the problems before the reader have to be carefully thought out before commencing reading.

Students may be given a problem question to research, or an essay to write. With both types of assessment activity, it is vital that the limits of the question are correctly identified by looking for clues in the grammar used to construct the question. Remember, the facts of problem cases are always set in the areas between decided cases where there is an area of 'unknown', an area that the student is expected to talk about confidently. Competent identification of the issues from the outset often determines the quality of the answer before any creative writing has begun.

The care given to the reading of cases and statutory provisions has *also* to be brought to the reading of secondary explanatory, interpretative or evaluative texts. Reading with an idea of *why* the text is being read as well as with a view to *what you hope to do with the extracted information will* enable the student to read with a mixture of skimming strategies, detailed reading strategies and notetaking.

The why can be as simple as 'I am reading to find out what this article is about' through to 'does this article support the argument that I am trying to construct?'. Many students, however, read blindly – 'This is on the reading list so I have to read it'. They do not fit their reading into a strategy: 'Am I reading this for description, information or analysis?' 'Am I seeking to find out basic things about the topic or am I trying to support propositions in my argument?'

It is essential to develop a reading strategy. There are some easy basic first steps which will be set out below. However, the most important issue to grasp is that reading can never be a purely passive act, for writing always seeks to engage the reader in active dialogue with the text. No one writes in order not to be read, and no one wishes to be read passively without thought entering into the reading process. It is necessary to become aware of an inner dialogue between self and text as reading progresses, or to acquire an inner dialogue if one is not present! The reader should be continually processing, reflecting, considering, agreeing or disagreeing as reading is in progress.

Readers should particularly note if other thoughts enter their head (like 'what's on TV?'!). If readers become frustrated with the text, the reading should stop and questions asked. Is the reader scared, threatened, annoyed with the text and, if so, why?

There are four main stages to any reading enterprise:

(a) preparation prior to reading:

- locating texts;
- ascertaining purpose for reading;

(b) methods of reading;

(c) understanding what is being read;

(d) evaluating what is being read.

These are deceptively easy to set out but much harder to utilise for the first time, especially if readers have already established ill-disciplined approaches to reading.

Each of the above stages can be split into sub-stages; such analysis is necessary to obtain the fullest comprehension of the text. The following strategy for competent reading demonstrates this.

A STRATEGY FOR COMPETENT READING

(a) Preparation prior to reading

- *reading intention*:
    - ○ why am I reading this text?;
    - ○ what do I hope to get out of it?;
- *reader prediction of use and content of text*:
    - ○ this involves a consideration of what the writer is saying. This can be judged from the subject matter and the title;
    - ○ the very act of choosing a text involves prediction:
        - – that this text is relevant;
        - – that the text will begin to answer some of the questions that you have in your mind.

(b) Methods of reading

- *skimming*:

    read very quickly and generally through a text noting:
    - ○ publication date – for the study of law, it is particularly vital to know which edition you are reading; texts can go out of date due to changes in the law in a matter of months;
    - ○ index;
    - ○ foreword;

- o any headings and sub-headings;
- o author details;
- o introductory paragraphs;
- o the first sentence or two of paragraphs following introductions;
- o look at concluding paragraphs.

This activity assists in deciding the potential relevance of the text;

- *scanning*:

unlike the general skim through, scanning involves quickly looking for specific words, phrases or information;

- *detailed reading*:

reading will allow attention to be given to secondary or subsidiary points in the text. Here, the reading is slower and careful. Check unfamiliar vocabulary. Some words and phrases become clear as more text is read.

Note the type of language used:

technical;

figurative;

journalistic;

academic;

personal (you must ...);

impersonal (one must or it is therefore);

intimate;

distanced.

Note how arguments are put together:
- are points backed up by reference to evidence?
- are points made left to stand alone without evidence?

(c) Understanding what you are reading

- *guessing words that you do not know*:

do not expect to know all the words read. Even as a more extensive vocabulary is acquired, there will be words that are not known;

- *identifying main ideas*:

  many main ideas will have been discovered on a first skimming. A second reading begins the process of identifying the main points made by the writer. This aids in the acquisition of a deeper understanding of the arguments presented in the text;

- *identifying subsidiary ideas*:

  as the main points are identified, it is possible to organise the information and classify secondary, subsidiary points;

- *identifying overall text organisation*:

  every writer has a different way of organising, classifying and structuring their work. This needs to be ascertained by any reader who wishes to break into the text successfully;

  An initial issue is to decide whether the writer is:

    o outlining an area;

    o discussing a specific problem;

    o proposing a solution to a problem;

    o comparing and contrasting ideas;

    o speaking of the present, future or the past.

(d) Evaluating what you are reading

- *ascertaining the purpose of the writer*:

    this is crucial.

  Does the writer want to inform you about something or try to persuade you of the correctness of a particular point of view?

    Often a writer will seek to both inform and persuade;

- *ascertaining the argument(s) of the writer*:

  some texts are said to be complex not because they use particularly difficult words or arguments but because, in order to understand the full detail of the writer's position, extensive knowledge of other areas within or outside the particular discipline will be required;

- *ascertaining the attitude of the writer*:

  writers are usually biased towards a certain view in their writing, although on occasion a writer may be neutral.

  You must be able to gain skill in identifying a writer's attitude to the ideas he or she is discussing.

  You must at least know whether the writer is neutral or biased;

Each of the above is interconnected and a good way of showing such interconnection is by using a diagram as in Figure 8.1.

Figure 8.1: diagrammatic summary of reading plan

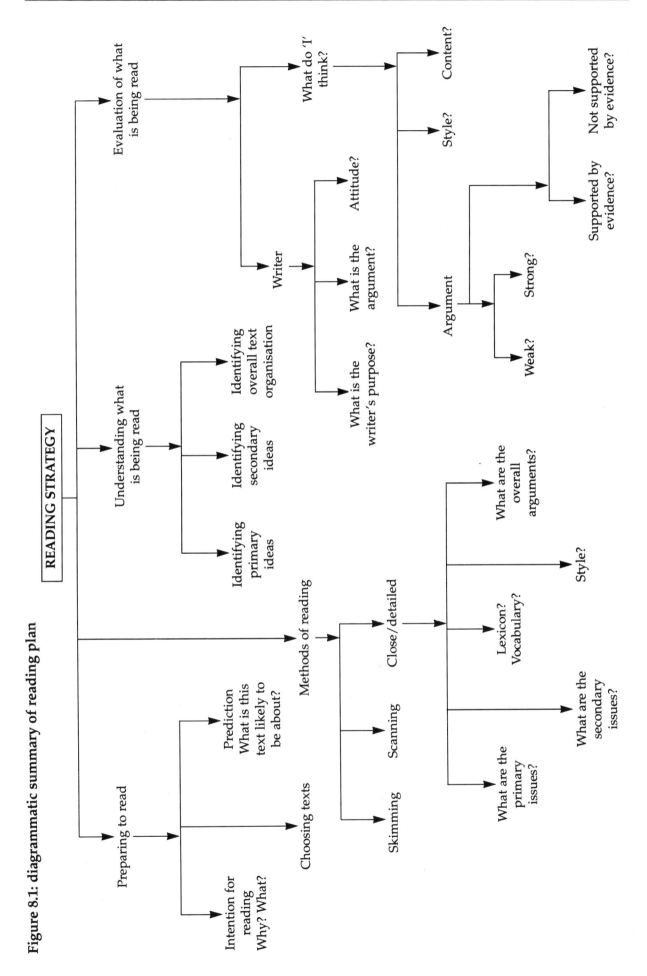

Practical demonstration of the strategy for reading: analysis of an article

Going through this approach in detail demonstrates that reading appropriately is a highly disciplined, complex and skilled process. To test the method it will be applied to an article, 'The European Union belongs to its citizens: three immodest proposals' by JHH Weiler; the full text can be found in Appendix 5.

Following the reading strategy above, read the article and insert, under each of the headings given in the reading strategy, appropriate responses.

(a) Preparation prior to reading

- *reading intention*:
  - o why am I reading this text?
    - – to learn how to read texts from the perspective of good legal method;
    - – this particular legal text is the one chosen!
  - o what do I hope to get out of it?
    - – a strategy for competent reading;
    - – some new knowledge from the article;
- *reader prediction of use and content of text*:
  - o this involves a consideration of what the writer is saying. This can be judged from the subject matter and the title.

    What does the title suggest?

It is about the European Union and is suggesting it 'belongs to its citizens'. What does one think about this claim – European Union citizen? The last phrase of the title is deliberately reversed 'three immodest proposals'. Usually, people will argue that they are only suggesting modest, small changes. Here, then, the suggestion is that the changes are large and perhaps outrageous. The title also sounds like a political slogan, a call to arms maybe 'The European Union belongs to its citizens.' So the article is, or should be, about proposals relating to the concept of the Union belonging to its citizens.

(b) Methods of reading

- *skimming*:

  read very quickly and generally through the text noting:
  - o **publication date**: 1997;
  - o **headings and sub-headings**:
    - – introduction;
    - – proposal 1: the European Legislative Ballot;
    - – proposal 2: Lexcalibur – The European Public Square;
    - – proposal 3: limits to growth;
  - o **author details.**

    Professor of Law and Jean Monnet Chair, Harvard University;

    Co-Director, Academy of European Law, European University Institute Florence;

    > NOTE: Jean Monnet was one of the original architects of the European Community in 1957.

  - o **introductory paragraphs:**

    para 1: asks the reader to recall days of the Maastricht treaty. Notes who was for and who against and raises doubts about understanding;

para 2: talks of:

- street reaction relating back to title;
- disempowerment of the individual European citizen;

para 3: gives three 'roots' of disempowerment:

    (i) democratic deficit;

para 4: states second root

    (ii) ever-increasing remoteness, opaqueness and inaccessibility of European governance;

para 5: third root:

    (iii) competencies of the Union;

para 6: one sentence: don't be surprised by the alienation;

para 7: says proposals of IGC 'very modest', with those who gain being governments, and consumers losing out;

para 8: says the author will give three proposals that can make a difference without a political fuss.

Already, from the heading above we know what they are:

- proposal 1: the European Legislative Ballot;
- proposal 2: Lexcalibur – the European Public Square;
- proposal 3: limits to growth;

  o   read the first sentence of two of the paragraphs following introductions;

  o   look at concluding paragraphs. Article does not have a signalled conclusion as it had a signalled introduction. But it does state:

The IGC has proclaimed that the European Union belongs to its citizens. The proof of the pudding will be in the eating [p 343].

IGC = Inter-Governmental Conference.

Note the use of the figurative language.

This activity assists in deciding the potential relevance of the text.

If the work in hand concerned the European citizen, enough has been gained by the introduction, headings and last paragraph to conclude that the article is relevant.

- **Scanning**

Unlike the general skim through, scanning involves quickly looking for specific words, phrases or information.

This would be used with this article if it was being scanned for potential relevancy.

- **Detailed reading**

Reading will allow attention to be given to identifying primary and secondary or subsidiary arguments properly in the text.

Here, the reading is slower and careful. Check out unfamiliar vocabulary. Some words and phrases become clear as more text is read.

For example:

  o   what does the word 'Lexcalibur' mean?;

  o   what does the phrase 'the European public square' mean?

Note the type of language used.

Thinking closely about the text the most obvious language usage is *figurative*. The writer uses short sentences, slogans, rhetorical questions, poetic language, metaphor, invents words.

For example:

Steel imagery	cast your mind back ...
Political imagery	the Mandarins heralded
Mathematical imagery	'what's-in-it-for-me?' calculus
Architectural/geological imagery	shaky foundation
Nature imagery	roots of disempowerment
Scientific imagery	the specific gravity of whom continues to decline
Nature imagery	the second root goes even deeper
Religious imagery	an apocryphal statement
Food imagery	it is End of Millennium Bread and Circus Governance
Elemental imagery	could be shielded behind firewalls
Grand teleological style	ours is a vision which tries to enhance human sovereignty, demystify technology and place it firmly as servant and not master
Food imagery	the European Court of Justice should welcome having this hot potato removed from its plate
Food imagery	the proof of the pudding will be in the eating.

Note how arguments are put together.

Scanning for argument: the argument was relatively well signalled by the introduction and the headings.

The following has been divided into proposition and evidence supporting it. Many readers do not differentiate the two which is a major error and leads to confusion and misunderstanding.

- o **Proposition**: the Maastricht treaty was not the remarkable diplomatic achievement it was claimed to be.

  Evidence: street reaction apathetic, confused, hostile, fearful:

  – Danes voted against it;

  – French approved it marginally (1%);

  – commentators say greater scrutiny in Great Britain and Germany would have meant outcome uncertain;

  – even those supporting it were greedy.

- o **Proposition**:

  (i) there was a growing disillusionment with the European construct as a whole;

  (ii) the moral and political legitimacy of the European construct is in decline.

  Evidence: reasons many. Especially due to a sense of disempowerment of the European citizen. Many roots, but three stand out:

> – democratic deficit;
>
> – remoteness;
>
> – competencies of union.
>
> o **Conclusion**: a package of three proposals (a limited ballot by citizens concerning legislation; internet access to European decision making; establishment of a constitutional council), taken from research, initiated by the European Parliament, can make a real difference to increase the power of the European citizen without creating a political drama.

The argument as set out in the introduction

The Maastricht Treaty was not the diplomatic achievement it was claimed to be. The European citizen continues to be disempowered. There remains a growing disillusionment with the European construct as a whole which is suffering from a decline in its moral and political legitimacy. However, a package of three proposals (a limited ballot by citizens concerning legislation; internet access to European decision making; establishment of a constitutional council), taken from research, initiated by the European Parliament, can make a real difference to increase the power of the European citizen without creating a political drama.

(c) Understanding what you are reading

- *guessing words that you do not know*:

  do not expect to know all the words read. Even as a more extensive vocabulary is acquired, there will be words that are not known;

- *identifying main ideas*:

  here, the main idea is that a package of three proposals (a limited ballot by citizens concerning legislation; internet access to European decision making; establishment of a constitutional council), taken from research, initiated by the European Parliament, can make a real difference to increase the power of the European citizen without creating a political drama;

- *identifying subsidiary ideas*

  here, that there could be potential clashes between the constitutional council and the function of the European Court of Justice;

- *identifying overall text organisation*:

  every writer has a different way of organising, classifying and structuring their work. This needs to be ascertained by any reader who wishes to break successfully into the text. Here the author has clearly indicated structure through the headings and has discussed points in the order indicated.

  The writer is:

  o discussing a specific problem; and

  o proposing a solution to a problem.

(d) Evaluating what you are reading

- *ascertaining the purpose of the writer*:

  the writer wants to inform about something and indicate the correctness of a particular point of view;

- *evaluating the argument(s) of the writer*:

  the argument here is relatively easy to extract because the article is written in a punchy, journalistic style while keeping to headings. What is clear, however, is that the detail given to setting out the three proposals is not given to indicating evidence to support propositions – perhaps because the writer feels that many of his propositions are self-evident.

Having ascertained the arguments, then it is up to the reader to decide what is thought.

A student's view of the argument of the writer is initially limited by their lack of knowledge of the issues spoken of. As research is continued in an area for an essay, more is learnt, more about competing views, and more about the area generally. Then, the student's view of the argument may change.

Even if an argument is preferred, it can still be a weak or strong argument either theoretically or practically. It can be weak because no evidence to show support for important propositions or ultimate conclusion has been put forward.

Students may need far more information before they can evaluate the writer's proposals concerning problems and solutions. The student may not agree with the problem. If a problem has been misdiagnosed, then the solution will not work. If the problem has been correctly identified, but the wrong causes attributed then, again, the solution will not work.

Reading is, therefore, a dynamic act, not a purely passive thing.

In any text identifying problems and putting forward solutions in argument or description formats, the following questions need to be asked:

- o is it plausible to classify these circumstances as a problem?;

- o is it plausible to maintain that these are the causes of the problem?;

- o given the view on the above two questions, is it plausible to offer these solutions?

Then ask: OK, is this conclusion plausible?

Do I agree with the conclusion to the argument?

If I do not, how do I attack it?

Do I agree with all of the propositions that are the building blocks in this argument?

Are the propositions strong or weak?

Ask these questions in relation to the article on the European Citizen.

Any area of lack of understanding, ask 'why?':

- o are there problems with the vocabulary, the concepts, too much presupposed information, etc?;

- *ascertaining the attitude of the writer*:

writers are usually biased towards a certain view in their writing, although on occasion a writer may be neutral.

You must be able to gain skill in identifying a writer's attitude to the ideas he or she is discussing.

You must at least know whether the writer is neutral or biased.

Having read this article, it is possible to represent this argument as a diagram which is a useful method of viewing all arguments unidimensionally which our brain cannot do with text. This is demonstrated in Figure 8.2

Furthermore, imagine that there are other articles about citizenship by authors X, Y and Z, the original article by Weiler could then be annotated according to whether X, Y or Z agree or disagree with Weiler's arguments and evidences. This is set out in Figure 8.3. Study these diagrams carefully and understanding will be gained in the area of the use of secondary texts.

Figure 8.2: diagram of arguments in article

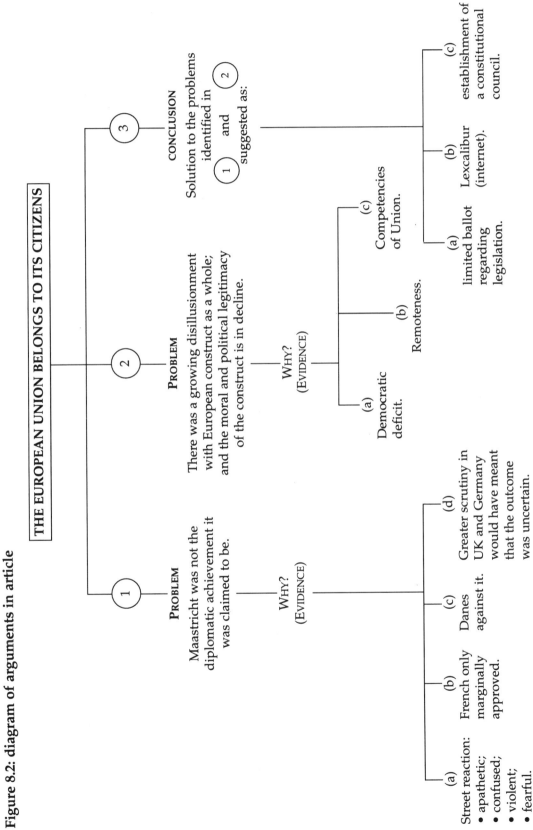

THE EUROPEAN UNION BELONGS TO ITS CITIZENS

① PROBLEM

Maastricht was not the diplomatic achievement it was claimed to be.

WHY? (EVIDENCE)

(a) Street reaction:
• apathetic;
• confused;
• violent;
• fearful.

(b) French only marginally approved.

(c) Danes against it.

(d) Greater scrutiny in UK and Germany would have meant that the outcome was uncertain.

② PROBLEM

There was a growing disillusionment with European construct as a whole; and the moral and political legitimacy of the construct is in decline.

WHY? (EVIDENCE)

(a) Democratic deficit.

(b) Remoteness.

(c) Competencies of Union.

③ CONCLUSION

Solution to the problems identified in ① and ② suggested as:

(a) limited ballot regarding legislation.

(b) Lexcalibur (internet).

(c) establishment of a constitutional council.

Figure 8.3: how to annotate a diagrammatic presentation of the argument of an article with other authors (X, Y and Z) who agree/disagree with the argument of the original article

NOTE: even when authors agree with a point in argument, they may disagree with evidence put forward for proving that point.

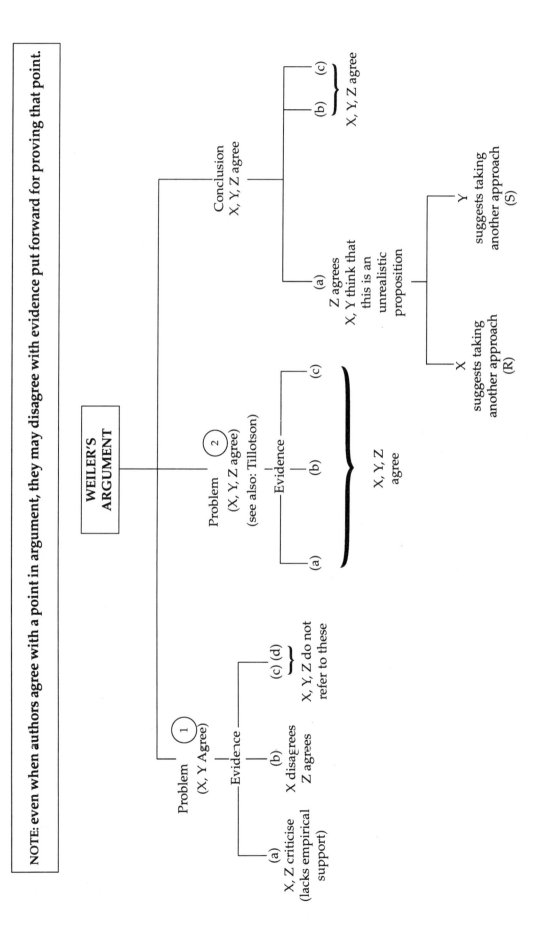

If one were marshalling evidence for an essay entitled 'Does the European Union belong to its citizens?', it would be possible to incorporate the views of Weiler, and authors X, Y and Z in such an essay by simply writing to the diagram. In addition, one would look in leading textbooks to see if those authors had anything to state, authors such as Tillotson (1996).

Having noted the areas of agreement and disagreement on the diagram, a clear view emerges of strong and weak arguments. Then, it is possible for the student to come to a personal conclusion.

The student may feel that it is not possible to come to a clear conclusion. This feeling can be right or wrong, depending upon the answers to the following questions:

(a) is there enough information collected to properly cover the area?;

(b) have all of the arguments put forward been understood?;

(c) is there a lack of empirical/practical evidence to support theoretical positions?

It is vital to decide whether there is enough information and this is often a subjective matter.

A brief conclusion to the above suggested essay follows below. It centres on Weiler's articles and the imaginary authors X, Y, Z. Hopefully, it forcefully illustrates how:

- identification;
- organisation;
- classification;
- competent reading strategy and notes;
- diagrams,

can work together to bring clarity of thought and expression. Textbooks are not included in the conclusion but if a textbook did comment on a theory or give useful insights, these could also be incorporated.

'The European Union belongs to its citizens.' Discuss.

Conclusion

Weiler (1995) argues that at present the European citizen does not exert power over policy and law making within the European Union. This indicates that the European Union certainly does not belong to its citizens. However, as noted above, he convincingly argues that with very little change the situation could be rectified. X (1997), Y (1998) and Z (1998), in large part, agree with Weiler, both in terms of the problems and solutions presented by him.

It is suggested that Weiler's argument is well set out and is essentially backed by supporting evidence and attainable solutions. It is further suggested that the evidence presented concerning proposition 1, that Maastricht was not the diplomatic achievement it was claimed to be, is weak. A point also noted by X (1997) and Y (1998).

Proposition 2 is strongly supported by the available evidence. If the governments of the Member States and the institutions of the European Community seriously consider the issue of the European citizen in terms of Weiler's problems and solutions, it may well be that, in the opening years of the new millennium, it will be possible to maintain that the European Union *does* belong to its citizens.

CHAPTER 9

HOW TO MANAGE A LARGE AMOUNT OF INFORMATION

INTRODUCTION

The key to successful evaluation or analysis of an issue lies in the initial competent identification, classification and summarising of relevant texts. When relevant texts are ready for evaluation, then the creative work of comparison, interpretation and argument construction begins. Unfortunately, many students think that the sheer effort involved in finding and reading is enough. But it is only enough to get to the beginning! Many students do not go beyond this – to analysis.

WIGMOREAN ANALYSIS – FACT MANAGEMENT

An important skill for anyone to develop, and most of all for law students to develop, is the management of facts. John Wigmore, in 1930s America, devised a complicated method for identifying, classifying and arranging factual information in a law case so that much of it could be viewed simultaneously.

One of the major difficulties when confronted with a problem, and needing to construct an argument, is dealing with a mass of information in such a way that interconnections and alternating arguments can be grasped.

Wigmore devised a chart composed entirely of numbers and symbols which could be accessed via a *key list*. Every number corresponded to a textual description of:

(a) *evidence*:

- documentary evidence, for example:
  - o maps;
  - o books, articles, lists, letters;
  - o financial statements of accounts;
  - o receipts;
  - o handwriting samples;
- forensic evidence, for example:
  - o DNA testing;
  - o fingerprints;
  - o blood, hair, skin, fibre, chemical, paint samples;
- testamentary evidence, for example:
  - o witness statements (eye witnesses, character witnesses, expert witnesses);
  - o statements of the parties to litigation or of the defendant in a criminal trial;
  - o police statements/reports;

(b) *facts*;

(c) *the elements of the legal rule involved in the case*;

(d) *argument*.

The chart, primarily a tree diagram, is constructed in such a way that, for every piece of information or allegation, one can trace the evidence in support, whether facts, legal rules or argument.

As initially conceived, the chart is far too complex and time consuming for use in all circumstances. However, William Twining and David Miers vastly simplified it for teaching purposes and, in their form, it is of enormous value for teaching students to use and manipulate data in order to classify, order, identify and manage a range of different types of information as a prelude to argument construction.

When problems occur and arguments are constructed to state that this happened, or that did not happen, a lot of different types of information is used. People will protest their innocence: 'I did not;' appeal perhaps to their past behaviour: 'You know that I never tell lies.' They may produce an alibi and say: 'It could not have been me; I was at the cinema.' Here, ideally, the other party would want not only to see the cinema ticket, but hear someone else say they saw the person at the cinema.

Real life is lived and, after the event, laywers construct arguments to explain what did, or did not, happen. Juries and courts have to decide which explanation is the 'truth'. The chosen explanation may or may not be the 'truth'. The court is not a place where mistakes never happen and innocent people have been sent to prison for crimes which later it is found they did not commit. Similarly, guilty people have been found not guilty. In the area of civil law, where there is less moral blame allocated to 'losers', results can sometimes seem unfair – the exemplary husband who, in a divorce settlement, loses everything; the employee who unfairly loses her job, but gets paltry compensation and is not given the job back; the accident victim who is so brave in the face of insurmountable pain and suffering he is awarded lower damages by the court!

All of the outcomes in court are the result of evidence formally presented and arguments weaving that evidence, with the assistance of inferences and persuasion, into a story of what happened.

The way to begin to win the argument is by gathering together and classifying the facts, rules, evidence already possessed. Then, when these are considered together with the possible argument that the laywer wishes to use, gaps in evidence and information can be ascertained.

So, the first task is knowing what is there, so that it can be evaluated. This is exactly what the Wigmore chart was primarily constructed to do.

This method allows:

(a) a complex set of interrelationships to be grasped;

(b) arguments to be built up;

(c) the indication of propositions in arguments not supported by evidence;

(d) the indication of propositions in arguments supported by evidence;

(e) the indication of propositions in arguments supported by weak or strong evidence;

(f) gaps in arguments for both sides notable;

(g) prediction of the strength and type of case to be presented by the opponent;

(h) assessment of the strength and type of case to be presented by the opponent.

As originally conceived, the chart had different symbols for:

(a) both parties;

(b) strong and weak evidence;

(c) inferences;

(d) any other issues.

Thus, one chart could be used for setting up the argument of both parties and assessing the value of each piece of evidence as weak or strong and for an overall evaluation of the strength of each case. Once the basic technique is learnt, it can also be utilised for other purposes, including assessment of competing theories, etc.

The chart can most easily be described as operating on different levels. There are no set number of levels, but normally the following would be found:

Level 1:   the assertion to be proved is set out.

Level 2:   the relevant legal rule is split into its constituent parts.

Level 3:   the facts of the case as known are classified according to the part in Level 2 that they substantiate; points of argument could be put in here too – most commonly one may find inferences used.

Level 4:   any available evidence backing up, or denying, the truth of the facts are classified and put on the chart underneath the relevant fact(s).

Level 5:   the sources of the evidence are noted on the chart under the evidence itself.

The chart argues from end to beginning. It starts from the final point through the stages of information. It is necessary to go through each level of the chart

Level 1: the assertion to be proved is set out

This has to be a simple clear *either/or assertion*. The determination of this point resolves the entire trial. It is therefore the end process in an argument; however, it is stated *first* and the chart proceeds from this point. In the words of John Wigmore, 'Level 1 is the *ultimate probandum*'.

The following assertions would be examples of the **ultimate probandum**:

> John murdered Sally.
>
> John did not murder Sally.
>
> Afzal stole a book contrary to the Theft Act 1968.
>
> Afzal did not steal a book contrary to the Theft Act 1968.

Level 2: the relevant legal rule is split into its constituent parts

In order to proceed further, it is necessary to be able to deconstruct common law and statutory rules into the parts needing to be proved. This is taught in substantive law courses, but often, students do not realise:

(a) what is being taught;

(b) how to do it for themselves; and

(c) how important it is.

Perhaps this is because, at the academic stage, it is difficult to project the dry legal rule into a life situation and the student does not automatically know what facts need to be fitted to which parts of the rule. Also, there is a tendency to set a rule as a simplistic whole: John is guilty of theft. Theft is defined in s 1 of the Theft Act 1986, but students do not see it as a series of parts to be proved before the theft can be said, at law, to be proved.

Given the work already done in this text on rules, perhaps the reader of this text can immediately comprehend why it is so important to be able to split a rule into its constituent parts.

It has already been noted at length, above, that a rule has to be understood to be interpreted. Rules are often constructed to resolve problems, hence rules are invariably solutions to problems. But, if someone is to call upon a rule to apply it to a given situation, it is necessary to know what it is that is to be applied. In a court of law, the trial judge will want to know why that rule applies to the facts of the case.

Understanding a rule in this way still remains essentially an issue of comprehension. For example, read the following definition of theft which is found in s 1 of the Theft Act 1986:

A person is guilty of theft if he dishonestly appropriates property belonging to another with the intention of permanently depriving the other of it.

Now, read the following scenario:

On Saturday, Mary decides to borrow some money from her friend Andrew's 'emergency' money jar in the kitchen. They share a flat with two other people. She wants to buy a new skirt at the local 'cash only' market and forgot to go to the bank on Friday. She knows Andrew will probably not miss it because he is away until Sunday night and, in any case, she is sure that if he was there he would have lent it to her. She can then go to the bank on Monday and replace the money. When Andrew returns on Sunday night he notices that the money is missing. He denies that he would have lent the money to Mary, saying that the point of an emergency jar is for emergencies, not trivialities like buying a skirt. He tells her that, as far as he is concerned, she is guilty of theft and she is very lucky that he does not report the matter to the police. Mary is furious with Andrew and tells him that she is not a thief.

(a) Is Mary guilty of theft?

(b) If so, why?

Now read the following imaginary conversation between the other two flatmates, William and Sarah, discussing whether Mary is guilty of theft.

William:	Yes, of course, she is guilty of theft. She took the money and it didn't belong to her did it?
Sarah:	Well no, it didn't belong to her, but she said she was only borrowing it, not stealing it.
William:	Look, the law in s 1 of the Theft Act doesn't suggest that the thief decides whether it is theft or borrowing does it? She said she borrowed, it but she stole it. She is a thief. It was theft!
Sarah:	No, s 1 doesn't suggest that the thief can decide if it is theft or borrowing. But it does say that the thief has to have the 'intention to permanently deprive'. She didn't, because it says that she was going to return the money on Monday.
William:	Aaah, I see what you mean. But, come on, she was dishonest and s 1 clearly talks about the dishonest appropriation of property. Surely it was dishonest to take the money without permission?
Sarah:	Well, usually, I would say 'yes', but in this case, maybe not, because she probably thought he would give permission.
William:	But he had not; was it reasonable for her to suppose he would? Does the section give any leeway for this?
Sarah:	Anyway, it doesn't matter if she did take it dishonestly, because she didn't have an intention to permanently deprive and, without that intention, she isn't guilty, so Andrew is just a bully.
William:	No, I don't accept this, she behaved in a way that is morally wrong.
Sarah:	Well, that's another story!

So – who is right, William or Sarah? The court always has to decide. It is never an option to have a final outcome that says 'We don't know'. For Sarah, much hangs upon the issue of the intention to permanently deprive. William feels uncomfortable with this and considers that Mary has behaved in a way that is morally wrong and places much upon her dishonesty, in taking the money without permission.

It is always useful to compose a diagram of elements to be proved so that all aspects of available evidence are covered.

What should have been noticed in the reading of the section from the Theft Act, or the reading of the conversation, is that there were two major issues:

(a) the physical *act* of taking (dishonestly appropriates);

(b) the mental aspect motivating the taking (the intention of permanently depriving the other of it).

Reading s 1 for those all important connectors, it is seen that the physical act is joined to the mental aspect by the connector **with**:

dishonestly appropriates property

with

the intention of permanently depriving.

NOTE: can you express s 1 as a tree diagram to understand the interconnections?

There is no way that it would be sufficient just *to dishonestly appropriate*, nor would it be sufficient just *to permanently deprive* (by breaking or taking) without the act of dishonesty.

Property *must* be taken and that property *must* 'belong to another'.

So, there are four elements to be proven in theft.

A person is guilty of theft **if:**

(1)   he dishonestly appropriates

(2)   property

(3)   belonging to another

with

(4)   the intention of permanently depriving the other of it.

All four elements have to be dealt with to build an argument. In a real case, there must be evidence available pointing at *all* aspects. A correct Wigmore chart, in fact, enables lawyers to identify missing evidence. If such evidence is not available, it may not necessarily mean that the case cannot be argued, the lawyer may be able to say that given facts (a), (b) and (c), the presence of intention can be strongly inferred.

Once the parts of the legal rule needing to be proved have been identified, they are placed at the next level on the Wigmore chart. These parts making up Level 2 are, in the words of John Wigmore, the penultimate probanda – propositions; those matters which, once proved, make the assertion forming the ultimate probandum automatically proved. Figure 9.1 demonstrates this in the chart format.

Figure 9.1: levels 1 and 2 of a simplified Wigmore chart

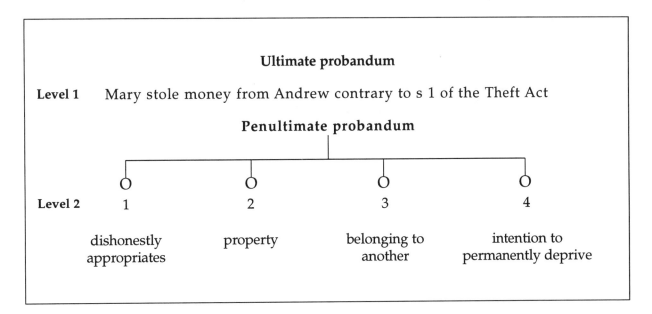

Recall that the entries on the chart should not be textual but just numeric and, where appropriate, symbolic.

So, the above Figure 9.1 would be represented as it is in Figure 9.2.

Figure 9.2: levels 1 and 2 and key list so far constructed

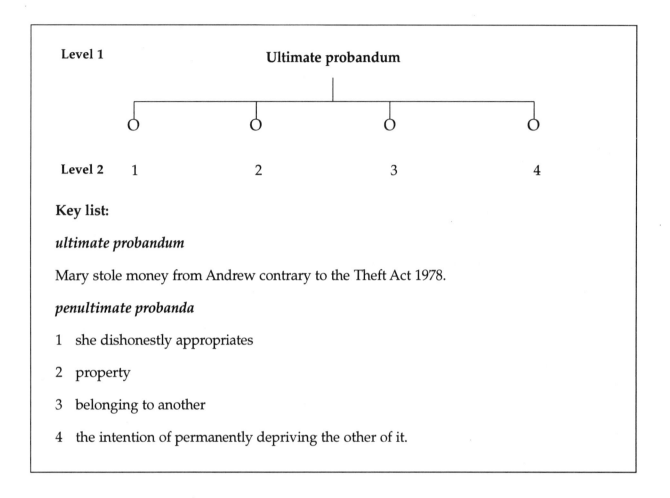

Level 1   **Ultimate probandum**

Level 2   1   2   3   4

Key list:

ultimate probandum

Mary stole money from Andrew contrary to the Theft Act 1978.

penultimate probanda

1   she dishonestly appropriates

2   property

3   belonging to another

4   the intention of permanently depriving the other of it.

Level 3: the facts of the case as indicated by the evidence are placed under the element that they substantiate

Figure 9.3 begins to do this and, again, for the first demonstration, the facts have been textually shown in their position on the chart. As the chart is studied, it will be noted that if more than one fact lends proof to a part of the legal rule; then they are placed alongside each other. Look at facts 5 and 6 under penultimate probanda 1 in Figure 9.3. They may both be needed to prove that part or they may both prove it independently. Every chart will be different because every case is different.

Start to look for patterns in the chart, for the patterns alone give information concerning the balance of the proof and the available raw material for argument construction.

Figure 9.3: levels 1, 2 and 3 and key list so far constructed

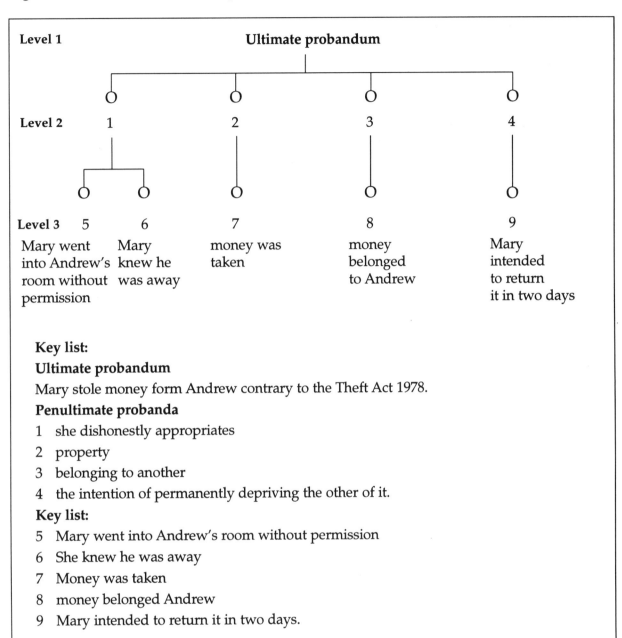

Level 1   **Ultimate probandum**

Level 2   1   2   3   4

Level 3   5   6   7   8   9

Mary went into Andrew's room without permission | Mary knew he was away | money was taken | money belonged to Andrew | Mary intended to return it in two days

Key list:
Ultimate probandum
Mary stole money form Andrew contrary to the Theft Act 1978.
Penultimate probanda
1   she dishonestly appropriates
2   property
3   belonging to another
4   the intention of permanently depriving the other of it.
Key list:
5   Mary went into Andrew's room without permission
6   She knew he was away
7   Money was taken
8   money belonged Andrew
9   Mary intended to return it in two days.

Figure 9.4 replicates the chart so far but in the form it should be in, just numbers.

Figure 9.4: levels 1, 2 and 3 of Figure 9.3 as they should be constructed

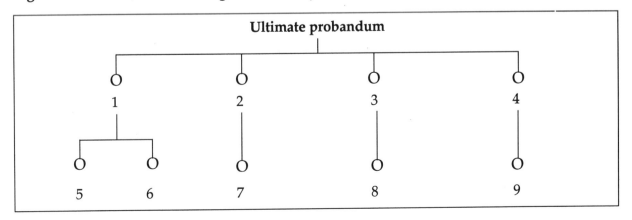

Ultimate probandum

1   2   3   4

5   6   7   8   9

Level 4: the sources of the evidence supporting the facts are noted underneath the facts

There may be one or two or more sources, of course. The more evidence there is across all of the elements in Level 2, the stronger the case for the correctness of the assertion forming the ultimate probandum.

Returning once more to our story, the evidence in relation to 5, 6 and 7 is Mary's own statement. Therefore, this is added to the chart as illustrated in Figure 9.5

Figure 9.5: chart with level 4 added

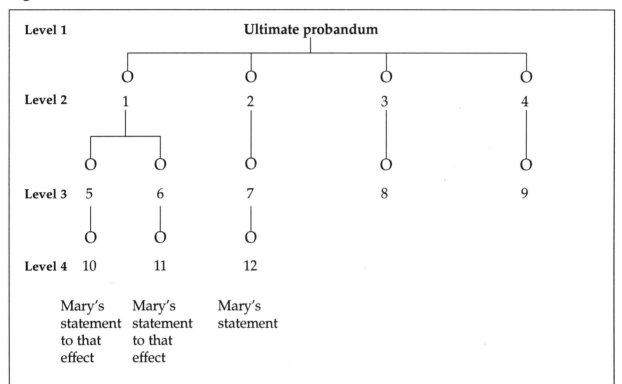

Key list:

Ultimate probandum

Mary stole money from Andrew contrary to the Theft Act 1978.

Penultimate probanda

1   she dishonestly appropriates
2   property
3   belonging to another
4   the intention of permanently depriving the other of it.

Key list:

5   Mary went into Andrew's room without permission
6   she knew he was away
7   money was taken
8   money belonged Andrew
9   Mary intended to return it in two days
10 (5 supported by) Mary's statement to that effect
11 (6 supported by) Mary's statement to that effect
12 (7 supported by) Mary's statement to that effect.

It is easier to read the key list where the evidence is under the facts, but it is necessary for the list to run numerically, therefore, it is better to change the numbers on the chart and key list to inset 10, 11 and 12 in better places for comprehension.

Figure 9.6, therefore, shows the revised chart and key list after renumbering.

Figure 9.6

Key list:
Ultimate probandum
Mary stole money form Andrew contrary to the Theft Act 1978.
Penultimate probanda
1   she dishonestly appropriates
2   property
3   belonging to another
4   the intention of permanently depriving the other of it.
Key list:
5   Mary went into Andrew's room without permission
6   Supported by Mary's statement to that effect
7   She knew he was away
8   Supported by Mary's statement to that effect
9   Money was taken
10 Supported by Mary's statement to that effect
11 Money belonged to Andrew
12 Mary intended to return it in two days.

And, finally, remember that the chart renumbered is not to contain text and Figure 9.9 therefore sets it out purely as a chart with numbers.

Figure 9.7

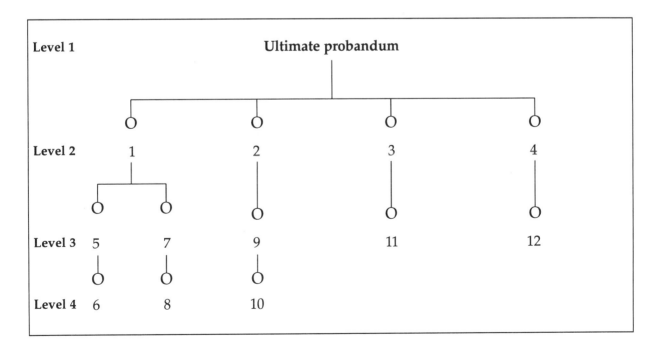

To construct such a chart takes time; data has to be manipulated, and constant updating and perhaps renumbering engaged in. However read the key list in Figure 9.6 from 1–12 and a clear argument is beginning to emerge in an objective manner.

Competence and excellence take *time*. There are no shortcuts to understanding. This is a time consuming exercise but will teach invaluable skills.

There are many other things that can be put in. For example, 'Mary took the money'. This has not been stated on the chart. The chart reveals in 5 and 7 that Mary went into the room without permission and knew that Andrew was away. There is a suggestion in 12 that Mary took the money, as it states that she intended to return it in two days.

But the chart is constructed from a story and there are no statements made and no forensic evidence produced. To enable this chart to be experienced and its value demonstrated, it is necessary to complete a chart that works from some materials closer to the type that would be dealt with in a real case.

For that purpose you will find below a range of vastly simplified witness statements that have been set out in the imaginary case of the *R v Jack*. Jack is accused of stealing a shirt, contrary to s 1 of the Theft Act, from a clothes shop. You are to put yourself in the shoes of the prosecution and construct a Wigmore chart to prove that Jack stole the shirt.

As theft is still being used, the first two levels are the same as in the case of Mary and Andrew (however, do not forget to change the names and the property stolen).

Method

(a) Read the witness statements carefully and construct the 'story' by extracting facts about what happened.

(b) List these facts. They belong to Level 3.

(c) Decide which of the identified facts belong to which parts of the penultimate probandum.

(d) Put the facts on the chart.

(e) List the evidence that is available.

(f) Classify the evidence as to whether it is testimonial, forensic, etc.

   (Look at the divisions of evidence at the beginning of this chapter.)

(g) Decide which piece(s) of evidence proves which fact:

   • there may be more that one piece of evidence for each part – this is acceptable;

   • there may be a piece of evidence that backs two facts – this is acceptable, but enter it on the chart twice and use different numbers.

Look at previous charts for the method.

Figure 9.8 sets out the chart for Levels 1 and 2; see how far you can get adding in Levels 3 and 4. Remember that you may have to renumber the chart to keep sense.

When you have completed your chart compare it to the partially completed chart of Figure 9.10. Much more could be added, however, it is the basic method that requires practice. If you have enjoyed this method and would like to read more, look at Anderson and Twining (1991), Chapter 3, 'Methods of Analysis'.

Figure 9.8: the ultimate probandum

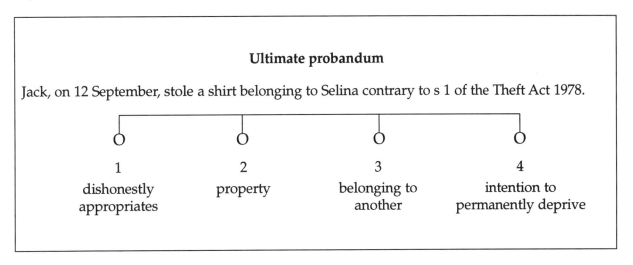

Ultimate probandum

Jack, on 12 September, stole a shirt belonging to Selina contrary to s 1 of the Theft Act 1978.

1	2	3	4
dishonestly appropriates	property	belonging to another	intention to permanently deprive

Figure 9.9: the ultimate probandum and key list

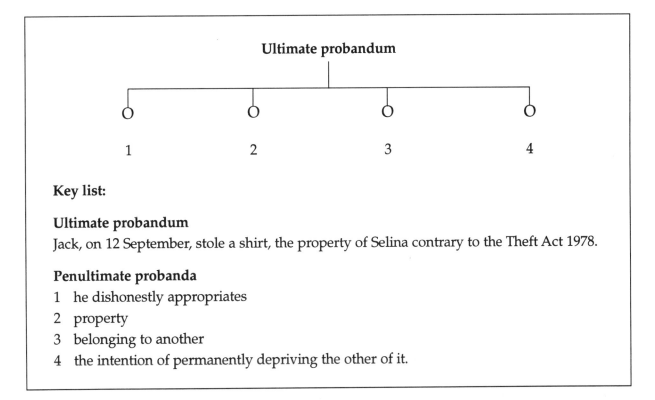

Ultimate probandum

Key list:

Ultimate probandum
Jack, on 12 September, stole a shirt, the property of Selina contrary to the Theft Act 1978.

Penultimate probanda
1 he dishonestly appropriates
2 property
3 belonging to another
4 the intention of permanently depriving the other of it.

R v Jack

Statements for Wigmore chart

Jack has been charged with the theft (under s 1 of the Theft Act 1968) of a shirt from the New Style Clothes Shop, on 12 September.

Below, you will find witness statements. Read them carefully and fill in Levels 3 and 4 of the Wigmore chart.

Selina (owner of the New Style Clothes Shop): witness statement

I am the owner of the New Style Clothes Shop in Norbury. After cashing up on the night of Saturday 12 September, I found my stock to be down, a man's shirt was missing. I immediately checked the security cameras. At 12 o'clock midday, I saw a male that I now know to be Jack leaving a changing room. He was acting suspiciously and holding his arm under his jacket. He walked out of the shop without returning any clothes to the assistant. I have heard his name mentioned around here as a thief. I phoned the police who arrested Jack.

Jack: statement given to defence solicitor

I did not steal the shirt, it is not my size or colour. Selina has a grudge against me and is trying to frame me. At 12 o'clock on Saturday, I was in the White Lies Pub with my friend, Frederick, who will support me on this. The first I knew about all this was when Constable Danger arrested me on Saturday evening. The search of my house did reveal a shirt but I had bought this a couple of days ago in the market, honestly. I admit I have a criminal record, but I have turned my back on all that now. I now have a steady job as a shop assistant in a book shop. But when they find out about this accusation, I will lose my job.

The ID parade was a fix, no one looked at all like me, so I stuck out as the tallest. I have brown hair, everyone else had black hair.

PC Danger: police statement

On the evening of 12 September, I was on my beat in London Road, Norbury, South London when I received a radio message to proceed to the address of Jack to arrest him on a charge of theft. I knocked on the door and Jack opened it and said 'Oh no, not you lot trying it on'. I immediately told him he was being arrested on suspicion of stealing a shirt, cautioned him, telling that he did not have to say anything but if he did it could be used against him. He said 'This is ridiculous. I know nothing about anything'. A subsequent search of the property revealed a shirt of the same design and make as that stolen from the New Style Clothes Shop.

Jack was taken to the Police Station where he refused to answer questions. He was charged with theft and released on bail.

Mary (part time sales assistant, the New Style Clothes Shop): witness statement

I am a student, but I work in the New style Clothes Shop to supplement my grant. It is very convenient for me as I can travel to work one stop on the train and the shop is about three to five minutes from Norbury Railway Station. The first time I knew anything was wrong on Saturday 12 September, was when we were cashing up in the evening and Selina, my boss, started shouting that the tills didn't balance. She went into the back room to play back the security cameras. We saw a figure leaving a changing room at 12.15 pm. My boss became suspicious and she said that the man looked like Jack, a well known local thief who is always hanging around. She phoned the police.

I don't know Jack but, at an ID parade, I identified Jack as the man who was on the video. I am sure the figure on the camera is the thief.

Frederick (best friend of Jack:) witness statement

I was with Jack in the White Lies Pub on Saturday 12 September. I can't remember the time I met him, but it was around midday. I spent the afternoon with him and then he went home. The next thing I knew was that he had been nicked. I went with him to the ID parade, which was a fix. He stuck out like a sore thumb.

Carl: owner of the White Lies Pub

I am the owner of the White Lies Public House, High Road, Norbury next door to the railway station. I recall seeing Jack and Frederick in the pub around 12.30 pm on Saturday 12 September.

> **Complete your own Wigmore chart by adding to Figure 9.9 and, only then, turn over for answer: Figure 9.10.**

Figure 9.10: the completed Wigmore chart in the case of *R v Jack*

Ultimate probandum: Jack stole a shirt belonging to Selina on 1 September contrary to Theft

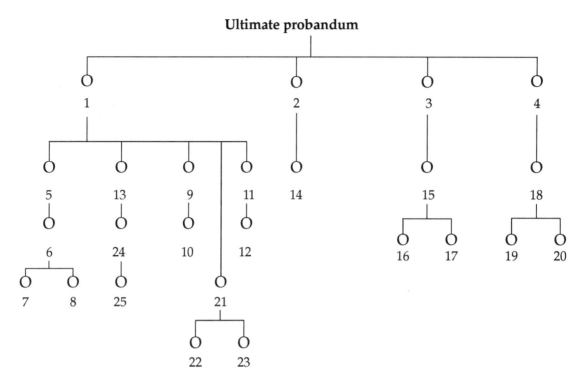

1   dishonestly appropriates
2   property
3   belonging to another
4   intention to permanently deprive
5   Jack was behaving suspiciously
6   evidenced by video film
7   supported by statement of Selina
8   supported by statement of Selina
9   Jack was in the shop that day at 12.15pm
10 supported by video film
11 a similar shirt found in Jack's flat
12 supported by statement of PC Danger
13 Jack had the opportunity
14 a shirt
15 shirt belongs to Selina
16 statement of Selina
17 statement of Mary
18 shirt in Jack's flat
19 statement of PC Danger
20 statement of Jack
21 Jack in the vicinity
22 statement of Frederick to that effect
23 statement by Carl
24 put only a few minutes from shop

PART IV

PUTTING IT ALL TOGETHER

PUTTING IT ALL TOGETHER

INTRODUCTION: THE AIM OF PART IV

The aim of this text was to be a 'How to' text – how to:

(a) competently develop reading strategies;

(b) write summaries and casenotes;

(c) identify arguments;

(d) construct arguments;

(e) evaluate arguments;

(f) deal with primary and secondary legal texts ;

(g) understand the relationship between law reports and statutes;

(h) organise and classify differing types of information,

in order to:

(a) develop confidence in handling information;

(b) gain an appreciation of the complex interrelationships between a range of different texts,

so that:

(a) a place of competent understanding can be reached;

(b) competent understanding can be demonstrated in written and oral assessments.

However, the 'million dollar' question is, how can all of the above skills be successfully amalgamated and processed in order to reach understanding and produce written or oral work that demonstrates such understanding?

Understanding, and the competent communication of understanding:

is

not only

the **outcome** of a **complex process**

it is

always

an **act** of personal **creativity.**

No two people will think and see in the same way. Therefore, no two people will understand in exactly the same way, using exactly the same words. Language is too flexible for that to occur. It is, therefore, essential for each person to uncover a personal, customised method for processing and evaluating the information in order to construct arguments, and to write.

In Chapter 1, a range of skills was identified as essential to competent legal study, but the requirement for a range of skills to be competently exercised for legal study is not a unique requirement to law.

All skills

in

any area

need to be **internalised** and **customised**

before competent creative use of skills may be achieved.

Consider the act of painting a room, this may involve:

(a) appreciation of design issues;

(b) learning about colour mixing;

(c) learning how to clean the surfaces properly before painting;

(d) learning how to strip off paint or paper and, if necessary, lining walls with paper for painting;

(e) learning about the various methods of applying paint (a brush, a roller, a sponge, paper, a rag, etc);

(f) learning about undercoats and top coats, silk or matt finishes, drying times and ideal conditions for painting/drying;

(g) practising a range of applying techniques to find the one most suited to the task (what finish is required, what are the wall surfaces like?) and the expertise of the painter.

The more practice acquired, the less concentration has to be given to various items along the way as methods begin to be internalised. Colour mixing, drying times, the range of techniques become second nature. Preferred methods of applying paint will develop. Techniques will be developed because of the uniqueness of the painter.

Similarly, the way that a law student puts together the mass of detail required for a given legal task will, over time, become that student's preferred method, a method rooted in good academic practice, but also a method that has been customised and is part second nature, part research and reflection, part personal style.

Consider the following list of *differences* between students' preferred customised methods of writing. Some students will:

(a) develop a written style based upon reference to technical words, Latin phrases, poetic language, short appropriate quotations from leading texts in the area;

(b) carefully translate all Latin phrases;

(c) ensure they use a concise, simple lexicon, avoiding one long word when two shorter ones will do;

(d) favour an historic perspective if one can be made appropriate to the essay;

(e) only want to discuss relevant legal rules and decided cases;

(f) produce an excellent essay based on a microscopic attention to the detail in one theoretical argument of relevance to an area and refuting or affirming it;

(g) produce an excellent essay by taking a macroscopic, approach identifying a range of plausible theories applicable to that given area, and refuting or affirming them.

All of these approaches are equally correct when used appropriately, either singly or in combination. However, the development of a writing style and preferred ways of doing things takes time. The grasping of the range of important and essential skills cannot be forced or rushed. They are deliberately developed out of practice, reflection, adaptation and more practice.

There are no short cuts; it takes time. These skills may not develop in a basic manner until towards the end of the first year of studies. They will certainly continue to develop throughout the lifetime of a student. Very few students, irrespective of age, go to university equipped with preferred methods and a writing style.

Constructing an argument from legal rules, facts of cases, available evidence, historical developments, texts on theories, texts about doctrines and practices, can be likened to doing a jigsaw. All of the different pieces of text have to be put together in the best way. Unlike a jigsaw, however, there is not just one way of fitting the pieces together! There are often at least two, if not more, plausible ways of putting the pieces together and constructing an argument!

There is *always* more than one plausible argument. Students have to learn to decide between competing arguments. They have to demonstrate they are in control!

This is why argument construction is so:

(a) creative;

(b) challenging;

(c) daunting.

This text has sought to indicate ways of moving towards an approach to answering questions and solving problems that demonstrates:

(a) attention to detail;

(b) an understanding of the differing nature, uses, functions and hierarchy of texts;

(c) an appreciation of context and the existence of other answers.

It has followed the process of:

(a) identification of issues raised by problem/question;

(b) research, location of materials;

(c) ordering;

(d) classification;

(e) reflection;

(f) comprehension;

(g) prediction;

(h) creation;

(i) evaluation;

(j) reflection;

(k) re-evaluation, analysis, critique.

These next and last chapters aim to begin to lay out the process whereby there can be engagement in the process of argumentation through the methodical deployment of an argument. Hopefully, they will demonstrate the methods of argumentation and the art of 'putting it all together' through the preparation of a limited number of texts (two reports and a few pages from a textbook) for the purposes of writing an essay.

CHAPTER 10

HOW TO IDENTIFY, EVALUATE, INTERPRET AND CONSTRUCT ARGUMENTS

'You did it!'

'No I didn't.'

'Yes you did.'

'No I didn't.'

'Prove it then!'

'Why should I? You prove I did.'

'No, why should I? You prove you didn't.'

What is clear by now is that lawyers must be competent argument constructors and dismantlers. An ability to construct a good argument is the core of successful study in any area. But what is an argument – let alone a good one? The word has a range of meanings, but all revolve around the concept of proving the validity of a view. Consider the following two diagrams which illustrate the various meanings of 'argue' and 'argument'.

Figure 10.1: to argue

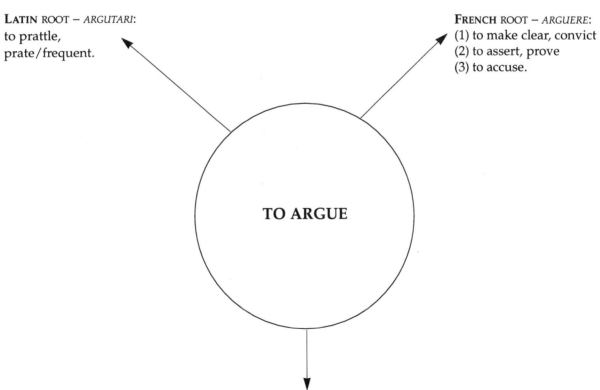

LATIN ROOT – *ARGUTARI*: to prattle, prate/frequent.

FRENCH ROOT – *ARGUERE*:
(1) to make clear, convict
(2) to assert, prove
(3) to accuse.

TO ARGUE

ENGLISH – TO ARGUE:
the root that acquired ascendancy in English is the French.
English meaning is now:
(1) to bring reasons to support or deny a proposition;
(2) to maintain that something is the case by the bringing of reasons to prove that it is so.

Figure 10.2: argument

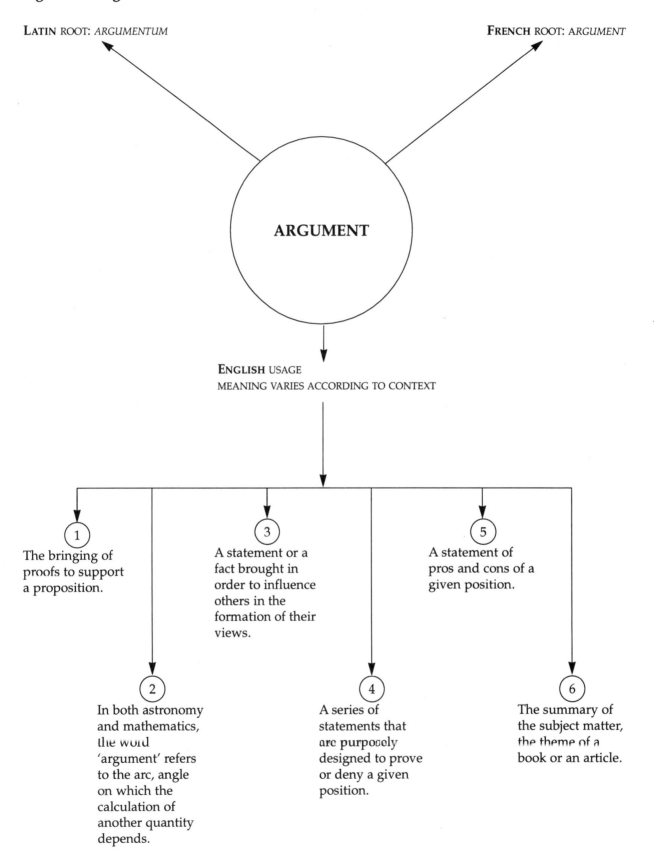

For our purposes, the following working definition of an argument will be used:

An argument is a series of statements, some backed by evidence, some not, that are purposely presented in order to prove, or disprove, a given position.

Such *given positions* could be:

(a) Mary is guilty of theft contrary to the Theft Act 1968;

(b) Jack is not guilty of theft contrary to the Theft Act 1968;

(c) the European Union does not belong to its citizens;

(d) the European Union does belong to its citizens.

To engage then in the *process* of argumentation is to deploy methodically a *series* of arguments. Note the words *process* and *series*.

To state a truism, all legal arguments take place through the mediating influence of language both oral and written. As already noticed, language is a notoriously flexible and subjective medium of communication. The consideration already given to statutory, European and common law rules, and the discretion language injects into the process of interpretation demonstrates this flexibility. This is what moulds the law and determines outcomes. How perilously we hover on the brink of another explanation when we engage in the interpretation of words.

An argument can be viewed as a journey *from* problem *to* solution. In the case of legal problems, this journey is through the medium of the interpretation and application of legal rules to problems that have been pre-classified as legal problems. It is a journey that requires a map; a map others can follow that allows the argument crafter to take the other exactly to the desired destination; a map that eloquently explains why it is not a good idea to take that side road or that alternative route; a map that also explains how, if matters were different, another route could have been taken.

However, this journey cannot be undertaken without preparation and if the preparation is not properly carried out then the end may not be reached.

Many students hate the preparation and the journey and do not see it as a challenge during the course of which their developing study, research, legal and language skills are further refined. If the preparation and the journey can be enjoyed, and not just endured, then the road is set for lifelong successful learning, learning that has good results.

An argument is only as good as the ability to hold in tension a range of issues, as illustrated in Figure 10.3.

Figure 10.3: argument construction

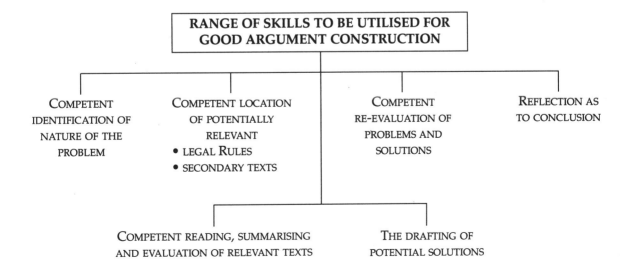

179

Before the process of argument is looked at in more depth, it is useful to revisit words with seemingly common meanings which are intimately related to legal argument.

PROBLEM(S) AND RULE(S)

What is a problem?

Before you have time to think, answer this question: are problems *good* or *bad*?

Probably, you thought '*bad*'. Some of you may have said 'sometimes they're *bad* and sometimes they're *good*'. A secondary question would be: 'are they good or bad for the individual or for society or for both? Who decides?'

Word on the street is that problems are bad – certainly, for the peace of mind of the student!

The standard definitions of problem are:

(a) a difficult question put forward for an answer or a scholastic disputation;

(b) the question asked in a standard formal logic example of the 'syllogism', the conclusion of which is also the answer to the problem;

(c) in mathematics and physics, an inquiry or a question which, starting from a given position, investigates some fact, result or law.

Nearly all of the tasks asked of students are problems awaiting a solution. But problems have a bad press; people think that problems are bad. But they are not all bad. There are different sorts of problems. Consider the following list:

Is there anything for dinner?

How can I murder Robert?

How can I write this essay?

Where can I find a book that does all the work for me?

How does this washing machine work?

Where is my pen?

Why don't we just get out of the European Community?

Can we go to the cinema?

Will you look after my child?

What is the time?

Where does all the time go?

Why don't I have a best friend?

Why does my mother hate me?

Why did you steal my money?

Why are you so sad?

What's the matter with you?

Where is the station?

How much is the fare to York?

What do you want from me?

When are the examinations?

Why don't I get distinctions for my essays?

What is time?

These questions can be re-classified under headings such as social, legal and so on, as in Figure 10.4. The problems presented by the questions can be re-classified as good social and bad social although this may depend on your moral position. Some may not see anything the matter with the question/problem: 'How can I murder Robert?'

Figure 10.4: classification of list

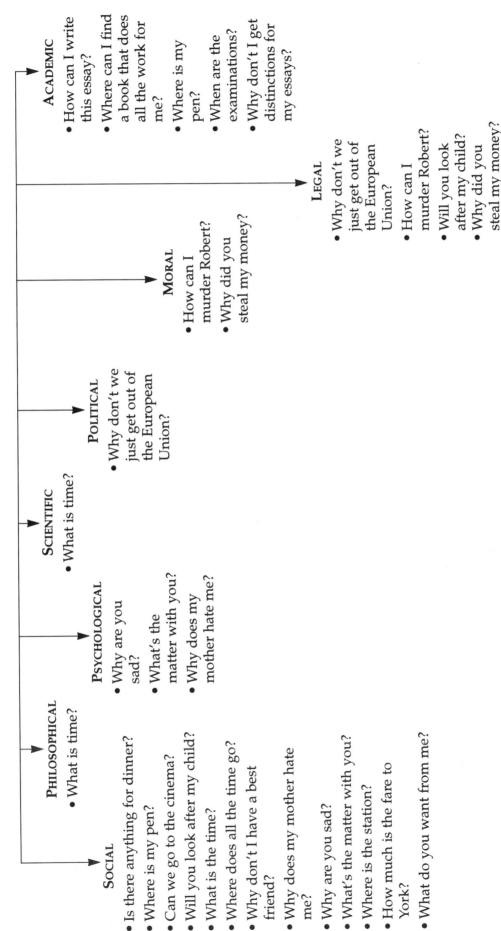

These questions can all be said to be describing problems, but they are not all bad. Some questions are practical, some theoretical, some may be both. This is explored using a Venn diagram in Figure 10.5.

Figure 10.5: Venn diagram – problems

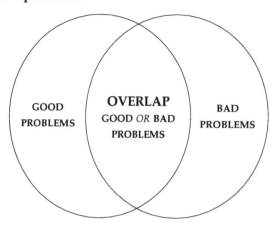

The above classifications could be further divided into arbitrary good/bad although, in reality, much depends on context

Of course, the real issue is how you move from problem to solution. Students often do not know how to go on the journey. They cannot see the 'start' and they miscalculate the length of the journey. By correctly identifying, classifying, interpreting, one begins to journey from problem to solution. But also solutions can involve *guessing* and *trying*.

Everything can be seen as a question awaiting an answer. Life itself could be described as a journey through questions and answers towards a solution. It is a risky business.

Solutions can be aimed at *dealing* with the problem, *or* making the problem solver *feel better*. Solutions aimed at making the problem solver feel better could include dong nothing, leaving, or it could include a reconciliation and extraction of a promise not to repeat the problematic behaviour. A parent who smacks a child for behaving in a manner unacceptable to the parent *may not have solved the problem* of the behaviour but the parent *may feel better*, thus, the problem of the parent feeling bad may have been solved.

Much depends on the role of the problem solver. Is the problem solver:

(a) a family member in a dysfunctional family;

(b) a teacher in a school;

(c) a defence lawyer in court;

(d) a judge in court;

(e) a politician in the cabinet,

(f) a scientist in a laboratory;

(g) a 'victim'?

Is the problem a purely paper issue or a personal issue? A seemingly simple problem can be complex for those seeking a solution. It has been said that no problems come as single units but as a series of interconnected issues and problems. Problems, like so many other issues, are *processes*, often *complex processes*.

If the nature of problems generally is not understood, it is difficult to understand the nature of legal rules, the complexities of using legal rules as solutions to problems perceived as legal.

Problem solving and problem management is a part of everyday life and the skills in these areas that have been developed automatically can assist students in turning their attention to a more methodical approach to dealing with complex legal problems.

But, to use knowledge, it is necessary to be aware that it is possessed. Often, people are not aware of the methods they have developed to solve problems. Some people develop bad problem solving techniques to deal with life (anger, fear, frustration, running away). It is equally possible to develop bad problem solving techniques for academic work (fear, running away, laziness, guilt, denial and frustration).

Problem solving involves accurately:

(a) seeing that there is a problem;

(b) deciding what type of problem it is (which determines much about the eventual solution);

(c) presenting a solution(s) to the problem.

What needs to be grasped immediately is that solutions are the *end product of a series of complicated interrelated operations* that range from the initial diagnosis of the problem to the ultimate purpose, function view of the problem solver.

Teenage alcoholism, as a problem, is viewed very differently according to whether one is:

(a) a teenager who drinks moderately, heavily, or not at all;

(b) a police officer;

(c) a legislator;

(d) a parent of a teenage alcoholic;

(e) a parent of a teenager who drinks illegally but within their limits;

(f) a parent of a teenager who does not drink;

(g) a teacher;

(h) a youth worker;

(i) a seller of alcohol;

(j) a member of the medical profession;

(k) a social worker;

(l) a counsellor.

In many disciplines, professionals use problem solving models which enable users to check certain steps along the road to eventual solution. One of the best known and most useful problem solving methods within legal education is the model devised by Twining and Miers (1991).

Seven steps from identification through diagnosis, prescription and implementation aimed at solution are given as follows.

Problem solving model

(1) **CLARIFICATION** of individuals:

standpoint, role, objectives, general position;

(2) **PERCEPTION** by individual of the facts constituting the situation;

(3) **EVALUATION** of one or more of the elements making the situation undesirable, obstructive, bad ... in other words, 'what's the problem?';

(4) **IDENTIFICATION** of a range of possible solutions to the perceived problem;

(5) **PREDICTION** of:

(a) the cost of each option;

(b) obstacles associated with each option;

(6) **PRESCRIPTION** choosing a solution to the problem; the construction of an effective policy for solving the problem;

(7) **IMPLEMENTATION** of that policy.

Things often go wrong because legislators, as well as problem solvers, often rather like impatient general practitioners:

- prescribe first; and

- diagnose later!

This course of action is a classic government response in a crisis, or student response when confronted with an essay.

Even when an attempt is made to follow a model or to try to cover all eventualities, solutions to problems often cause more problems. Because one searches deeper into a problem, it is usually observed to be a cluster of problems with a range of causes, and a range of potential solutions, each with a different set of obstacles and costs.

Much of a lawyer's job, like that of many other people, involves solving or managing such problems. They tend to be drawn into solving problems in a range of ways, mostly revolving around the application and meaning of legal rules. So, it is worthwhile paying some attention to what is meant by a rule.

What is a rule?

There are many meanings to rule. A rule can be a principle, a maxim governing individual or group conduct in life or in a game. It can be a system that creates a way of life. Within monastic life, the way of life according to rules can mean that the group itself is defined and described as the rule – the rule of St Benedict, for example. Some rules only have force within religious or social settings; others have effect within legal settings.

Some rules only have force within a given academic discipline, philosophy, law or indeed legal method. Language itself is subject to rule formation in its rules of grammar, rules that some literary stars have attempted to subvert. James Joyce in *Ulysses* or in *Finnegan's Wake*, for example.

Other rules constitute a standard against which correct behaviour is judged – religious rules. for example.

A basic definition for legal purposes could be that a legal rule is:

an oral or

written statement

↓

guiding the conduct of individuals and/or groups

infringement of which

↓

may or

may not

↓

result in

compulsory or

discretionary

↓

action being taken to

enforce observance

of the rule.

A rule often represents the view of a group concerning lawful, moral, social, acceptable, good action.

The same rule can carry out several functions. 'Do not kill' has a moral function, backed by a range of religious or philosophical groups worldwide. It also has a social function. To enable it to be enforced, it has been given a legal base. Infringement can lead to severe penalties.

Moral rules are created by a range of groups, both religious and social. Social rules are similarly created by social groupings. A rule that has not been created by the law making process or accepted by those empowered to create law is not deemed to be a legal rule.

Rules in general – and legal rules are no exception – are concerned with saying people:

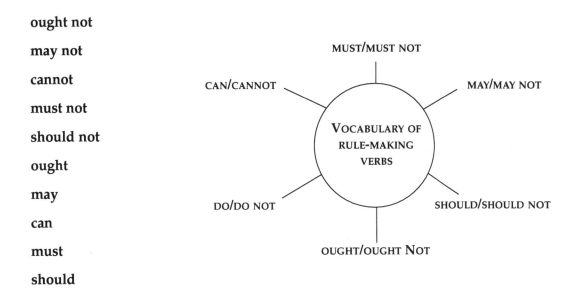

ought not

may not

cannot

must not

should not

ought

may

can

must

should

engage in certain activity either in thought, or word or deed.

Rules often also contain statements about values. They are vehicles for communicating statements about justice, ethics, equality, fairness.

They stop	(they are **prescriptive**);
They guide	(they are **normative**);
They allow	(they are **facilitative**).

All legal rules are created by state authorised groups and are all given the full force of the State. Often, the difficulty with legal rules is that they are general and need to be applied to specific situations.

Statutory rules in our simple majority democracy often reflect the political values of the party in power. They can, therefore, be described as instruments of policy. Whatever the original intention of the political designers of the statutory rule, when users of these rules come to interpret them, defects in design are always apparent because words can, so often, be made to mean what the utterer did not intend them to mean: another reminder that language is flexible.

The judges in the courts have constructed rules of interpretation of statutes which have. for nearly 100 years, taken as their predominant attitude the view that legal rules are to be interpreted without recourse to the reason, motive, or policy of the creator. The argument has a certain force, for a statutory rule can change during its passage through the Houses of Parliament.

Figure 10.5: classification of rules according to their nature

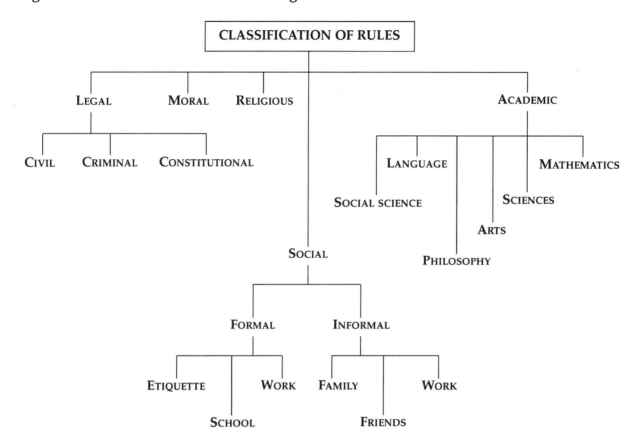

CONSTRUCTING ARGUMENTS

So, now that a little thought has been given to:

(a) the meaning of argument;

(b) the nature of **problems** and **rules**;

(c) the mediating power of language,

it is hoped that the complexity of any attempt to solve problems by recourse to rules is fully appreciated.

Despite the difficulties it is essential that lawyers are able to construct arguments, to fully engage in the process of effective reasoning. Without that core skill, a lawyer lacks competence.

Argument construction utilises a number of preparatory skills:

(a) summarising texts;

(b) choosing amongst appropriate texts for the most useful;

(c) research and organisation of texts;

(d) critique and analysis;

(e) the appropriate collection of materials in order to persuade the listener of the validity of the arguments presented.

A specifically legal argument is often a delicate balance of facts and/or theories and the application of existing rules connected by reasoned comments to persuade of the validity of adopting the outcome suggested. In the court room, both parties put forward arguments and the judge chooses the argument that is either the most persuasive or that is the closest to the judge's own belief concerning the outcome of the case.

So far, in this text, there have been opportunities to read judgments and the judges have presented their decisions in the form of reasoned responses to the questions posed by the case. In the classroom, students are constantly called upon to practise and refine their skills in legal problem solving by engaging in reasoning processes leading to full scale argument construction.

For the practising lawyer, a valid argument is of the utmost importance. Decisions as to right action can only be made by people who are able to distinguish between competing arguments and determine that, in a given set of circumstances, one argument is more valid than another. Judges are, of course, the ultimate arbiters of the acceptable decision. Sometimes, this decision is quite subjective.

Argument and logic

It is generally believed that academic and professional lawyers and, indeed, law students, are well skilled in the art of reasoning. Furthermore, it is believed that they are people who argue 'logically'.

To most, the term 'logical' indicates a person who can separate the relevant from the irrelevant, and come to an objective view, based often on supposedly objective formula. Colloquially, people accuse others, who change their mind or who are emotional in their arguing, of allowing their emotions to get the better of them, of 'not being logical'.

The dictionary defines logic as the science of reasoning, thinking, proof or inference. More than that, logic is defined as a science in its own right – a sub-section of philosophy dealing with scientific method in argument and the uses of inference. Hegel called logic the fundamental science of thought and its categories. It certainly claims to be an accurate form of reasoning: its root is found in the Greek word *logos* meaning reason.

Figure 10.6: a definition of logic

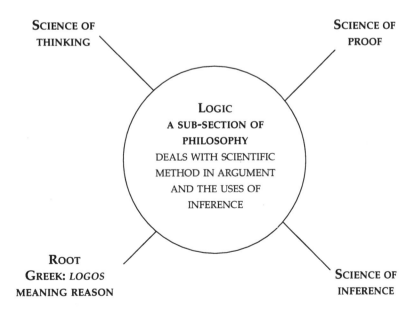

The lawyer, like a scientist, spends time considering the importance of supporting all statements with evidence and considers how one might weigh evidence on a scale of weak to strong. What is it that is actually proved by the evidence?

However, the lawyer deals in words, reports, reconstructions; the lawyer was not present observing the wrong, the accident, the incident. The scientist can always replay the event, observe the event. So, there is not a strict correlation between the lawyer and the scientist.

The logician, like the lawyer, deals in statements expressed in words and symbols called propositions. In the context of logic, the word 'proposition' only means making a statement or an assertion about something. Essentially, logic is the study of propositions and how conclusions may be correctly obtained from propositions in the process of reasoned argument.

There are two main types of logic: deductive and inductive, and a third process: abduction. Each of these processes will be briefly explained. In addition, 'analogic argument' (which is really a form of inductive reasoning) will be discussed, because analogic reasoning is the type of reasoning used within the English legal system where the courts argue from precedent to precedent.

Reasoning itself is analogous to a journey:

(a) prepare/collect information;

(b) order/organise information;

(c) start working through the information once the direction of travel is clear.

When people set out on a journey, they normally have an idea of where they are going. If they do not know where they are going, this is usually a matter of deliberate choice. When people begin to consider argument construction, they need to know where they are going. Many students, however, do not know where they are going, hope they will know when they get there, and often give up exhausted and arbitrarily state 'Therefore, this is the end'!

It is not possible to craft a good argument by accident. Useful information to include as evidence for an argument may be uncovered accidentally; however, the argument *can never* be accidentally constructed.

Deductive argument

Formal logic only allows rigid propositions to be made. Propositions which are of limited assistance to the lawyer's search for validity and truth. Everything in formal logic rests on structure, and structure is not truth.

The structure is as follows:

Every	X	is a	Y
Some	Zs	are	Xs
Therefore, some	Zs	are	Ys

Each letter of the alphabet is a symbol. It signifies the place where words can be inserted that retain the sense of the proposition and guarantee the *internal* correctness of the conclusion. The argument does not depend on the subject matter inserted in place of the signs X, Y, Z but on the *form*.

An argument reproduced in the above form is valid. Not necessarily *true, but incontrovertibly* valid.

For example:

Proposition 1: every	**X**	**is a**	**Y**
every	female	is a	human

X marks the spot where the logician can insert a *subject* (dog, cat, God, man, woman, car, etc).

Y marks the spot where X can always be said to be described as something else as well (mammal, non-human, human, machine).

The rules would dictate that X should be capable of being Y.

Proposition 2: **some**	**Zs**	**are**	**Xs**
some	children	are	female

Z marks the spot for the insertion of a new subject (Z) that is *also* capable of being *sometimes X, the subject of the first proposition*. Only *sometimes*, as the word 'Every' *is not used but the word* 'Some'.

Proposition 3: **some**	**Zs**	**are**	**Ys**
Therefore, some	children	are	human

We happen to know the conclusion is flawed. All children are human. But the conclusion is valid.

Would it make a difference if just a little change was made? If the form was:

Every	X	is a	Y
Some	Zs	are	Ys
Therefore, some	Zs	are	Xs

Surely not? Let us experiment:

Proposition 1: **every**	**X**	**is a**	**Y**

The rules would dictate that X should be capable of being Y.

It would be flawed and pointless to say:

every X (pig) is a Y (cat)

This simply is never the case.

But correct to state:

every X (pig) is a Y (mammal).

It is at least now possible to give a clearer idea of what it means to argue logically. It means to argue according to correct rules of reasoning.

Proposition 2: **Some**	**Zs**	**are**	**Ys**

It is important that the insertion here is a new subject (Z) also capable of being sometimes Y. It is not *every* but *some*.

Some Zs (winged creatures) are Ys (mammals)

Proposition 3:   is the conclusion based on propositions 1 and 2.

The conclusion is undeniable and is a purely grammatical exercise.

Therefore, some Zs are Xs.

Some winged creatures are pigs.

And there we have it – after this sophisticated process, the compelling conclusion is that:

Pigs can fly!

However the inference from the two statements leading to the conclusion is invalid. We know pigs cannot fly. It is the only inference possible, but it is invalid. It is invalid because of the structure which has compelled that conclusion. The conclusion is false because proposition 2 is in error. Winged creatures are not mammals.

However, the movement through the propositions from 1, 2 to 3 is a good demonstration of inference.

Also, it demonstrates that there are different places to attack an argument:

- the proposition;
- the conclusion.

It is through the science of logic that the forms of argument have been identified, classified and evaluated. These provide models, or frames of reference for the evaluation of claims to truth.

All those who engage in argument construction want their arguments to be valid. From logic, it is learnt that essentially there are two main forms of valid argument.

This type of reasoning comes in several forms: forms where it can be said that the conclusion is not a valid inference from the propositions and forms where the conclusion is a valid inference from the propositions:

- when the propositions can be said to be true; and
- the conclusion is a logically correct inference from the conclusion;
- the argument is sound.

Test: is the following argument sound?

Every pig is a mammal.

Some winged creatures are mammals.

Therefore, some winged creatures are pigs.

Answer: this is unsound

WHY?

Well, we know pigs can't fly, even if we have a saying '... and pigs might fly!'.

Where's the problem? The conclusion is not a logically correct inference.

The indisputable logic of the conclusion can be demonstrated to be *valid* in relation to the grammar of the sentences and absolutely *invalid* in relation to scientific knowledge.

Logical *and* crazy – so do not be seduced by the apparent desirability of logic. Logic alone does not suffice. But its discipline can be instructive.

How can one attack such an argument?

Easy: you cannot attack the conclusion, it is openly available to be formally extracted from the propositions. However, can you attack the propositions? If the propositions are framed incorrectly this needs to be proved.

Deductive argument involves drawing out what is already in the premise. Its weakness is that the premise may be false or the reasoning invalid. Over time, set formulae have been established as the framework for deductive reasoning. Deductive reasoning is *not* concerned with persuasion, for that is the task of rhetoric (which is the general art of persuasion). The most utilised formula is that of syllogism. A syllogism is an argument which consists of two propositions (or statements), leading to a conclusion which is made up of the subject of the second statement and the predicate of the first statement. In other words:

1.   (a)   if $A = B$ **major premise;**

    (b)   and $B = C$ **minor premise;**

    (c)   then $A = C$ **conclusion.**

2.   (a)   **no scientists are children;**

    (b)   **some infants are children;**

    (c)   **some infants are not scientists.**

(a) and (b) are the premises and (c) is the conclusion; (a) and (b) are evidence of (c).

If the premises are correctly drawn, the conclusion follows of necessity and is conclusive. This chain of reasoning is often expressed using words such as 'if', 'then', 'since', 'therefore'. A deductive argument can be identified by considering the nature of the conclusion. If it is compelled by the propositions, that is no other conclusion is possible, it is an inductive argument.

Inductive logic

There is another form of arguing which involves arguments that put forward some general proposition (the conclusion) from fact or facts that seem to provide some evidence for the general given proposition or group of propositions (the premises).

This is perhaps the closest to the everyday legal argument when decisions are made concerning which side of a dispute is accorded the privileging of their story in terms of the law's authority to provide an declaration of right followed by sanction and/or compensation.

Inductive reasoning is similar to deductive reasoning in so far as the conclusions are based on premises. However, in inductive reasoning, the conclusion reached extends beyond the facts in the premise. The premise supports the conclusion, it makes it *probable*. Therefore, there is less certainty and it is possible that another conclusion exists.

A sub-division of inductive reasoning is reasoning by analogy or analogous reasoning, this being the method best known to English legal method.

The difference between deductive and inductive reasoning is that deductive reasoning is a closed system of reasoning, from the general to the general or the particular, and includes cases where *the conclusion is drawn out; it is, therefore, analytical,* whereas inductive reasoning is an open system of reasoning. It involves finding a general rule from particular cases and is *inconclusive* which suggests the end processes of legal judgments are inconclusive. However, when it is, the courts ensure that inconclusive reasoning can be enforced!

Like deductive reasoning, the logic of inductive reasoning has no interest in the *actual truth* of the propositions that are the premises or the conclusion.

Just because a logical form is correctly constructed, it does not mean that the conclusion expressed is *true*. The truth of a conclusion depends upon whether the major and minor premises express statements that are *true*. The statements may be false.

Much time is spent by lawyers in court attempting to prove the truth of statements used as building blocks in the construction of arguments.

In an inductive argument, the premises only tend to support the conclusions, but they do not *compel* the conclusion. By tradition, the study of inductive logic was kept to arguments by way of analogy, or methods of generalisation, on the basis of a *finite* number of observations.

Argument by analogy is the most common form of argument in law. Such an argument begins by stating that two objects are observed to be similar by a number of attributes. It is concluded that the two objects are similar with respect to a third. The strength of such an argument depends upon the *degree* of relationship.

Lawyers are advisers and they offer predictive advice based on how previous similar cases have been dealt with. All advice is based on the lawyers' perception of what would happen in court; this is usually enough to ensure that, in the vast majority of civil cases, matters between disputants are settled. The lawyers' perception is based upon their experience of how judges reason.

Although deductive reasoning lends support to the Blackstonian theory that the law is always there to be found, there is room for the judge to exercise discretion. A judge will have to find the major premise. The judge may do this by looking at statutes or precedent. In the absence of statute, precedent or custom, he or she may need to create one by analogy or a process of induction. Once the judge has stated the major premise the judge will need to examine the facts of the case to ascertain if they are governed by the major premise. If this has been established, the conclusion will follow syllogistically.

In the vast majority of cases, the conclusion will simply be an application of existing law to the facts. Occasionally, the decision creates a new law which may or may not be stated as a proposition of law. To ascertain whether a new law has been stated may require a comparison between the material facts implied within the major premise and the facts which make up the minor premise.

To summarise, judges are involved in a type of inductive reasoning called reasoning by analogy. This is a process of reasoning by comparing examples. The purpose is to reach a conclusion in a novel situation. This process has been described as a three stage process:

(1) the similarity between the cases is observed;

(2) the rule of law (*ratio decidendi*) inherent in the first case is stated. Reasoning is from the particular to the general (deduction);

(3) that rule is applied to the case for decision. At this point, reasoning is from the general to the particular (induction).

Abduction

Another reasoning process which needs to be discussed is the process of abductive reasoning.

At the pre-trial stage, a lawyer will need to construct 'a story' or argument from available data in an effort to persuade the courts or tribunal to find in favour of the client. Before attempting this, the data will need to be tested. Is the available data sufficient to support the argument or is additional information required?

If so, how can this additional data be obtained? The data may suggest alternative, and more plausible, hypotheses which may or may not damage the client. At this stage of the process, the lawyer is involved in abductive reasoning, a creative process which produces new hypotheses or explanations.

Let us consider a legal problem before a criminal court. Sarah has been accused of shoplifting. She denies it. The defence, looking at formal deductive logic, can argue the following:

Major premise:	theft is against the law.
Minor premise:	Sarah did not commit theft.
Conclusion:	Sarah did not break the law.

The prosecution case can be just as easily stated as:

Major premise:	theft is against the law.
Minor premise:	Sarah committed theft.
Conclusion:	Sarah did break the law.

However, neither of these arguments would be accepted by a jury without more detail and without proof. It's tantamount to saying:

'I didn't do it!'

'Yes you did.'

What is the evidence for the major premise?

Find a copy of the Theft Act 1968 and locate the section dealing with the *definition* of theft. It is then easy to prove the validity of this statement. Theft is against the law. (Refer back to p 159 for the full text of s 1 of the Theft Act.) However, in the court, more problematic questions will be considered, relating to the definition of words.

For example, what is the meaning of:

(a) 'intention to permanently deprive'?

(b) 'dishonestly'?

(c) 'property'?

Sometimes, these words will be defined in the statute. But you may also have to consider any cases clarifying the definitions.

What is the evidence for the minor premise?

Facts, with evidence in support of facts, are needed to determine whether this premise is true in relation to the defence of the prosecution (whatever 'true' may mean).

What is the evidence for the conclusion?

No evidence is needed, for the conclusion is inescapable – it flows out of the information contained in the two premises. The conclusion is valid because there is no other conclusion to be drawn.

Question: how does one *attack* a deductive syllogism?

One *attacks* the premises. There is no point in attacking the conclusion of a deductive syllogism because the conclusion will always be *valid* internally. All that a deductive syllogism is claiming is that a conclusion is *internally valid*. It is not claiming that the conclusion is true.

So, attacking the premise as not true allows one to say the conclusion may be valid but it is false, it is not correct, it is not a reflection of truth because the validity of the premise is in doubt. No, that is not the law, therefore the conclusion, although valid, is not of use in arguing the case. Or no, those are not the provable facts, therefore, the conclusion, although valid, is not of use in arguing the case.

The deductive syllogism could be expressed another way:

- dishonestly taking property belonging to another with the intention of permanently depriving that other is theft;
- Sarah dishonestly took property belonging to another with the intention of permanently depriving the other of it;
- therefore, Sarah has committed theft.

It is just as unhelpful as before; *however*, it more clearly expresses the premise that needs unpacking:

Sarah took property belonging to another with the intention of permanently depriving that other.

If this premise is correct the conclusion is correct (so long as the other premise is correct, which classifies this behaviour as theft!).

Deduction here may help clarify the issues but it proves nothing. In relation to law, deduction – although logical – is not a useful argumentative devise. Because logic, it can be seen, is not connected necessarily to truth but only to the *validity* of an argumentative structure.

Lawyers primarily resort to inductive reasoning: the setting up of an argument that points to a conclusion that may or may not be the case. There may be other conclusions that could be drawn from the circumstances, facts, evidence.

However, law is not a series of scientifically correct arguments. Court room decisions about legal disputes involve predictions (guesswork), facts, evidence, discretion, inference, assertion. It is not a forgone conclusion; it is not a simple matter of the straightforward application of rules to facts. If this were possible, it would have been scientifically applied outside the courtroom in the situation in which the dispute arose, or perhaps in the lawyer's office.

Indeed, it is worth remembering that over 97% of all known disputes of a legal nature do not go to court. Bargains are struck with the law as the backdrop, with economics and convenience, as well as fairness, as motivating factors in ultimate decision making by the parties ,guided by their advisors.

The starting point for the inductive argument is usually the minor premise in the classic legal deductive syllogism. Taking only the prosecution argument going from the two deductive syllogisms, above, these would be either:

(a) Sarah committed theft; or

(b) Sarah dishonestly took property belonging to another with the intention of permanently depriving that other of it.

Both allege the same thing. However, notice that the inescapable conclusion of the first deductive syllogism is: 'therefore, Sarah broke the law'. The inescapable conclusion of the second deductive syllogism is that 'therefore Sarah committed theft'. Choices are therefore available in the manner in which deductive syllogisms are constructed.

Either 'Sarah committed theft' or 'Sarah dishonestly took property belonging to another' could be the *ultimate probandum* of a Wigmore chart. You then realise how much work needs to be done before the *ultimate probandum* can be proved!

Each element in the minor premise needs to be proved. These can be set out as assertions for clarification:

(a) Sarah acted dishonestly (how is this known?);

(b) Sarah took property (how is this known?);

(c) the property Sarah took belonged to another (how is this known?);

(d) Sarah intended to deprive that other of it permanently (how is this known?).

It may well be the case that an inductive syllogism could be set up for *each one* of the above four assertions, each being a mixture, perhaps, of hard proof and inference. In any case, it would be unusual for incontrovertible evidence to be available to prove every element making up the legal rule broken. The lawyer argues from the position they are in with the information that they have.

The essential quality of a well structured argument is that it takes the reader/listener from the beginning to the end and makes them hold to the opinion that the argument is correct or the most plausible argument. Sometimes, the process of argument uses bridges from one fact to another that are not made of evidence but of inference.

It is not wrong to assert a proposition that is not backed by evidence, but an adjudicating body is not compelled to accept the validity of an unproved proposition. It is difficult to refute a proposition backed by strong evidence but of course evidence is not always strong, it may be tenuous, or medium strong, etc. So, there are many variables present in an argument. One has to look for the weak points. Most adjudicating bodies have elements of discretion and can accept the tenuous but plausible explanatory bridge from one proven fact to another as the argument progresses to conclusion. Much depends on the minor or major nature of the proposition asserted. If it is pivotal for the case, then it must be backed by evidence. Lawyers will tend to take the little jumps with plausibility and, hopefully, the big jumps with proven propositions.

At the everyday level of explanation an argument tends to say:

- **This happened ...**
- **The following law states that this behaviour is illegal in certain circumstances.**
- **These witnesses, these official documents, this forensic evidence prove that it happened.**
- **It can be proved that ...**
- **... therefore broke the law .**

An essay may argue about theory, rather than fact, but the structures remain the same.

Argument construction is not difficult if there has been meticulous preparation of information. The argument will be basic or elegant depending upon the development of skills, understanding of the law, the level of preparation, thought and reflection that has gone into the argument construction. What one gets back is proportional to the quality of what has gone in. A strong argument may ultimately be rejected if there is a fair amount of discretion, but the person who has forwarded it will know it is good. Indeed, often an adjudicator, even when deciding against an argument, will compliment the argument constructor on the art with which it was done.

CHAPTER 11

USING PRIMARY AND SECONDARY TEXTS TO CONSTRUCT ARGUMENTS AND ANSWER QUESTIONS

Not only are there are a set number of places to look for information, and some reasonably set methods of identifying and classifying existing arguments, there are also a large number of ways of using and drawing on material to construct arguments.

It is also appropriate for the student to consider the available material with a view to raising new issues for reflection. In doing this, the student begins to move beyond the texts, beyond summarising, identifying and classifying, even beyond predicting, and is actively engaged in producing something that is backed by the evidence of the texts but is nonetheless new.

Not all written or oral work demands this and not all students can do this on a consistent basis. Those who can, if they create rationally on the basis of existing theory, texts and practice, usually generate final results in the distinction range.

Those who try to be creative, but can demonstrate no plausible evidence for their argument, construct weak pieces of written work that are borderline. This group of students is not demonstrating understanding by application, interpretation, prediction and creativity. They are usually demonstrating incomprehension of the task before them!

Ideally, in an essay, articles in the area would be researched and, if relevant, included. These have been excluded from the limited texts used for the exercise in this chapter in order to work with a manageable number of pages.

In fact, students regularly abuse the concept of researching articles by being tempted only to try to find articles that answer the question for them; they then précis the articles and hope 'it will do'. They often throw in a few quotes for good measure. It often does *not* 'do', simply because the student has not put in the work to understand the essay question and the articles read!

This is a good moment to repeat that there are:

no

> **short cuts**

>> **to**

>>> **excellent work.**

Intellectual Health Warning!

NOTE: essay preparation, construction and writing is a time consuming task.

BUT

putting in the time to:

(a) understand the basic issues;

(b) appreciate the interconnectedness of the text;

(c) determine your view;

(d) compare it with that of others,

enables students to control the information. Once the student is in control of the texts, they can be played with, alternative arguments can be constructed and understanding increased.

Often, a student merely hands in a précis of a string of articles, texts and case notes. This is not an essay offering a serious argument for consideration, and it will not attract a good mark.

A useful method for preparation, construction and writing up of essays is set out below.

METHOD FOR THE PREPARATION AND CONSTRUCTION OF ESSAYS

(a) Carefully reflect on the question

- What is being asked?
- How many issues are raised?

This is an exercise in basic English comprehension. The question has to be deconstructed. It is very useful to convert it into a **tree diagram** that can be annotated as texts are collected.

The actual essay question must be constantly borne in mind as texts are read and research is conducted.

(b) Search for relevant texts

- Cases.
- Textbooks.
- Articles.
- Handouts, lecture notes.

(c) Carefully reflect on the material collected

Précis them, extract arguments presented and **reconsider the** question.

(d) Begin to form a view of possible answers to the question

Add these to the tree diagram.

(e) Reconsider the texts

How strong is your argument.

(f) Reconsider the argument so far constructed

(g) Begin to write the essay plan

Look at:

- the diagram of the question;
- the notes of cases and other texts;
- the notes of **your personal ideas/argument.**

(h) Reflect

Reflect on the essay plan, the texts read and the question.

(i) Begin to write the first draft of the essay

Begin with the middle section, review everything for your conclusion; write the introduction **last**.

(j) Reflect on the draft

- Pay particular attention to the conclusion and thoughts on the introduction.
- Also review the argument. Is there evidence to back it up? Have opposing views been dealt with?

(k) Consider whether there is a need to search for any more texts

(l) Begin to write the final version of the essay

This method can be represented as a flow chart. See Figure 11.1.

Figure 11.1: flow chart for the preparation and construction of essays

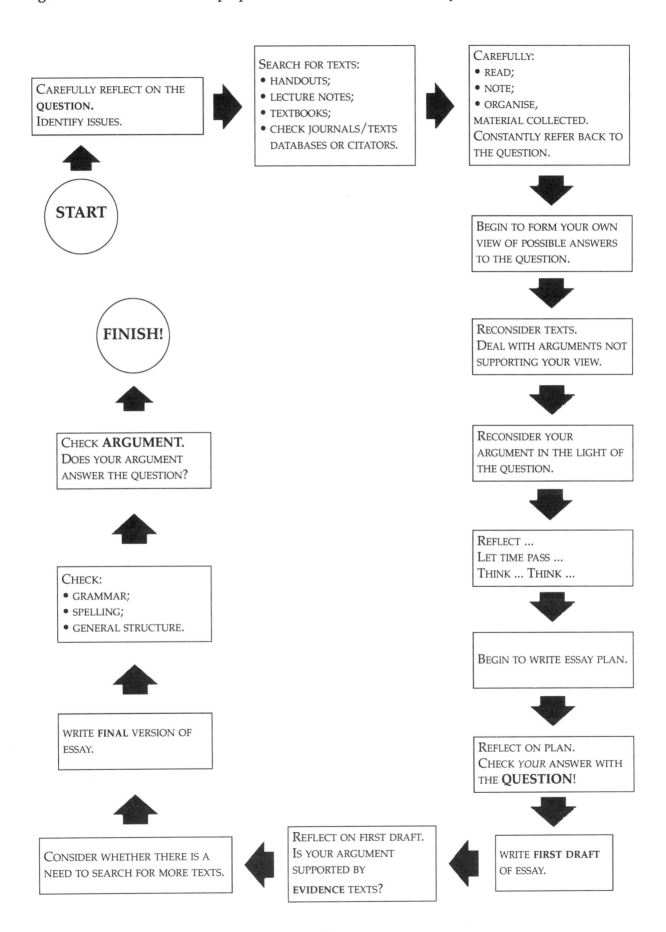

The essay question that is the vehicle for demonstrating 'putting it all together' is as follows:

> In *R v Secretary of State ex p Factortame (No 1)* and *(No 2)*, the English courts and the European Court of Justice made it clear that not only do English courts have the power to suspend Acts of Parliament conflicting with European Community law but that European Community law demands that the provisions of lawfully enacted Acts of the UK Parliament be overturned and the European Court can even dictate what national remedies should be available.
>
> Discuss solely by reference to the following texts:
>
> (a) extracts from *R v Factortame (No 1)*;
>
> (b) extracts from *R v Factortame (No 2)*;
>
> (c) extracts from Tillotson, J, *European Community Law: Text, Cases and Materials*, 2nd edn, 1996, London: Cavendish Publishing.
>
> **Note: texts (a), (b) and (c) can be located in Appendix 4.**

The question is slightly artificial in that it is limiting the choice of texts, and cutting out research. This has been done in order to carefully monitor the handling, interpretation and evaluation of the texts by the student, so that the following can be considered:

- what arguments were located in those texts?;
- how were they found?;
- what arguments in the given texts were missed?;
- why were they missed?;
- how were arguments finally constructed?;
- which lower order skills still need work (summarising, and so on)?;
- which higher order skills still need work (analysis)?

The essay is set in the area of European law as it touches upon UK law. As has already been discussed, the relationship between Community law and English law is a complex matter and could involve the side by side consideration of all or some of the following texts:

- UK statutes;
- UK delegated legislation;
- UK case law;
- articles in European Community treaties;
- European Community legislation;
- opinions of the European Court of Justice (ECJ);
- decisions by the domestic courts of Member States in similar areas;
- explanations in textbooks;
- arguments in specialist articles.

In addition the student has to:

- keep the doctrines and principles of the two legal orders (the Community's and the UK's) in tension;
- determine areas of merging, of discretion and of separation,

and **still** remember to answer the **specific** question asked!

This can seem a daunting task, but if the lower order skills of:

- organisation;
- classification;
- identification; and
- summarising,

are methodically deployed, then the texts will be broken into and sifted and made ready for answering a specific question. The competent execution of the lower order skills allows the higher level cognitive skills of:

- analysis;
- evaluation;
- critique; and
- argument construction,

to be commenced.

Once the texts have been carefully prepared by ordering and summarising:

- potential arguments can be reflected upon;
- arguments can be compared;
- differences of opinion expressed by judges and academics considered.

At this point, the student can indeed begin to have a personal view and write about it.

The initial task is to:

- understand each text as far as it is possible standing alone;
- consider the interconnections between the texts.

Law cases and texts that conflict are as intimately interconnected as law cases that agree with each other.

The student needs to be able to put together:

- cases and arguments that are the same;
- cases and arguments that are different;
- cases and arguments that are mixed in that in some areas they agree and in some areas they disagree.

The section on identifying and constructing arguments demonstrated that no problem is ever a simple unitary matter; that problems come in bundles. Whilst questions posed may appear simple and unitary, they never are.

Not only is there no such thing as a simple question, there is no such thing as a simple answer. All questions are complex and, of necessity, all answers are complex. It is never sufficient to give as an answer a purely descriptive commentary. No questions posed to test understanding will require only description. They will require evaluation and critique as well.

The student has to make choices. Decide what issues are most relevant; and what can, and what cannot, be discussed in the answer to the question.

The method set out above for the preparation and construction of essays is one suggestion for 'putting it all together'. That method will now be deployed for the preparation of the given texts and for the construction of the arguments that could be used in answer to the given essay question.

SO LET'S BEGIN!

(a) Carefully reflect on the question

- What is being asked?
- How many issues are raised?

This is an exercise in basic English comprehension. Here, the way forward is to textually deconstruct the question and then convert it into a tree diagram that can be annotated as other information and arguments, are collected from the texts. Efficient use of textual notation without a diagram would be as useful at this stage. When the level of attention to detail is realised, the methodology finally adopted depends on the development of personal preference.

The actual essay question must be constantly borne in mind as texts are read and research is conducted.

The first task, therefore, is to set the question out and annotate it.

Which ones?

More connectors:
• and;
• but;
• maybe.

You will note these are English cases. How is ECJ involved?

In *R v Secretary of State ex p Factortame (No 1)* and *(No 2),*

the English courts and the ECJ made it clear that not only

Signals first issue (the power to suspend).

do English courts have the power to suspend Acts of

Parliament conflicting with European Community law but

Signals second issue (EC law demands).

that European Community law demands that the

provisions of lawfully enacted Acts of the UK Parliament

Signals third issue (ECJ can even dictate ...).

be overturned and the European Court can even dictate

what national remedies should be available'.

This is an open invitation to say something analytic. It is suggesting: locate issues and debate. See diagram for detail of word.

Discuss solely by reference to the following texts:

(a) extracts from *R v Factortame (No 1);*

(b) extracts from *R v Factortame (No 2);*

(c) extracts from Tillotson, J, *European Community Law Text, Cases and Materials,* 2nd edn, 1996, London: Cavendish Publishing.

When precise instructions are given, students get NO credit for doing more. Command here is NOT to look at other texts.

Note: texts (a), (b) and (c) can be located in Appendix 4.

From the above annotation, several issues are beginning to emerge.

Issues

The question seems to be suggesting that, in the *Factortame* cases:

- **English and European courts made it clear that English courts can suspend Acts of Parliament;**
- **European law demands that conflicting UK legislation must be overturned;**
- **the ECJ can dictate what national remedies should be available.**

These issues have been set out as assertions, although it is left to the student to determine whether these assertions legitimately describe the views of the relevant courts as set out in the two cases.

Tree diagram of issues raised by the essay question

The next step in deconstructing the question is to look at the text of the question again, together with the annotations, and turn it into a tree diagram. This can be used to put page references, quotes, arguments onto a grid that will assist in mapping out the arguments of the essay.

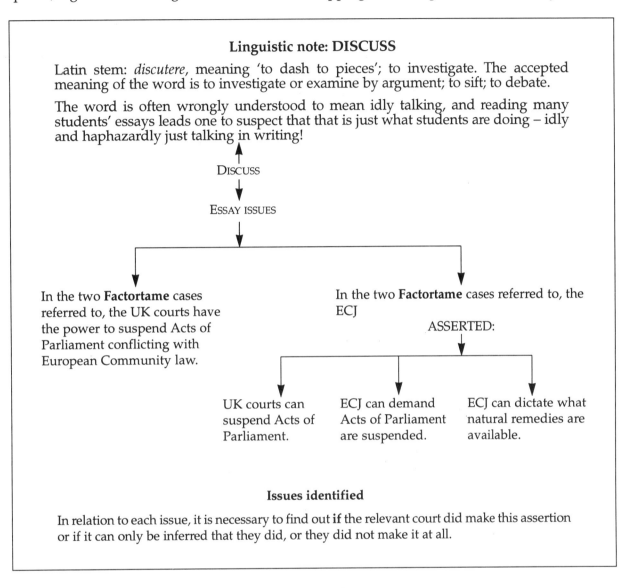

Linguistic note: DISCUSS

Latin stem: *discutere*, meaning 'to dash to pieces'; to investigate. The accepted meaning of the word is to investigate or examine by argument; to sift; to debate.

The word is often wrongly understood to mean idly talking, and reading many students' essays leads one to suspect that that is just what students are doing – idly and haphazardly just talking in writing!

DISCUSS

ESSAY ISSUES

In the two **Factortame** cases referred to, the UK courts have the power to suspend Acts of Parliament conflicting with European Community law.

In the two **Factortame** cases referred to, the ECJ

ASSERTED:

UK courts can suspend Acts of Parliament.

ECJ can demand Acts of Parliament are suspended.

ECJ can dictate what natural remedies are available.

Issues identified

In relation to each issue, it is necessary to find out **if** the relevant court did make this assertion or if it can only be inferred that they did, or they did not make it at all.

> NOTE: reflect on how much work has been done on the question before any reading has been engaged in. All that has happened so far is a careful deconstruction along purely linguistic lines. However, a lot is now known about the question.

(b) Search for relevant texts

This has, of course, already been determined in this case. Normally, however, once the issues raised by the question have been discovered and preliminary reading undertaken in the textbooks, it is useful to scan the following:

- handouts from tutors;
- articles mentioned in the **footnotes** or **endnotes** in set textbooks;
- available database or relevant indexes of law journals;
- available database or Current Law Citator for up to date law cases, legislation and so on.

(c) Carefully read, note, and reflect on the materials collected

- Précis them.
- Extract arguments presented.
- **Reconsider the** question.

Here, it is relevant to turn to the limited materials used for this essay – the extracts from the two cases and the textbook by Tillotson.

The first task is reading, asking the basic questions detailed below in relation to cases and texts, all the time recalling the actual issues detailed in the essay question, otherwise, relevant details could be missed. As you read texts, you need to ask yourself questions:

- **law reports:**

  what are the facts?;

  what legal rules have been applied and why?;

  what aspects of this case is of relevance to my essay?;

  how do the arguments presented assist me in my current essay?;

- **textbooks:**

  what is being described?;

  do I understand?;

  does it fit my understanding of the cases?;

  have I properly grasped the issues involved?;

  what is of relevance to my essay?;

- **articles:**

  what is the writer's argument?;

  is it well supported by the evidence?;

  does the writer's argument support or deny my argument in the essay?

Is there a majority view developing in the texts concerning any of the issues raised by the question?

Go back to the diagram of the questions. Note, beside the various issues, aspects of the texts that are of relevance to the issues identified as requiring discussion to answer the question. It is important to remain open to the possibility that personal ideas may change as more research is conducted and some texts present persuasive arguments that had not been previously considered.

Law reports

The reports of the law cases given will appear extremely complex initially. However, it is worth remembering that basic skills have already begun to develop. Experience has been commenced in the following areas:

(a) reading English and European Community law reports and making case notes;

(b) argument identification, organisation;

(c) argument deconstruction/construction;

(d) knowledge of the hierarchy of courts;

(e) knowledge of the relationship between UK (domestic) legislation and European law.

The basic questions that need to be answered to ensure a firm grasp of the law report are:

(a) what are the facts?;

(b) what legal rules have been applied and why?;

(c) what aspects of this case are of relevance to my essay?;

(d) how do the arguments presented assist me in my current essay?

The extracts from the two law cases are set out in Appendix 4; turn to them now and read through them. Be warned, however, that these are long cases; therefore, if you take one minute to read a page – which is quite fast – it would take 75 minutes to read it all. This puts the task into context. So make sure that you have enough time to do this task.

The cases are also of invaluable assistance for the microanalysis of legal method – how to break into a highly complex set of cases giving vast amounts of information running to hundreds of pages.

The length of the report is daunting and the language and content of the text formidable. However, persistence will allow the refinement of your developing skills of organising, comparing, describing, classifying and identifying facts and legal rules.

Initial challenge: how to break into the text

How can one begin to break into this text? It is complex, long, and a mixture of common law and civil law styles as case *(No 2)* includes the ECJ rulings under Art 177 (the preliminary reference). Such a daunting case will not come your way too often as an undergraduate and, when it does, it will be in the context of a substantive law subject such as constitutional law or Community law.

The approach taken in the text here is like being thrown into the deep end, but with a life buoy in place. The purpose of choosing a difficult set of texts is to demonstrate that:

(a) utilising sophisticated comprehension skills;

(b) recognising textual intraconnections;

(c) being able to classify, identify, organise texts,

enables a relatively firm grasp of what is going on to be ascertained even by beginners. Indeed, beginners viewing this as a comprehension exercise with fresh eyes can often obtain a more secure grasp than many law students specialising in the area will ever be able to attempt because beginners are open to legal method skills.

In *George Mitchell* (1983) in Chapter 4 and the *Van Gend en Loos* case (Case 26/62) in Chapter 7, paragraph markers were taken. This was relatively easy with the short case of *George Mitchell*, a little more tricky with the length of *Van Gend en Loos*, although a table format simplified matters.

Here, a paragraph précis would create a book and not be very helpful. Yet the markers are useful. Paragraph clusters can be considered dealing with particular issues. The approach taken to this series of cases will be:
- skim read: literally imagine that you have a pile of papers and are flicking them through your hands. But skim read a little more slowly than this! Do not stop to read in detail. Look out for:
  - headings;
  - courts, to find out the procedural history;
  - dates, get a feel for the chronology of events;
  - what are the issues in the case?

Do not proceed until you have skim read the cases and taken notes according to the above guidance: Note how long it takes you to do so. Read the cases with your deconstruction of the question to hand so that you can ensure that you are constantly reading with a view also to the question.

Having looked at the cases quickly note down:
  - *your* immediate reactions to the texts, to the issues, to the things you understood and to the things that you did not understand;
  - what you think the cases were about.

Make notes and be prepared to use them.

> **PROMISE: if you successfully break into these cases and understand the outline of what is going on, no law report will ever defeat you.**

Reaction:

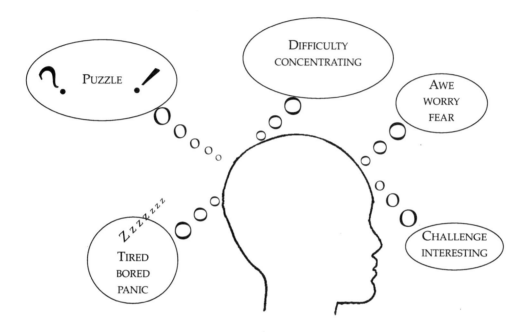

Now re-read the cases in detail for the purposes of casenoting.

Here there must be:

(1) a meticulous précis of the facts of the case;

(2) careful ascertainment of the issues involved; what questions are before the relevant courts;

(3) careful listing of legal rules of relevance to the case;

(4) the decision of the court and the reasoning for that decision.

Each of these four areas will now be considered in a little detail.

(1) A meticulous précis of the facts of the case

In an English case, the facts are usually presented early on in the first judgment. Consider *Factortame (No 1)*. From the skim reading of the extracts from the cases, and from reading Tillotson, it should be clear that **all** the cases revolve around the same facts.

Problem: missing the information that ALL *Factortame* cases revolve around the same facts

If you missed this point, then you are not reading with the proper attention to detail. Retrace your steps by skim reading again if you did not pick up this point. Find out why you missed it – although, in the end, the reason is always the same: reading with insufficient care and attention.

> Reading **words** but not reading for **sense**.

If you ascertained that all the cases involve the same facts, what are the facts? Turn back to the extract of *Factortame (No 1)*. Where are the facts to be found?

Look at p 253: is there anything about the information on this page that strikes you as odd, unusual, unexpected, confusing?

THINK CAREFULLY!

The case is called *Regina v Secretary of State for Transport ex p Factortame Limited and Others* and it is being heard in the Court of Appeal. It is on appeal from the first instance court, the Queen's Bench Divisional Court, and it is an action for judicial review. The Secretary of State for Transport has powers that will result in the ending of the applicant's ability to apply for a licence to fish. The applicants want the legislation and the power of the Secretary of State reviewed in the light of their assertion that the action is based on the authority of domestic legislation that conflicts with European Community law.

The next 25 pages of the Court of Appeal report set out the judgment in the Divisional Court of the Queen's Bench by Neill LJ. This is in the High Court and, from this information, it is realised that this must be the report of the judgment in the original hearing. A student who is not properly reading, and thinking about, the heading could miss this and think that they are reading the Court of Appeal judgment. This judgment in the Queen's Bench Division is going to be where the initial recounting of the facts is to be found.

> **NOTE:** it's worth remembering that this version of the facts is the judge's version. This is the official, influential version. In this case, as it turned out, the facts were not disputed. In cases where the facts are disputed, the judge decides which is the 'true' version.

Practical exercise before moving on

Now locate the facts, read them, underline any points, make notes and write a concise summary of the facts. No more that 25 lines. Now check your summary of the facts against the summary at the end of this chapter:

- have you missed out any facts? If so how did that happen?;
- have you more facts than in the summary? Why did you add in facts not in the summary?;
- is your summary longer than 25 lines? Why is this the case?

Look at your extra facts again. Are they really facts? Or have you misidentified, or misclassified. For example, the following matters, although relevant, do not constitute facts:

- political background: talking about the UK Government's view of the Common Fisheries Policy? This is background context which is useful but *not facts* of the case;
- the procedural history: which courts the case has been in;
- the legal issues: both UK law and European Community law.

All of the above matters are highly relevant but they are not facts.

Q Why does it matter that only the facts are put into this part of the summary?

A It matters because clarity of understanding will never be achieved if separate matters are confused and intertwined. How can issues raised, or legal rules, be applied to the facts if the student has confused issues or history *as* facts.

If facts are missed out, check to see why this is the case. Was the mistake due to inattention during reading or confusion as to the difference between facts, issues and procedural history. Rectify and make sure that it does not happen again.

(2) Careful ascertainment of the legal issues involved. What questions are before the relevant courts? and

(3) Careful listing of legal rules of relevance to the case

The following explanation incorporates items (2) and (3) above. In order to properly appreciate the nature of the legal issues raised in an appeal, it is essential to understand the nature of the legal issues raised at the original trial, as the appeal is a consequence of the trial! As an appeal progresses, there may be changes to the grounds of the appeal. If the developmental history of the appeal is not properly understood, important changes may even be missed.

(a) Go back to the judgment of Neill LJ and set out as concisely as you can:
- who were the applicants?;
- why did the applicants appeal?;
- what exactly did the applicants want the court to do?;
- what legal rules were being relied on by the applicants?

(b) Read the Court of Appeal judgment and set out as concisely as you can the answers to the following questions:
- who were the appellants?;
- why did the appellants appeal?;
- what exactly did the appellants want the court to do?;
- what legal rules were being relied on by the appellants?

(c) Now read the House of Lords' judgment:

    o   who were the appellants?;

    o   why did the appellants appeal?;

    o   why is there an opinion by the ECJ in this judgment?;

NOTE: Lord Goff refers to an interim order by the European Court **in another action brought against the UK by the European Commission under Art 169 of the Treaty of Rome** (the plot thickens). This required the UK to suspend the **nationality** requirements in the Merchant Shipping Act 1988.

The UK Parliament amended s 14 to bring it in line with the interim order by regulations ratified 2 November 1989. This made the appellants appeal as stated unnecessary.

So ... WHY did the applicants in this case still proceed with their appeal?

---

    o   what exactly did the appellants want the court to do?;

    o   what legal rules were being relied on by the appellants?

As this is such a complex case, further clarification can be obtained by methodically listing, preferably in chronological order, all UK and European Community law involved. Just go through the High Court judgments and note down **ALL** references to legislative rules in both the UK and EC as well as all references to Articles in treaties. (Do not get confused by the fact that subdivisions in a **regulation** are also referred to as Articles.) This will include UK legislation and delegated legislation, EC Treaty Articles and EC legislation created by the institutions. Once set out as **separate** lists, they can be converted into a composite diagram that also relates legal rules to relevant issues (see Figures 11.4 and 11.5).

The answers to the various questions asked concerning the cases in (a), (b) and (c) above should now be carefully considered and each set out as tree diagrams. When you have constructed a tree diagram using the questions asked of the cases as headings, a comparison of all three courts will encapsulate the most important aspects of the case. These diagrams are set out at the end of this chapter in Figures 11.6–11.10. They also include the information noted in response to (4) below.

Intellectual Health Warning!

Make the summaries and construct the diagrams before checking the diagrams in the text.

The diagrams are useful for broad, yet in depth, comparisons and for self-diagnosis:

- what was found?;
- what was missed?;
- what is now understood?

> **NOTE:** the most important matters are:
> - those that you did not see; or
> - relevant matters that you decided were not relevant.
>
> **If you missed out issues, or thought relevant matters were irrelevant, you must ask yourself:** *why did I do that?*

(4) The decision of the court and the reasoning for that decision

Recall when issues relating to use of rules to solve problems were being discussed. It was stated that problems do not come in simple, single units, and neither do solutions. When the reasons for decisions are analysed, sometimes it is easy to forget this point. Judges sometimes present simple problems by their interpretation of the issues. However, in these cases, no one is pretending the outcome is simple.

In sorting out:

- the facts;
- the applicants or appellants;
- the issues in the main case;
- the grounds of appeal,

much information will also have been assimilated concerning the reasoning of the court in response to the issues raised.

As students read judgments with the facts, issues and relationships between legal rules in place, then it becomes an easier task to isolate the text relating to the reasoning process. As the text is mentally ordered and classified, relevant aspects of the judgment in relation to reasoning can be identified, weak reasoning can also be considered. It is then less daunting to deal with a line of cases changing legal rules or the interpretation of legal rules.

If a statistical breakdown of the parts of any judgment was conducted, it would be found that a relatively small percentage of the judgment is related to reasoning. But, in an English law report knowledge of the reasoning process of the court is said to be the most vital element of the report.

In reading these judgments, much information can be gathered on the attitudes of the senior English judiciary concerning the relationship between European Community law and UK law. For example, careful reading will have noted that all judges accept, without question, that, in cases of clear infringement of European Community law by UK law, then UK law must be disapplied. Noting this will make the student question the interpretation of the case put forward by the essay question that they are essential about 'disapplying English statutes'.

An appreciation of the correct issue (can a court disapply as an interim measure before a rule has been held to conflict with EC law?) suggests the necessity for a vital yet subtle difference between what the question is suggesting and what the case is about.

The reasoning of the courts can only be obtained by reading all judgments.

Go back over the information gathered in relation to the procedural history of these cases and, incorporating information in the cases, construct a diagram of the actions.

Final consideration of the cases by reflecting on textual notes and diagrams

The three diagrams contain the basic reasoning behind the decision for you to check your findings against.

It is useful here to look at all the diagrams:

Figure 11.3:	the list of UK law and EC law;
Figure 11.4:	UK and EC legal rules of relevance;
Figure 11.5:	provisions of the EC Treaty of relevance to the *Factortame* cases;
Figure 11.6:	the issues raised by the question;
Figures 11.7–11.9:	the three diagrams concerning the grounds of appeal, decision and reasoning in all three courts, including indication of grounds of preliminary ruling;
Figure 11.10:	the diagram of the actions in the case.

On only nine pages there is now an ordered summary of the essay question and the 72 page cases extract. Looking at these diagrams, it would be appropriate to write the case notes of the cases.

Textbook and articles

Next read the extract from Tillotson, *European Community Law: Text, Cases and Materials*. Try to understand what he is describing and fit the cases into the commentary. There are other cases in the 'Factortame saga'.

The following preliminary questions should be answered by reading the text:

- what is being described?
- do I understand?
- does it fit with my understanding of the cases?
- have I properly grasped the issues involved?
- what is of relevance to my essay?

At the end of this stage, there will be an appreciation of how the textbook and the extracts from the law reports fit together. This is an appropriate time to ask if there is a majority view developing in the texts concerning any of the issues raised by the question?

Go back to the diagram of the question. Note beside the various issues aspects of the texts, with page references, that are of relevance to each point that you have identified. It is now possible to begin to develop a view as to which parts of the texts deal with which issue.

(d) Begin to form a view of possible answers to the question

The completion of the analysis of the cases and the textbook should have communicated a relatively strong grasp of the issues raised by these cases and the political background against which they were decided.

The work on the issues raised by the essay questions, together with the issues raised in the cases, should have revealed the subtle distinction that the cases revolve around the issue of the ability or otherwise of the UK courts to disapply a UK statute when it is only *suspected* of infringing European law. This point has not been decided before by the courts. The cases are therefore about the viability of disapplying national legislation as an interim measure awaiting final determination. The urgency behind the application by *Factortame* and others is that irreparable damage will be done to their businesses even if they win the final case because:

- **they could not get damages against the Crown as the law then stood;**
- **they would, therefore, go bankrupt before the matter was finally determined, as it would occur well after they had been unable to register.**

Ascertaining these points allows much to be said in your essay.

The reading shows that, at a broad level, no English judge disputes the fact that EC law obliges English courts to disapply a national law if it conflicts with EC law. Neither does the UK Government dispute this. That is why it is essential that the *narrower* issue is picked up. That the case concerns disapplying UK legislation by an English court as an *interim* measure awaiting final determination of the main issue concerning European Community law and its infringement.

Look at the diagrammatic version of the essay question set out below in Figure 11.6 and the way in which the limited knowledge so far obtained has been added to it. The diagrams of the cases in relation to issues, grounds and reasoning have been used to attach points to the issues raised by the question in Figure 11.6.

What judges say constitutes powerful evidence for an argument. It can be seen that the cases can be allocated to issues and arguments formed to agree or disagree, to agree in part or to agree in total.

(e) Reconsider the texts

Intellectual Health Warning!

Texts which deny your argument are not to be ignored, they are to be dealt with. You can argue that they are unreliable (for example, you may argue that the argument is pure theory with no evidence to back it up); you can argue that it is one possible plausible interpretation but that you are presenting another equally plausible interpretation. If you cannot explain away an argument denying your view, then perhaps you should reconsider your view. How strong is your argument?

(f) Reconsider the argument

Look at all the diagrams and the argument constructed. Refine the argument. Look back now to the textual deconstruction of the question and deal with *each* assertion.

Issues:

The question seems to be suggesting that, in the '*Factortame* cases':

Issue 1   **English and European courts made it clear that English courts can suspend Acts of Parliament**

   Essay discussion: (Précis form)

   This point was well established by the UK and EC courts *before* the case of *Factortame* was brought to court. The judges treat this point as uncontroversial and taken-for-granted in the case of *Factortame*. The courts did make it clear but only by re-stating the position already existing. The issue in this case was whether the court could order legislation to be disapplied as an interim measure when the main case concerned an application that there was a potential conflict with EC law. The sticking point being that at the time of the disapplication there was **no** conflict proved.

   Evidences: quote from the cases briefly and summarise briefly the view of the judges. Refer to earlier cases deciding these points; refer to Tillotson.

Issue 2   **European law demands that conflicting UK legislation must be overturned**

   Yes, it does; the courts accepted this before *Factortame* so this is stating the obvious.

Evidence: s 2 of the European Community Act 1972.

Quote from cases; Tillotson.

Issue 3   the ECJ can dictate what national remedies should be available

No, the case determined that the ECJ cannot. The ECJ stated in the preliminary ruling **requested** by the House of Lords that the absence of interim orders by way of a national remedy would be an injustice and would make the resort to European law non-viable in certain types of case. They did not say what remedies should be available. Indeed, the ECJ actually said that it was beyond its powers to say **what** remedies and **what** criteria should apply to them. They did, however, say that there should be remedies.

Evidence: direct quotations and brief summaries.

So, in brief, the argument of your essay is that the quotation is misleading for the reasons outlined. The word **'discuss'** allows the essayist to expand or contract issues as is wished and armed with all the information the writer is in control!

Intellectual Health Warning!

In an exam situation and in an essay situation, many students would have merely spent pages discussing the facts and the outcomes, demonstrating, however, little appreciation of the issues raised by the cases and little understanding of the question. This is not because they are not capable of understanding, but because they did not spend enough time thinking about what the question was asking and preparing the texts to be used.

(g) Begin to write the essay plan

Look at:

- all the diagrams;
- notes of cases and other texts;
- notes of **your own ideas/argument.**

(h) Reflect

Reflect on the essay plan, the texts read and the question.

(i) Begin to write the first draft of the essay

- Begin with the middle section.
- Review everything for the conclusion.
- Write the introduction last.

(j) Reflect on the draft

- Pay attention to the argument – does it clearly present itself?
- Pay particular attention to the conclusion and thoughts on the introduction.
- Also, review the argument. Is there evidence to back it up? Have opposing views been dealt with?

(k) Consider whether you need to search for any more texts

This is irrelevant here for the purposes of this exercise, but if the texts had not been pre-ordained it is highly likely that a first trawl through would demand further reading and/or research.

(l) Begin to write the final version of the essay

This method can be represented as a cyclical process as seen in Figure 11.1.

Breakdown and ordering of material/essay question

(a) Summaries.

(b) Diagrams.

(a) Summaries

- **Summary of the facts:**

  the action revolved around a dispute between the British Government and Spanish companies legitimately registered to fish under the Merchant Shipping Act 1894 carrying on business in England. The majority of the directors and shareholders were Spanish and were resident outside the UK.

  The UK introduced new conditions for granting licences in the Merchant Shipping Act 1988 which laid down that 75% of the directors and shareholders must be British nationals and reside in the UK. All vessels had to re-register as their existing licences expired on 31 March 1989.

  The applicants could not comply with the new conditions for registration, their vessels would have to stop fishing and the companies would face financial disaster.

- **Summary of the political background as set out in the cases:**

  if students had been searching for their own texts, they might have, quite legitimately, chosen to research the political background in more detail.

  The UK joined the European Community in 1973 and the powers of ministers regarding fishing contained in the Sea Fish (Conservation) Act 1967 subject to the Common Fisheries Policy of European Community. Around the UK was a 200 mile European Community fishing zone.

  The European Community had introduced a system of fishing quotas for each Member State. For the purposes of calculating whether a quota had been exceeded, foreign vessels registered with Member States had their load calculated against the quotas of that State.

  The British Government had expressed concern that the full benefit of the quotas therefore was not going to British interests but to foreign economic interests. The British Government was of the opinion that local fishing communities were suffering from such invasion of their waters and that they needed special protection.

- **Summary of the issue in the application for judicial review:**

  the applicants alleged that the British Government, by stipulating that 75% of the shareholders and directors had to be of British nationality, were unnecessarily acting out of all proportion to the problem. Furthermore, they had infringed their Community obligations by passing a statute that contained provisions in direct contravention of the Treaty of Rome – notably that Member States cannot discriminate against each other (see Arts 7, 52 and 221 of the Treaty of Rome).

- **Summary of procedural history:**

Factortame applied to the High Court for an order that the contravening sections of the statute, together with parts of accompanying regulations passed to implement the statute, should be disapplied pending a full hearing of the matter.

The High Court considered that the dispute raised a question requiring the interpretation of some of the articles in the EC Treaty and decided to operate their discretion to ask the European Court for a preliminary ruling under Art 177 to the question whether s 14 of the Merchant Shipping Act 1988 infringed Arts 7, 52 and 221 of the EEC Treaty.

This case commenced in December 1988 but the court decided to seek a preliminary ruling from the European Court and this was sent on 10 March 1989.

The High Court ordered the application of the statute to be suspended on the grounds:

o of changes brought about by entry into the EC;

o of s 2(1) and (4) of the ECA 1972;

o that the applicants stood a good chance of winning the case and, if they had to await a ruling, the case could take two years:

> if they were unable to register and therefore unable to fish they would be bankrupt;

o that this case for judicial review was not a case in which damages was a remedy on offer.

The Government appealed on the grounds that an English court cannot suspend an Act of the English Parliament before it has even been determined to be in conflict with European law. The Court of Appeal agreed with the Government.

The applicants were forced to appeal to the House of Lords who said that, as far as the law as they saw it was concerned, the High Court could not suspend a statute. However, as the final court of appeal, they were obliged to seek a preliminary ruling on the matter from the ECJ under Art 177, concerning whether a national court had to give relief pending a reference in a main action and, if it gave relief, did Community law give it the power to grant interim protection?

The ECJ replied in the affirmative and stated that if a national law stood in the way of interim relief then that national law must be set aside. So the House of Lords further ordered on 9 July 1990 that, as the applicants' case was strong, interim relief, in the form of the suspension of s 14 of the Act, was granted.

By then, the Commission for the EC had commenced an action against the British Government stating that s 14 of the Merchant Shipping Act 1988 infringed its treaty obligations under the founding Treaty of Rome 1957, Arts 7, 52 and 221. The Commission also applied to the ECJ for interim relief requiring the UK to suspend s 14 of the Merchant Shipping Act. The ECJ granted this on 10 October 1989. The UK complied by an Order in Council dated 2 November 1989.

- **Skim read of the cases:**
  The skim reading should have revealed most of the following.

	HEADINGS

Case 2 (yes, 2!)
 An appeal against interim order made in
 Case 1
 Case 2 is really an *interlocutory matter*
 Court of Appeal
	Regina v Secretary of State for Transport ex p
	 Factortame Limited and Others
	 Before the English Court of Appeal:
	 On appeal from the English High Court:
	 • Community law and national law;
	    priority of Community law;
	    European Court National Courts;
	    Priority of Community law.
	    Interim measure.
	 • Constitutional law:
	    UK Acts of Parliament;
	    Priority of Community law.

Case 1: the trial **High Court** Printed in full prior to the judgments in the appeal on interlocutory matters.	**Judgment of the Divisional Court** Neill LJ The application for interim relief. Hodgson LJ
OUTCOME	**Reference made to the European Court** **under Art 177.** **Interim order made suspending the operation** **of the contentious part of the Merchant** **Shipping Act 1988 and the accompanying** **regulations.**

Case 2
 Court of Appeal
 22 March 1989
	Appeal by Secretary of State against the
	 interim order
	 Judgment of the Court of Appeal
	 The Master of the Rolls
	    The application.
	    The appeal.
	    Reasons.
	 Bingham LJ

OUTCOME	**APPEAL ALLOWED**

Case 3 **House of Lords** **Appeal on the interlocutory matter the subject of Case 2**	On appeal by the applicants from the Court of Appeal's decision to allow the appeal of the Secretary of State.
	Regina v Secretary of State for Transport ex p Factortame Ltd and Others (No 2) House of Lords I Background to the dispute
11 May 1989	II The House of Lords judgment of 18 May 1989 III Course of the procedure
4 August 1989	Commission of European Community takes the UK to the European Court under Art 169 of the EEC Treaty for a declaration that s 14 of the Merchant Shipping Act infringes the UK's obligations under Arts 7, 51 and 221 of the EEC Treaty.
4 August 1989	Commission seeks an interim order from the European Court to suspend the application of s 14 of the Merchant Shipping Act 1988.
2 November 1989	Order in Council by the UK Government comes into force amending s 14 to take account of the interim relief ordered by the European Court. IV Written observations Second question
European Court **17 May 1990** **European Court** **19 June 1990**	**Reference under Art 177 to enable House of Lords to proceed to judgment** 17 May, Mr Advocate General Tesauro. 19 June, judgment delivered in Luxembourg.
House of Lords **11 October 1990**	**Their Lordships took time for consideration** 11 October, Lord Bridge of Harwich Lord Brandon of Oakbrook Lord Oliver of Aylmerton Lord Goff of Chieveley Lord Jauncey of Tullichettle (1) the threshold; (2) have the applicants crossed the threshold?; (3) balance of convenience.
OUTCOME	**APPEAL ALLOWED**

Figure 11.3: UK legislation/delegated legislation and European Community Treaty Articles and legislation of institutions

(a)	**(i)**	**English legislation**
	•	Part IV of the Merchant Shipping Act 1894 (Pt IV MCA 1894)
	•	Section 4 of the Sea Fish (Conservation) Act 1967, as amended
	•	European Communities Act 1972
	•	Parts II, s 14(1), (2), (3), (4), (7) of the Merchant Shipping Act 1988
	(ii)	**English delegated legislation**
	•	Merchant Shipping (Registration of Fishing Vessels)
	•	Part VII, reg 66 of the Regulations 1988

(b) Community law

(i) **Treaties**

• The Treaty of Rome 1957:
  ○ Art 7
  ○ Art 34, para 1

Pt II

Title II
  ○ Art 38, para 1
  ○ Art 39, para 1
  ○ Art 40, para 3

Title III

Chapter 1

Chapter 2
  ○ Art 52
  ○ Art 58, Chapter 3
  ○ Art 221
  ○ Art 177

Resolutions

Hague Resolution, November 1976

Declarations

Council's Declaration on Common Fisheries Policy Brussels 30 May 1980

Acts

Acts of Accession 1985

(ii) **Regulations**

Regulation 2141/70

2142/70

101/76 (replacing 2141/70 above)

First five recitals of 101/76

2057/82 First recital, Arts 3, 6, 10

170/83 First recital, sixth recital, twelfth recital, and Arts 1, 4 and 5 of that Regulation

172/83

2241/87 Art 11 (was Art 10, para 1 of reg 2057/82)

THE DIAGRAMS

Figure 11.4: diagram of UK and European Community legal rules of relevance in the cases (key law indicated by circles)

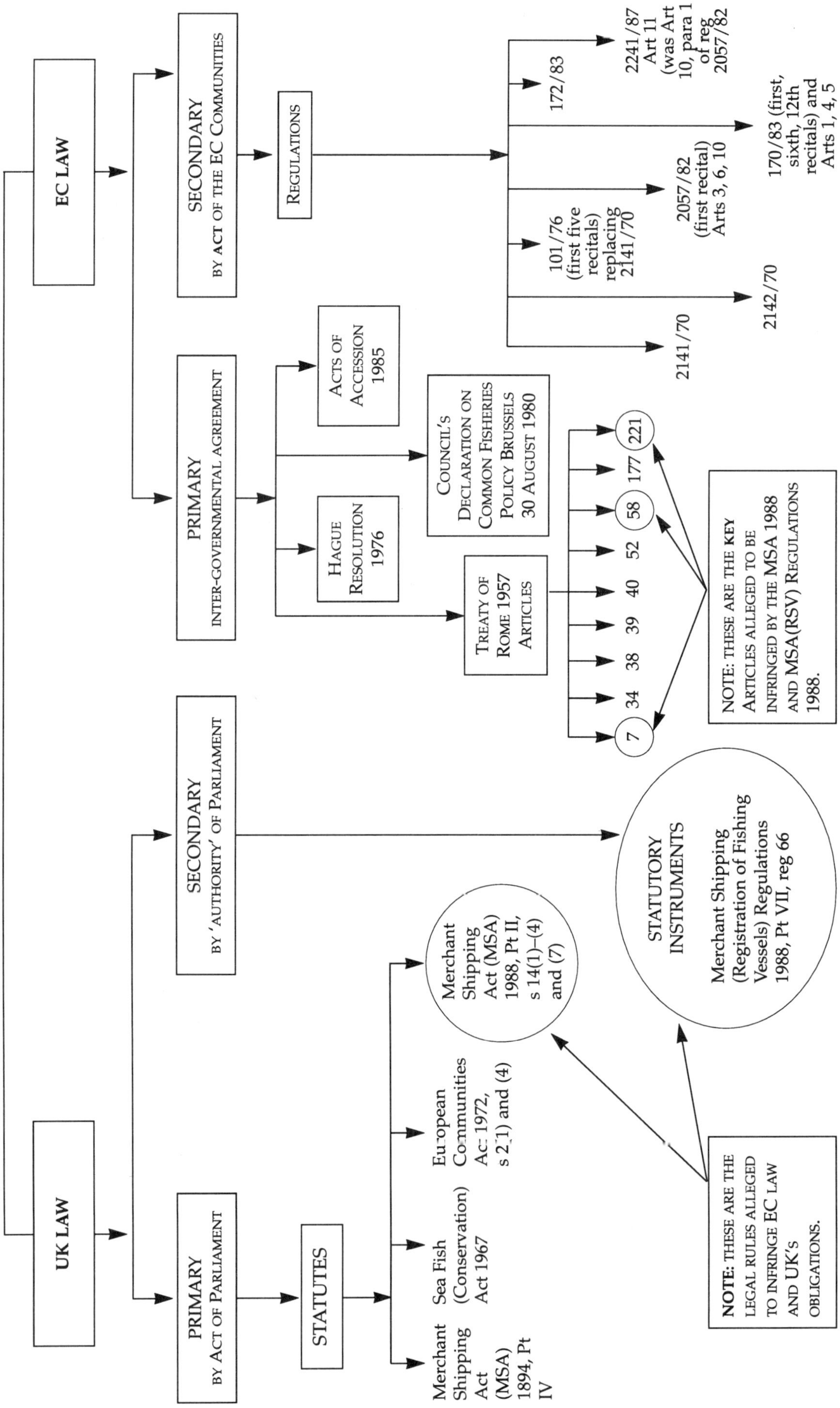

Figure 11.5: provisions in Treaty of Rome 1957 of relevance to the *Factortame* cases

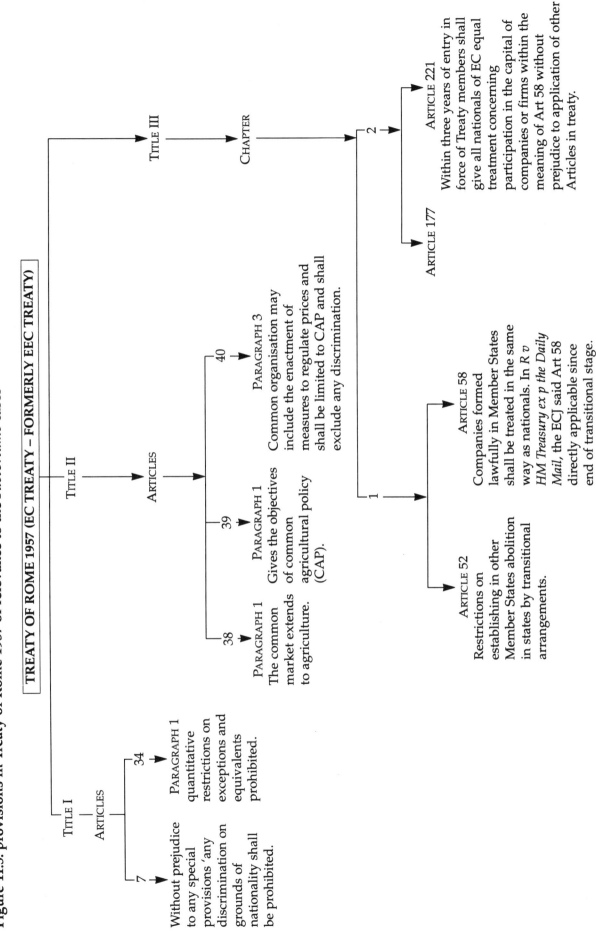

Figure 11.6: diagram of issues raised by the question with attached relevant references to cases

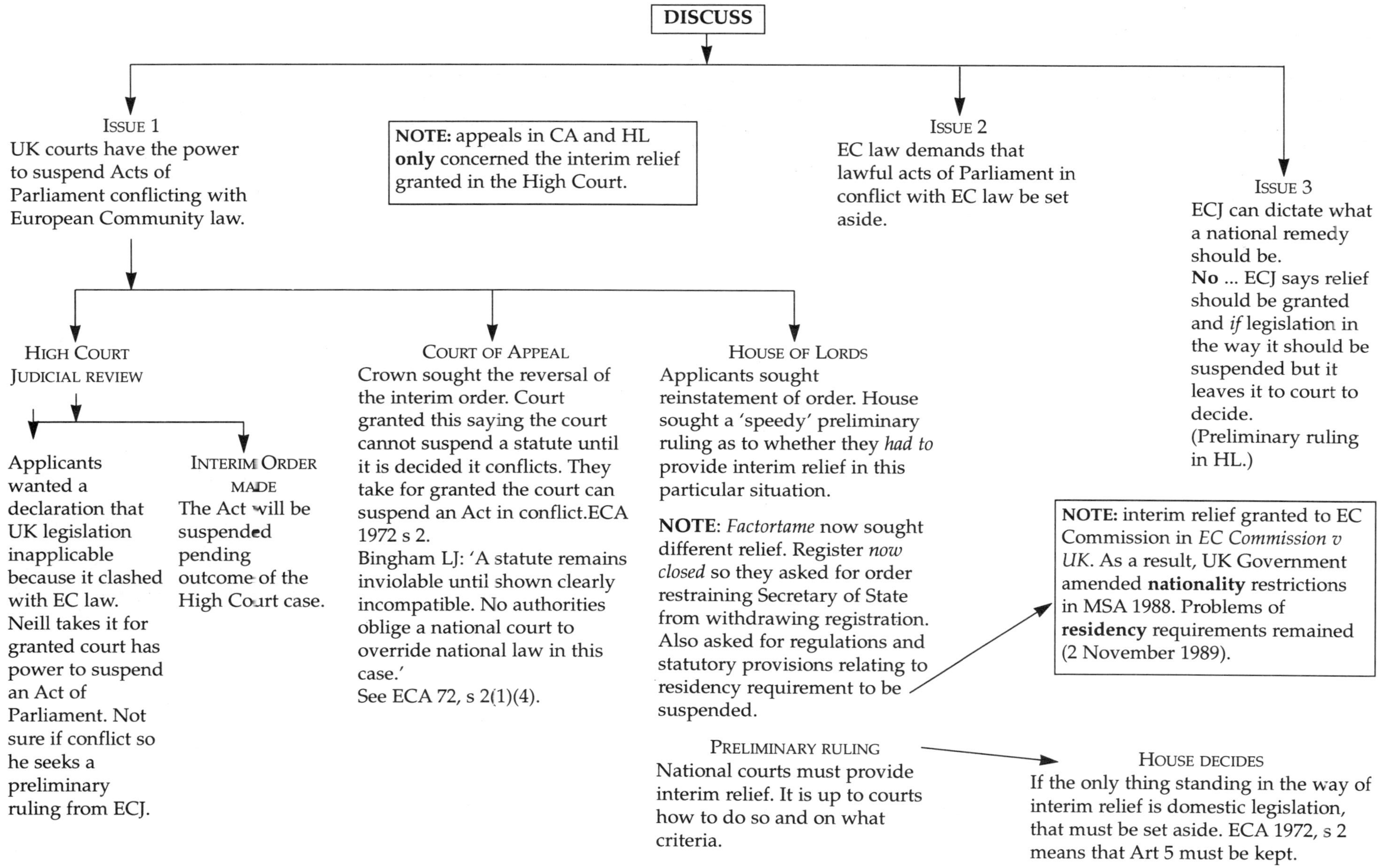

DISCUSS

ISSUE 1
UK courts have the power to suspend Acts of Parliament conflicting with European Community law.

ISSUE 2
EC law demands that lawful acts of Parliament in conflict with EC law be set aside.

ISSUE 3
ECJ can dictate what a national remedy should be.
No ... ECJ says relief should be granted and *if* legislation in the way it should be suspended but it leaves it to court to decide.
(Preliminary ruling in HL.)

NOTE: appeals in CA and HL **only** concerned the interim relief granted in the High Court.

HIGH COURT
JUDICIAL REVIEW

Applicants wanted a declaration that UK legislation inapplicable because it clashed with EC law. Neill takes it for granted court has power to suspend an Act of Parliament. Not sure if conflict so he seeks a preliminary ruling from ECJ.

INTERIM ORDER
MADE
The Act will be suspended pending outcome of the High Court case.

COURT OF APPEAL
Crown sought the reversal of the interim order. Court granted this saying the court cannot suspend a statute until it is decided it conflicts. They take for granted the court can suspend an Act in conflict. ECA 1972 s 2.
Bingham LJ: 'A statute remains inviolable until shown clearly incompatible. No authorities oblige a national court to override national law in this case.'
See ECA 72, s 2(1)(4).

HOUSE OF LORDS
Applicants sought reinstatement of order. House sought a 'speedy' preliminary ruling as to whether they *had to* provide interim relief in this particular situation.

NOTE: *Factortame* now sought different relief. Register *now closed* so they asked for order restraining Secretary of State from withdrawing registration. Also asked for regulations and statutory provisions relating to residency requirement to be suspended.

PRELIMINARY RULING
National courts must provide interim relief. It is up to courts how to do so and on what criteria.

NOTE: interim relief granted to EC Commission in *EC Commission v UK*. As a result, UK Government amended **nationality** restrictions in MSA 1988. Problems of **residency** requirements remained (2 November 1989).

HOUSE DECIDES
If the only thing standing in the way of interim relief is domestic legislation, that must be set aside. ECA 1972, s 2 means that Art 5 must be kept.

Figure 11.7: diagram of the High Court decision in *Factortame*

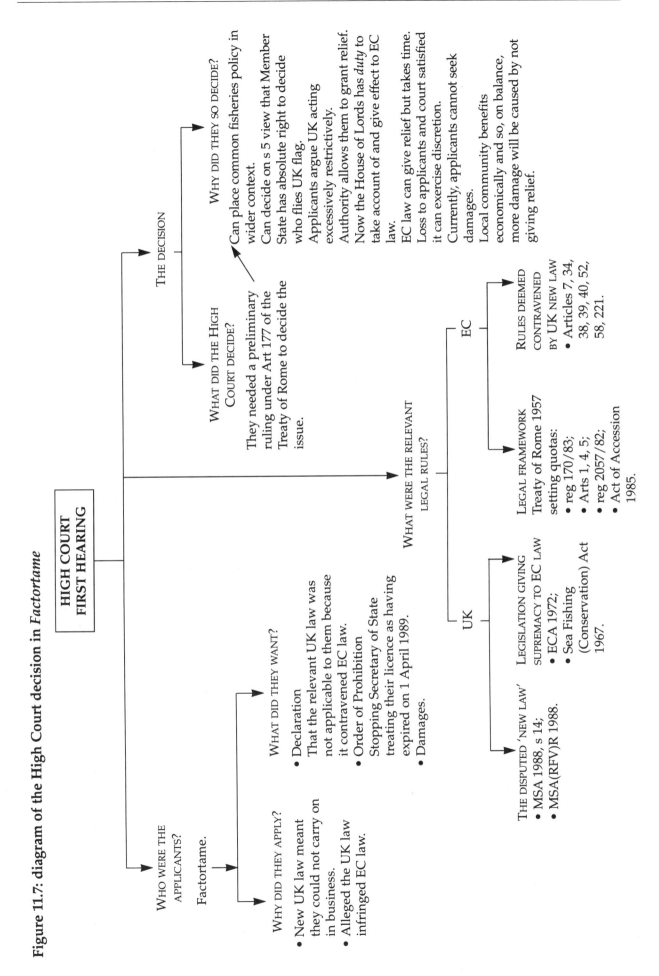

Figure 11.8: diagram of the Court of Appeal decision in relation to the injunction in *Factortame*

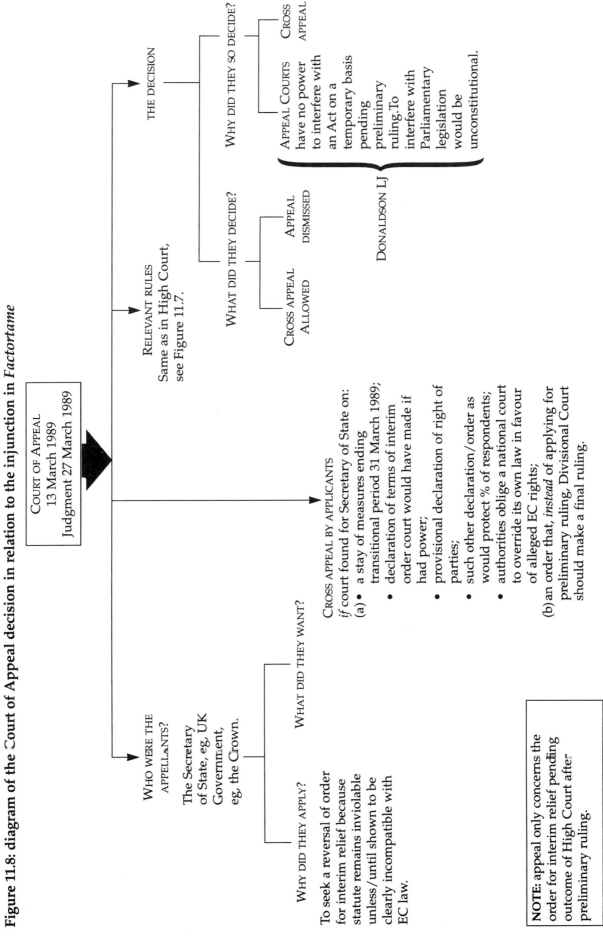

COURT OF APPEAL
13 March 1989
Judgment 27 March 1989

THE DECISION

WHY DID THEY SO DECIDE?

CROSS APPEAL

APPEAL COURTS have no power to interfere with an Act on a temporary basis pending preliminary ruling. To interfere with Parliamentary legislation would be unconstitutional.

DONALDSON LJ

WHAT DID THEY DECIDE?

APPEAL DISMISSED

CROSS APPEAL ALLOWED

RELEVANT RULES
Same as in High Court, see Figure 11.7.

WHO WERE THE APPELLANTS?

The Secretary of State, eg, UK Government, eg, the Crown.

WHAT DID THEY WANT?

WHY DID THEY APPLY?

To seek a reversal of order for interim relief because statute remains inviolable unless/until shown to be clearly incompatible with EC law.

CROSS APPEAL BY APPLICANTS
if court found for Secretary of State on:
(a) • a stay of measures ending transitional period 31 March 1989;
• declaration of terms of interim order court would have made if had power;
• provisional declaration of right of parties;
• such other declaration/order as would protect % of respondents;
• authorities oblige a national court to override its own law in favour of alleged EC rights;
(b) an order that, *instead* of applying for preliminary ruling, Divisional Court should make a final ruling.

NOTE: appeal only concerns the order for interim relief pending outcome of High Court after preliminary ruling.

222

Figure 11.9: diagram of the House of Lords in relation to the granting of the injunction in *Factortame*

Preamble: reading the first few pages of this report, it becomes apparent that this House of Lords report is the second of a process. The case came before the House of Lords on 18 May 1989 and they decided it was appropriate to seek a preliminary ruling from ECJ on the issue of whether (given UK court had no power under UK law to grant type of interim relief required) UK court obliged to grant relief or whether EC law gave power to grant relief – and, if it gave power without obligations, what were the criteria to be applied in deciding whether or not to grant such interim relief protection.

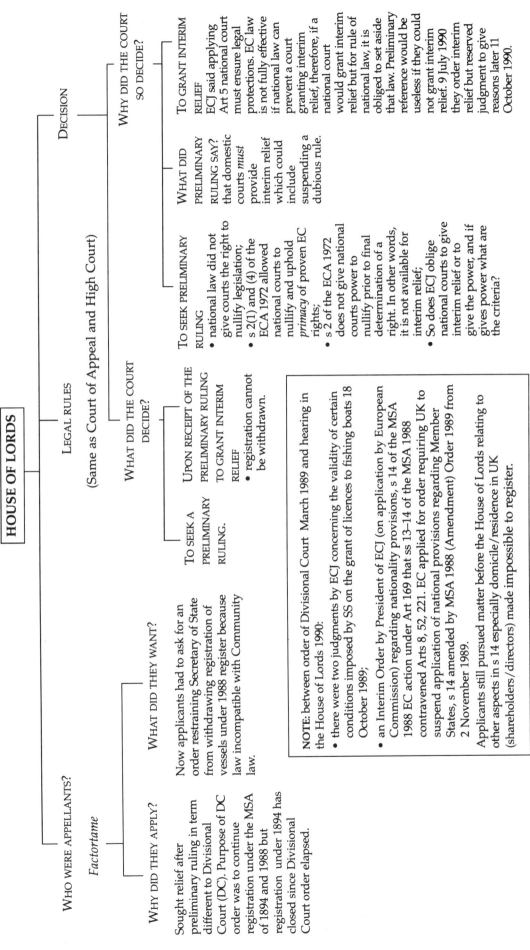

HOUSE OF LORDS

WHO WERE APPELLANTS?

Factortame

WHY DID THEY APPLY?

Sought relief after preliminary ruling in term different to Divisional Court (DC). Purpose of DC order was to continue registration under the MSA of 1894 and 1988 but registration under 1894 has closed since Divisional Court order elapsed.

WHAT DID THEY WANT?

Now applicants had to ask for an order restraining Secretary of State from withdrawing registration of vessels under 1988 register because law incompatible with Community law.

LEGAL RULES

(Same as Court of Appeal and High Court)

WHAT DID THE COURT DECIDE?

TO SEEK A PRELIMINARY RULING.

UPON RECEIPT OF THE PRELIMINARY RULING TO GRANT INTERIM RELIEF
• registration *cannot* be withdrawn.

NOTE: between order of Divisional Court March 1989 and hearing in the House of Lords 1990:
• there were two judgments by ECJ concerning the validity of certain conditions imposed by SS on the grant of licences to fishing boats 18 October 1989;
• an Interim Order by President of ECJ (on application by European Commission) regarding nationality provisions, s 14 of the MSA 1988 EC action under Art 169 that ss 13–14 of the MSA 1988 contravened Arts 8, 52, 221. EC applied for order requiring UK to suspend application of national provisions regarding Member States, s 14 amended by MSA 1988 (Amendment) Order 1989 from 2 November 1989.

Applicants still pursued matter before the House of Lords relating to other aspects in s 14 especially domicile/residence in UK (shareholders/directors) made impossible to register.

DECISION

WHY DID THE COURT SO DECIDE?

TO SEEK PRELIMINARY RULING
• national law did not give courts the right to nullify legislation;
• s 2(1) and (4) of the ECA 1972 allowed national courts to nullify and uphold *primacy* of proven EC rights;
• s 2 of the ECA 1972 does not give national courts power to nullify prior to final determination of a right. In other words, it is not available for interim relief;
• So does ECJ oblige national courts to give interim relief or to give the power, and if gives power what are the criteria?

WHAT DID PRELIMINARY RULING SAY? that domestic courts *must* provide interim relief which could include suspending a dubious rule.

TO GRANT INTERIM RELIEF
ECJ said applying Art 5 national court must ensure legal protections. EC law is not fully effective if national law can prevent a court granting interim relief, therefore, if a national court would grant interim relief but for rule of national law, it is obliged to set aside that law. Preliminary reference would be useless if they could not grant interim relief. 9 July 1990 they order interim relief but reserved judgment to give reasons later 11 October 1990.

Figure 11.10: diagram indicating actions/processes/issues/rules involved in *Factortame* and *Factortame (No 2)* (information solely derived from the cases and Tillotson)

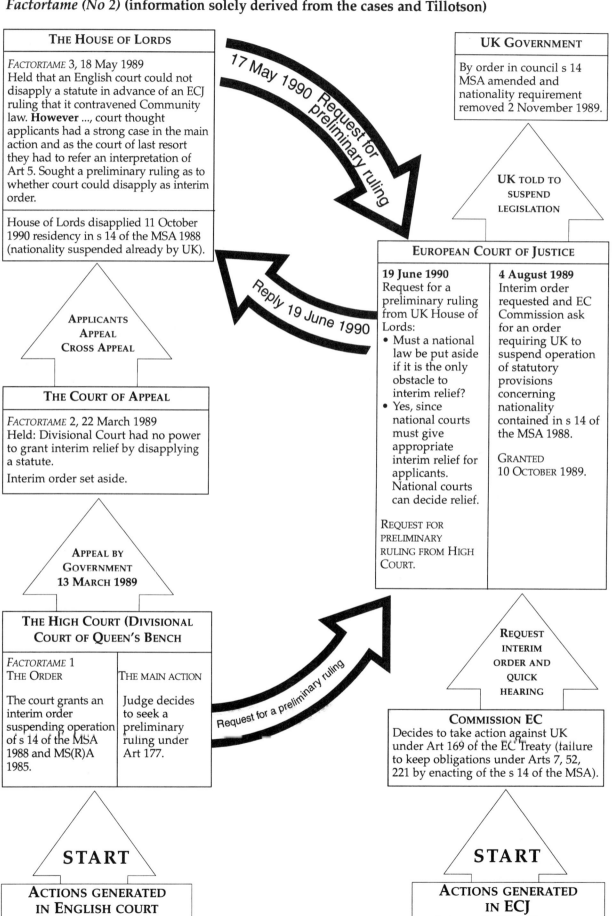

CHAPTER 12

CONCLUSIONS

This text has attempted to provide a clearer view of the practicalities of reading legal texts, both primary and secondary. Ways have been suggested of 'breaking into' texts, to understand the flexibility, and the inherent unreliability of language.

The power of 'the word' and of language generally were signalled at the beginning. The conclusion finishes by signalling – and no more, for this text is eminently a practical manual – that only a partial understanding is reached if one does not consider the particular power of law, of the power of the authority of law, attached to the flexibility of words; the power of law's context, of status; the power of the privileging of law over other institutions, over other words. Law is applied, used or created by people in roles dealing with the memories of the law. 'The question of interpretation is that of whose memory, whose order of reference, does the law institute' (Goodrich, 1990, p 253).

Much time has been spent looking at mechanistic schemes for understanding legal words, legal texts, intertextual and intratextual links signalled as signposts along the way to that understanding, or even finding, the arguments for the outcome of the case. But, as Goodrich has stated, 'reading is never innocent' (Goodrich, 1990, p 231).

There are vast dimensions of analysis untouched, ready for the politician, the philosopher, feminist, criminologist, sociologist. There is a range of ever present yet buried motivational issues – why did the judge adopt that interpretation? Which rationale for adopting that interpretation do 'I' believe? (The rationale about political decision making or the rationale about the literal meaning or some other rationale.)

We have considered raw legal arguments and have noted the reasons given to support outcomes. Valuable issues can be raised by asking: 'OK, but why didn't the judge take another plausible interpretation?'

Judgments are the end process after parties and witnesses put their side, via official and tortuous questioning. In places where rules of evidence, magistrates and judges control what is and what is not said; by whom and how it is said. From the stilted collection of words, judgment is seamlessly created. Lawyers, judges, officials control definitions too – as well as choose interim and ultimate interpretations.

Legal texts are never unambiguous representations of the law, they are the words from which interpretations flow. At the level of the obvious, the voice of consensus states '*we* all *know* what this means, *don't we*?'. Equally, this can be said in a tone of incredulity, or of ridicule, '*we* all *know* what this means, don't we?' – everything in the authoritative accent and tone.

In our texts, we built one story, one ending. The story could be different and so could the ending. Our bricks are words and slips. After all this practicality – of study skills, English language skills, legal method skills and their interrelationship with substantive law and solving legal problems – all these little building bricks, there is the landscape that decides it all: the officials; the institutions; politics; the judiciary; the police; policy. Why this interpretation and not another?

The critical thinker has to remain engaged not only in micro questions within the text, both at the superficial and the deep readings, but also engage in macro questions at the level of law, politics and culture; at the level of text as social fact, as the product of a culture; continuing the search for underlying assumptions.

Much law degree study will revolve around fighting with cases, reconciling, distinguishing and/or following them and explaining differences of interpretation where some might say there are no differences. Students learn an increasingly larger body of rules and, more and more, the overarching context of institutions and culture shrinks into the background. They are interesting from an academic perspective, but cultural legal content has no place in the everyday life of the law and its mediation of competing interests, and it is in the interest of these legal institutional values that the legal 'story' is the one that covers all. There is a danger that the daily process of doing the law blinds the 'doers' who are on the street (the practitioners) to the motivational influences of some institutional 'doers'.

When deciding what words mean in court, judges make far reaching decisions and maintain that they do not do so on grounds of morality, religion, justice or ethics, but purely as a true interpretation of the words. They support the view that one must believe in the ultimate good of the law and the ultimate ability of the law to determine what the law means. A problem can now be seen. As pointed out above, the law is not an autonomous neutral agent, it is used by people in a social role. Legal texts can be analysed as social texts created by social actors. They are statutory texts communicated via words created by politicians in compromise, they are interpreted by judges for a range of reasons some explicit some not.

The orthodox view is that law is a neutral instrument for the good moral society. Law is objective, rational and logical. Can discussions about law ever be justifiably separated from discussions about power, from discussions of law maintaining society and its political ideology? Access to law making power is only available to players in the higher levels of the political machinery or professionals in the higher judiciary.

Critical thinkers look for hidden assumptions underlying the face value explanations of the neutrality and objective logic of the language, argument and outcomes of the law.

Law is not logical, nor does it have to be. There is social agreement that, for a range of reasons – political, social and moral – English law should be seen to be fair and outrage when it is thought to be not fair. Statutory rules have attempted to engage in behaviour re-direction.

But to apply a rule to a problem requires the clarification of the problem and proof that the facts of the problem as presented are the facts that occurred. Rules have developed which state what must be proved by testimonial or forensic evidence and when evidence itself must be backed up.

Due to the developmental strategies of the common law, its orality of proceeding, the breaking away of the courts from the royal household, the ultimate ascendancy of statutory law and the complete reorganisation of the courts of England and Wales in 1875 and 1978, we now have a system of law which is based upon the reaction to arguments presented to those officials who decide which argument is legitimate, be they negotiators in offices, tribunals and juries, magistrates and appellate courts. This system is being challenged, stretched and changed by the new political and legal order of the European Community.

The English legal system has a concept of legal decision making that masks much discretion with its assertion of logical argument, objectivity, and discriminatory 'common sense'.

The law as language is to be read, interpreted, questioned and seen in its fragmented contexts, to be the object of a healthy scepticism. It should not be invested with qualities it cannot control. Law is not justice – for indeed justice may demand that there be no law.

But that's another story!

PART V

APPENDICES

UNFAIR CONTRACT TERMS ACT 1977

1977 CHAPTER 50

An Act to impose further limits on the extent to which under the law of England and Wales and Northern Ireland civil liability for breach of contract, or for negligence or other breach of duty, can be avoided by means of contract terms and otherwise, and under the law of Scotland civil liability can be avoided by means of contract terms.

[26 October 1977]

Be it enacted by the Queen's most Excellent Majesty by and with the advice and consent of the Lords Spiritual and Temporal, and Commons, in this present Parliament assembled, and by the authority of the same, as follows:

PART I

AMENDMENT OF LAW FOR ENGLAND AND WALES AND NORTHERN IRELAND

Introductory

Scope of Part I

1.– (1) For the purposes of this Part of this Act, 'negligence' means the breach–

(a) of any obligation, arising from the express or implied terms of a contract, to take reasonable care or exercise reasonable skill in the performance of the contract;

(b) of any common law duty to take reasonable care or exercise reasonable skill (but not any stricter duty);

(c) of the common duty of care imposed by the Occupiers' Liability Act 1957 or the Occupiers' Liability Act (Northern Ireland) 1957.

(2) This Part of this Act is subject to Part III; and in relation to contracts, the operation of sections 2 to 4 and 7 is subject to the exceptions made by Schedule 1.

(3) In the case of both contract and tort, sections 2 to 7 apply (except where the contrary is stated in section 6(4)) only to business liability, that is liability for breach of obligations or duties arising—

(a) from things done or to be done by a person in the course of a business (whether his own business or another's); or

(b) from the occupation of premises used for business purposes of the occupier,

and references to liability are to be read accordingly.

(4) In relation to any breach of duty or obligation, it is immaterial for any purpose of this Part of this Act whether the breach was inadvertent or intentional, or whether liability for it arises directly or vicariously.

Negligence liability

Avoidance of liability for negligence, breach of contract, etc.

2.– (1) A person cannot by reference to any contract term or to a notice given to persons generally or to particular persons exclude or restrict his liability for death or personal injury resulting from negligence.

(2) In the case of other loss or damage a person cannot so exclude or restrict his liability for negligence except in so far as the term or notice satisfies the requirement of reasonableness.

(3) Where a contract term or notice purports to exclude or restrict liability for negligence a person's agreement to or awareness of it is not of itself to be taken as indicating his voluntary acceptance of any risk.

Liability arising in contract

3.– (1) This section applies as between contracting parties where one of them deals as consumer or on the other's written standard terms of business.

(2) As against that party, the other cannot by reference to any contract term–

(a) when himself in breach of contract, exclude or restrict any liability of his in respect of the breach; or

(b) claim to be entitled–

(i) to render a contractual performance substantially different from that which was reasonably expected of him, or

(ii) in respect of the whole or any part of his contractual obligation, to render no performance at all,

except in so far as (in any of the cases mentioned above in this subsection) the contract term satisfies the requirement of reasonableness.

Unreasonable indemnity clauses

4.– (1) A person dealing as consumer cannot by reference to any contract term be made to indemnify another person (whether a party to the contract or not) in respect of liability that may be incurred by the other for negligence or breach of contract, except in so far as the contract term satisfies the requirement of reasonableness.

(2) This section applies whether the liability in question–

(a) is directly that of the person to be indemnified or is incurred by him vicariously;

(b) is to the person dealing as consumer or to someone else.

Liability arising from sale or supply of goods

'Guarantee' of consumer goods

5.– (1) In the case of goods of a type ordinarily supplied for private use or consumption, where loss or damage–

(a) arises from the goods proving defective while in consumer use; and

(b) results from the negligence of a person concerned in the manufacture or distribution of the goods,

liability for the loss or damage cannot be excluded or restricted by reference to any contract term or notice contained in or operating by reference to a guarantee of the goods.

(2) For these purposes–

(a) goods are to be regarded as 'in consumer use' when a person is using them, or has them in his possession for use, otherwise than exclusively for the purposes of a business; and

(b) anything in writing is a guarantee if it contains or purports to contain some promise or assurance (however worded or presented) that defects will be made good by complete or partial replacement, or by repair, monetary compensation or otherwise.

(3) This section does not apply as between the parties to a contract under or in pursuance of which possession or ownership of the goods passed.

Sale and hire-purchase

6.– (1) Liability for breach of the obligations arising from–

(a) section 12 of the Sale of Goods Act 1893 (seller's implied undertakings as to title. etc)

(b) section 8 of the Supply of Goods (Implied Terms) Act 1973 (the corresponding thing in relation to hire-purchase),

cannot be excluded or restricted by reference to any contract term.

(2) As against a person dealing as consumer, liability for breach of the obligations arising from–

(a) section 13, 14 or 15 of the 1893 Act (seller's implied undertakings as to conformity of goods with description or sample, or as to their quality or fitness for a particular purpose);

(b) section 9, 10 or 11 of the 1973 Act (the corresponding things in relation to hire-purchase), cannot be excluded or restricted by reference to any contract term.

(3) As against a person dealing otherwise than as consumer, the liability specified in subsection (2) above can be excluded or restricted by reference to a contract term, but only in so far as the term satisfies the requirement of reasonableness.

(4) The liabilities referred to in this section are not only the business liabilities defined by section 1(3), but include those arising under any contract of sale of goods or hire-purchase agreement.

Miscellaneous contracts under which goods pass

7.– (1) Where the possession or ownership of goods passes under or in pursuance of a contract not governed by the law of sale of goods or hire purchase, subsections (2) to (4) below apply as regards the effect (if any) to be given to contract terms excluding or restricting liability for breach of obligation arising by implication of law from the nature of the contract.

(2) As against a person dealing as consumer, liability in respect of the goods' correspondence with description or sample, or their quality or fitness for any particular purpose, cannot be excluded or restricted by reference to any such term.

(3) As against a person dealing otherwise than as consumer, that liability can be excluded or restricted by reference to such a term, but only in so far as the term satisfies the requirement of reasonableness.

(4) Liability in respect of–

(a) the right to transfer ownership of the goods, or give possession; or

(b) the assurance of quiet possession to a person taking goods in pursuance of the contract, cannot be excluded or restricted by reference to any such term except in so far as the term satisfies the requirement of reasonableness.

(5) This section does not apply in the case of goods passing on a redemption of trading stamps within the Trading Stamps Act 1964 or the Trading Stamps Act (Northern Ireland) 1965.

Other provisions about contracts

Misrepresentation

8.– (1) In the Misrepresentation Act 1967, the following is substituted for section 3–

Avoidance of provision excluding liability for misrepresentation

3.   If a contract contains a term which would exclude or restrict–

(a) any liability to which a party to a contract may be subject by reason of any misrepresentation made by him before the contract was made; or

(b) any remedy available to another party to the contract by reason of such a misrepresentation, that term shall be of no effect except in so far as it satisfies the requirement of reasonableness as stated in section 11(1) of the Unfair Contract Terms Act 1977: and it is for those claiming that the term satisfies that requirement to show that it does.'

(2) The same section is substituted for section 3 of the Misrepresentation Act (Northern Ireland) 1967.

Effect of breach

9.– (1) Where for reliance upon it a contract term has to satisfy the requirement of reasonableness, it may be found to do so and be given effect accordingly notwithstanding that the contact has been terminated either by breach or by a party electing to treat it as repudiated.

(2) Where on a breach the contract is nevertheless affirmed by a party entitled to treat it as repudiated, this does not of itself exclude the requirement of reasonableness in relation to any contract term.

Evasion by means of secondary contract

10. A person is not bound by any contract term prejudicing or taking away rights of his which arise under, or in connection with the performance of, another contract, so far as those rights extend to the enforcement of another's liability which this Part of this Act prevents that other from excluding or restricting.

Explanatory provisions

The 'reasonableness' test

11.–(1) In relation to a contract term, the requirement of reasonableness for the purposes of this Part of this Act, section 3 of the Misrepresentation Act 1967 and section 3 of the Misrepresentation Act (Northern Ireland) 1967 is that the term shall have been a fair and reasonable one to be included having regard to the circumstances which were, or ought reasonably to have been, known to or in the contemplation of the parties when the contract was made.

(2) In determining for the purposes of section 6 or 7 above whether a contract term satisfies the requirement of reasonableness, regard shall be had in particular to the matters specified in Schedule 2 to this Act; but this subsection does not prevent the court or arbitrator

from holding, in accordance with any rule of law, that a term which purports to exclude or restrict any relevant liability is not a term of the contract.

(3) In relation to a notice (not being a notice having contractual effect), the requirement of reasonableness under this Act is that it should be fair and reasonable to allow reliance on it, having regard to all the circumstances obtaining when the liability arose or (but for the notice) would have arisen.

(4) Where by reference to a contract term or notice a person seeks to restrict liability to a specified sum of money, and the question arises (under this or any other Act) whether the term or notice satisfies the requirement of reasonableness, regard shall be had in particular (but without prejudice to subsection (2) above in the case of contract terms) to–

(a) the resources which he could expect to be available to him for the purpose of meeting the liability should it arise; and

(b) how far it was open to him to cover himself by insurance.

(5) It is for those claiming that a contract term or notice satisfies the requirement of reasonableness to show that it does.

'Dealing as consumer'

12.-(1) A party to a contract 'deals as consumer', in relation to another party if–

(a) he neither makes the contract in the course of a business nor holds himself out as doing so; and

(b) the other party does make the contract in the course of a business:, and

(c) in the case of a contract governed by the law of sale goods or hire-purchase, or by section 7 of this Act, the goods passing under or in pursuance of the contract are of a type ordinarily supplied for private use or consumption.

(2) But on a sale by auction or by competitive tender the buyer is not in any circumstances to be regarded as dealing as consumer.

(3) Subject to this, it is for those claiming that a party does not deal as consumer to show that he does not.

Varieties of exemption clause

13.-(1) To the extent that this Part of this Act prevents the exclusion or restriction of any liability it also prevents–

(a) making the liability or its enforcement subject to restrictive or onerous conditions;

(b) excluding or restricting any right or remedy in respect of the liability, or subjecting a person to any prejudice in consequence of his pursuing any such right or remedy;

(c) excluding or restricting rules of evidence or procedure,

and (to that extent) sections 2 and 5 to 7 also prevent excluding or restricting liability by reference to terms and notices which exclude or restrict the relevant obligation or duty.

(2) But an agreement in writing to submit present or future differences to arbitration is not to be treated under this Part of this Act as excluding or restricting any liability.

Interpretation of Part I

14.-In this Part of this Act–

'business' includes a profession and the activities of any government department or local or public authority;

'goods' has the same meaning as in the Sale of Goods Act 1893;

'hire purchase agreement' has the same meaning as in the Consumer Credit Act 1974;

'negligence' has the meaning given by section 1(1);

'notice' includes an announcement, whether or not in writing, and any other communication or pretended communication; and

'personal injury' includes any disease and any impairment of physical or mental condition.

PART II

AMENDMENT OF LAW FOR SCOTLAND

Scope of Part II

15.–(1) This Part of this Act applies only to contracts, is subject to Part III of this Act and does not affect the validity of any discharge or indemnity given by a person in consideration of the receipt by him of compensation in settlement of any claim which he has.

(2) Subject to subsection (3) below, sections 16 to 18 of this Act apply to any contract only to the extent that the contract–

(a) relates to the transfer of the ownership or possession of goods from one person to another (with or without work having been done on them);

(b) constitutes a contract of service or apprenticeship;

(c) relates to services of whatever kind, including (without prejudice to the foregoing generality) carriage, deposit and pledge, care and custody. mandate, agency, loan and services relating to the use of land;

(d) relates to the liability of an occupier of land to persons entering upon or using that land;

(e) relates to a grant of any right or permission to enter upon or use land not amounting to an estate or interest in the land.

(3) Notwithstanding anything in subsection (2) above, sections 16 to 18–

(a) do not apply to any contract to the extent that the contract–

(i) is a contract of insurance (including a contract to pay an annuity on human life);

(ii) relates to the formation, constitution or dissolution of any body corporate or unincorporated association or partnership;

(b) apply to–

a contract of marine salvage or towage;

a charter party of a ship or hovercraft;

a contract for the carriage of goods by ship or hovercraft; or,

a contract to which subsection (4) below relates,

only to the extent that–

(i) both parties deal or hold themselves out as dealing in the course of a business (and then only in so far as the contract purports to exclude or restrict liability for breach of duty in respect of death or personal injury); or

(ii) the contract is a consumer contract (and then only in favour of the consumer).

(4) This subsection relates to a contract in pursuance of which goods are carried by ship or hovercraft and which either–

(a) specifies ship or hovercraft as the means of carriage over part of the journey to be covered; or

(b) makes no provision as to the means of carriage and does not exclude ship or hovercraft as that means, in so far as the contract operates for and in relation to the carriage of the goods by that means.

[Remainder of Part II omitted.]

SCHEDULES

SCHEDULE 1

SCOPE OF SECTIONS 2 TO 4 AND 7

1. Sections 2 to 4 of this Act do not extend to–

(a) any contract of insurance (including a contract to pay an annuity on human life);

(b) any contract so far as it relates to the creation or transfer of an interest in land, or to the termination of such an interest, whether by extinction, merger, surrender, forfeiture or otherwise;

(c) any contract so far as it relates to the creation or transfer of a right or interest in any patent, trade mark, copyright, registered design, technical or commercial information or other intellectual property, or relates to the termination of any such right or interest;

(d) any contract so far as it relates–

(i) to the formation or dissolution of a company (which means any body corporate or unincorporated association and includes a partnership), or

(ii) to its constitution or the rights or obligations of its corporators or members;

(e) any contract so far as it relates to the creation or transfer of securities or of any right or interest in securities.

2. Section 2(1) extends to–

(a) any contract of marine salvage or towage;

(b) any charter party of a ship or hovercraft; and

(c) any contract for the carriage of goods by ship or hovercraft,

but subject to this sections 2 to 4 and 7 do not extend to any such contract except in favour of a person dealing as consumer.

3. Where goods are carried by ship or hovercraft in pursuance or a contract which either–

(a) specifies that as the means of carriage over part of the journey to be covered; or

(b) makes no provision as to the means of carriage and does not exclude that means,

then sections 2(2), 3 and 4 do not, except in favour of a person dealing as consumer, extend to the contract as it operates for and in relation to the carriage of the goods by that means.

4. Section 2(1) and (2) do not extend to a contract of employment, except in favour of the employee.

5. Section 2(1) does not affect the validity of any discharge and indemnity given by a person, on or in connection with an award to him of compensation for pneumoconiosis

attributable to employment in the coal industry, in respect of any further claim arising from his contracting that disease.

SCHEDULE 2

'GUIDELINES' FOR APPLICATION OF REASONABLENESS TEST

The matters to which regard is to be had in particular for the purposes of sections 6(3), 7(3) and (4), 20 and 21 are any of the following which appear to be relevant–

(a) the strength of the bargaining positions of the parties relative to each other, taking into account (among other things) alternative means by which the customer's requirements could have been met;

(b) whether the customer received an inducement to agree to the term, or in accepting it had an opportunity of entering into a similar contract with other persons, but without having to accept a similar term;

(c) whether the customer knew or ought reasonably to have known of the existence and extent of the term (having regard, among other things, to any custom of the trade and any previous course of dealing between the parties);

(d) where the term excludes or restricts any relevant liability if some condition is not complied with, whether it was reasonable at the time of the contract to expect that compliance with that condition would be practicable;

(e) whether the goods were manufactured, processed or adapted to the special order of the customer.

SCHEDULE 3

AMENDMENT OF ENACTMENTS

In the Sale of Goods Act 1893–

(a) in section 55(1), for the words 'the following provisions of this section' substitute 'the provisions of the Unfair Contract Terms Act 1977';

(b) in section 62(l), in the definition of 'business', for 'local authority or statutory undertaker' substitute 'or local or public authority'.

In the Supply of Goods (Implied Terms) Act 1973 (as originally enacted and as substituted by the Consumer Credit Act 1974–

(a) in section 14(1) for the words from 'conditional sale' to the end substitute 'a conditional sale agreement where the buyer deals as consumer within Part I of the Unfair Contract Terms Act 1977 or, in Scotland, the agreement is a consumer contract within Part II of that Act;

(b) in section 15(l), in the definition of 'business', for 'local authority or statutory undertaker' substitute 'or local or public authority'.

GEORGE MITCHELL (CHESTERHALL) LTD V FINNEY LOCK SEEDS LTD

HOUSE OF LORDS

LORD DIPLOCK, LORD SCARMAN, LORD ROSKILL, LORD BRIDGE OF HARWICH AND LORD BRIGHTMAN

23, 24 MAY, 30 JUNE 1983

...

Lord Diplock: My Lords, this is a case about an exemption clause contained in a contract for the sale of goods (not being a consumer sale) to which the Supply of Goods (Implied Terms) Act 1973 applied. In reliance on the exemption clause the sellers sought to limit their liability to the buyers to a sum which represented only 0.33% of the damage that the buyers had sustained as a result of an undisputed breach of contract by the sellers. The sellers failed before the trial judge, Parker, who, by placing on the language of the exemption clause a strained and artificial meaning, found himself able to hold that the breach of contract in respect of which the buyers sued fell outside the clause. In the Court of Appeal both Oliver LJ and Kerr LJ, by similar processes of strained interpretation, held that the breach was not covered by the exemption clause; but they also held that if the breach had been covered it would in all the circumstances of the case not have been fair or reasonable to allow reliance on the clause, and that accordingly the clause would have been unenforceable under the 1973 Act. Lord Denning MR was alone in holding that the language of the exemption clause was plain and unambiguous, that it would be apparent to anyone who read it that it covered the breach in respect of which the buyers' action was brought, and that the passing of the Supply of Goods (Implied Terms) Act 1973 and its successor, the Unfair Contract Terms Act 1977, had removed from judges the temptation to resort to the device of ascribing to the words appearing in exemption clauses a tortured meaning so as to avoid giving effect to an exclusion or limitation of liability when the judge thought that in the circumstances to do so would be unfair. Lord Denning MR agreed with the other members of the court that the appeal should be dismissed, but solely on the statutory ground under the 1973 Act that it would not be fair and reasonable to allow reliance on the clause.

My Lords, I have had the advantage of reading in advance the speech to be delivered by my noble and learned friend Lord Bridge in favour of dismissing this appeal on grounds which reflect the reasoning although not the inimitable style of Lord Denning MR's judgment in the Court of Appeal.

I agree entirely with Lord Bridge's speech and there is nothing that I could usefully add to it; but I cannot refrain from noting with regret, which is, I am sure, shared by all members of the Appellate Committee of this house, that Lord Denning MR's judgment in the instant case, which was delivered on 29 September 1982, is probably the last in which your Lordships will have the opportunity of enjoying his eminently readable style of exposition and his stimulating and percipient approach to the continuing development of the common law to which he has himself in his judicial lifetime made so outstanding a contribution.

Lord Scarman: My Lords, I have had the advantage of reading in draft the speech to be delivered by my noble and learned friend Lord Bridge. I agree with it, and for the reasons which he gives would dismiss the appeal.

Lord Roskill: My Lords, I have had the advantage of reading in draft the speech to be delivered by my noble and learned friend Lord Bridge. I agree with it, and for the reasons which he gives I would dismiss the appeal.

Lord Bridge of Harwich: [1] My Lords, the appellants are seedmerchants. The respondents are farmers in East Lothian. In December 1973 the respondents ordered from the appellants 30 lb of

Dutch winter white cabbage seeds. The seeds supplied were invoiced as Finney's Late Dutch Special'. The price was £201.60. Finney's Late Dutch Special was the variety required by the respondents. It is a Dutch winter white cabbage which grows particularly well in the acres of East Lothian where the respondents farm, and can be harvested and sold at a favourable price in the spring. The respondents planted some 63 acres of their land with seedlings grown from the seeds supplied by the appellants to produce their cabbage crop for the spring of 1975. In the event, the crop proved to be worthless and had to be ploughed in. This was for two reasons. First, the seeds supplied were not Finney's Late Dutch Special or any other variety of Dutch winter white cabbage, but a variety of autumn cabbage. Second, even as autumn cabbage the seeds were of very inferior quality.

[2] The issues in the appeal arise from three sentences in the conditions of sale indorsed on the appellants' invoice and admittedly embodied in the terms on which the appellants contracted. For ease of reference it will be convenient to number the sentences. Omitting immaterial words they read as follows:

> [1] In the event of any seeds or plants sold or agreed to be sold by us not complying with the express terms of the contract of sale ... or any seeds or plants proving defective in varietal purity we will, at our option, replace the defective seeds or plants, free of charge to the buyer or will refund all payments made to us by the buyer in respect of the defective seeds or plants and this shall be the limit of our obligation. [2] We hereby exclude all liability for any loss or damage arising from the use of any seeds or plants supplied by us and for any consequential loss or damage arising out of such use or any failure in the performance of or any defect in any seeds or plants supplied by us or for any other loss or damage whatsoever save for, at our option, liability for any such replacement or refund as aforesaid. [3] In accordance with the established custom of the seed trade any express or implied condition, statement or warranty, statutory or otherwise, not stated in these Conditions is hereby excluded.

I will refer to the whole as 'the relevant condition' and to the parts as 'cll 1, 2, and 3' of the relevant condition.

[3] The first issue is whether the relevant condition, on its true construction in the context of the contract as a whole, is effective to limit the appellants' liability to a refund of £201.60, the price of the seeds (the common law issue). The second issue is whether, if the common law issue is decided in the appellants' favour, they should nevertheless be precluded from reliance on this limitation of liability pursuant to the provisions of the modified s 55 of the Sale of Goods Act 1979 which is set out in para 11 of Sched I to the Act and which applies to contracts made between 18 May 1973 and 1 February 1978 (the statutory issue).

[4] The trial judge, Parker J, on the basis of evidence that the seeds supplied were incapable of producing a commercially saleable crop, decided the common law issue against the appellants on the ground that

> ... what was supplied... was in no commercial sense vegetable seed at all [but was] the delivery of something wholly different in kind from that which was ordered and which the defendants had agreed to supply.

He accordingly found it unnecessary to decide the statutory issue, but helpfully made some important findings of fact, which are very relevant if that issue falls to be decided. He gave judgment in favour of the respondents for £61,513.78 damages and £30,756 interest. Nothing now turns on these figures, but it is perhaps significant to point out that the damages awarded do not represent merely 'loss of anticipated profit', as was erroneously suggested in the appellants' printed case. The figure includes, as counsel for the appellants very properly accepted, all the costs incurred by the respondents in the cultivation of the worthless crop as well as the profit they would have expected to make from a successful crop if the proper seeds had been supplied.

[5] In the Court of Appeal, the common law issue was decided in favour of the appellants by Lord Denning MR, who said ([1983] 1 All ER 108, p 113; [1983] QB 284, p 296):

On the natural interpretation, I think the condition is sufficient to limit the seed merchants to a refund of the price paid or replacement of the seeds.

Oliver LJ decided the common law issue against the appellants primarily on a ground akin to that of Parker J, albeit somewhat differently expressed. Fastening on the words 'agreed to be sold' in cl 1 of the relevant condition, he held that the clause could not be construed to mean 'in the event of the seeds sold or agreed to be sold by us not being the seed agreed to be sold by us'. Clause 2 of the relevant condition he held to be 'merely a supplement' to cl 1 He thus arrived at the conclusion that the appellants had only succeeded in limiting their liability arising from the supply of seeds which were correctly described as Finney's Late Dutch Special but were defective in quality. As the seeds supplied were not Finney's Late Dutch Special, the relevant condition gave them no protection. Kerr LJ, in whose reasoning Oliver LJ also concurred, decided the common a law issue against use appellants on the ground that the relevant condition was ineffective to limit appellants' liability for a breach of contract which could not have occurred without negligence on the appellants' part, and that the supply of the wrong variety of seeds was such a breach.

[6] The Court of Appeal, however, was unanimous in deciding the statutory issue against the appellants.

[7] In his judgment, Lord Denning MR traces, in his uniquely colourful and graphic style, the history of the courts' approach to contractual clauses excluding or limiting liability, culminating in the intervention of the legislature, first, by the Supply of Goods (Implied Terms) Act 1973, and second, by the Unfair Contract Term Act 1977. My Lords, in considering the common law issue, I will resist the temptation to follow that fascinating trail, but will content myself with references to the two recent decisions of your Lordship's House commonly called the two Securicor cases: *Photo Production Ltd v Securicor Transport Ltd* [1980] 1 All ER 996; [1980] AG 827 and *Ailsa Craig Fishing Co Ltd v Malvern Fishing Co Ltd* [1983] 1 All ER 101.

[8] The *Photo Production* case gave the final quietus to the doctrine that a 'fundamental breach' of contract deprived the party in breach of the benefit of clauses in the contract excluding or limiting his liability. The *Ailsa Craig* case drew an important distinction between exclusion and limitation clauses This is clearly stated by Lord Fraser ([1983] 1 All ER 101, p 105):

> There are later authorities which lay down very strict principles to be applied when considering the effect of clauses of exclusion or of indemnity: see particularly the Privy Council case of *Canada Steamship Lines Ltd v R* [1952] I All ER 305 at 310 [1952] AC 192, 208, where Lord Morton, delivering the advice of the Board, summarised the principles in terms which have recently been applied by this House in *Smith v UMB Chrysler (Scotland) Ltd* 1978 SC (HL) 1. In my opinion these principles are not applicable in their full rigour when considering the effect of conditions merely limiting liability. Such conditions will of course be read contra proferentem and must be clearly expressed, but there is no reason why they should be judged by the specially exacting standards which arc applied to exclusion and indemnity clauses.

[9] My Lords, it seems to me, with all due deference, that the judgments of the trial judge and of Oliver LJ on the common law issue come dangerously near to reintroducing by the back door the doctrine of 'fundamental breach' which this House in the *Photo Production* case had so forcibly evicted by the front. The judge discusses what I may call the 'peas and beans' or 'chalk and cheese' cases, ie, those in which it has been held that exemption clauses do not apply where there has been a contract to sell one thing, eg, a motor car, and the seller has supplied quite another thing, eg, a bicycle. I hasten to add that the judge can in no way be criticised for adopting this approach since counsel appearing for the appellants at the trial had conceded 'that, if what had been delivered had been beetroot seed or carrot seed, he would not be able to rely on the clause'. Different counsel appeared for the appellants in the Court of Appeal, where that concession was withdrawn.

[10] In my opinion, this is not a 'peas and beans' case at all. The relevant condition applies to 'seeds'. Clause 1 refers to 'seeds sold' and 'seeds agreed to be sold.' Clause 2 refers to 'seeds supplied'. As I have pointed out, Oliver LJ concentrated his attention on the phrase 'seeds agreed to be sold'. I can see no justification, with respect, for allowing this phrase alone to dictate the interpretation of the relevant condition, still less for treating cl 2 as 'merely a supplement' to cl 1.

Clause 2 is perfectly clear and unambiguous. The reference to 'seeds agreed to be sold' as well as to 'seeds sold' in cl 1 reflects the same dichotomy as the definition of 'sale' in the Sale of Goods Act 1979 as including a bargain and sale as well as a sale and delivery. The defective seeds in this case were seeds sold and delivered, just as clearly as they were seeds supplied, by the appellants to the respondents. The relevant condition, read as a whole, unambiguously limits the appellants' liability to a replacement of the seeds or refund of the price. It is only possible to read an ambiguity into it by the process of strained construction which was deprecated by Lord Diplock in the *Photo Production* case [1980] 1 All ER 556, p 568, [1980] AC 82, p 851 and by Lord Wilberforce in the *Ailsa Craig* case [1983] 1 All ER 101, p 102.

[11] In holding that the relevant condition was ineffective to limit the appellants' liability for a breach of contract caused by their negligence, Kerr LJ applied the principles stated by Lord Morton giving the judgment of the Privy Council in *Canada Steamship Lines Ltd v R* [1952] 1 All ER 303, p 310; [1952] AC 192, p 208. Kerr LJ stated correctly that this case was also referred to by Lord Fraser in the *Ailsa Craig* case [1983] 1 All ER 101, p 105. He omitted, however, to notice that, as appears from the passage from Lord Fraser's speech which I have already cited, the whole point of Lord Fraser's reference was to express his opinion that the very strict principles laid down in the *Canada Steamship Lines* case as applicable to exclusion and indemnity clauses cannot be applied in their full rigour to limitation clauses. Lord Wilberforce's speech contains a passage to the like effect, and Lord Elwyn Jones, Lord Salmon and Lord Lowry agreed with both speeches Having once reached a conclusion in the instant case that the relevant condition unambiguously limited the appellants' liability, I know of no principle of construction which can properly be applied to confine the effect of the limitation to breaches of contract arising without negligence on the part of the appellants. In agreement with Lord Denning MR, I would decide the common law issue in the appellants' favour.

[12] The statutory issue turns, as already indicated, on the application of the provisions of the modified s 55 of the Sale of Goods Act 1979, as set out in para 11 of Sched I to the Act. The 1979 Act is a pure consolidation. The purpose of the modified s 55 is to preserve the law as it stood from 18 May 1973 to 1 February 1978 in relation to contracts made between those two dates. The significance of the dates is that the first was the date when the Supply of Goods (Implied Terms) Act 1973 came into force containing the provision now re-enacted by the modified s 55, the second was the date when the Unfair Contract Terms Act 1977 came into force and superseded the relevant provisions of the 1973 Act by more radical and far-reaching provisions in relation to contracts made thereafter.

[13] The relevant subsections of the modified s 55 provide as follows:

(1) Where a right, duty or liability would arise under a contract of sale of goods by implication of law, it may be negatived or varied by express agreement ..., but the preceding provision has effect subject to the following provisions of this section ...

(4) In the case of a contract of sale of goods, any term of that or any other contract exempting from all or any of the provisions of s 13, 14 or 15 above is void in the case of a consumer sale and is, in any other case, not enforceable to the extent that it is shown that it would not be fair or reasonable to allow reliance on the term.

(5) In determining for the purposes of sub-s (4) above whether or not reliance on any such term would be fair or reasonable regard shall be had to all the circumstances of the case and in particular to the following matters – (a) the strength of the bargaining positions of the seller and buyer relative to each other, taking into account, among other things, the availability of suitable alternative products and sources of supply; (b) whether the buyer received an inducement to agree to the term or in accepting it had an opportunity of buying, the goods or suitable alternatives without it from any source of supply; (c) whether the buyer knew or ought reasonably to have known of the existence and extent of the term (having regard, among other things, to any previous course of dealing between the parties); (d) where the term exempts from all or any of the provisions of s 13, 14 or 15 above if any condition is not complied with, whether it was reasonable at the time of the contract to expect that compliance with that condition would be practicable; (e) whether the goods were manufactured, processed, or adapted to the special order of the buyer ...

(9) Any reference in this section to a term exempting from all or any of the provisions of any section of this Act is a reference to a term which purports to exclude or restrict, or has the effect of excluding or restricting, the operation of all or any of the provisions of that section, or the exercise of a right conferred by any provision of that section, or any liability of the seller for breach of a condition or warranty implied by any provision of that section ...

[14] The contract between the appellants and the respondents was not a 'consumer sale', as defined for the purpose of these provisions. The effect of cl 3 of the relevant condition is to exclude, *inter alia*, the terms implied by ss 13 and 14 of the Act that the seeds sold by description should correspond to the description and be of merchantable quality and to substitute therefor the express but limited obligations undertaken by the appellants under cl 1 and 2. The statutory issue, therefore, turns on the words in s 55(4) 'to the extent that it is shown that it would not be fair or reasonable to allow reliance on this restriction of the appellants' liabilities, having regard to the matters referred to in sub-s (5).

[15] This is the first time your Lordships' House has had to consider a modern statutory provision giving the court power to override contractual terms excluding or restricting liability, which depends on the court's view of what is 'fair and reasonable'. The particular provision of the modified s 55 of the 1979 Act which applies in the instant case is of limited and diminishing importance. But the several provisions of the Unfair Contract Terms Act 1977 which depend on 'the requirement of reasonableness', defined in s 11 by reference to what is 'fair and reasonable', albeit in a different context, are likely to come before the courts with increasing frequency. It may, therefore, be appropriate to consider how an original decision what is 'fair and reasonable' made in the application of any of these provisions should be approached by an appellate court. It would not be accurate to describe such a decision as an exercise of discretion. But a decision under any of the provisions referred to will have this in common with the exercises of a discretion, that, in having regard to the various matters to which the modified s 55(5) of the 1979 Act, or s 11 of the 1977 Act direct attention, the court must entertain a whole range of considerations, put there in the scales on one side or the other and decide at the end of the day on which side the balance comes down. There will sometimes be room for a legitimate difference of judicial opinion as to what the answer should be, where it will be impossible to say that one view is demonstrably wrong and the other demonstrably right. It must follow, in my view, that, when asked to review such a decision on appeal, the appellate court should treat the original decision with the utmost respect and refrain from interference with it unless satisfied that it proceeded on some erroneous principle or was plainly and obviously wrong.

[16] Turning back to the modified s 55 of the 1979 Act, it is common ground that the onus was on the respondents to show that it would not be fair or reasonable to allow the appellants to rely on the relevant condition as limiting their liability. It was argued for the appellants that the court must have regard to the circumstances as at the date of the contract, not after the breach. The basis of the argument was that this was the effect of s 11 of the 1977 Act and that it would be wrong to construe the modified s 55 of the Act as having a different effect. Assuming the premise is correct, the conclusion does not follow The provisions of the 1977 Act cannot be considered in construing the prior enactment's now embodied in the modified s 55 of the 1979 Act. But, in any event, the language of sub-ss (4) and (9) of that section is clear and unambiguous. The question whether it is fair or reasonable to allow reliance on a term excluding or limiting liability for breach of contract can only arise after the breach. The nature of the breach and the circumstances in which it occurred cannot possibly be excluded from 'all the circumstances of the case' to which regard must be had.

[17] The only other question of construction debated in the course of the argument was the meaning to be attached to the words 'to the extent that' in sub-s (4) and, in particular, whether they permit the court to hold that it would be fair and reasonable to allow partial reliance on a limitation clause and, for example, to decide in the instant case that the respondents should recover, say, half their consequential damage. I incline to the view that, in their context, the words are equivalent to 'in so far as' or 'in circumstances in which' and do not permit the kind of judgment of Solomon illustrated by the example.

[18] But for the purpose of deciding this appeal I find it unnecessary to express a concluded view on this question.

[19] My Lords, at long last I turn to the application of the statutory language to the circumstances of the case. Of the particular matters to which attention is directed by paras (a) to (e) of s 55(5) only those in paras (a) to (c) are relevant. As to para (c), the respondents admittedly knew of the relevant condition (they had dealt with the appellants for many years) and, if they had read it, particularly cl 2, they would, I think, as laymen rather than lawyers, have had no difficulty in understanding what it said. This and the magnitude of the damages claimed in proportion to the price of the seeds sold are factors which weigh in the scales in the appellants' favour.

[20] The question of relative bargaining strength under para (a) and of the opportunity to buy seeds without a limitation of the seedsman's liability under para (b) were interrelated. The evidence was that a similar limitation of liability was universally embodied in the terms of trade between seedsmen and farmers and had been so for very many years. The limitation had never been negotiated between representative bodies but, on the other hand, had not been the subject of any protest by the National Farmers' Union. These factors, if considered in isolation, might have been equivocal. The decisive factor, however, appears from the evidence of four witnesses called for the appellants, independent seedsmen, the chairman of the appellant company, and a director of a sister company (both being wholly-owned subsidiaries of the same parent). They said that it had always been their practice, unsuccessfully attempted in the instant case, to negotiate settlements of farmers claims for damages in excess of the price of the seeds, if they thought that the claims were 'genuine' and 'justified'. This evidence indicated a clear recognition by seedsmen in general, and the appellants in particular, that reliance on the limitation of liability imposed by the relevant condition would not be fair or reasonable.

[21] Two further factors, if more were needed, weigh the scales in favour of the respondent The supply of autumn, instead of winter cabbage seed was due to the negligence of the appellants' sister company. Irrespective of its quality, the autumn variety supplied could not, according to the appellants' own evidence, be grown commercially in East Lothian. Finally, as the trial judge found, seedsmen could insure against the risk of crop failure caused by supply of the wrong variety of seeds without materially increasing the price of seeds.

[22] My Lords, even if I felt doubts about the statutory issue, I should not, for the reasons explained earlier, think it right to interfere with the unanimous original decision of that issue by the Court of Appeal. As it is, I feel no such doubts. If I were making the original decision, I should conclude without hesitation that it would not be fair or reasonable to allow the appellants to rely on the contractual limitation of their liability.

I would dismiss the appeal.

Lord Brightman: My Lords, I would dismiss this appeal for the reasons given by my noble and learned friend Lord Bridge.

Appeal dismissed.

Solicitors: *Davidson Doughty & Co* (for the appellants); *McKenna & Co* (for the respondents).

Mary Rose Plummer, Barrister

VAN GEND EN LOOS

In Case 26/62

(1) Reference to the Court under sub-paragraph (a) of the first paragraph and under the third paragraph of Article 177 of the Treaty establishing the European Economic Community by the Tariefcommissie, a Netherlands administrative tribunal having final jurisdiction in revenue cases, for a preliminary ruling in the action pending before that court between

(2) NV Algemene Transport-En Expeditie Onderneming Van Gend en Loos, having its registered office at Utrecht, represented by HG Stibbe and LFD ter Kuile, both Advocates of Amsterdam, with an address for service in Luxemburg at the Consulate-General of the Kingdom of the Netherlands

AND

(3) Nederlandse Administratie Der Belastingen (Netherlands Inland Revenue Administration), represented by the Inspector of Customs and Excise at Zaandam, with an address for service in Luxemburg at the Netherlands Embassy

(4) on the following questions:

    (1) whether Article 12 of the EEC Treaty has direct application within the territory of a Member State, in other words, whether nationals of such a State can, on the basis of the article in question, lay claim to individual rights which the courts must protect;

    (2) in the event of an affirmative reply, whether the application of an import duty of 8% to the import into the Netherlands by the applicant in the main action of ureaformaldehyde originating in the Federal Republic of Germany represented an unlawful increase within the meaning of Article 12 of the EEC Treaty or whether it was in this case a reasonable alteration of the duty applicable before 1 March 1960, an alteration which, although amounting to an increase from the arithmetical point of view, is nevertheless not to be regarded as prohibited under the terms of Article 12.

(5) THE COURT

composed of: AM Donner (President), L Delvaux and R Rossi (Presidents of Chambers), O Riese, ch, L Hammes (Rapporteur), A Trabucchi and R Lecourt (Judges)

Advocate-General K Roemer

Registrar: A Van Houtte

gives the following

JUDGMENT

Issues of fact and of law

I   FACTS AND PROCEDURE

(6) The facts and the procedure may be summarised as follows:

1   On 9 September 1960 the Company NV Algemene Transport-en Expeditie Onderneming Van Gend en Loos (hereinafter called 'Van Gend en Loos'), according to a customs declaration of 8 September on form D.5061 imported into the Netherlands from the Federal Republic of Germany a quantity of ureaformaldehyde described in the import document as 'Harnstoffharz (UF resin) 70, aqueous emulsion of ureaformaldehyde'.

(7) 2   On the date of importation, the product in question was classified in heading 39.01-a-1 of the tariff of import duties listed in the 'Tariefbesluit' which entered into force on 1 March 1960. The

nomenclature of the 'Tariefbesluit' is taken from the protocol concluded between the Kingdom of Belgium, the Grand Duchy of Luxemburg, and the Kingdom of the Netherlands at Brussels on 25 July 1958, ratified in the Netherlands by the Law of 16 December 1959.

(8) 3 The wording of heading 39.01-a-1 was as follows:

Product of condensation, poly-condensation, and poly-addition, whether modified or not, polymerized, or linear (phenoplasts, aminoplasts, alkyds, allylic polyesters and other non-saturated polyesters. silicones, etc ...):

(a) Liquid or paste products, including emulsions, dispersions, and solutions

	Duties applicable	
	gen %	spec %
1 Aminoplasts in aqueous emulsions, dispersions, or solutions	10%	8%

(9)   4   On this basis, the Dutch revenue authorities applied an ad valorem import duty of 8 per cent to the importation in question.

(10) 5   On 20 September 1960 Van Gend en Loos lodged an objection with the Inspector of Customs and Excise at Zaandam against the application of this duty in the present case. The company put forward in particular the following arguments:

(11) On 1 January 1958, the date on which the EEC Treaty entered into force, aminoplasts in emulsion were classified under heading 279-a-2 of the tariff in the 'Tariefbesluit' of 1947, and charged with an ad valorem import duty of 3%. In the 'Tariefbesluit' which entered into force on 1 March , heading 279-a-2 was replaced by heading 39.01-a.

(12) Instead of applying, in respect of intra-Community trade, an import duty of 3 per cent uniformly to all products under the old heading 279-a-2, a subdivision was created: 39.01-a-1, which contained only aminoplasts in aqueous emulsions, dispersions, or solutions, and in respect of which import duty was fixed at 8 per cent. For the other products in heading 39.01-a, which also had been included in the old heading 279-a-2, the import duty of 3% applied on 1 January 1958 was maintained.

(13) By thus increasing the import duty on the product in question after the entry into force of the EEC Treaty, the Dutch Government infringed Article 12 of that Treaty, which provides that Member States shall refrain from introducing between themselves any new customs duties on imports or exports or any charges having equivalent effect, and from increasing those which they already apply in their trade with each other.

(14) 6   The objection of Van Gend en Loos was dismissed on 6 March 1961 by the Inspector of Customs and Excise at Zaandam on the ground of inadmissibility, because it was not directed against the actual application of the tariff but against the rate.

(15) 7   Van Gend en Loos appealed against this decision to the Tariefcommissie, Amsterdam, on 4 April 1961.

(16) 8   The case was heard by the Tariefcommissie on 21 May 1962. In support of its application for the annulment of the contested decision Van Gend en Loos put forward the arguments already submitted in its objection of 20 September 1960. The Nederlandse Administratie der Belastingen replied in particular that when the EEC Treaty entered into force the product in question was not charged under the heading 279-a-2 with a duty of only 3% but, because of its composition and intended application, was classified under heading 332 bis ('synthetic and other adhesives, not stated or included elsewhere') and charged with a duty of 10 per cent so that there had not in fact been any increase.

(17) 9   The Tariefcommissie, without giving a formal decision on the question whether the product in question fell within heading 332 bis or heading 279-a-2 of the 1947 'Tariefbesluit', took the view that the arguments of the parties raised questions concerning the interpretation of the EEC Treaty. It therefore suspended the proceedings and, in conformity with the third paragraph of Article 177 of the Treaty referred to the Court of Justice on 16 August 1962, for a preliminary ruling on the two questions set out above.

(18) 10   The decision of the Tariefcommissie was notified on 23 August 1962 by the Registrar of the Court to the parties to the action, to the Member States, and to the Commission of the EEC.

(19) 11   Pursuant to Article 20 of the Protocol on the Statute of the Court of Justice EEC written observations were submitted to the Court by the parties to the main action, by the Government of the Kingdom of Belgium, the Government of the Federal Republic of Germany the Commission of the EEC and the Kingdom of the Netherlands.

(20) 12   At the public hearing of the Court on 29 November 1962, the oral submissions of the plaintiff in the main action and of the Commission of the EEC were heard. At the same hearing questions were put to them by the Court. Written replies to these were supplied within the prescribed time.

(21) 13   The Advocate-General gave his reasoned oral opinion at the hearing on 12 December 1962, in which he proposed that the Court should in its judgment only answer the first question referred to it and hold that Article 12 of the EEC Treaty imposes a duty only on Member States.

II   ARGUMENTS AND OBSERVATIONS

(22) The arguments contained in the observations submitted in accordance with the second paragraph of Article 20 of the Protocol on the Statute of the Court of Justice of the European Economic Community by the parties to the main action, the Member States, and the Commission may be summarised as follows.

A   THE FIRST QUESTION

Admissibility

(23) The Netherlands Government, the Belgian Government, and the Nederlandse Administratie der Belastingen (which in its statement of case declared that it was in complete agreement with the observations submitted by the Netherlands Government) confirm that the main complaint of Van Gend en Loos against the Government of the Benelux countries is that by the Brussels protocol of 25 July 1958 they infringed Article 12 of the EEC Treaty by increasing after its entry into force a customs duty applied in their trade with other Member States of the communities.

(24) The Netherlands Government disputes whether an alleged infringement of the Treaty by a Member State can be submitted to the judgment of the Court by a procedure other than that laid down by Articles 169 and 170, that is to say on the initiative of another Member State or of the Commission. It maintains in particular that the matter cannot be brought before the Court by means of the procedure of reference for a preliminary ruling under Article 177.

(25) The Court, according to the Netherlands Government, cannot, in the context of the present proceedings, decide a problem of this nature, since it does not relate to the interpretation but to the application of the Treaty in a specific case.

(26) The Belgian Government maintains that the first question is a reference to the Court of a problem of constitutional law, which falls exclusively within the jurisdiction of the Netherlands court.

(27) That court is confronted with two international treaties both of which are part of the national law. It must decide under national law – assuming that they are in fact contradictory which treaty prevails over the other or more exactly whether a prior national law of ratification prevails over a subsequent one.

(28) This is a typical question of national constitutional law which has nothing to do with the interpretation of an Article of the EEC Treaty and is within the exclusive jurisdiction of the Netherlands court, because it can only be answered according the constitutional principles and jurisprudence of the national law of the Netherlands.

(29) The Belgian Government also points out that a decision on the first question referred to the Court is not only unnecessary to enable the Tariefcommissie to give its judgment but cannot even have any influence on the solution to the actual problem which it is asked to resolve.

(30) In fact, whatever answer the Court may give, the Tariefcommissie has to solve the same problem: has it the right to ignore the law of 16 December 1959 ratifying the Brussels Protocol, because it conflicts with an earlier law of 5 December 1957 ratifying the Treaty establishing the EEC?

(31) The question raised is not therefore an appropriate question for a preliminary ruling, since its answer cannot enable the court which has to adjudicate upon merits of the main action to make a final decision in the proceedings pending before it.

(32) The Commission of the EEC, on the other hand, observes that the effect of the provisions of the Treaty on the national law of Member States cannot be determined by the actual national law of each of them but by the Treaty itself. The problem is therefore without doubt one of interpretation of the Treaty.

(33) Further the Commission calls attention to the fact that a finding of inadmissible would have the paradoxical and shocking result that the rights of individuals would be protected in all cases of infringement of Community law except in the case of infringement by a Member State.

On the substance

(34) Van Gend en Loos answers in the affirmative the question whether the article has internal effect.

It maintains in particular that:
- Article 12 is applicable without any preliminary incorporation in the national legislation of Member States, since it only imposes a negative obligation;
- it has direct effect without any further measures of implementation under Community legislation, as all the customs duties applied by Member States in their trade with each other were bound on 1 January 1957 (Article 14 of the Treaty);
- although the Article does not directly refer to the nationals of Member States but to the national authorities, infringement of it adversely affects the fundamental principles of the Community, and individuals as well as the Community must be protected against such infringements;
- it is particularly well adapted for direct application by the national court which must set aside the application of customs duties introduced or increased in breach of its provisions.

(35) The Commission emphasises the importance of the Court's answer to the first question. It will have an effect not only on the interpretation of the provision at issue in a specific case and on the effect which will be attributed to it in the legal systems of Member States but also on certain other provisions of the Treaty which are as clear and complete as Article 12.

(36) According to the Commission an analysis of the legal structure of the Treaty and of the legal system which it establishes shows on the one hand that the Member States did not only intend to undertake mutual commitments but to establish a system of Community law, and on the other hand that they did not wish to withdraw the application of this law from the ordinary jurisdiction of the national courts of law.

(37) However, Community law must be effectively and uniformly applied throughout the whole of the Community.

(38) The result is first that the effect of Community law on the internal law of Member States cannot be determined by this internal law but only by Community law, further that the national courts are bound to apply directly the rules of Community law, and finally that the national court is bound to ensure that the rules of Community law prevail over conflicting national laws even if they are passed later.

(39) The Commission observes in this context that the fact that a community rule is, as regards its form, directed to the States does not of itself take away from individuals who have an interest in it the right to require it to be applied in the national courts.

(40) As regards more particularly the question referred to the Court, the Commission is of the opinion that Article 12 contains a rule of law capable of being effectively applied by the national court.

(41) It is a provision which is perfectly clear in the sense that it creates for Member States a specific unambiguous obligation relating to the extension of their internal law in a matter which directly affects their nationals and it is not affected or qualified by any other provision of the Treaty. It is also a complete and self-sufficient provision in that it does not require on a Community level any new measure to give concrete form to the obligation which it defines.

(42) The Netherlands Government draws a distinction between the question of the internal effect and that of the direct effect (or direct applicability), the first, according to it, being a precondition of the second.

(43) It considers that the question whether a particular provision of the Treaty has an internal effect can only be answered in the affirmative if all the essential elements, namely the intention of the contracting parties and the material terms of the provision under consideration, allows such a conclusion.

(44) With regard to the intention of the parties to the Treaty the Netherlands Government maintains that an examination of the actual wording is sufficient to establish that Article 12 only places an obligation on Member States, who are free to decide how they intend to fulfil this obligation. A comparison with other provisions of the Treaty confirms this finding.

(45) As Article 12 does not have internal effect it cannot, *a fortiori*, have direct effect.

(46) Even if the fact that Article 12 places an obligation on Member States were to be considered as an internal effect, it cannot have direct effect in the sense that it permits the nationals of Member States to assert subjective rights which the courts must protect.

(47) Alternatively, the Netherlands Government argues that, so far as the necessary conditions for its direct application are concerned, the EEC Treaty does not differ from a standard international treaty. The conclusive factors in this respect are the intention of the parties and the provisions of the Treaty.

(48) However, the question whether under Netherlands constitutional law Article 12 is directly applicable is one concerning the interpretation of Netherlands law and does not come within the jurisdiction of the Court of Justice.

(49) Finally, the Netherlands Government indicates what the effect would be, in its view of an affirmative answer to the first question put by the Tariefcommissie:

- it would upset the system which the authors of the Treaty intended to establish;
- it would create, with regard to the many provisions in Community regulations which expressly impose obligations on Member States, an uncertainty in the law of a kind which could call in question the readiness of these States co-operation in the future;
- it would put in issue the responsibility of States by means of a procedure which was not designed for this purpose.

(50) The Belgian Government maintains that Article 12 is not one of the provisions:
- which are the exception in the Treaty;
- having direct internal effect.

(51) Article 12 does not constitute a rule of law of general application providing that any introduction of a new customs duty or any increase in an existing duty is automatically without effect or is absolutely void. It merely obliges Member States to refrain from taking such measures.

(52) It does not create therefore a directly applicable right which nationals could invoke and enforce. It requires from Governments action at a later date to attain the objective fixed by the Treaty. A national court cannot be asked to enforce compliance with this obligation.

(53) The German Government is also of the opinion that Article 12 of the EEC Treaty does not constitute a legal provision which is directly applicable in all Member States. It imposes on them an international obligation (in the field of customs policy) which must be implemented by national authorities endowed with legislative powers.

(54) Customs duties applicable to a citizen of a Member State of the Community, at least during the transitional period, thus do not derive from the EEC Treaty or the legal measures taken by the institutions, but from legal measures enacted by Member States. Article 12 only lays down the provisions with which they must comply in the customs legislation.

(55) Moreover the obligation laid down only applies to the other contracting Member States.

(56) In German law a legal provision which laid down a customs duty contrary to the provisions of Article 12 would be perfectly valid.

(57) Within the framework of the EEC Treaty the legal protection of nationals of Member States is secured, by provisions derogating from their national constitution system, only in respect of those measures taken by the institutions of the Community which are of direct and individual concern to such nationals.

B   THE SECOND QUESTION

Admissibility

(58) The Netherlands and Belgian Governments are of the opinion that the second as well as the first question is inadmissible.

(59) According to them the answer to the question whether in fact the Brussels Protocol of 1958 represents a failure by those states who are signatories to fulfil the obligations laid down in Article 12 of the EEC Treaty cannot be given in the context of a preliminary ruling, because the issue is the application of the Treaty and not its interpretation. Moreover such an answer presupposes a careful study and a specific evaluation of the facts and circumstances peculiar to a given situation, and this is also inadmissible under Article 177.

(60) The Netherlands Government emphasises, furthermore, that if a failure by a State to fulfil its Community obligations could be brought before the Court by a procedure other than those under Articles 169 and 170 the legal protection of that State would be considerably diminished.

(61) The German Government, without making a formal objection of inadmissibility, maintains that Article 12 only imposes an international obligation on States and that the question whether national rules enacted for its implementation do not comply with this obligation cannot depend upon a decision of the Court under Article 177 since it does not involve the interpretation of the Treaty.

(62) Van Gend en Loos also considers that the direct form of the second question would necessitate an examination of the facts for which the Court has no jurisdiction when it makes a ruling under Article 177. The real question for interpretation according to it [the firm] could be worded as follows:

(63) Is it possible for a derogation from the rules applied before 1 March 1960 (or more accurately, before 1 January 1958) not to be in the nature of an increase prohibited by Article 12 of the Treaty, even though this derogation arithmetically represents an increase?

Grounds of judgment

I PROCEDURE

(64) No objection has been raised concerning the procedural validity of the reference to the Court under Article 177 of the EEC Treaty by the Tariefcommissie, a court or tribunal within the meaning of that Article. Further, no grounds exist for the Court to raise the matter of its own motion.

II THE FIRST QUESTION

A JURISDICTION OF THE COURT

(65) The Government of the Netherlands and the Belgian Government challenge the jurisdiction of the Court on the ground that the reference relates not to the interpretation but to the application of the Treaty in the context of the constitutional law of the Netherlands, and that in particular the Court has no jurisdiction to decide, should the occasion arise, whether the provisions of the EEC Treaty prevail over Netherlands legislation or over other agreements entered into by the Netherlands and incorporated into Dutch national law. The solution of such a problem, it is claimed, falls within the exclusive jurisdiction or the national courts, subject to an application in accordance with the provisions laid down by Articles 169 and 170 of the Treaty.

(66) However in this case the Court is not asked to adjudicate upon the application of the Treaty according to the principles of the national law of the Netherlands, which remains the concern of the national courts, but is asked, in conformity with sub-paragraph (a) of the first paragraph of Article 177 of the Treaty, only to interpret the scope of Article 12 of the said Treaty within the context of Community law and with reference to its effect on individuals. This argument has therefore no legal foundation.

(67) The Belgian Government further argues that the Court has no jurisdiction on the ground that no answer which the Court could give to the first question of the Tariefcommissie would have any bearing on the result of the proceedings brought in that court.

(68) However, in order to confer jurisdiction on the Court in the present case it is necessary only that the question raised should clearly be concerned with the interpretation of the Treaty. The considerations which may have led a national court or tribunal to its choice of questions as well as the relevance which it attributes to such questions in the context of a case before it are excluded from review by the Court of Justice.

(69) It appears from the wording of the questions referred that they relate to the interpretation of the Treaty. The Court therefore has the jurisdiction to answer them. This argument, too, is therefore unfounded.

B ON THE SUBSTANCE OF THE CASE

(70) The first question of the Tariefcommissie is whether Article 12 of the Treaty has direct application in national law in the sense that nationals of Member States may on the basis of this article lay claim to rights which the national courts must protect.

(71) To ascertain whether the provisions of an international treaty extend so far in their effects it is necessary to consider the spirit, the general scheme, and the wording of those provisions.

(72) The objective of the EEC Treaty, which is to establish a Common Market, the functioning of which is of direct concern to interested parties in the Community, implies that this Treaty is more than an agreement which merely creates mutual obligations between the contracting States. This view is confirmed by the preamble to the Treaty which refers not only to governments but to

peoples. It is also confirmed more specifically by the establishment of institutions endowed by the sovereign rights, the exercise of which affects Member States and also their citizens. Furthermore, it must be noted that the nationals of the states brought together in the Community are called upon to co-operate in the functioning of this Community through the intermediary of the European Parliament and the Economic and Social Committee.

(73) In addition, the task assigned to the Court of justice under Article 177, the object of which is to secure uniform interpretation of the Treaty by national courts and tribunals, confirms that the states have acknowledged that Community law has an authority which can be invoked by their nationals before those courts and tribunals.

(74) The conclusion to be drawn from this is that the Community constitutes a new legal order of international law for the benefit of which the States have limited their sovereign rights, albeit within limited fields, and the subjects of which comprise not only Member States but also their nationals. Independently of the legislation of Member States, Community law therefore not only imposes obligations on individuals but is also intended to confer upon them rights which become part of their legal heritage. These rights arise not only where they are expressly granted by the treaty, but also by reason of obligations which the Treaty imposes in a clearly defined way upon individuals as well as upon the Member States and upon the institutions of the Community.

(75) With regard to the general scheme of the Treaty as it relates to customs duties and charges having equivalent effect it must be emphasised that Article 9, which bases the Community upon a customs union, includes as an essential provision the prohibition of these customs duties and charges. This provision is found at the beginning of the part of the Treaty which defines the 'Foundations of the Community'. It is applied and explained by Article 12.

(76) The wording of Article 12 contains a clear and unconditional prohibition which is not a positive but a negative obligation. This obligation, moreover, is not qualified by any reservation on the part of States which would make its implementation conditional upon a positive legislative measure enacted under national law. The very nature of this prohibition makes it ideally adapted to produce direct effects in the legal relationship between Member States and their subjects.

(77) The implementation of Article 12 does not require any legislative intervention on the part of the States. The fact that under this article it is Member States who are made the subject of the negative obligation does not imply that their nationals cannot benefit from this obligation.

(78) In addition the argument based on Articles 169 and 170 of the Treaty put forward by the three Governments which have submitted observations to the Court in their statements of case is misconceived. The fact that these Articles of the Treaty enable the Commission and the Member States to bring before the Court a State which has not fulfilled its obligations does not mean that individuals cannot plead these obligations, should the occasion arise, before a national court, any more than the fact that the Treaty places at the disposal of the Commission ways of ensuring that obligations imposed upon those subject to the Treaty are observed, precludes the possibility, in actions between individuals before a national court, of pleading infringements of these obligations.

(79) A restriction of the guarantees against an infringement of Article 12 by Member States to the procedures under Articles 169 and 170 would remove all direct legal protection of the individual rights of their nationals. There is the risk that recourse to the procedure under these Articles would be ineffective if it were to occur after the implementation of a national decision taken contrary to the provisions of the Treaty.

(80) The vigilance of individuals concerned to protect their rights amounts to an effective supervision in addition to the supervision entrusted by Articles 169 and 170 to the diligence of the Commission and of the Member States.

(81) It follows from the foregoing considerations that, according to the spirit, the general scheme, and the wording of the Treaty, Article 12 must be interpreted as producing direct effects and creating individual rights which national courts must protect.

(82) **III THE SECOND QUESTION**

A THE JURISDICTION OF THE COURT

According to the observations of the Belgian and Netherlands Governments, the wording of this question appears to require, before it can be answered, an examination by the Court of the tariff classification of ureaformaldehyde imported into the Netherlands, a classification on which Van Gend en Loos and the Inspector of Customs and Excise at Zaandam hold different opinions with regard to the 'Tariefbesluit' of 1947. The question clearly does not call for an interpretation of the Treaty but concerns the application of Netherlands customs legislation to the classification of aminoplasts, which is outside the jurisdiction conferred upon the Court of Justice of the European Communities by sub-paragraph (a) of the first paragraph of Article 177.

(83) The Court has therefore no jurisdiction to consider the reference made by the Tariefcommissie.

(84) However, the real meaning of the question put by the Tariefcommissie is whether, in law, an effective increase in customs duties charged on a given product as a result not of an increase in the rate but of a new classification of the product arising from a change of its tariff description contravenes the prohibition in Article 12 of the Treaty.

(85) Viewed in this way the question put is concerned with an interpretation of this provision of the Treaty and more particularly of the meaning which should be given to the concept of duties applied before the treaty entered into force.

(86) Therefore, the Court has jurisdiction to give a ruling on this question.

B ON THE SUBSTANCE

(87) It follows from the wording and the general scheme of Article 12 of the Treaty that, in order to ascertain whether customs duties of charges having equivalent effect have been increased contrary to the prohibition contained in the said Article, regard must be had to the customs duties and charges actually applied at the date of the entry into force of the Treaty.

(88) Further, with regard to the prohibition in Article 12 of the treaty such an illegal increase may arise from a rearrangement of the tariff resulting in the classification of the product under a more highly taxed heading and from an actual increase in the rate of customs duty.

(89) It is of little importance how the increase in customs duties occurred when, after the Treaty entered into force, the same product in the same Member State was subjected to a higher rate of duty.

(90) The application of Article 12, in accordance with the interpretation given above, comes within the jurisdiction of the national court which must enquire whether the dutiable product, in this case ureaformaldehyde originating in the Federal Republic of Germany, is charged under the customs measures brought into force in the Netherlands with an import duty higher than that with which it was charged on 1 January 1958.

(91) The Court has no jurisdiction to check the validity of the conflicting views on this subject which have been submitted to it during the proceedings but must leave them to be determined by the national courts.

IV COSTS

(92) The costs incurred by the Commission of the EEC and the Member States which have submitted their observations to the Court are not recoverable, and as these proceedings are, in so far as the parties to the main action are concerned, a step in the action pending before the Tariefcommissie, the decision as to costs is a matter for that court.

(93) On those grounds:

upon reading the pleadings;

upon hearing the report of the Judge-Rapporteur;

upon hearing the parties;

upon hearing the opinion of the Advocate-General;

having regard to Articles 9, 12, 14, 169, 170 and 177 of the Treaty establishing the European Economic Community;

having regard to the Protocol on the Statute of the Court of Justice of the European Economic Community;

having regard to the Rules of Procedure of the Court of Justice of the European Communities;

THE COURT

(94)   in answer to the questions referred to it for a preliminary ruling by the Tariefcommissie by decision of 16 August 1962, hereby rules:

(95)   1   Article 12 of the Treaty establishing the European Economic Community produces direct effects and creates individual rights which national courts must protect.

(96)   2   In order to ascertain whether customs duties or charges having equivalent effect have been increased contrary to the prohibition contained in Article 12 of the Treaty, regard must be had to the duties and charges actually applied by the Member State in question at the date of the entry into force of the Treaty.

Such an increase can arise both from a rearrangement of the tariff resulting in the classification of the product under a more highly taxed heading and from an increase in the rate of customs duty applied.

(97)   3   The decision as to costs in these proceedings is a matter for the Tariefcommissie.

R v SECRETARY OF STATE FOR TRANSPORT EX P FACTORTAME LTD AND OTHERS

[1989] 2 CMLR 353

REGINA V SECRETARY OF STATE FOR TRANSPORT EX P FACTORTAME LIMITED AND OTHERS

BEFORE THE ENGLISH COURT OF APPEAL

(Lord Donaldson MR; Lord Justice Bingham and Lord Justice Mann)

22 March 1989

[Gaz: GB890322]

ON APPEAL FROM THE ENGLISH HIGH COURT (QUEEN'S BENCH DIVISIONAL COURT)

(Lord Justice Neill and Mr Justice Hodgson)

10 March 1989

[Gaz: GB890310]

JUDGMENT (OF THE DIVISIONAL COURT)

Neill LJ: [1] The applicants in these proceedings comprise a number of companies incorporated under the laws of the United Kingdom and also the directors and shareholders of those companies. An amended list of these companies and individuals is now contained in Annex I to the application.

[2] Apart from three of the applicant companies, which carry on business as managers, the applicant companies are the owners of fishing vessels registered in the United Kingdom and authorised to fish under licence granted by the United Kingdom authorities. The applicants also now include Rawlings (Trawlings) Ltd and its directors and shareholders. Leave was given to join these additional parties as applicants at the outset of the hearing of the appeal on Monday 27 February 1989. At the same time, however, leave was given to Rawlings to be separately represented as the facts relating to this company are different in a number of respects from those relating to the other applicant companies.

[3] The relief sought by the applicants can be stated shortly as follows:

1 A declaration that the provisions of Part II of the Merchant Shipping Act 1988 (the 1988 Act) and the provisions of Part VII of the Merchant Shipping (Registration of Fishing Vessels) Regulations 1988 (the 1988 Regulations) may not be applied to the applicants on the grounds that such application is contrary to the law of the European Economic Community (EEC law) as given effect by the European Communities Act 1972.

2 An order of prohibition prohibiting the Secretary of State for Transport from treating the existing registration of the applicant vessels under Part IV of the Merchant Shipping Act 1894 as having ceased from 1 April 1989 unless the applicants satisfy the conditions of eligibility set out in Part II of the 1988 Act and Part VII of the 1988 Regulations.

[4] Part II of the 1988 act, which came into force on 1 December 1988, introduced a new system of registration of British fishing vessels. It also provided that any registration of a fishing vessel under the relevant provisions of the Merchant Shipping Act 1894 should not continue beyond the end of a period to be subsequently prescribed. By regulation 66 of the 1988 Regulations the end of this period has been prescribed as being 31 March 1989.

[5] The applicant companies between them own or manage 95 British fishing vessels, which are registered under the Merchant Shipping Act 1894. Fifty-three of these vessels were originally

registered in Spain and flew the Spanish flag. Between 1980 and 1983 43 of these 53 vessels were registered as British fishing vessels under the Merchant Shipping Act 1894. Since 1983 the other 10 vessels, which were originally Spanish, have been similarly registered as British fishing vessels under the 1894 Act. The remaining 42 vessels have always been British fishing vessels. These vessels have been purchased by the applicants at various dates, mainly since 1983.

[6] It is common ground that, if the 1988 Act and the 1988 Regulations do apply to the applicants, it will not be possible for these vessels to remain registered or to be re-registered as British fishing vessels after 31 March 1989 so long as they remain in the ownership of the applicant owner companies as at present constituted. The reason is that most of the directors and shareholders of the applicant companies are Spanish citizens. None of the applicant Companies as at present constituted can satisfy the conditions required for a qualified company, as defined in section 14(7) of the 1988 Act. Nor do those directors or shareholders who are Spanish citizens, or who are resident or domiciled in Spain, satisfy the tests therein prescribed for a qualified person. Section 14 of the 1988 Act, so far as is material, provides as follows:

(1) Subject to subsections (3) and (4), a fishing vessel shall only be eligible to be registered as a British fishing vessel if–

    (a) the vessel is British-owned;

    (b) the vessel is managed, and its operations are directed and controlled, from within the United Kingdom; and

    (c) any charterer, manager or operator of the vessel is a qualified person or company.

(2) For the purposes of subsection (1)(a) a fishing vessel is British-owned if

    (a) the legal title to the vessel is vested wholly in one or more qualified persons or companies; and

    (b) the vessel is beneficially owned–

        (i) as to not less than the relevant percentage of the property in the vessel, by one or more qualified persons, or

        (ii) wholly by a qualified company or companies, or

        (iii) by one or more qualified companies and, as to not less than the relevant percentage of the remainder of the property in the vessel, by one or more qualified persons.

(3) The Secretary of State may by regulations specify further requirements which must be satisfied in order for a fishing vessel to be eligible to be registered as a British fishing vessel, being requirements imposed–

    (a) in connection with the implementation of any of the requirements specified in subsection (1)(a) to (c), or

    (b) in addition to the requirements so specified, and appearing to the Secretary of State to be appropriate for securing that such a vessel has a genuine and substantial connection with the United Kingdom.

(4) Where, in the case of any fishing vessel, the Secretary of State is satisfied that–

    (a) the vessel would be eligible to be registered as a British fishing vessel but for the fact that any particular individual, or (as the case may be) each of a number of particular individuals, is not a British citizen (and is accordingly not a qualified person), and

    (b) it would be appropriate to dispense with the requirement of British citizenship in the case of that individual or those individuals, in view of the length of time he has or they have resided in the United Kingdom and been involved in the fishing industry of the United Kingdom,

    the Secretary of State may determine that that requirement should be so dispensed with; and, if he does so, the vessel shall, so long as paragraph (a) above applies to it and any such determination remains in force, be treated for the purposes of this Part as eligible to be registered as a British fishing vessel.

Finally I should read subsection (7) of section 14. That provides as follows:

(7) In this section–

'qualified company' means a company which satisfies the following conditions, namely–

    (a) it is incorporated in the United Kingdom and has its principal place of business there;

    (b) at least the relevant percentage of its shares (taken as a whole), and of each class of its shares, is legally and beneficially owned by one or more qualified persons or companies; and

(c) at least the relevant percentage of its directors are qualified persons;

'qualified person' means–

(a) a person who is a British citizen resident and domiciled in the United Kingdom, or

(b) a local authority in the United Kingdom; and

'the relevant percentage' means 75% or such greater percentage (which may be 100 per cent) as may for the time being be prescribed.

[7] The reasons why the British Government have thought it necessary to introduce this new system of registration were explained in the first affidavit sworn by Mr George William Noble on behalf of the Secretary of State on 3 February 1989 as follows, in paragraph 33:

First it is to ensure that the catch of all vessels on the United Kingdom Register, and consequently fishing against United Kingdom quotas, should enure to the benefit of the United Kingdom fishing industry in general and to local communities dependent on fishing in particular. Secondly, it will enable the United Kingdom authorities to exercise effective control over the activities of United Kingdom registered vessels from the point of view of safety. Thirdly the more effective policing which is now possible will help to achieve the EC conservation objectives and those of the [Common Fishing Policy] and maintain 'the relevant stability' of fishing operations throughout the Community.

It is clear that the Secretary of State relies primarily on the first of these reasons.

[8] The applicants' case is that the conditions imposed by section 14 of the 1988 Act, and the detailed provisions made thereunder in the 1988 Regulations, offend against the basic principles of the Treaty of Rome and against a number of specific articles of the Treaty.

[9] For the respondent Secretary of State it is argued, on the other hand:

1 That Community law does not in any way restrict a Member State's rights to decide who is entitled to be a national of that State, or who is entitled to fly its flag.

2 That, in any event, the new legislation is in conformity with Community law and, indeed, is designed to achieve the Community purposes enshrined in the Common Fisheries Policy.

[10] 1 shall have to look at these rival arguments again later, but first it is necessary to refer to the provisions in the Treaty of Rome on which the applicants rely and to trace, as shortly as possible, the history of the Common Fisheries Policy.

[11] The first Article to which our attention was particularly drawn is Article 7 of the Treaty, which is in these terms:

Within the scope of application of this Treaty, and without prejudice to any special provisions contained therein, any discrimination on grounds of nationality shall be prohibited.

The applicants place great reliance on this article. Next I should refer to Article 34. Paragraph 1 of this Article reads:

Quantitative restrictions on exports, and all measures having equivalent effect, shall be prohibited between Member States.

Title II, in Part Two of the Treaty of Rome, is concerned with agriculture, and we were referred to Articles 38, 39 and 40 in particular in that Title. Article 38 provides, in paragraph 1:

The common market shall extend to agriculture and trade in agricultural products. 'Agricultural products' means the products of the soil, of stock-farming and of fisheries and products of first-stage processing directly related to these products.

In paragraph I of Article 39 are set out the objectives of the Common Agricultural Policy. They are important but, for the purposes of this judgment, I do not think it is necessary for me to set them out *in extenso*. Article 40 provides for the establishment of a common organisation and we were referred in particular to paragraph 3 of Article 40 which provides:

The common organisation established in accordance with paragraph 2 [of Article 40] may include all measures required to attain the objectives set out in Article 39, in particular regulation of prices, aids for the production and marketing of the various products, storage and carry-over arrangements and common machinery for stabilising imports or exports.

The common organisation shall be limited to pursuit of the objectives set out in Article 39 and shall exclude any discrimination between producers or consumers within the Community.

Title III of the Treaty is concerned with the free movement of persons, services and capital. Chapter 1 of this Title relates to workers, Chapter 2 is headed 'Right of Establishment', Chapter 3 is headed 'Services'. We were referred in particular to Articles 52 and 58 in Chapter 2. I should read those two articles:

> Article 52 Within the framework of the provisions set out below, restrictions on the freedom of establishment of nationals of a Member State in the territory of another Member State shall be abolished by progressive stages in the course of the transitional period. Such progressive abolition shall also apply to restrictions on the setting up of agencies, branches, or subsidiaries by nationals (of any Member State established in the territory of any Member State.

> Freedom of establishment shall include the right to take up and pursue activities as self-employed persons and to set up and manage undertakings, in particular companies or firms within the meaning of the second paragraph of Article 53, under the conditions laid down for its own nationals by the law of the country where such establishment is effected, subject to the provisions of the Chapter relating to capital.

Article 58, which deals with companies or firms, is in these terms:

> Companies or firms formed in accordance with the law of a Member State and having their registered office, central administration or principal place of business within the Community shall, for the purposes of this Chapter, be treated in the same way as natural persons who are nationals of Member States.

> 'Companies or firms' means companies or firms constituted under civil or commercial law, including co-operative societies, and other legal persons governed by public or private law, save for those which are non-profit making.

[12] Pausing there, it is relevant to note that in *R v Her Majesty's Treasury ex p the Daily Mail*, the European Court said this about Article 52:

> ... the Court must first point out, as it has done on numerous occasions, that freedom of establishment constitutes one of the fundamental principles of the Community and that the provisions of the Treaty guaranteeing that freedom have been directly applicable since the end of the transitional period. Those provisions secure the right of establishment in another Member State not merely for Community nationals but also for the companies referred to in Article 58.

[13] I come finally to Article 221, which is concerned with the participation in the capital of companies or firms. That article provides as follows:

> Within three years of the entry into force of this Treaty, Member States shall accord nationals of the other Member States the same treatment as their own nationals as regards participation in the capital of companies or firms within the meaning of Article 58, without prejudice to the application of the other provisions of this Treaty.

[14] On the basis of these articles it was argued on behalf of the applicants that they had a number of relevant rights under Community law, including the following:

- (a) the right not to be discriminated against on the grounds of nationality (Article 7);
- (b) the right in the case of the individuals to establish a business anywhere in the EEC (Article 52) (including the right to carry on fishing at sea) and, in the case of the companies (Article 58); and
- (c) the right in the case of the individual applicants to participate in the capital of the applicant companies (Article 221).

[15] It was further argued that these provisions of Community law were provisions which had direct effect and that the applicants' rights would be infringed by the application to them of the 1988 Act and the 1988 Regulations. It was submitted that these rights were fundamental rights which could not be swept away or submerged by the Common Fisheries Policy and that all provisions of the Common Fisheries Policy had to be read subject to these fundamental provisions.

[16] On behalf of the Secretary of State, on the other hand, it was argued that the provisions of the Treaty were of no direct relevance in this case because each Member State has a sovereign right to decide questions of nationality: that is, who are permitted to be nationals and who are permitted to fly the national flag. In the alternative, it was argued, the whole matter was governed by the Common Fisheries Policy, which was established to cope with the special problems in the fishing industry and which recognised the importance, and the need for protection, of national fishing

fleets and national fishing communities, and that the legislation merely gave effect to the Common Fisheries Policy and was therefore wholly consistent with the Community law.

[17] It is therefore necessary to make some reference to the history and purpose of the Common Fisheries Policy. The Common Fisheries Policy was established in October 1970 before the United Kingdom acceded to the Common Market. We were referred to Regulation 2141/70 of 20 October 1970, which laid down a common structural policy for the fishing industry. We were also referred to Regulation 2142/70 of the same date in 1970, which established the common organisation of the market in fishery products. The recitals in these regulations are of importance but, as they are reflected in later regulations, for the sake of brevity 1 shall not refer to them *in extenso* in this judgment.

[18] The United Kingdom acceded to the EEC on 1 January 1973. Since that time the powers of Ministers contained in the Sea Fish (Conservation) Act 1967, as amended, to regulate fisheries has been subject to the provisions of the Common Fisheries Policy.

[19] In 1976 Regulation 2141/71 was repealed and replaced by Regulation 101/76. It will be convenient, to indicate the nature of the Common Fisheries Policy, to refer to the first five recitals in that 1976 Regulation:

> Whereas the establishment of a common organisation of the market in fishery products must be supplemented by the establishment of a common structural policy for the fishing industry;

> Whereas sea fisheries form the most important part of the fishing industry as a whole; whereas they have their own social structure and fish under special conditions;

> Whereas, subject to certain specific conditions concerning the flag or the registration of their ships, Community fishermen must have equal access to and use of fishing grounds in maritime waters coming under the sovereignty or within the jurisdiction of Member States;

> Whereas the Community must be able to adopt measures to safeguard the stocks of fish present in the waters in question;

> Whereas it is important that the fishing industry should develop along rational lines and that those who live by that industry should be assured of a fair standard of living; whereas, to that end, Member States should be authorised to grant financial aid so that these aims may be achieved in accordance with Community rules to be laid down; whereas, moreover, common action to achieve these aims may be financed by the Community, if it relates to the aims referred to in Article 39(1)(a) of the Treaty.

[20] When the Common Fisheries Policy was first established it was then contemplated that the vessels of all Member States should be free to fish up to the beaches of other Member States. In time, however, this policy was changed. By the Hague Resolution of November 1976 the Common Fisheries Policy was extended so as to create a two hundred mile fishing zone in the Community with effect from 1 January 1977. At the same time the Council was empowered to conduct negotiations with other countries outside the EEC with a view to reaching agreement about the use by these countries of their traditional fishing grounds, which fell within the new two hundred mile limit.

[21] The basic rules of the current Common Fisheries Policy are contained in Regulation 170/83, dated 25 January 1983. I shall have to refer to some of the provisions of this regulation in a moment. First, however, I should refer to the Council's declaration on the Common Fisheries Policy which was made in Brussels on 30 May 1980. That provides as follows:

> 1   The Council agrees that the completion of the common fisheries policy is a concomitant part in the solution of the problems with which the Community is confronted at present. To this end the Council undertakes to adopt, in parallel with the application of the decisions which will be taken in other areas, the decisions necessary to ensure that a common overall fisheries policy is put into effect at the latest on 1 January 1981.

> 2   In compliance with the Treaties and in conformity with the Council Resolution of 3 November 1976 (the 'Hague agreement'), this policy should be based on the following guidelines–

>> (a) rational and non discriminatory Community measures for the management of resources, and conservation and reconstitution of stocks so as to ensure their exploitation on a lasting basis in appropriate social and economic conditions;

>> (b) fair distribution of catches having regard most particularly to traditional fishing activities, to the special needs of regions where the local populations are particularly dependent upon fishing and industries allied thereto and to the loss of catch;

    (c) effective controls on the conditions applying to fisheries;

    (d) adoption of structural measures which include a financial contribution by the Community;

    (e) establishment of securely-based fisheries relations with third countries and implementation of agreements already negotiated. In addition, endeavours should be made to conclude further agreements on fishing possibilities, in which the Community – subject to the maintenance of stability on the Community market could also offer trade concessions.

I do not think it is necessary to read paragraphs 3 and 4 of that Regulation. I come back now to Regulation 170/83. The first recital was in these terms:

> Whereas the Council of the European Communities has agreed that the Member States should act in concert to extend their fishing zones to 200 nautical miles with effect from 1 January 1977 along their North Sea and North Atlantic coastlines, without prejudice to action of the same kind in respect of other fishing zones within their jurisdiction, in particular in the Mediterranean; whereas, since that time and on this basis, the Member States concerned have also extended their fishing limits in certain areas of the West Atlantic, the Skagerrak and the Kattegat and the Baltic Sea; over-fishing of stocks of the main species, it is essential that the Community, in the interests of both fishermen and consumers, ensure by an appropriate policy for the protection of fishing grounds that stocks are conserved and reconstituted; whereas it is therefore desirable that the provisions of Council Regulation 101/76 of 19 January 1976 laying down a common structure policy for the fishing industry be supplemented by the establishment of a Community system for the conservation and management of fishery resources that will ensure balanced exploitation ...

Then there are further recitals which refer to provision about regulation of overall catches. The fourth recital says this:

> Whereas the overall catch should be distributed among the Member States.

And the sixth recital says:

> Whereas, in other respects, that stability, given the temporary biological situation of stocks, must safeguard the particular needs of regions where local populations are especially dependent on fisheries and related industries as decided by the Council in its resolution of 3 November 1976 and in particular Annex VII thereto.

The twelfth recital, which I think is the only other one that I need read for present purposes, provides:

> Whereas the creation of a Community system for the conservation and management of fishery resources should be accompanied by the institution of an effective system of supervision of activities in the fishing grounds and on landing.

Three of the Articles of that regulation are relevant. Article 1 provides:

> In order to ensure the protection of fishing grounds, the conservation of the biological resources of the sea and their balanced exploitation on a lasting basis and in appropriate economic and social conditions, a Community system for the conservation and management of fishery resources is hereby established.
>
> For these purposes, the system will consist, in particular, of conservation measures, rules for the use and distribution of resources, special provisions for coastal fishing and supervisory measures.

Article 4 provides:

> 1 The volume of the catches available to the Community referred to in Article 3 shall be distributed between the Member States in a manner which assures each Member State relative stability of fishing activities for each of the stocks considered.

Article 5 provides:

> 1 Member States may exchange all or part of the quotas in respect of a species or group of species allocated to them under Article 4 provided that prior notice is given to the Commission.
>
> 2 Member States shall determine, in accordance with the applicable Community provisions, the detailed rules for the utilisation of the quotas allocated to them. Detailed rules for the application of this paragraph shall be adopted, if necessary, in accordance with the procedure laid down in Article 14.

In addition, we were referred to Regulation 2057/82, made in June 1982 to establish certain control measures for fishing activities for fishing vessels of the Member States. I draw attention to this regulation, because it refers to fishing vessels 'flying the flag' of a Member State. The first recital is in these terms:

> Whereas for catches by fishing vessels flying the flag of, or registered in, a Member State it is important to adopt rules for the control of catches in order to ensure that the limits fixed elsewhere for permissible levels of fishing are observed.

We were referred to a number of other recitals in that regulation, which I do not propose to read at this stage. Title I of the regulation was concerned with the inspection of fishing vessels and their activities and, by Article 1, each Member State was required, within ports situated within its territory and within its maritime waters, to inspect their fishing vessels 'flying the flag of, or registered' in a Member State. Our attention was also drawn to other references to 'fishing vessels flying the flag of or registered in a Member State' contained in Articles 3, 6 and 10 of Regulation 2057/82. Particular importance in this context was attached to paragraph 1 of Article 10 of this regulation, which has now been reproduced as Article 11 of Regulation 2241/87. These Articles are in these terms:

> All catches of a stock or group of stocks subject to quota made by fishing vessels flying the flag of a Member State or registered in a Member State shall be charged against the quota applicable to that State for the stock or group of stocks in question, irrespective of the place of landing.

Regulation 172/83 is also of importance. That regulation fixed the total allowable catches for 1982 and the share of those catches available to the Community, the allocation of that share between Member States and the conditions under which the total allowable catches might be fished. The recitals for this regulation refer to the interests of fishermen, to the fair allocation of total allowable catches among the Member States and, in the fourth recital, provided that particular account was to be taken of traditional fishing activities, the specific needs of areas particularly dependent on fishing and its dependent industries, and the loss of fishing potential in the waters of third countries.

[22] On the basis of these regulations, to which I have drawn attention, and later regulations including Regulation 2241/87, it was emphasised on behalf of the Secretary of State that these regulations repeatedly underlined the importance of the protection of traditional fishing activities, the special needs. of regions where local populations depended upon fishing and industries allied thereto, and the importance of distributing the available fish between the Member States in a manner which ensured each Member State relative stability of fishing activities for each of the stocks which was subject to protection. The regulations, as I have already noted, also made reference to fishing vessels 'flying the flag' of a Member State.

[23] The system adopted by the Council to ensure fair distribution was by the establishment of national quotas. These national quotas were directly linked to vessels flying the flag or registered in the individual Member State. As I have already observed, in Article 10 of the 1983 and Article 11 of the 1987 Regulations, all relevant fish caught by vessels flying the flag counted against the quota of that State. In order to decide how to share out the available fish between Member States the Council took into account the quantities of fish which had been caught, on average, by the fishing fleets of the relevant State between 1973 and 1978.

[24] Once the area governed by the Common Fisheries Policy was extended as from January 1977 to a range of two hundred miles from the coastline of Member States, the Common Fisheries policy began to make an impact on areas of the Eastern Atlantic, including the Western Approaches, which had traditionally been fished by Spanish fishing vessels. Prior to the accession of Spain to the Community in 1986, the rights of Spain to fish in the waters of the Member States was governed by an agreement reached between the EEC and Spain in 1980. This agreement laid down strict limits on fishing by Spanish registered boats.

[25] The principle of national quotas was incorporated into the Act of Accession of 1985 whereby Spain and Portugal became members of the EEC. The Act of Accession prohibited more than 150 Spanish fishing vessels fishing in specified areas.

[26] From about 1980 onwards the applicants and others began to register vessels which had formerly been Spanish fishing vessels (that is, vessels which had formerly flown the flag of Spain)

as British fishing vessels under the Merchant Shipping Act 1894. Some 53 of these vessels are those owned by the applicants. In addition, the applicants and others bought British fishing vessels with a view to using them for fishing in the area covered by the Common Fisheries Policy. The fish were, in the main, destined for the Spanish market.

[27] As time went by the United Kingdom Government became concerned at the growth of the practice whereby Spanish interests were either buying British fishing vessels or re-registering Spanish vessels under the Merchant Shipping Act 1894. The United Kingdom Government therefore decided to make use of the powers contained in section 4 of the Sea Fish (Conservation) Act 1967 to impose some additional conditions for the licences which are required before fishing for stocks which are subject to quotas under the Common Fisheries Policy by vessels ten metres length and over.

[28] These new conditions were announced on 6 December 1985. The conditions were of three kinds; operating, crewing and social security. The conditions were described by Mr Noble in his first affidavit in paragraph 22, and can be summarised as follows. The operating conditions were designed to ensure that the vessels concerned had a real economic link with the United Kingdom ports. That link was to be demonstrated in one of two ways; firstly, by selling a portion of the catch in the United Kingdom (the landing test) or, secondly, by making a specified number of visits to the United Kingdom (the visiting test). The crewing condition required that at least 75% of the crew should he made up of EEC nationals (excluding, for a period, nationals of Spain, Greece and Portugal) ordinarily resident in the United Kingdom. The social security condition required that all the crew should contribute to the United Kingdom's National Insurance Scheme. These conditions came into force in January 1986. They have been challenged by Spanish interests in the European Court in Luxembourg. It has been contended that they are contrary to Community law. The decision of the European Court in the two relevant references is now awaited. The cases have been brought respectively, at the suit of a company called Agegate Ltd and another company called Jaderow Ltd.

[29] In the course of the argument we were referred to the opinions in these two cases of Mischo AG in which he expressed views about the validity of the conditions. In summary, his opinion was this: that the crewing and social security conditions were valid, that the visiting test would be valid provided it did not interfere with exports, but that the landing test (included as part of the operating conditions) was in breach of Article 34 of the EEC Treaty. It should be remembered that earlier I referred to the terms of Article 34.

[30] It has been the contention of the Secretary of State that these conditions have not been observed by the applicants and that the further measures prescribed in the 1988 Act and the 1988 Regulations have been necessary to secure that the purposes of the Common Fisheries Policy are duly carried out, and also to ensure that proper policing and safety control are improved.

[31] Such then, in summary, is the background to this case and these are the relevant provisions both of the Treaty and of the Common Fisheries Policy to which our attention was particularly directed.

[32] In these circumstances, the first question for the consideration of this court is whether it would be right to try to resolve the issues between the parties ourselves or whether we should make a reference to the European Court in accordance with Article 177. In many cases it is right for a court of first instance to attempt to reach a conclusion itself and leave it to a higher court to make a reference to Luxembourg if that is thought appropriate. In the present case, however, I have no hesitation whatever in concluding that we should make a reference now. It is appropriate to look at the terms of Article 177, which provides as follows:

The Court of Justice shall have jurisdiction to give preliminary rulings concerning:

(a) the interpretation of this Treaty;

(b) the validity and interpretation of acts of the institutions of the Community;

(c) the interpretation of the statutes of bodies established by an act of the Council, where those statutes so provide.

> Where such a question is raised before any court or tribunal of a Member State, that court or tribunal may, if it considers that a decision on the question is necessary to enable it to give judgment, request the Court of Justice to give a ruling thereon.

It is apparent, therefore, that before a reference could be made two matters call for consideration. First, the court can only refer the matter to the European Court if it considers that a decision on the question is 'necessary to enable it to give judgment'. It is common ground in the present case that it is necessary to reach a decision on a question of Community law for the purpose of resolving the present case. Thus, it is necessary to determine the interrelation between Community law and the right of a Member State to determine nationality and the conditions which it can impose on those who wish to fly the national flag. It is also necessary to determine the interrelation between Community law as expressed in the Treaty and the special provisions of the Common Fisheries Policy.

[33] Once it has been established that a decision on the question is necessary, it is then for consideration whether the court in the exercise of its discretion should make the reference. The guidelines on the way in which this discretion should be exercised have been laid down in a number of cases, including in particular, *Bulmer v Bollinger* [1974]; *Customs & Excise Commissioners v Samex* [1983]; and *R v Pharmaceutical Society of Great Britain* [1987]. It will be convenient to refer to the judgment of Kerr LJ in the *Pharmaceutical Society* case at p 970, where he says this:

> Many factors may be relevant in considering the exercise of the discretion under the penultimate paragraph of Article 177. The judgment of Lord Denning MR, in *Bulmer Ltd v Bollinger SA* contains a useful list of guidelines which have stood the test of time. They were helpfully reviewed by Bingham J in the Commercial Court in *Customs and Excise Commissioners v Samex*. I do not find it necessary for present purposes to go through these. But I think that the following short extract from this valuable judgment is of considerable relevance to the present case. At p 1055G Bingham J said:
>
> > Sitting as a judge in a national court, asked to decide questions of Community law, I am very conscious of the advantages enjoyed by the Court of Justice. It has a panoramic view of the Community and its institutions, a detailed knowledge of the Treaties and of much subordinate legislation made under them, and an intimate familiarity with the functioning of the Community market which no national judge denied the collective experience of the Court of Justice could hope to achieve. Where questions of administrative intention and practice arise the Court of Justice can receive submissions from the Community institutions ... Where the interests of Member States are affected they can intervene to make their views known. That is a material consideration in this case since there is some slight evidence that the practice of different Member States is divergent.

Later Kerr LJ added this:

> The English authorities show that our courts should exercise great caution in relying on the doctrine of 'acte clair' as a ground for declining to make a reference.

[34] In the present case the Court in Luxembourg is, in my view, in a much better position than any national court to place the provisions of the Common Fisheries Policy in the wider context of the Treaty provisions as a whole. It can also examine, from the point of view of the Community, the important and far-reaching submissions put forward on behalf of the Secretary of State that a Member State is free to determine who is to fly the national flag of a commercial fishing vessel irrespective of any restraints which might appear to be enshrined in the Treaty. I should record that on this aspect of the case the Solicitor General attaches great importance to paragraphs 7 and 9 of the opinion of the Advocate General in the *Jaderow* case, and to a passage in the judgment of *Pesca Valentia Ltd v Minister for Fisheries* [1988]. It is sufficient at this stage merely to cite the opening sentence of paragraph 7 of the Advocate General's opinion:

> The Community law does not there restrict the power which each Member State has under public international law to determine the conditions on which it allows a vessel to fly its flag.

Furthermore, the European Court is much better placed than we are to consider the issue of proportionality. Thus the applicants seek to contend that, in any event, the desired objectives for protecting the fishing communities could be achieved by less restrictive measures. It is also to be assumed that in the present case other Member States, including perhaps Ireland and Spain, may wish to intervene.

[35] Having reached a clear and unambiguous conclusion on that aspect of the case, I must therefore turn to a question of greater difficulty; namely, whether this court has any jurisdiction to grant interim relief pending the determination of the reference. The question of interim relief is, it is said, of crucial importance in the present case because, according to the information which was given to us during the course of the hearing of the appeal, a decision may not be reached by the Court in Luxembourg until about the beginning of 1991.

The application for interim relief

[36] It is accepted on behalf of the Secretary of State that, at any rate in this court, there is binding authority for the proposition that in proceedings for judicial review interim relief by way of an injunction or stay of proceedings is available against the Crown. In *R v Licensing Authority ex p Smith Kline & French Laboratories (No 2)* [1989] the Court of Appeal by a majority approved the decision of my Lord, Hodgson J, in *R v Home Secretary ex p Herbage* [1987]. At p 393G Woolf LJ adopted the reasoning of Hodgson J in *Herbage* at p 886 of the Queen's Bench Report, and Taylor LJ expressed his concurrence at pages 395 to 396.

[37] I understand that the Secretary of State may seek to argue elsewhere that the decision on this matter in Herbage and the majority decision in *Smith, Kline & French (No 2)* are wrong. For present purposes, however, I must proceed on the basis that there is jurisdiction in an appropriate case to grant interim relief against the Crown.

[38] The submission on behalf of the Secretary of State is that, even if interim relief may be available in other cases, the court has no jurisdiction to grant such relief in the present case. In the alternative, it is submitted that as a matter of discretion such relief should not be granted.

[39] The submission on jurisdiction has been put forward on the following lines, which are conveniently summarised in paragraphs in Part 5 of the skeleton argument which has been put before us as follows:

> In the case of delegated legislation [that is the Regulations] it is a well established principle of English law that duly passed legislation is to be enforced unless and until it is declared invalid.

> The court cannot grant interim relief in respect of an Act of Parliament [the Merchant Shipping Act 1988].

> In any event the position in respect of an Act of Parliament must be stronger than the position in respect of delegated legislation.

> There is nothing in Community law which requires the granting of interim relief against a measure which is alleged to be contrary to the Treaty.

[40] The Solicitor General has referred us to the speeches in the House of Lords in *Hoffmann-La Roche v Secretary of State for Trade and Industry* [1975] AC 295 in support of the proposition that, unless and until a statutory instrument is declared to be invalid, it is effective and has the full force of law. This proposition must also apply, even more strongly, in the case of an Act of Parliament: unless and until an Act of Parliament has been disapplied the court cannot make any order which has the effect of preventing the law as declared by Parliament being enforced. It may be, it was said, that in certain circumstances the court will not grant an injunction to enforce a statutory instrument which is impugned as being contrary to Community law, but this does not mean that an English court can take some step by way of injunction or otherwise to prevent the enforcement of a statutory instrument, yet alone the enforcement of a statute.

[41] I should refer to the passages in *Hoffmann-La Roche* on which the Solicitor General placed particular reliance. Lord Reid said this:

> It must be borne in mind that an order made under statutory authority is as much the law of the land as an Act of Parliament unless and until it has been found to be *ultra vires*.

Lord Morris said:

> The order [one which has been affirmed by resolution both in the House of Commons and the House of Lords] then undoubtedly had the force of law. Obedience to it was just as obligatory as would be obedience to an Act of Parliament. There was only the difference that whereas the courts of law could

not declare that an Act of Parliament was *ultra vires* it might be possible for courts of law to declare that the making of the order (even though affirmatively approved by Parliament) was not warranted within the terms of the statutory enactments from which it purported to derive its validity.

Finally, a passage in the speech of Lord Diplock where, under the heading 'The legal status of the order' he said this:

My Lords, in constitutional law a clear distinction can be drawn between an Act of Parliament and subordinate legislation, even though the latter is contained in an order made by statutory instrument approved by resolutions of both Houses of Parliament. Despite this indication that the majority of members of both Houses of the contemporary Parliament regard the order as being for the common weal, I entertain no doubt that the courts have jurisdiction to declare it to be invalid if they are satisfied that in making it the Minister who did so acted outwith the legislative powers conferred upon him by the previous Act of Parliament under which the order purported to be made, and this is so whether the order is ultra vires by reason of its contents (patent defects) or by reason of defects in the procedure followed prior to its being made (latent defects). In so far as there are passages in the judgment of Lord Denning MR in the instant case which may appear to suggest the contrary. I think that they are wrong. Under our legal system, however, the courts as the judicial arm of government do not act on their own initiative. Their jurisdiction to determine that a statutory instrument is ultra vires does not arise until its validity is challenged in proceedings inter partes either brought by one party to enforce the law declared by the instrument against another party or brought by a party whose interests are affected by the law so declared sufficiently directly to give him locus standi to initiate proceedings to challenge the validity of the instrument. Unless there is such a challenge and, if there is, until it has been upheld by judgment of the court, the validity of the statutory instrument and the legality of acts done pursuant to the law declared by it are presumed.

It followed, submitted the Solicitor General, that if the court referred the question of the validity of section 14 and the Regulations to the European Court and made no decision itself, the 1988 Act and the 1988 Regulations remained in full force and effect meanwhile.

[42] I find this a very formidable submission. I am not satisfied, however, that this approach takes sufficient account of the new state of affairs which came into being when the United Kingdom became a Member State of the European Community in January 1973. Twenty years ago the idea that the High Court could question the validity of an Act of Parliament or fail, having construed it, to give effect to it would have been unthinkable. But the High Court now has the duty to take account of and to give effect to European Community law and, where there is a conflict, to prefer the Community law to national law. The judgment of the European Court in *Simmenthal* 1978 is clear. At p 644 appears this passage:

every national court must, in a case within its jurisdiction, apply Community law in its entirety and protect rights which the latter confers on individuals and must accordingly [disapply] any provision of national law which may conflict with it, whether prior or subsequent to the Community rule.

The reason for this is that since the European Communities Act 1972 came into force Community law has been part of English law; where it applies it takes precedence over both primary and secondary legislation. I should refer to part of section 2 of the European Communities Act 1972. Section 2(1) is in these terms:

All such rights, powers. liabilities. obligations and restrictions from time to time created or arising by or under the Treaties, and all such remedies and procedures from time to time provided for by or under the Treaties, as in accordance with the Treaties are without further enactment to be given legal effect or used in the United Kingdom shall be recognised and available in law, and be enforced, allowed and followed accordingly; and the expression 'enforceable Community right' and similar expressions shall be read as referring to one to which this subsection applies.

I should read part of subsection 4:

... any enactment passed or to be passed, other than one contained in this Part of this Act, shall be construed and have effect subject to the foregoing provisions of this section; but, except as maybe provided by any Act passed after this Act, Schedule 2 shall have effect in connection with the powers conferred by this and the following sections of this Act to make Orders in Council and regulations.

The effect of that central part of subsection (4), together with section 2(1) is this, as I understand it: that directly applicable Community provisions are to prevail not only over existing but also over future Acts of Parliament (that is, Acts subsequent to 1972) in so far as those provisions may be inconsistent with such enactments.

[43] For my part, I do not propose to express even a tentative view of the likely result in the present reference, but neither side's arguments in my judgment can be described as weak. They both merit the most careful scrutiny. The applicants' contentions invoke the support of fundamental principles of the Treaty of Rome. The Solicitor General relies on sovereign rights over nationality, and on the special provisions of the Common Fisheries Policy. In these circumstances I think it is right to look at the matter on the basis that the cogent and important arguments put forward on behalf of the applicants are to be set against arguments of a like weight urged with equal force on behalf of the Secretary of State.

[44] What follows from this? In my view, one cannot overemphasise the importance of the principle that, where applicable, Community law is part of the law of England. I should refer to a short passage in the judgment of Lord Denning MR in *Macarthys Ltd v Smith*. In that case the Court of Appeal referred certain questions to the European Court as to the effect of Article 119 of the Treaty on the provisions of the Equal Pay Act 1970. The European Court made a ruling in the matter. It came back to the Court of Appeal and Lord Denning said this:

> It is important now to declare – and it must be made plain – that the provisions of Article 119 of the EEC Treaty take priority over anything in our English statute on equal pay which is inconsistent with Article 119. That priority is given by our own law. It is given by the European Communities Act 1972 itself. Community law is now part of our law; and whenever there is any inconsistency Community law has priority. It is not supplanting English law. It is part of our law which overrides any other part which is inconsistent with it.

Then he turned to consider the facts of that case.

[45] At this stage no decision has been made. Is there some presumption in those circumstances in favour of the recent statute? The Solicitor General in the course of his argument placed reliance on a passage in the decision of the Court of Appeal in *Portsmouth City Council v Richards* which, as far as I know, is not reported but of which we have been provided with a transcript. Judgment was given on 16 November 1988. In the course of his judgment in that case Kerr LJ referred to a statement made by Lord Donaldson MR on the application which had come before the Court of Appeal earlier to adjourn the appeal. Kerr LJ said this:

> Secondly, I echo four sentences from the judgment of the Master of the Rolls on the application to adjourn the appeal in this case, which I have already read; but I repeat them for convenience:
>
> > It is unarguably the case that the mere fact that [there is] a pending reference to the European Court is no ground for refusing interlocutory relief on the basis that the European Court of Justice may say that the Act is void. I can see no difference between the position of the European Court of Justice and the House of Lords. We must continue to enforce the law as it appears to us until we are informed otherwise.

On behalf of the applicants, on the other hand, reliance was placed on the decision in *Polydor Ltd v Harlequin Record Shops Ltd*, where the Court of Appeal refused to grant an injunction to enforce a prohibition on importation contained in section 16(2) of the Copyright Act 1956.

[46] From these cases I obtain this guidance. If the applicants for interim relief have only a weak case the court should not, and probably cannot, grant relief. In the words of the Master of the Rolls, as cited by Kerr LJ in the *Portsmouth* case, the court must enforce the law as it appears to the court to be. The decision in Polydor is really to the same effect. In that case the court took the view that Article 14 of the Portuguese Treaty was indistinguishable from Article 30 of the Treaty of Rome and that therefore, though the final decision rested with the European Court, the plaintiffs claim to have certain rights under the English statute should not be enforced. It appeared to the court that the law was that contained in the provisions of the Treaties.

[47] In the present case, however, I find myself unable at this stage to say what law ought to be enforced. Is section 14 to be applied *simpliciter* unless and until it is disapplied, or should it be read provisionally as being subject to an unexpressed exception excluding those who may have superior rights by virtue of section 2 of the 1972 Act and the relevant articles the Treaty? The European Court itself can make interim orders, as is set out in Articles 185 and 186, but we were not referred to any authorities which show in what circumstances orders under these Articles are made. In any event, it would be some time before this case could come before the Court in Luxembourg, even on an interlocutory basis.

[48] In these circumstances I am satisfied that there is jurisdiction to grant interim relief. It exists in the national court to ensure that justice can be done. Moreover, it is to be remembered that the effect of any interim order in this case is only to suspend the coming into force of the time limit prescribed by statutory instrument. The court is not in a position at this stage to decide what the law is but, in my view, it can preserve the position for the time being if, in the exercise of its discretion, it considers it right to do so.

[49] I turn therefore to the issue of discretion. It is said on behalf of the applicants that if no interim relief is granted the financial consequences for them would be disastrous. The vessels would either have to be sold or laid up and substantial unemployment would be an inevitable consequence. It is stressed that the applicants have no alternative grounds in which they can fish. Moreover, as the law stands at present the applicants have no prospects – at any rate, in any court below the House of Lords recovering damages if they are ultimately successful before the European Court (see *Bourgoin SA v Ministry of Agriculture, Fisheries And Food*).

[50] It is further argued that in the case of certain ports, and, in particular, Milford Haven, the activities of some of the applicants bring substantial benefits to the local community. Details of this contention are set out in the supporting affidavits, including those of Mr John Couceiro, a director of Jaderow Ltd.

[51] At this stage I should also refer to the special position of Rawlings, which is explained by Mr Ramon Yllera, the Managing Director of that company, in his affidavit sworn on 20 February 1989. I should read some of the paragraphs of that affidavit to explain the facts relevant to that company:

> 3 Rawlings is a limited company incorporated in the UK in April 1980. Rawlings is the legal and beneficial owner of the fishing vessel '*Brisca*' which is currently a British fishing boat within the meaning of the 1983 Act being registered under Part IV of the Merchant Shipping Act 1894.

> 4 Rawlings is a company the business of which is wholly carried on in the UK and which is controlled from the UK. It thus satisfies the first test of 'qualified company' in section 14(7)(a). However, although the two directors of Rawlings are both resident in the UK, the condition as to the relevant percentage of the director being of British nationality is not satisfied. This is because I am a Spanish citizen, though I have lived in Milford Haven with my wife and family since June 1986. The other director is John Edwin Crawford, a British citizen who resides in Neyland, Pembrokeshire and who satisfies, I believe, the test in the 1988 Act of a qualified person.

Then he sets out in paragraph 5 the fact that Rawlings employ 14 people, most of whom live in the Milford Haven area. He points out that the *Brisca* is the only vessel which, at the moment, Rawlings owns and operates. Then, in the subsequent paragraphs (particularly at paragraph 15) he sets out the operations of *Brisca* and the difficulties which would result if no interim relief were granted. He says that it would have serious and immediate financial consequences, and also draws attention to the fact that, because of the conditions attaching to the grants for the construction of the vessel, Rawlings cannot dispose of the vessel without the permission of the relevant authorities. Again, for the sake of brevity, I do not propose to read any other part of the affidavit; it can be referred to for the particular facts which are relevant to the case of that applicant.

[52] It is said on behalf of the Secretary of State, on the other hand, that the activities of the applicants are causing very considerable damage to what is described as 'the genuine British fleet', the concern of the Crown is more fully explained in the affidavits which have been sworn by Mr Noble, to which reference can be made. I merely summarise some of the contentions, which are as follows:

(1) the applicants are not part of the genuine British fleet;

(2) the activities of the applicants are hard to police;

(3) in the past (although, it is right to say, now to a lesser degree) fishing by the applicants and other Spanish owned vessels has led to the British quotas being exceeded, particularly in the case of Western Hake, which is a variety of fish which attracts a good price on the Spanish market;

(4) the suggested benefits to which reference was made on behalf of the applicants, to British ports (including, in particular, Milford Haven) are much exaggerated by the applicants and do little, it is said. to reduce the damage to the genuine fishing communities.

[53] In addition, it is submitted on behalf of the Secretary of State that, as this is a public law measure, the ordinary principles laid down in *American Cyanamid* have to be modified to take account of the public interest as expressed both in the Act and, as it is said, in the Common Fisheries Policy, which is specifically designed to protect national communities.

[54] There remain some issues of fact between the parties as to the extent to which the applicants are complying with conditions relating to visits and such matters its periodic surveys. The area of dispute has, however, now been much reduced and it seems that in broad terms the conditions which the Secretary of State seeks to impose are being observed to a substantial degree. The details are set out in schedules which have been put before the court, and to which reference has been made. It is also relevant to record that the applicants have stated that, in so far as any conditions which may be in dispute in the two pending references before the European Community are upheld as valid, they will comply with these conditions.

[55] I see the force of the argument that, if the Common Fisheries Policy is intended to protect traditional fishing communities of the Member States, great importance must be given to any measures which are designed for that purpose. In the present case, however, I am not in the end persuaded on the present evidence that there are identifiable persons or communities whose activities or livelihood are at present being so seriously damaged, or will be so seriously damaged, as to outweigh the very obvious and immediate damage which would be caused by these new provisions if no interim relief were granted to the applicants. The present state of affairs has continued for some time. The applicants are making efforts to comply with the conditions to which they have for the time being agreed, and they have expressed a willingness to comply with all such conditions as may be upheld in the two outstanding references. It is also relevant to note the opinion expressed by the Advocate General in paragraph 41 of his opinion in the *Jaderow* case: the condition that 75% of the fishermen fishing against the quotas of a Member State must ordinarily reside in that Member State and the rule requiring a vessel's periodic presence in a port of that country seems to me sufficient to ensure that the benefit of that Member State's quota actually goes to those truly forming part of that Member State's fishing Community.'

[56] I would therefore exercise my discretion in favour of granting some interim relief. The exact terms of this relief may require to be further considered. I would, however, make two further observations.

1 For my part, I would expect it to be very unusual for a court to exercise its discretion in favour of granting relief against the application of a statute or statutory instrument. In the present case, however, there is a European dimension of great importance, and the whole matter has to be looked at in the context of a gradually developing problem of significance not only to this country but to other countries as well.

2 The continuance of any interim relief should, in my view, be dependent on the proper observance by the applicants of the condition of their licences which may from time to time be lawfully imposed.

[57] Subject to these matters, I would refer the case to the European Court in accordance with Article 177 of the Treaty and, in the meantime, would grant interim relief to the applicants.

Hodgson J: [58] The applicants, with leave, seek judicial review of two decisions of the respondent Secretary of State and of Part II of the Merchant Shipping Act 1988. The relief sought is a declaration backed by prohibition and damages. It is clear that if, now or hereafter, we grant relief the grant will involve holding that the provisions of an Act of Parliament which, in terms, apply to the applicants do not so apply because they contravene Community law.

[59] It is, I think, important to remember that the applicants are seeking a final order. These are not interlocutory proceedings. Were it not for the provisions of Article 177 we should be required today either to grant relief or dismiss the application. Article 177 however, uniquely in English law,

gives the court a discretion to refer questions to another court, that of Europe. If we do refer that will mean that we cannot give the decision now which hereafter we shall have to give. By the court's own motion the parties' right to a decision will be delayed.

[60] The first question to which, therefore, we must address ourselves is whether or not at this stage to make a reference under Article 177. After several days of argument, and the citation of much European authority, we are as well equipped to resolve what is or may be conflict between United Kingdom measures and directly effective provisions of EEC law as an English court could be. Nevertheless, I have no doubt that we ought to make a reference. I so conclude for these reasons:

(1) Speaking entirely for myself, I realise that I am not well qualified 'to place in its context every provision of Community law nor to interpret it in the light of Community law as a whole'. I take that quotation from CILFIT, Case 283/81, paragraph 20. The whole paragraph is even more intimidating to an English judge. It reads:

> Finally, every provision of Community law must be placed in its context and interpreted in the light of the provisions of Community law as a whole, regard being had to the objectives thereof and to its state of evolution at the date on which the provision in question is to be applied.

The relationship between the Common Fisheries Policy and the articles of the Treaty of Rome, in particular Article 7 (discrimination on grounds of nationality), Article 52 (right of establishment) and Article 221, the extent to which the provisions of the Treaty affect the right a Member State to determine the conditions of eligibility for fishing vessels to have access to its flag and questions of proportionality seem to me to be matters much better left to the European Court's decision.

(2) It is of great importance that decisions in the field of administrative law should be given as speedily as possible. It is abundantly clear that, sooner or later, there will be a reference to the European Court. It seems to me that the sooner it is done the better.

(3) It seems to me also that most of the criteria referred to by Lord Denning MR in *HP Bulmer Ltd v J Bollinger SA*, which favour a reference, apply to this case. The answers to the questions to be asked will be conclusive, there have been no previous rulings on the points raised in the case, no one suggests they are acte claire, the facts are sufficiently decided and the questions can be formulated clearly. I do not think anyone underestimates the difficulty and importance of the issues raised.

[61] If we make a reference under Article 177 two things remain to be decided. First, do we have jurisdiction to make an interim order pending an answer to the questions referred? Second, if we have jurisdiction, should we in our discretion exercise it?

[62] The question whether a court has jurisdiction to make an interim order to retain the status quo pending a reference under Article 177 is, of course, one that would never have arisen before the United Kingdom's accession to the Treaty of Rome. Before that a court had no need to consider the question. It was obliged to give its decision there and then, and there was no room for the grant of interim relief. It is not, therefore, surprising that there is a lack of authority on the question.

[63] The respondents rely mainly of [*sic*] the decision of the House of Lords in *Hoffmann-La Roche v Secretary of State for Trade* to support their submission that the court had no jurisdiction to grant interim relief. I do not think that that decision addressed, or is more than marginally relevant to the question which faces us. It was decided at a time when it was unthinkable that there should be in an English court a higher authority than an Act of Parliament: but there is now in English law such a higher authority. My Lord, Neil LJ has cited the dictum of Lord Denning MR in *Macarthys v Smith* which explains the position with his habitual clarity. *Hoffmann-La Roche* was concerned not with primary but with delegated legislation, which can be struck down by the courts on limited grounds. The whole thrust of most of the argument was that while primary legislation is inviolable, delegated legislation is not (see in particular the passage from the speech of Lord Diplock to which my Lord has referred). Primary legislation is still inviolable, save that primacy over all other law is now given to the Treaty and Community law by the European Communities Act 1972.

[64] In *Polydor Ltd and RSO Records v Harlequin Record Shops Ltd*, the plaintiffs had obtained an interlocutory injunction restraining the defendants from importing gramophone records into the United Kingdom, on the grounds that they infringed section 16(2) of the Copyright Act 1956. The Court of Appeal referred the question whether section 16(2) was equivalent to a quantitative restriction on trade under Article 30 of the Treaty to the European Court, but refused to continue the injunction so that, in effect, the English statute was not enforced during the period between reference and decision. It is true that both Ormrod LJ and Templeman LJ (as he then was) thought, erroneously as it turned out, that the plaintiffs had no case and that there was no triable issue, and on that ground the case was distinguished by Kerr LJ in *Portsmouth City Council v Richards*, of which we have been provided with a transcript. But at paragraph 63 of *Polydor*, Templeman LJ said:

> In any event, it seems to me if there had been a triable issue I would have reached the conclusion that the balance of convenience requires no injunction.

[65] *Polydor* was, of course, the obverse of the problem which faces us. There, by not continuing the injunction, the court temporarily prevented an English statute being effected, whereas we are asked to bring about the same result by granting interim relief. But I would have thought that, if the respondents' contention is the correct one, the court in *Polydor* ought to have continued the injunction. The respondent seeks to distinguish *Polydor* on the ground that the litigation was between two private individuals. That is a distinction which in my judgment, since the decision of the Court of Appeal in *R v Licensing Authority ex p Smith Kline and French (No 2)*, we are not entitled to make.

[66] In any case I find it difficult to believe that a court which has jurisdiction to make a final order disapplying the provisions of an English statute does not also have jurisdiction in a proper case to make an interim order to the same temporary effect. If the court is not constrained by authority, and I believe it is not, it seems to me clear that to deny the court the power to make an interim order would be wrong.

[67] The final question, therefore, is whether the court should make an interim order to protect the applicants during the period between our reference and the answers to our questions. Not surprisingly, there is little guidance in the cases as to what guidelines should apply. The situation is novel in two ways: first, because the possibility of a final decision being delayed because of a reference under Article 177 only arose after the United Kingdom accession to the Treaty and the passing of the European Communities Act 1972; secondly, because, until my decision in *R v Home Secretary, ex p Herbage* and its subsequent approval by the Court of Appeal in *Smith Kline and French*, it was not thought to be possible to obtain an interim injunction against a Minister.

[68] In parenthesis, I may say that I share Woolf LJ's difficulty, expressed in *Smith Kline and French*, in envisaging any good reason why (as recommended by the Law Commission) a court should not be entitled to make an interim declaration.

[69] In *Polydor*, which was a case between individuals, the Court of Appeal seems to have assumed that the principles laid down in *American Cyanamid v Ethicon* would guide the decision whether to grant interim relief in the period between reference and answer. But, in my judgment, the fact that here the interim relief is sought against a Minister greatly alters the situation. In *Herbage* I expressed the view that, in such cases, the principles governing interim injunctions in civil proceedings are not particularly helpful. I added that clearly the apparent strengths and weaknesses of the two opposing cases ought to be considered. I adhere to both those opinions.

[70] Some guidance may be obtained from two decisions of the Court of Appeal in cases where interlocutory injunctions were sought against local authorities. In *R v Westminster City Council ex p Sierbien*, Dillon LJ referred to the early authority. He said this:

> The position where there is a public element and an interlocutory injunction is sought was considered by the court in the case of *Smith v Inner London Education Authority* [1978] 1 All ER 411. That was concerned with the closure of the St Marylebone Grammar School. Certain parents were challenging the Education Authority's decision to close the school. They were doing so by action rather than by application for judicial review. In the state of the law at that time, that was a possible course. They had sought an interlocutory injunction. This court refused the injunction, primarily, I think, on the

view of all the members of the court that the plaintiffs in that case had not shown a serious question to be tried within the straight *Cyanamid* test. But Lord Denning (as he then was) saw merit in the suggestion that the ordinary *Cyanamid* test could not really apply to cases against local authorities in public law, and Browne LJ agreed with that and took the view that the public aspect was of considerable importance. I myself feel that in a case where what is sought to be restrained is the act of a public authority in a matter of public law, the public interest is very important to be considered and the ordinary financial considerations in the *Cyanamid* case, though no doubt to some extent relevant, must be qualified by a recognition of the public interest.

I think these principles apply equally when the relief sought is against a Minister.

[71] In my judgment, the first step is to consider the prima facie cases of each side and their respective strength. Unless the court is satisfied that an applicant has a strong prima facie case, I think it should hesitate long before granting interim relief in the form of an injunction or stay against a Minister.

[72] It seems to me that, doing the best I can with my inadequate qualifications, the applicants have a strong prima facie case on each of the three main areas of contention. In so far as the most extreme position taken by the respondent is concerned, I think it faces substantial difficulties. I confess that it was only at a late stage in the argument that I appreciated that it was being contended that, in laying down the flag conditions for fishing vessels, the United Kingdom's rights were completely untrammelled by any considerations of discrimination, the right of establishment, or, indeed, any of the fundamental Articles in the Treaty.

[73] To test this submission in argument, I asked whether it would be permissible in Community law to add to the Act a fourth condition of eligibility for registration, that the crew of the vessel should at all times consist only of British citizens resident and domiciled in the United Kingdom. I did not, I think, receive any satisfactory answer to this question; perhaps because the answer is provided by the case of *EC Commission v France* (Case 167/73), and is 'No'.

[74] We have heard much argument as to the relationship between the Common Fisheries Policy and the main body of Community law. I consider, without elaboration, that on this part of the case also the applicants have prima facie strong arguments to advance.

[75] So far as the impact of the Community law principle of proportionality is concerned, I am of the same opinion. In my view the applicants can draw much comfort from the opinion of Mischo AG where he says, at paragraph 41 in the *Jaderow* reference that, first, the condition that 75% of the fishermen fishing against the quotas of the Member State must ordinarily reside in that Member State, and the rule requiring a vessel's periodic presence in a port of that county, seems to be sufficient to ensure that the benefit of that Member State's quota actually goes to those truly forming part of that Member State's fishing community.

[76] Next it is necessary to consider the public interest, which comprehends both the United Kingdom interests and the interests of the Community.

[77] I do not myself think that the impact of a standstill for some two years, which seems to be the most pessimistic forecast for an answer from the European Court, will seriously affect either interest if the respondents succeed on the reference. In the United Kingdom the only people who will suffer if the Spanish shareholders eventually assigned their shares to United Kingdom domiciled residents, are those unidentifiable United Kingdom nationals who, without a standstill, might have benefited earlier from a forced sale of Spanish owned shares. I do not see how the United Kingdom fishing interest itself would be affected.

[78] So far as Community interest is concerned, although the UK quota would continue, no doubt, to be fished to capacity, there are clearly already in place effective means both at national and Community level to ensure that it is not exceeded.

[79] Lastly one has, in my judgment, to look and balance against each other what the results will be if one or other of the conflicting arguments eventually prevails. If the applicants' argument eventually prevails but no standstill is provided, they will, unless they risk defying domestic United Kingdom law, suffer serious, irreversible and perhaps uncompensatable injury, I say perhaps uncompensatable because of the decision of the Court of Appeal in *Bourgoin*, Oliver LJ (as

he then was) dissenting. If the answers from Europe are in the applicants' favour they will come back to this court and ask for declaratory relief, but they will want damages too which we should be constrained by authority from awarding.

[80] Against that, if the respondents' arguments prevail the UK fishing industry will only suffer the deferment for two years of the transfer of share capital from Spanish to United Kingdom nationals.

[81] In my judgment, the balance of fairness is really all one way and I would, without hesitation, make an interim order sufficient to maintain the status quo until the European Court answers the questions posed to it. [The order finally made is set out in the Court of Appeal judgment.]

JUDGMENT (OF THE COURT OF APPEAL)

The Master of the Rolls: [1] The background to this appeal is the Common Market Fishing Policy. If stocks of fish, or at all events stocks of some varieties of fish, are to continue to exist in the seas around Europe, some system has to be devised to prevent overfishing. This in turn involves the need for fixing quotas for national fishing fleets limiting the amount of fish which each may catch.

[2] Given a quota for the British fishing fleet, the Government has been concerned to ensure that all the vessels operating as part of this fleet can properly be regarded as British. To that end in 1985 new licence conditions were established under the Sea Fish (Conservation) Act 1967.

[3] Under that system certain conditions had to be fulfilled before a vessel registered as British under the Merchant Shipping Act 1894 could fish. These licence conditions related to such matters as the proportion of the catch which was landed in the United Kingdom, the frequency with which the vessel visited the United Kingdom, the proportion of the crew who were EEC nationals and the liability of the crew to contribute to the United Kingdom social security scheme.

[4] That 1985 licensing system has been the subject of a challenge in the European Court of Justice on the grounds that it contravenes European law. A decision on this is awaited.

[5] Last year the Government came to the conclusion that the 1985 licence conditions were not sufficiently restrictive for the protection of British fishing interests and it invited Parliament to enact, and Parliament did enact, the Merchant Shipping Act 1988 which, inter alia, empowered the Secretary of State to make regulations introducing a new register of British fishing vessels. The applicants are either unable, or would have great difficulty, to comply with the 1988 Scheme as formulated under the 1988 Act and the Merchant Shipping (Registration of Fishing Vessels) Regulations 1988, The obstacles which confront them arise out of the definitions of 'qualified company' and 'qualified person' in section 4 of the 1988 Act which import conditions relating to British citizenship and domicile. That Act and those regulations taken together wound up the register established by the 1894 Act and, if valid, might well force the applicants to sell or to reflag their vessels.

The application

[6] The applicants took the view that Part II of the 1988 Act which deals with the registration of British fishing vessels and those regulations conflicted with European law. They therefore applied for judicial review. The matter was, and is, of considerable urgency because section 13 of the Act read with the regulations will close the register established by the 1894 Act as from 31 March 1989. Thereafter, no vessel previously on that register and no other fishing vessel will be able to fish commercially unless they are qualified for entry in, and are entered in, the new register.

[7] The application was heard by Neill LJ and Hodgson J. In judgments of conspicuous clarity, they set out the facts, the relevant law, their conclusions and the reasons for those conclusions. Those conclusions were that:

 (a) it was necessary to enable [the court] to give judgment on the applications to seek certain preliminary rulings from the European Court of Justice; and

(b) in the circumstances of this case the court was competent to grant and should grant interim relief in the form of orders that:

1 Pending final judgment or further order herein, the operation of Part II of the Merchant Shipping Act 1988 and the Merchant Shipping (Registration of Fishing Vessels) Regulations 1988 be disapplied, and the Secretary of State be restrained from enforcing the same, in respect of any of the applicants and any vessel now owned (in whole or in part), managed, operated or chartered by any of them, so as to enable registration of any such vessel under the Merchant Shipping Act 1894 and/or the Sea Fishing Boats (Scotland) Act 1886 to continue in being.

2 The Secretary of State does have liberty to apply to, the court in the event of non-compliance by any of the applicants' vessels with conditions of their fishing licenses, save that the enforcement of these conditions shall be subject where applicable to the provisions of the *Jaderow* Agreement and to any judgment or order made by the European Court of Justice in the *Agegate* and *Jaderow* cases.

3 Liberty to apply generally.

The appeal

[8] The Secretary of State appealed to this court seeking a reversal of the interim relief granted. The applicants' primary contention was that the decision of the Divisional Court was correct. However they served a notice of cross appeal to take effect if we were not prepared to uphold the Divisional Court's order. In this event they sought:

(a) (i) a stay of the measures bringing the transitional period referred to in section 13(3)(b) of the Merchant Shipping Act 1988 to an end on 31 March 1989 pursuant to Order 53 rule 3(10)(a) of the rules of the Supreme Court (in so far as the Order made by the Divisional Court does, not amount to an interim stay), or

(ii) a declaration of the terms of the interim Order which the court would have made if the court had had power to make such Order, or

(iii) a provisional declaration of the rights of the parties, or

(iv) such other declaration or Order as would protect the interests of the Respondents pending the judgment of the Court of justice; or

(b) an order that the Divisional Court instead of referring the questions to the Court of Justice under Article 177 give final judgment.

[9] In view of the urgency of the matter we announced our decision at the conclusion of the argument and said that we would put our reasons into writing for delivery at a later date. This we now do. Our decision was that the appeal should be allowed and the cross appeal dismissed, but that the applicants should have leave to appeal to the House of Lords. We declined to make any interim order pending such appeal.

Reasons

[10] It would unduly lengthen this judgment if I sought to summarise the reasons given by Neill LJ and Hodgson J for their decision on interim, relief and I do not consider that such a summary would do them justice. Accordingly, I give my own reasons on the assumption that copies of their judgments will be available to the reader, notwithstanding that they have not yet been reported

[11] The Solicitor General appearing for the Secretary of State did not seek to urge us not to follow the decision of this court in *R v Licensing Authorities ex p Smith, Kline & French Laboratories (No 2)* that in proceedings for judicial review interim relief by way of an injunction, or stay or proceedings was available against the Crown. He indicated that in other circumstances he might have wished to argue that the decision was not binding on this court, because it was obiter, and that he might well wish to argue in the House of Lords that it was wrongly decided. So be it, but for our purposes we can accept this as a binding authority.

[12] The Solicitor General also accepted that the Divisional Court was in no position to dismiss the application for judicial review without first seeking a ruling from the European Court of Justice. In other words, it was not 'clear' that the applicants were wrong or wholly wrong in their contentions. For the applicants, Mr David Vaughan QC and Mr Nicholas Forwood QC made the

same concession substituting 'right' for 'wrong' subject in each case to the qualification that if we concluded that interim relief could not be given, the potential hardship to their clients and, in particular, to Rawlings (Trawlings) Ltd for the reasons set out in the judgment of Neill LJ was such that the Divisional Court should have given a final ruling, preferably in favour of their clients, leaving it to an appellate court so make an application for a ruling from the European Court of Justice.

[13] The essential difference between the two parties on 'clarity' was that the Solicitor General was content to accept Neil LJ's formulation that 'I find myself unable at this stage to say what law ought to be enforced' and that for the applicants it was submitted that Hodgson J somewhat understated the position when he said that 'the applicants have a strong prima facie case on each of the three main areas' of contention'.

[14] Accepting, as I do, the extreme hardship which the applicants will suffer if they are required to give up fishing at the end of this month and accepting, as I also do, that the Government has some reason to claim that any failure to give effect to the 1988 Scheme would have adverse consequences for others engaged in, or who would wish to be engaged in, fishing against the British quota, I would have liked to have been able to give some degree of interim relief limited to maintaining the status quo for two or three months. This would have enabled the EC Commission to bring proceedings against the United Kingdom Government and to seek interim relief from the European Court of Justice. If the Commission failed to bring such proceedings or the European Court was unable or unwilling to grant interim relief, I would have been satisfied that European law had been given a reasonable opportunity of asserting itself and that the applicants would have had no reasonable cause for complaints against the British courts and British law for failing to assist them further.

[15] Underlying the whole of this problem is the unusual (to a British lawyer) nature of Community law, which is long on principle and short on specifics. This is intended as a statement of fact rather than a criticism. Indeed my own view is that Parliament would render a service to the nation if it moved slightly more in the direction of Community law and thus enabled the judiciary more easily and appropriately to apply the law to unusual or unforeseen circumstances. However. the result is often that the British courts are faced with an undoubted right or duty under British law and a claim that an inconsistent right or duty exists under Community law. If the British court can ascertain the nature and extent of this competing right or duty, there is little difficulty in resolving any inconsistency on the basis that Community law is paramount. This is the 'acte clair' situation, but it is a comparative rarity. Much more commonly the British court cannot ascertain the nature and extent of the competing right or duty and it is to meet this problem that the right to seek a ruling by the European Court is provided under Article 177 of the Treaty of Rome. But it would be a mistake to think of that Court merely as having a greater expertise in Community law than a British court, although this is undoubtedly true, whatever the formal position its true function inappropriate cases is actually to make new law by the application of principle to specific factual situations. A challenge to national law based upon community law may, when properly analysed, amount to a submission not that the national law is inconsistent with Community law as it then exists, but that upon a reference being made to the European Court, that court will give a ruling creating new and inconsistent rights and duties: arising out of settled principles albeit with retroactive effect. In other words, national law is effective at present, but its life span is predictably short.

[16] Notwithstanding that I suspect that this is the position in the instant appeal. I would have been very willing to require the Secretary of State to hold his hand pending a ruling by the European Court (provided that this could be obtained within a reasonably short time). But this would only be possible if the 1988 legislation had called for any further action upon his part to enable the 1894 Act register to be wound up and the 1988 Scheme to come into force. But that is not the position. Part II of the 1988 Act and, in particular, section 3(2) and (3), is designed to produce an automatic ending of the 1894 register and an equally automatic creation of the 1988 Scheme, subject to a transitional period, the whole process being triggered by the making of

regulations. Nothing happens before these regulations are made. Once they are made, that change is a *fait accompli*. The regulations concerned are SI 1988/1926 which were made on 2 November and came into force on 1 December 1988.

[17] We are thus faced with a situation in which positive action will have to be taken if the status quo is to be maintained after 31 March 1989. It was suggested that the Secretary of State could be required by the court to keep the 1894 register temporarily in force. However this would be contrary to principle, since the court would be requiring him to do an act for which he had no authority whatsoever. Furthermore, the mere maintenance of the register would not legalise fishing in the face of the provisions of the 1988 Act. I also considered whether it would be possible to quash the regulations which triggered the demise of the 1894 register and the birth of the 1988 Scheme which would undoubtedly have achieved the desired result. This is, however, impossible. The making of these regulations was not *ultra vires* unless the 1988 Act itself can be attacked. It was not *Wednesbury* unreasonable and there was no procedural irregularity.

[18] The ultimate question is thus whether the courts of this country have any power to interfere with the operation of the 1988 Act itself, either by modifying its operation or striking it down, and of doing so not on a permanent basis founded upon Community law or the British European Communities Act 1972 but on a temporary basis pending a ruling by the European Court of Justice. The answer to this question, I have no doubt, is in the negative, whether we base ourselves on national or on Community law or both.

[19] Looking at British national law without reference to the European Communities Act 1972, it is fundamental to our (unwritten) constitution that it is for Parliament to legislate and for the judiciary to interpret and apply the fruits of Parliament's labours. Any attempt to interfere with primary legislation would be wholly unconstitutional. That apart, there is a well settled principle of British national law that the validity of subordinate legislation and the legality of acts done pursuant to the law declared by it are presumed unless and until its validity has been challenged in the courts and the courts have fully determined its invalidity (see *Hoffmann-La Roche v Secretary of State for Trade, per* Lord Diplock). The position in relation to primary legislation must be the same. It appears that the European Court of Justice applying Community law reaches the same conclusion. Thus paragraph 4 of the Court's decision in the *Granaria* case (Case 101/781) states: 'Every regulation which is brought into force in accordance with the Treaty must be presumed to be valid so long as a competent court has not made a finding that it is invalid.'

[20] Accordingly, albeit with some reluctance, I have come to the conclusion that in the circumstances of this case there is no juridical basis upon which interim relief can be granted by the British courts. If the applicants have a remedy, it can only be provided by the European Court of Justice either in the form of a ruling in response to the reference made by the Divisional Court or in the form of interim relief in proceedings, not yet instituted by the Commission against the United Kingdom Government.

Bingham LJ: [21] The economic ideal upon which the European Community is founded is that there should within its frontiers be free competition not distorted by protective tariffs, quantitative restrictions, discriminatory practices or state subsidies but subject only to objectively justifiable constraints such as are to be found, for example, in Article 36 of the Treaty of Rome. To make this ideal effective in practice, a number of important and directly enforceable rights are conferred on the nationals or Member States by the Treaty, among their rights of equal and non-discriminatory treatment, rights of establishment, rights to provide services, rights of participation, and so on. It would, at first blush, seem inconsistent with this ideal that particular areas of economic activity should be reserved for the enjoyment of particular Member States to the exclusion of others, or that Member States should be free to discriminate in favour of their own nationals.

[22] A common structural policy for the fishing industry was first adopted in 1971. This was in accordance with the Treaty, which extended the common market to agriculture, including fisheries, and required establishment of a common agricultural policy. But the problem of fisheries acquired a new immediacy with the accession of the United Kingdom, Ireland and Denmark and the

expected accession of Norway, all of them countries with long coast-lines and established fishing industries. Neill LJ has most helpfully and comprehensively identified the historical landmarks and legislative milestones leading to the Common Fisheries Policy which exists today, and I shall not attempt to repeat his summary. It is however, common knowledge that the achievement of a common fisheries policy has been more than ordinarily difficult. To this difficulty two factors, among others have contributed. The first was that fish are not an inexhaustible resource. At certain times some species have been over-fished to the verge of extinction. As was recognised in Article 102 of the Treaty of Accession, it was therefore necessary to take steps to conserve the biological resources of the sea. This could only be done by limiting the total allowable catches or the various species of fish. But how, within the overall total, should Member States compete? In the absence of some, regulation a disorderly and potentially sanguinary free-for-all would have seemed likely. The second difficulty was that certain areas and communities within Member States, often in economically disadvantaged regions, were to an unusual degree dependent on the fishing industry. A sudden cessation, or sharp reduction, in activity would cause great hardship, both economically and socially.

[23] The solution adopted, as Neill LJ's summary makes clear, was based on total allowable catches for the different species and national quotas related to the level of past fishing activity. This solution is probably regarded as unsatisfactory by most of those involved in the fishing industry, but no doubt represents the best available compromise of an intractable problem. It does not, however, seem to accord closely with the prevailing free market philosophy of the Treaty.

[24] The problem of Community law at the heart of this case concerns the reconciliation of this free market philosophy, on which (and the directly enforceable rights expressed in the Treaty) the applicants rely, with the more regulatory framework of the common fisheries policy, on which the Secretary of State relies. More particularly, the question is whether, in the steps taken to ensure that its fishing quota is enjoyed beneficially and not merely nominally by British interests, the United Kingdom has contravened the prohibition of discrimination deeply embedded in Community law. Both judges in the Divisional Court thought this a difficult and important question on which a decision was necessary to enable them to give judgment. I agree, and no criticism has been addressed to that part of their judgments. Like Neill LJ I shall not express even a tentative view on the likely outcome of the reference to the European Court of Justice which the Divisional Court rightly ordered. Both sides accept that the answer to the Community law problem raised in the case is not acte clair. The major issue argued before us has accordingly been whether the Divisional Court was entitled, and if entitled right, to grant the applicants interim relief to protect their interests during the period of perhaps two years which will elapse before the European Court answers the question to be referred to it.

[25] The Secretary of State challenges the existence of any power in the court to grant interim relief by way of injunction against the crown or any officer of the crown even in judicial review proceedings. The Solicitor General who appears for him accepts, however, that we in this court are bound by *R v Licensing Authority ex p Smith Kline & French Laboratories Ltd (No 2)* to reject that challenge. We accordingly heard no argument on the question and must for present purposes assume that in judicial review proceedings an interim injunction can generally be granted against the crown or one of its officers.

[26] The order made by the Divisional Court provided that 'the operation of Part II of the Merchant Shipping Act 1988 and the Merchant Shipping (Registration of Fishing Vessels) Regulations 1988 be disapplied, and the Secretary of State be restrained from enforcing the same ...' The Solicitor General's first submission is that there is no jurisdiction in the Court to disapply an Act of Parliament unless and until incompatibility with Community law has been established. The relief sought and obtained by the applicants, he submits, involves disapplication of the 1988 Act. That Act has not been shown to conflict with Community law. The court could not, therefore, disapply it.

[27] The Solicitor General's argument was launched from a secure base. Although in medieval times judges claimed and exercised a discretion to dispense with statutes if they thought fit, the

supremacy of statute quickly became a cornerstone of British constitutional law. Coke said: 'Of the power and jurisdiction of the Parliament for making of laws, it is so transcendent and absolute as it cannot be confined either for causes or persons within any bounds.' The Bill of Rights 1688 declared unlawful the pretended power of dispensing with laws or the execution of laws by royal authority. According to Blackstone, 'True it is, that what the Parliament doth, no authority upon earth can undo'. Dicey stated that 'there is no power which, under the English constitution, can come into rivalry with the legislative sovereignty of Parliament' and listed as one of the three traits of parliamentary sovereignty as it exists in England 'the non-existence of any judicial or other authority having the right to nullify an Act of Parliament, or to treat it as void or unconstitutional'. The grant of relief such as the applicants obtained would not before 1973 have been thinkable, as I am sure they would accept.

[28] The applicants, however, contend that the European Communities Act 1972 implicitly confers jurisdiction on the court to grant such relief. Section 2(1) provides that all directly enforceable rights created or arising by or under the Treaties shall be given legal effect and enforced in the United Kingdom, and by section 2(4) any legal enactment is to take effect subject to the provisions of the section. The effect of the Act has been to incorporate the law of the Community into the law of the United Kingdom and to ensure that if any inconsistency arises between the domestic law of the United Kingdom and the law of the Community the latter shall prevail. This has been loyally and unreservedly accepted by the English courts. In *The Siskina*, Lord Hailsham said: 'it is the duty of the courts here and in other Member States to give effect to Community law as they interpret it in preference to the municipal law of their own country over which *ex hypothesi* Community law prevail'. Lord Denning MR in *Macarthys v Smith* was equally forthright:

> It is important now to declare – and it must be made plain – that the provisions of Article 119 of the EEC Treaty take priority over anything in our English statute on equal pay which is inconsistent with Article 119. That priority is given by our own law. It is given by the European Communities Act 1972 itself. Community law is now part of our law; and whenever there is any inconsistency, Community law has priority. It is not supplanting English law. It is part of our law which overrides any other part which is inconsistent with it.

As the European Court pointed out in *Van Gend en Loos v Nederlandse Administratie Der Belastingen*, 'the Community constitutes a new legal order of international law for the benefit of which the States have limited their sovereign rights, albeit within limited fields ...'. This reasoning was carried further in *Costa v ENEL* where the European Court said:

> By creating a Community of unlimited duration, having its own institutions, its own personality, its own legal capacity and capacity of representation on the international plane and, more particularly, real powers stemming from a limitation of sovereignty or a transfer of powers from the States to the Community, the Member States have limited their sovereign rights, albeit within limited fields, and have thus created a body of law which binds both their nationals and themselves.

> The integration into the laws of each Member State of provisions which derive from the Community, and more generally the terms and the spirit of the Treaty, make it impossible for the States, as a corollary, to accord precedence to a unilateral and subsequent measure over a legal system accepted by them on a basis of reciprocity. Such a measure cannot therefore be inconsistent with that legal system. The executive force of Community law cannot vary from one State to another in deference to subsequent domestic laws, without jeopardising the attainment of the objectives of the Treaty set out in Article 5(2) and giving rise to the discrimination prohibited by Article 7.

> The obligation undertaken under the Treaty establishing the Community would not be unconditional, but merely contingent if they could be called in question by subsequent legislative acts of the signatories. Wherever the Treaty grants States the rights to act unilaterally, it does this by clear and precise provisions (for example, Articles 15, 93(3), 223, 224 and 225). Applications by Member States for authority to derogate from the Treaty are subject to a special authorisation procedure (for example, Articles 8(4), 17(4), 25, 26, 73, the third sub-paragraph of Article 93(2), and 226) which would lose their purpose if the Member States could renounce their obligations by means of an ordinary law.

> The precedence of Community law is confirmed by Article 189, whereby a regulation 'shall be binding' and 'directly applicable in all Member States'. This provision, which, is subject to no reservation, would be quite meaningless if a State could unilaterally nullify its effects by means of a legislative measure which could prevail over Community law.

It follows from all these observations that the law stemming from the Treaty, an independent source of law, could not, because of its special and original nature, be overridden by domestic legal provisions, however framed, without being deprived of its character as Community law and without the legal basis of the Community itself being called into question.

The matter could not be more clearly or authoritatively put than it was by the European Court in *Amministrazione delle Finanze dello Stato v Simmenthal SpA*:

The main purpose of the *first question* is to ascertain what consequences flow from the direct applicability of a provision of Community law in the event of incompatibility with a subsequent legislative provision of a Member State. Direct applicability in such circumstances means that rules of Community law must be fully and uniformly applied in all the Member States from the date of their entry into force and for so long as they continue in force.

These provisions are therefore a direct source of rights and duties for all those affected thereby whether Member States or individuals, who are parties to legal relationships under Community law.

This consequence also concerns any national court whose task it is as an organ of a Member State to protect, in a case within its jurisdiction, the rights conferred upon individuals by Community law.

Furthermore, in accordance with the principle of the precedence of Community law, the relationship between provisions of the Treaty and directly applicable measures of the institutions on the one hand and the national law of the Member States on the other is such that those provisions and measures not only by their entry into force render automatically inapplicable any conflicting provisions of current national law but – in so far as they are an integral part of, and take precedence in the legal order applicable in the territory of each of the Member States – preclude the valid adoption of new national legislative measures to the extent to which they would be incompatible with Community provisions.

Indeed, any recognition that national legislative measures which encroach upon the field within which the Community exercises its legislative power or which are otherwise incompatible with the provisions of Community law had any legal effect would amount to a corresponding denial of the effectiveness of obligations undertaken unconditionally and irrevocably by Member States pursuant to the Treaty and would thus imperil the very foundations of the Community.

The same conclusion emerges from the structure of Article 177 of the Treaty which provides that any court or tribunal of a Member State is entitled to make a reference to the Court whenever it considers that a preliminary ruling on a question of interpretation or validity relating to Community law is necessary to enable it to give judgment.

The effectiveness of that provision would be impaired if the national court were prevented from forthwith applying Community law in accordance with the decision or the case law of the Court.

It follows from the foregoing that every national court must, in a case within its jurisdiction, apply Community law in its entirety and protect rights which the latter confers on individuals and must accordingly set aside any provision of national law which may conflict with it, whether prior or subsequent to the Community rule.

Accordingly any provision of a national legal system and any legislative, administrative or judicial practice which might impair the effectiveness of Community law by withholding from the national court having jurisdiction to apply such law the power to do everything necessary at the moment of its application to set aside national legislative provisions which might prevent Community rules having full force and effect are incompatible with those requirements which are the very essence of Community law.

This would be the case in the event of a conflict between a provision of community law and a subsequent national law if the solution of the conflict were to be reserved for an authority with a discretion of its own, other than the court called upon to apply Community law, even if such an impediment to the full effectiveness of Community law were only temporary.

The first question should therefore be answered to the effect that a national court which is called upon, within the limits of its jurisdiction, to apply provisions of Community law is under a duty to give full effect to those provisions, if necessary refusing of its own motion to apply any conflicting provision of national legislation, even if adopted subsequently, and it is not necessary for the court to request or await the prior setting aside of such provision by legislative or other constitutional means.

[24] [*sic*] In the face of this jurisprudence the Solicitor General was bound to accept, as he readily did, that if the answer given by the European Court to the question referred to it by the Divisional Court under Article 177 proves unfavourable to him, the Divisional Court will be obliged to give effect to that ruling by upholding any rights the applicants might be shown, in accordance with that ruling, to have, and this it will be obliged to do even though the 1988 Act had not been

repealed and even though its decision involves dispensing with (or disapplying) express provisions of the statute.

[30] I have no doubt this is the law. Where the law of the Community is clear, whether as a result of a ruling given on an Article 177 reference or as a result of previous jurisprudence or on straightforward interpretation of Community instruments, the duty of the national court is to give effect to it in all circumstances. Any rule of domestic law which prevented the court from, or inhibited it in, giving effect to directly enforceable rights established in Community law would be bad. To that extent a United Kingdom statute is no longer inviolable as it once was. But the point upon which the Solicitor General takes his stand is that a statute remains inviolable unless or until it is shown to be incompatible with the higher law of the Community. A statute does not, he argues, lose its quality of inviolability enshrined in our domestic law so long as it remains unclear, as it does in this case or in any other case which is, not acte clair, whether the statute is incompatible with Community law or not. I am persuaded, contrary to my initial view, that that argument is correct.

[31] We start from a position (before 1973) in which the court had no jurisdiction to dispense with the operation of a statute. If, therefore, the court now has such jurisdiction one must find the source of such additional jurisdiction. The authorities already cited not only entitle but oblige the court to give effect to Community rights, even if that means dispensing with the operation of a statute. But none of these authorities obliges a national court to override its own domestic law in favour of what is no more than an alleged or putative Community right, and if the English court is not obliged so to act it is not in my opinion, as the law now stands, entitled (under our own domestic law, which remains effective until displaced) to do so. I find no such obligation, expressly or impliedly, in the Treaty itself, or in the European Communities Act 1972, or in the jurisprudence of the European Court, or in any judgment of our own courts. If, of course, the European Court were to rule, as a matter of Community law, that the law obliged or entitled national courts to override national laws, whether statutory or otherwise, where to do so was judged necessary or desirable for the protection of claimed but unestablished Community rights, the situation would be quite different. But unless or until such ruling is given this court is in my view bound to hold that it has no jurisdiction to grant the interim relief which the applicants sought and the Divisional Court granted.

[32] Recognising the danger of this argument, the applicants contended that the interim relief sought involved not dispensing with the operation of the 1988 Act but staying the operation of regulation 66 of the 1988 Regulations. Statutory instruments, they pointed out, are subordinate legislation and have always (unlike statutes) been regarded as amenable to judicial review. This is of course so. It is not, however, suggested that regulation 66 or any other part of the Regulations is outside the powers conferred by the 1988 Act, nor is it suggested that the Regulations are invalidated by any procedural impropriety in their making. If the Act is unimpeachable there is no ground for impeaching the Regulations. The ground upon which the applicants sought and obtained interim relief was that the conditions imposed by section 13 on eligibility to be registered as a British fishing vessel are contrary to Community law. Interim relief could not be granted without temporarily dispensing with the operation of the Act, as the order of the Divisional Court in my view quite rightly recognised.

[33] I would for my part allow the Secretary of State's appeal on this jurisdictional ground alone. The applicants argued that if the Divisional Court could not grant the interim relief sought. then it should have ruled in the applicants' favour on the Community law point and dispensed with the operation of the Act and regulation 66 as part of a final judgment. This argument was not pressed and is in my view untenable. Hodgson J preferred the applicants' submissions on Community law, and may well have been right to do so. Neill LJ was neutral, regarding the arguments on both sides as formidable. Neither judge thought the answer to the Community law issue was obvious, and neither felt able to say what it was. It would have been quite wrong for the judges to leap sightless into the dark in order to protect rights which the applicants might turn out not to have.

[34] If, contrary to the view I have expressed, this court has jurisdiction to dispense with the operation of a statute to protect rights alleged but not established to exist in Community law, and assuming that there is jurisdiction to grant an interlocutory injunction against the Crown or one of its officers, the question remains whether (within the margin of appreciation accorded to it) the Divisional Court properly exercised its discretion to grant such relief.

[35] On a simple *American Cyanamid* approach to the problem the case for granting interlocutory relief was very strong, if not overwhelming. There was without doubt a serious issue to be determined and the applicants had a real prospect of success. If the Act and the Regulation took effect, the applicants stood to suffer very serious loss before the earliest date at which the European Court could, if they were right, rule in their favour. Such loss would, on existing English authority, be irreparable: *Bourgoin SA v Ministry of Agriculture, Fisheries and Food*. This would bear very hardly on all the applicants, and particularly hardly on Rawlings (Trawling) Ltd who are fully integrated with the United Kingdom fishing fleet, who have received grants from HMG, and from the Community as part of that fleet and whose activities form no part of the mischief (if it is mischief) at which the Act is directed. By contrast, the Secretary of State will himself suffer little or no detriment for two years or so, and an injury suffered by the United Kingdom fishing industry which he is concerned to protect will, because more diffused, be less acute than that suffered by the applicants. Maintenance of the status quo means continuing the current registration of the applicants' vessels until the legality of the statutory conditions making the applicants' vessels ineligible for registration is ruled upon.

[36] The Solicitor General contends that this simple and familiar approach is not the correct one because it fails to take account of the important principle that a law must be recognised and enforced as such unless and until it is overruled or invalidated. In support of this principle he referred us to *Hoffmann La-Roche & Co AG v Secretary of State for Trade and Industry* where the Secretary of State sought and obtained an injunction to enforce a statutory instrument the legality of which was challenged. Lord Reid said:

> It must be borne in mind that an order made under statutory authority is as much the law of the land as an Act of Parliament unless and until it has been found to be *ultra vires*. But I think it is for the person against whom the interim injunction is sought to show special reason why justice requires that the injunction should not be granted or should only be granted on terms.

Lord Morris said:

> ... the order then undoubtedly had the force of law. Obedience to it was just as obligatory as would be obedience to an Act of Parliament.

Lord Diplock said:

> Unless there is such challenge and, if there is, until it has been upheld by a judgment of the court the validity of the statutory instrument and the legality of acts done pursuant to the law declared by it are presumed.

These observations are, I think, fully consistent with familiar legal principles. An injunction may be wrongly granted, but until discharged it binds. A judgment may be wrongly given, but unless stayed it takes effect. In *Inland Revenue Commissioners v Rossminster Ltd* Lord Scarman gravely doubted the wisdom of interim relief against the Crown. 'The State's decisions must be respected unless and until they are shown to be wrong.' In *Nottinghamshire County Council v Secretary of State for the Environment* Lord Scarman elaborated these doubts, concluding:

> Judicial review is a great weapon in the hands of the judges; but the judges must observe the constitutional limits set by our parliamentary system upon their exercise of this beneficent power.

[37] There is some doubt how far the simple *American Cyanamid* approach is appropriate where the public interest is involved, and the existence of that interest is a very material consideration: *Smith v Inner London Education Authority*. In *R v Westminster City Council ex p Herbien*, Dillon LJ, referring to that decision, said:

> But Lord Denning MR (as he then was) saw merit in the suggestion that the ordinary *Cyanamid* test could not really apply to cases against local authorities in public law, and Browne LJ agreed with that and look the view that the public aspect was of considerable importance. I myself feel that in a case

where what is sought to be restrained is the act of a public authority in a matter of public law the public interest is very important to be considered and the ordinary financial considerations in the *Cyanamid* case, though no doubt to some extent relevant, must be qualified by a recognition or the public interest.

The applicants fairly urge that in a case such as this the public interest must embrace the Community interest. But they face the difficulty that whereas the national public interest (as seen by Parliament) is plain, the Community interest is as yet problematical.

[38] It would not be accurate or fair to suggest that these considerations were ignored by the Divisional Court. The authorities I have mentioned were referred to in the judgments and the same passages (more fully) cited. But I do, with respect, think that the Divisional Court erred in failing to direct itself that in all save the most exceptional case preponderant weight must be given to the rule that a statute, duly enacted, must be taken to represent the law unless or until displaced. I do not think the Divisional Court was correct to weigh equally in the scales an Act of Parliament, which might in future be held unlawful, and a Community right, which might in future be upheld. I do not think the Divisional Court acknowledged the constitutional enormity, as the law stands, of requiring a Secretary of State to act contrary to the clearly expressed will of Parliament when the unlawfulness of that expression has yet to be established. Nor do I think that the Divisional Court, in its references to *Simmenthal* and *Macarthys v Smith*, fully recognised that in those cases, unlike the present, the relevant Community law had been clearly and authoritatively established.

Article 155 of the Treaty provides that in order to ensure the proper functioning and development of the Common Market the Commission shall: ensure that the provisions of this Treatment and the measures taken by the institutions pursuant thereto are applied. Under Article 169 the Commission may, if it considers that a Member State has failed to fulfil an obligation under the Treaty, take the matter up with the Member State and if necessary bring the matter before the European Court. In a case so brought before it the Court may under Article 186 prescribe any necessary interim measures. If an order is to be made dispensing with the operation of the 1988 Act I think it much preferable that this should be made by the European Court in an action (if brought) by the Commission against the United Kingdom than by this court in this action. I take that view for two reasons:

(1) This is not a local problem confined to the United Kingdom and these applicants. It is a Community-wide problem. The Commission can make an objective appraisal of the competing interests of the various Member States and their citizens in a way in which we cannot. If the applicants' case on the law and the merits is strong, I see no reason why the Commission should hesitate to take appropriate action.

(2) If, on a preliminary consideration the Court were to conclude that the applicants have an apparently strong case. I see no reason why interim relief should be denied on application by the Commission acting as the guardian of Community interests. The Court is better placed than this court to assess whether the conditions for granting interim relief are met and whether the interests of the Community and its Member States and citizens call for the granting of such relief.

[41] For these reasons, as well as those of the Master of the Rolls (which I have had the advantage or reading in draft and with which I agree), I would allow the Secretary of State's appeal against the Divisional Court's grant or interim relief.

Mann LJ: [42] I have had the advantage of reading in draft the judgments of my Lord, the Master of the Rolls, and of my Lord, Bingham LJ I agree with them.

[43] The Merchant Shipping Act 1988, Part II, was enacted in accordance with our constitutional procedures. It was brought into force by regulations which were within the regulation-making power. This court is obliged to defer to the Sovereignty of the Queen in Parliament. We can only not so defer where legislation is inconsistent with the United Kingdom's obligations under the Treaty of Rome. I cannot in this case detect an inconsistency with the United Kingdom's obligations under the Treaty of Rome. It may be that the European Court of Justice can make such a detection.

Along with Lord, [*sic*] the Master of the Rolls, I think that if the applicants do have a remedy it can only be provided by the European Court of Justice either in the form of a ruling in response to the reference made by the Divisional Court or in the form of interim relief in proceedings which have not yet been instituted by the Commission against Her Majesty's Government.

[44] I would allow this appeal

Appeal allowed.

EUROPEAN COURT OF JUSTICE

REGINA V SECRETARY OF STATE FOR TRANSPORT EX P FACTORTAME LTD AND OTHERS (NO 2)

(Case C213/89)

1990 April 5:	President O Due
May 17:	Presidents of Chambers Sir Gordon Slynn, CN Kakouris,
June 19:	FA Shockweiler and M Zuleeg, Judges CF Mancini,
	R Joliet, JC Moitinho de Almeida,
	GC Rodriguez Iglesius, F Grevise and M de Valacso
	Advocate General C Tesauro

[HOUSE OF LORDS]

1990 July 2, 3, 4, 5, 9, 25	Lord Bridge of Harwich, Lord Brandon of Oakbrook
October 11	Lord Olive of Aylmerton, Lord Goff of Chieveley
	and Lord Jauncey of Tullichettle

...

REFERENCE by the House of Lords under Article 177 of the EEC Treaty.

The report for the hearing before the Court of Justice prepared by the Judge Reporter, Judge Kakouris, states:

I – BACKGROUND TO THE DISPUTE

1 The applicants in the main proceedings, including Factortame Ltd, were a number of companies incorporated under the laws of the United Kingdom and also the directors and shareholders or those companies, most of whom were Spanish nationals. Those Companies between them owned or managed 95 fishing vessels which were until 31 March 1989 registered as British fishing vessels under the Merchant Shipping Act 1894. Of those vessels, 53 were originally registered in Spain and flew the Spanish flag. Those 53 vessels were registered under the Act of 1894 at various dates from 1980 onwards. The remaining 42 vessels had always been British. They had been purchased by the appellants at various dates, mainly since 1983.

2 The statutory system governing the registration of British fishing vessels was radically altered by Part II of the Merchant Shipping Act 1988 and the Merchant Shipping (Registration or Fishing Vessels) Regulations 1988 (SI 1988/1926). It was common ground that the United Kingdom amended the previous legislation in order to put a stop to the practice known as 'quota hopping' whereby (according to that state) its fishing quotas were 'plundered' by fishing vessels flying the British flag but lacking any genuine link with the United Kingdom.

3 The Act of 1988 provided for the establishment of a new register of all British fishing vessels including those registered in the old register maintained under the Act of 1894. However, only fishing vessels fulfilling the conditions laid down in section 14 of the Act of 1988 could be registered in the new register.

4 Briefly the conditions laid down in section 14 of the new Act, which had to be fulfilled cumulatively, were as follows: (a) nationality: the legal title to the vessel had to be vested wholly in qualified British citizens or companies, at least 75% of the beneficial ownership of the vessel must be vested in qualified British citizens or companies; a company was 'qualified' if it was incorporated in the United Kingdom and had its principal place of business there, and if at least 75% of its shares were held by legal owners and beneficial owners who were British citizens; furthermore, at least 75% of its directors had to be British citizens, the figure of 75% may be raised provisionally to 100%, pursuant to regulations adopted under the Act of 1988; the United Kingdom had not yet availed itself of this possibility that nationality requirement also applied to a charterer

281

or operator of the vessel, whether he was a natural person or a company; (b) residence and domicile: this is a further requirement along with nationality. (c) direction and control: the vessel must be managed, and its operations directed and controlled, from the United Kingdom.

5 The Act of 1988 and the regulations of 1988 came into force on 1 December 1988. However, under section 13 of the Act of 1988, the validity of registrations made under the previous Act had been extended for a transitional period until 31 March 1989.

6 At the time of the institution of the proceedings in which the appeal arose the 95 fishing vessels of the applicants failed to satisfy one or more of the conditions for registration under section 14(1) of the Act of 1988 and thus failed to qualify for registration. Since those vessels could no longer engage in fishing as from 1 April 1989, the companies in question sought by means of an application for judicial review to challenge the compatibility of Part II of the Act of 1988 with Community law.

7 In particular, in their application of 16 December 1988 to the High Court of Justice, Queen's Bench Division, the applicants sought: (i) a declaration that the provisions of Part II of the Act of 1988 should not 'apply to them' on the grounds that such application would be contrary to Community law, in particular Articles 7, 52, 58 and 221 of the EEC Treaty; (ii) an order prohibiting the Secretary of State from treating the existing registration of their vessels (under the Act of 1894) as having ceased from 1 April 1989; (iii) damages; and (iv) interim relief pending final determination of the issues.

8 The Divisional Court of the Queen's Bench Division gave judgment on 10 March 1989, in which it: (i) decided that it was unable to determine the issues of Community law raised in the proceedings without making a reference under Article 177 of the EEC Treaty (now Case 221/89. currently pending before the Court of Justice); and (ii) ordered that, pending final judgment or further order by the court, the operation of Part II of the Act of 1988 and of the Regulations of 1988 be disapplied and the Secretary of State should be restrained from enforcing it in respect of any of the applicants and any vessel owned (in whole or in part), managed, operated or chartered by any of them so as to enable registration of any such vessel under the Act of 1894 to continue in being.

9 On 13 March 1989 the Secretary of State appealed against the Divisional Court's order for interim relief. By judgment of 22 March 1989 the Court of Appeal held unanimously that under the British constitution the courts had no power to disapply Acts of Parliament on a temporary basis. It therefore set aside the Divisional Court's order and granted leave to appeal to the House of Lords.

II – THE HOUSE OF LORDS JUDGMENT OF 18 MAY 1989

10 In its judgment of 18 May 1989 (*Factortame Ltd v Secretary of State for Transport* [1990] 2 AC 85) the House of Lords found in the first place that the applicants' claims that they would suffer irreparable damage if the interim relief which they sought was not granted and they were successful in the main proceedings were well founded.

11 With regard to the question whether the British courts were empowered to suspend on a temporary basis the operation of an Act and to issue an interim injunction to that effect against the Secretary of State so as to protect the rights claimed by a party under directly enforceable provisions of Community law. The House of Lords found in the first place that, under national law, the British courts had no power to grant interim relief in a case such as the present. The considerations on which that finding of the House of Lords was based might be summarised as follows.

12 In the first place, the presumption that an Act of Parliament was compatible with Community law unless and until declared to be incompatible did not permit the British courts to grant interim relief suspending the operation of the Act in question. In that connection the House of Lords pointed out that an order granting the applicants the interim relief which they sought would only serve their purpose if it declared that which Parliament had enacted to be the law not to be the law until some uncertain future date. Any such order would irreversibly determine in the

applicants' favour for a period of some two years rights which were necessarily uncertain until a preliminary ruling had been given by the Court of Justice.

13 Secondly, the old common law rule that a court had no jurisdiction to grant an interlocutory injunction against the Crown, that is to say against the government, also precluded the grant of interim relief in the main proceedings. The House of Lords pointed out in that connection that in *Regulation v Secretary of State for the Home Department ex p Herbage* [1987] QB 872, the Divisional Court of the Queen's Bench Division took the view that section 31 of the Supreme Court Act 1981 (which provided that the High Court of Justice might grant interim relief, where it would be just and convenient to do so, in all cases in which an application for judicial review had been made) had removed the Crown's immunity from interim relief and that was subsequently affirmed by the Court of Appeal in *Regulation v Licensing Authority Established under Medicines Act 1968 ex p Smith, Kline & French Laboratories Ltd (No 2)* (1990) 1 QB 574. According to the House of Lords, however, those judgments were based on an erroneous construction of the Supreme Court Act 1981. It therefore overruled them in its judgment in the present case and came to the conclusion that, as a matter of English law, the courts had no jurisdiction to grant interim injunctions against the Crown.

14 Next, the House of Lords turned to the question whether Community law empowered the national courts to grant interim relief of the kind forming the subject matter of the main proceeding, regardless of what was laid down by national law, in order to protect rights which were defensible on serious grounds but whose existence had yet to be established and which were claimed by a party under Community law.

15 After setting out the position of the parties on that point, the House of Lords pointed out in *Regulation v Secretary of State for Transport ex p Factortame Ltd* [1990] 2 AC 85, 151, *per* Lord Bridge of Harwich, that 'Community law embodies a principle which appears closely analogous to the principle of English law that delegated legislation must be presumed to be valid unless and until declared invalid' and referred to the Court of Justice's judgment in *Granaria BV v Hoofdproduktschap voor Akkerbouwprodukten* (Case 101/78) [1979] ECR 623. Next, it referred to paragraph 19 of the judgment in *Foto-Frost v Hauptzollamt Lubeck-Ost* (Case 314/85) [1987] ECR 4199, 4232 in which the Court of Justice stated, at paragraph 19, that 'the rule that national court may not themselves declare Community acts invalid may have to be qualified in certain circumstances in the case of proceedings relating to an application for interim measures.

16 In those circumstances, the House of Lords considered that the dispute raised an issue concerning the interpretation of Community law and it therefore decided, pursuant to Article 177 of the EEC Treaty, to stay the proceedings until the Court of Justice had given a preliminary ruling on the following questions:

> [1] Where: (i) a party before the national court claims to be entitled to rights under Community law having direct effect in national law ('the rights claimed'); (ii) a national measure in clear terms will, if applied, automatically deprive that party of the rights claimed; (iii) there are serious arguments both for and against the existence of the rights claimed and the national court has sought a preliminary ruling under Article 177 as to whether or not the rights claimed exist; (iv) the national law presumes the national measure in question to be compatible with Community law unless and until it is declared incompatible; (v) the national court has no power to give interim protection to the rights claimed by suspending the application of the national measure pending the preliminary ruling; (vi) if the preliminary ruling is in the event in favour of the rights claimed, the party entitled to those rights is likely to have suffered irremediable damage unless given such interim protection, does Community law either (a) oblige the national court to grant such interim protection of the rights claimed, or (b) give the court power to grant such interim protection of the rights claimed? [2] If question 1(a) is answered in the negative and question 1(b) in the affirmative, what are the criteria to be applied in deciding whether or not to grant such interim protection of the rights claimed?

III – COURSE OF THE PROCEDURE

17 The judgment of the House of Lords was received at the Court Registry on 10 July 1989.

18 On 4 August 1989, that is to say while the written procedure in the present case was in progress, the Commission of the European Communities brought an action before the Court of

Justice under Article 169 of the EEC Treaty for a declaration that by imposing the nationality requirements laid down in section 14 of the Act of 1988, the United Kingdom had failed to fulfil its obligations under Articles 7, 52 and 221 of the EEC Treaty (Case 246/89), now pending. In a separate document, lodged at the Court Registry on the same date, the Commission applied to the Court of Justice for an interim order requiring the United Kingdom to suspend the application or those nationality requirements as regards the nationals of other Member States and in respect of fishing vessels which until 31 March 1989 were fishing under the British flag and under a British fishing licence. By order of 10 October 1989, the President of the Court of Justice granted that application. Pursuant to that order, the United Kingdom made an Order in Council amending section 14 of the Act of 1988 with effect from 2 November 1989.

19 In accordance with Article 20 of the Protocol on the Statute of the Court of Justice of the EEC, written observations were lodged on 26 October 1989 by the Commission or the European Communities, on 8 November by Ireland, on 9 November by the United Kingdom, and also on 9 November by the applicants in these proceedings.

20 In its order for reference, the House of Lords expressed the wish that the Court of Justice should give priority to the case. The President of the Court of Justice decided, in accordance with the second paragraph of Article 55(1) of the Rules of Procedure, that this case should be given priority.

21 On hearing the report of the Judge Rapporteur and the views of the Advocate General, the Court of Justice decided to open the oral procedure without any preparatory inquiry.

IV – WRITTEN OBSERVATIONS

22 The United Kingdom began by describing the judicial remedies available in the United Kingdom. It pointed out that in proceedings for judicial review, the British courts were empowered to quash the acts of public authorities on grounds including illegality arising from a breach of Community law. The effectiveness of such jurisdiction was enhanced by liberal rules as to locus standi and by the fact that such proceedings could be conducted expeditiously.

23 With regard to legislation, the courts did not have the right, under the British constitution, to nullify an Act of Parliament or to treat it as void or unconstitutional. It was otherwise in the case of legislation which was contrary to Community law since section 2(1) and (4) of the European Communities Act 1972 empowered the courts to uphold the primacy of rights arising from Community law. However, Parliament conferred that power on the courts only at the stage when the matter was finally determined and not for the grant of interim relief.

24 The rules of English law which in the present case precluded the grant of interim relief, namely the presumption that an Act of Parliament was compatible with community law and the immunity of the Crown from interim relief, were not discriminatory because they did not draw any distinction between rights arising under domestic law and those arising under Community law.

25 With regard to the argument put forward by the applicants in the main proceedings to the effect that, in a criminal prosecution against them, those proceedings and consequently the application of the relevant legislation were suspended in the event of a reference being made for a preliminary ruling, the United Kingdom pointed out that in those circumstances it was the proceedings initiated before the national court that were suspended and not the application of the law.

26 The impossibility of securing interim relief of the kind sought in the present case was justified by important considerations of public policy, such as compliance with the fundamental limits of the judicial function and the need for legal certainty.

27 Furthermore. in terms of Community law, individuals did not normally have *locus standi* under Article 173 of the EC Treaty to challenge Community legislation. It followed that they could not obtain from the Court of Justice the suspension of Community legislative measures, however serious the effects of such measures on their business might be. Admittedly, Community

legislation could also be challenged in the national courts, but the Court of Justice had held that every regulation which was brought into force in accordance with the EEC Treaty must be presumed to be valid as long as a competent court had not made a finding that it was invalid: see the *Granaria* case [1979] ECR 623. Although the Court of Justice had not ruled out the possibility that a national court might have jurisdiction temporarily to suspend a provision of Community law (see the *Foto-Frost* case [1987] ECR 4199 and *Zuckerfabrik Suderdithmarshen AG* (Case 143/88) now pending before the Court of Justice), the United Kingdom doubted whether it would be consistent with the principle of legal certainty to give the national courts such interim jurisdiction.

28 Following a brief survey or the laws of other Member States on interim relief, the United Kingdom found that in the majority of those countries it did not seem possible to secure, by means of an application for the grant of interim measures, an order suspending the operation of primary legislation. In the Federal Republic of Germany, the Netherlands and Portugal, where there appeared to be certain wider procedures for challenging legislation and granting interim relief, it was not clear that the courts had jurisdiction to grant a mandatory order of the kind sought in the main proceedings.

29 Next, the United Kingdom dealt with the Court of Justice's case law on national remedies for the infringement of Community law. It pointed out that, according to the Court of Justices' judgments in *Comet BV v Productschap voor Siergewassen* (Case 45/76) [1976] ECR 2043 and in *Rewe-Zentralfinanz eG v Landwirtschaftskammer für Saarland* (Case 33/76) [1976] ECR 1989, in the absence of Community harmonisation such remedies were a matter for the national legal system, provided that (a) such remedies were no less favourable than those governing domestic disputes of the same type (principle of non-discrimination), and (b) national rules of procedure did not make it impossible in practice to exercise the rights which the national courts had a duty to protect (principle of effectiveness). Furthermore, it was apparent from paragraph 12 of the judgment in *Express Dairy Foods Ltd v Intervention Board for Agricultural Produce* (Case 130/79) [1980] ECR 1887 that it was not for the Court of Justice to lay down general rules of substance or procedural provisions which only the competent institutions might adopt.

30 According to the United Kingdom, the concept of the direct effect of certain EEC Treaty provisions could not create new remedies in national law. It emphasised that this position was confirmed by the Court of Justice in its judgment in *Rewe-Handelsgesellschaft Nord mbH v Hauptzollamt Kiel* (Case 158/80) [1981] ECR 1805, 1838, at paragraph 44, according to which the EEC Treaty 'was not intended to create new remedies in the national courts to ensure the observance of Community law other than those already laid down by national law.'

31 The Court of Justice therefore acknowledged by implication that the scope of the protection of directly effective rights would vary from one member state to another, pending harmonisation by Community legislation. The only requirement of Community law was that existing remedies should not be emasculated to the point at which there was, in practice, no remedy at all. That was the effect of national legislation, particularly in *Amministrazione delle Finanze dello Stato v SpA San Giorgio* (Case 199/82) [1983] ECR 3595 and in *Les Fils de Julies Bianco SA and J Girard Fils SA v Directeur Général des Douanes et Droits Indirect* (Cases 331, 376 and 378/85) [1988] ECR 1099.

32 Finally, the principle laid down by the Court of Justice in *Amministrazione delle Finanze dello Stato v Simmenthal SpA* (Case 106/77) [1978] ECR 629, according to which a national court was under a duty to give full effect to provisions of Community law and to protect the rights which those provisions conferred on individuals, if necessary refusing of its own motion to apply any conflicting provision of national legislation, was fully recognised in United Kingdom law. In the *Simmenthal* case the rights in question were not theoretical, because they had been established by the Court of Justice in an earlier judgment (*Simmenthal SpA v Italian Minister for Finance* (Case 35/76) [1976] ECR 1871); furthermore, the action brought by Simmenthal before an Italian court was a well-established remedy in the national legal order. The contrast with the present case was therefore striking.

33 It followed from the foregoing that the United Kingdom's position with regard to remedies was fully in accordance with Community law. None of those remedies had been withheld or

fettered in the present case. In an exceptional case such as the present, the protection of individuals might be ensured by the Court of Justice's ability to expedite any reference for a preliminary ruling submitted by a national court (Article 55 of the Rules of Procedure) and by the Commission's ability to obtain interim measures under Articles 169 and 186 of the EEC Treaty, as in the present case.

34 In conclusion, the United Kingdom submitted that the answer to question 1(b) should be as follows: 'Community law does not itself confer on a national court a jurisdiction to grant an interim order to suspend national legislative measures on the basis of claimed or putative rights under Community law having direct effect, if no such remedy exists as a matter of national law.'

35 Ireland pointed out, as a preliminary remark, that what was at issue in the present case was not the enforcement of established rights enjoyed by the applicants in the main proceedings under provisions of Community law which had direct effect, but whether interim protection might or must be granted before the national court decided whether the applicants enjoyed those rights and, if so, whether such rights had been infringed.

36 Ireland went on to state that the Court of Justice had consistently been reluctant to intervene in the sphere of national remedies for the enforcement of rights conferred on individuals by Community law, even where such rights (or their infringement) had been established. Ireland referred in that regard to the judgment in the *Rewe-Zentralfinanz* case [1976] ECR 1989 in which the Court of Justice ruled that, in the absence of Community rules on remedies in the national courts, it was for the domestic legal system of each member state to ensure the protection of the rights arising from the direct effect of Community law.

37 Furthermore, the Court of Justice ruled in the *Rewe-Handelsgesellschaft* case [1981] ECR 1805 that the EEC Treaty was not intended to create new remedies in the national courts to ensure the observance of community law. The Irish Government emphasised that, if it were otherwise, there would be an unwarranted interference by the Court of Justice in the manner in which national courts applied Community law according to internal procedures.

38 According to Ireland, it did not follow from the case law of the Court of Justice concerning the principle of effectiveness (the *Comet* case [1976] ECR 2043, and *Amministrazione delle Finanze v Mireco SaS* (Case 26/79) [1980] ECR 2559) that there was a right to interim protection.

39 Finally, Ireland submitted that it would be wholly inappropriate to require the creation of new remedies in national law. Divergences between the national systems as to the right to interim protection could be removed only by legislation on the part of the Council of the European Communities. In the absence of a Community measure of that kind, any problem raised in that regard by national law might be dealt with in the context of a direct action brought by the Commission against the Member State in question.

40 In conclusion, Ireland submitted that the answer to question 1 should be as follows: '(a) Community law does not in the circumstances described in this question oblige the national courts to grant interim protection of the rights claimed where the national court has no obligation or power under national law to grant such protection, (b) Community law does not in such circumstances give the national court power to grant interim protection of the rights claimed if the national court has no power to grant such interim protection under national law.'

41 The applicants pointed out, as a preliminary remark, that they had never suggested that in the ordinary event the grant of interim protection should be mandatory. However, in the light of the specific circumstances of this case, they contended that the national court was obliged in the present case to make an appropriate protection order.

42 The applicants went on to survey the Court of Justice's case law concerning 'directly effective' provisions of Community law and the role of the national courts with regard to the rights conferred on individuals by those provisions.

43 The applicants pointed out that, according to that case law, rules of Community law which were of 'direct effect' must be uniformly applied in all the Member States from the date of their entry into force and for as long as they continued in force: see *Amministrazione delle Finanze dello*

Stato v Ariete SpA (Case 811/79) [1980] ECR 2545, the *Mireco* case [1980] ECR 2559, and the *Simmenthal* case [1978] ECR 629. Those rules constituted a direct source of rights and duties for all those affected thereby (the Simmenthal case) and formed part of the citizens' legal heritage: see *NV Algemene Transport-en Expeditie Onderneming van Gend en Loos v Nederlandse Administratie der Belastingen* (Case 26/62) [1963] ECR 1. The rights arising therefrom for individual citizens were created by the provisions of Community law themselves and not by decisions of the Court of Justice which interpreted those provisions; see *Procureur de la Republic v Waterkeyn* (Cases 314/81, 315/81, 316/81, 83/82) [1982] ECR 4337.

44 It was upon the national courts that the obligation of ensuring the legal protection which individuals derived from directly effective provisions of Community law was imposed: see the *Rewe-Zentralfinanz* case [1976] ECR 1989 (the *Comet* case [1976] ECR 2043, and *Amministrazione delle Finanze dello Stato v Denkavit Italiana Srl* (Case 61/79) [1980] ECR 1205. That obligation on the part of the national courts could not be diminished or avoided on the ground that the Commission was empowered to take action against a Member State under Article 169 of the EEC. Treaty or that it might, within the framework of such proceedings, obtain interim measures from the Court of Justice pursuant to Article 186 of the EEC Treaty. That followed from the Court of Justice's judgments in the *Van Gend en Loos* case and in *Molkerei-Zentrale/Westfalen Lippe GmbH v Hauptzollamt Paderborn* (Case 28/67) [1969] ECR 143.

45 The applicants emphasised that the protection afforded to individuals by the national courts must be effective (see *Bozzetti v Invernizzi SpA* (Case 179/84) [1985] ECR 2301, 2317–2318, paragraph 17) and not merely symbolic. Such protection also had to be 'direct and immediate': see *Salgoil SpA v Italian Ministry for Foreign Trade* (Case 13/68) [1968] ECR 453, 462, 463). A temporary impediment to the full effectiveness of Community law was not permitted: see the *Simmenthal* case [1978] ECR 629, 644, paragraph 23. Consequently, any provision of a national legal system and any legislative administrative or judicial practice which might impair the effectiveness of Community law by withholding from the national courts the power to give appropriate protection was itself incompatible with Community law: see the *Simmenthal* case [1978] ECR 629, *von Colson and Kamann v Land Nordrhein-Westfalen* (Case 14/83) [1984] ECR 1891, and *Johnston v Chief Constable of the Royal Ulster Constabulary* (Case 222/84) [1987] QB 129.

46 That was the case with regard to two rules of English law which precluded the grant of the interim relief sought by the applicants.

47 In particular, a reference for a preliminary ruling on the substance of the case was rendered pointless by the presumption of compatibility, because that presumption prevented the national court from safeguarding the position until such time as the Court of Justice gave judgment. Since that presumption restricted the freedom of the national courts to refer to the Court of Justice any question of Community law which needed to be resolved in order to enable it to give judgment, it was incompatible with the principle of 'effective protection' and with the second paragraph of Article 177 of the EEC Treaty.

48 The paramount importance attributed by Community law to the protection of rights conferred on individuals by its provisions in the period between the submission of a reference for a preliminary ruling and the decision of the Court of Justice was confirmed by the judgment in the *Foto-Frost* case [1987] ECR 4199, 4232, paragraph 19.

49 With regard to the rule concerning the Crown's immunity from interim relief, the applicants pointed out that that obstacle was artificial because, if they disregarded the Act of 1988 and were prosecuted by the Crown for infringing it, the Crown would be unable to enforce that Act since the national court, by making a reference to the Court of Justice pursuant to Article 177 of the EEC Treaty, would suspend the proceedings and protect the rights claimed by the applicants.

50 In any event, the rule concerning the immunity of the Crown constituted an anomaly as regards the exercise of rights arising from provisions of Community law, in that (a) interim relief was available against all other defendants, with the exception of the Crown, although more often than not it was in fact against the authorities of the state, namely the Crown, that rights conferred by Community law had to be enforced, and (b) final relief was available against the Crown.

51 According to the applicants, Community law rendered inapplicable the two rules of English law which removed the possibility of obtaining interim relief of the kind sought in the main proceedings. They emphasised that, if it were otherwise, the United Kingdom would be able flagrantly to disregard Community law in cases such as the present, whilst at the same time taking advantage of the fact that, since a reference was likely to be made to the Court of Justice for a preliminary ruling, holders of rights conferred by Community law would be deprived of the right of exercising them in the interim period. Such deprivation of rights would in practice be permanent in cases where, as in the main proceedings, an action for damages was not available (since, as English law stood at present on the authority of *Bourgoin SA v Minister of Agriculture, Fisheries and Food* [1986] QB 716, no action for damages lay against the Crown for infringing an EEC Treaty provision, unless bad faith on the part of the Crown was established) and where the rights of applicants could never be given full retroactive protection in any other way when the final decision actually came to be made. All those considerations revealed the extent of the need, particularly in cases such as the main proceedings, for effective protection to be made available by way of interim relief.

52 Finally, the applicants pointed out that there were a number of reasons why it was entirely misplaced for the United Kingdom to rely on the Court of Justice's judgment in the *Rewe-Handelsgesellschaft* case [1981] ECR 1805 in order to justify the impossibility of obtaining interim relief. In the first place, there was no question of there being any need to create new remedies in the national courts in order to provide appropriate interim relief since the remedies which already existed under English law were perfectly adequate; it was sufficient for the two rules concerning the presumption of compatibility and Crown immunity to be disapplied. Secondly, and in any event, the *dicta* in that judgment were subject to the proviso, laid down by the Court of Justice in its judgments in the *Comet* case [1976] ECR 2043 and in the *Rewe-Zentralfinanz* case [1976] ECR 1989 and reiterated in its judgment in the *San Giorgio* case [1983] ECR 3595 and elsewhere, that in no circumstances might national measures be such as to render it impossible in practice or excessively difficult for the rights conferred on individuals by Community law to be protected. It was inconceivable that the Court of Justice would apply that proviso to cases of procedural, evidential and limitation rules, but not to a rule of locus standi such as that which was in issue in the *Rewe-Handelsgesellschaft* case [1981] ECR 1805.

53 In conclusion, the applicants submitted that the answer to question 1 should be that, in the circumstances referred to therein, 'Community law requires the courts of the Member States to have the duty (or at least the power) to grant such interim protection as is appropriate and to disapply to the extent necessary all national legislative measures, roles and judicial practices which constitute obstacles to the grant of effective protection to those such as the applicants in the present case, who rely on directly effective Community law rights.'

54 The Commission began with a comparative survey of Community legislation and the national legislation of the Member States on interim relief.

55 It pointed out that, in so far as Community law was concerned, Article 185 of the EEC Treaty provided, in proceedings for annulment, for the possibility of suspending a Community measure even with respect to primary legislation.

56 On the basis of its survey of national legislation, the Commission came to the conclusion that the laws of all the Member States other than Denmark and the United Kingdom empowered the courts to suspend measures which were open to challenge before them. Even in Denmark the courts had jurisdiction to grant such interim relief in certain limited classes of public law proceedings.

57 Next, the Commission referred to the case law of the Court of Justice on protection by the national courts of the rights which Community law conferred on individuals.

58 In the first place. the Court of Justice had emphasised the need for a remedy of a judicial nature against any decision of a national authority refusing to grant an individual the benefit of a right conferred by Community law: see *Union Nationale des Entraineurs et Cadres Techniques*

Professionnels du Football v Heylens (Case 222/86) [1987] ECR 4097, and *Johnston's* case [1987] 1 QB 179.

59 Furthermore, it followed from the case law of the Court of Justice on actions brought by individuals in a national court in order to protect the rights conferred upon them by Community law (see the *Comet* case [1976] ECR 2043 and the *Rewe-Zentralfinanze* case [1976] ECR 1989) that, in the absence of Community rules, the procedures relating to such actions were governed by national law, subject to compliance with the principles of non-discrimination and effectiveness.

60 The principle of non-discrimination was not directly applicable to the present case since the British courts had no jurisdiction to grant interim relief against the Crown, even in cases involving English law alone. In contrast, the principle of effectiveness was directly relevant to the present case. The Member States were bound to observe that principle quite independently of the principle of non-discrimination. Accordingly, when a rule contravened the principle of effectiveness, it was no answer to argue that in equivalent cases involving national law alone the rule applied in exactly the same way, see the *San Giorgio* case [1983] ECR 3595.

61 According to the Commission, the most important judgment ever delivered on the scope of the principle of effectiveness was that in the *Simmenthal* case [1978] ECR 629, pp 643, 644, paragraphs 15, 16 and 21–23. That ruling made it abundantly clear that the principle of effectiveness was an immediate and inevitable consequence of the concept of direct applicability. It would be nonsense to state that certain provisions of Community law might be relied upon before the national courts if any attempts to rely on them could in fact be thwarted by national rules on remedies or procedure.

62 It followed that the national courts were required to ensure that the parties who relied in proceedings before them on provisions of Community law having direct effect had an effective remedy in national law whereby effect might be given to their rights under those provisions. According to the Commission, the national courts must be empowered to grant interim relief, but without being required to do so in every case in which a plaintiff relied on a directly applicable provision of Community law.

63 The fact that in national law the contested national measure was presumed to be compatible with Community law unless and until it was declared incompatible constituted no logical obstacle to the grant of interim relief suspending its application. The same presumption existed in Community law (see the *Granaria* case [1979] ECR 623) but that did not prevent the Court of Justice from suspending, pursuant to article 185 of the EEC Treaty, the application of Community measures by way of interim relief. In English law also there was a presumption that measures adopted by local authorities were lawful, but that did not prevent the courts from suspending their application by the grant of interim injunctions: see *De Falco v Crawley Borough Council* [1980] QB 460, and also *Regulation v Kensington and Chelsea Royal London Borough Council ex p Hammel* [1989] QB 518.

64 The Commission pointed out that, according to the House of Lords, the damage suffered by the applicants was likely to be irremediable unless they were granted the interim protection sought and they were successful in their main action, since they would probably have no remedy in damages in view of the judgment of the Court of Appeal in the *Bourgoin* case [1986] QB 716.

65 According to the Commission, it could be argued that the likelihood of irremediable damage necessarily implied that the only effective remedy was interim relief. If a party could neither obtain interim relief in order to prevent the damage from occurring nor recover damages *ex post facto*, the Commission submitted that on any view he was deprived of any effective remedy whereby effect might be given to his rights. That situation could not be justified by the fact that the absence of any remedy was only temporary since, according to paragraph 23 of the judgment in the *Simmenthal* case [1978] ECR 629, even the temporary absence of an effective remedy was contrary to the principle of effectiveness.

66 In conclusion, the Commission submitted that question 1 should be answered as follows: 'The obligation on national courts to apply Community law having direct effect and to protect rights which the latter confers on individuals includes the obligation to consider whether interim

protection of the rights claimed against the authorities of a Member State should be granted in order to avoid irremediable damage and, where appropriate, to grant such interim relief.'

Second question

67 The United Kingdom pointed out that in view of the proposed answer to question 1(b) there was no need to answer the other questions submitted by the House of Lords.

68 Ireland submitted that the second question need not be answered in the light of the answer proposed to the first question. However, if the Court of Justice were to give an answer that question, Ireland suggested that it should be as follows: 'The conditions for the granting by a national court of such interim relief are a matter solely for national law, subject only to the qualifications that such conditions must not discriminate against Community law by comparison with national law, and must not infringe the prohibition of discrimination on grounds of nationality contained in Article 7 of the EEC Treaty.'

69 The applicants pointed out that if the Court of Justice's answer to the first question were that the national courts were empowered to grant interim relief, the answer to the second question should be that Community law left the Member States free to determine the criteria upon which that power was to be exercised, provided always that the criteria were not defined or applied in any respect (a) less favourably than would be the case if rights under Community law were not involved, or in any event (b) so as to render protection of the rights impossible in practice or excessively difficult to achieve.

70 On that basis the appropriate criteria would be those which the English courts currently applied with regard to interim relief and which involved the court asking itself (a) whether there was a serious issue to be tried, or, in other words, whether the action had a 'real prospect of success' (in that regard the applicants referred in particular, to the decision of the House of Lords in *American Cyanamid Co v Ethicon Ltd* [1975] AC 396); (b) if so, whether damages were obtainable and, if they were, whether they constituted an adequate remedy for one side or the other; (c) if not, where the balance of convenience lay as between the parties. In considering the latter question, the court should, in particular, weigh the consequences for the applicant if interim relief were not granted against the consequences for the defendant if interim relief were granted. It could also take into account any other relevant factors such as, for example, the applicant's delay in seeking an interim remedy, or the interaction of private rights with public interests, which was pertinent to this case.

71 Next, the applicants explained in detail the reasons why they satisfied all the aforesaid criteria.

72 The Commission pointed out, as a preliminary remark, that the criteria for the grant of interim relief by the Court of Justice in accordance with Article 83(2) of the Rules of Procedure, as interpreted by the Court of Justice, were that the applicant must make out a prima facie case and show the existence of urgency such that interim measures were necessary to avoid serious and irreparable harm. Although Article 86(2) of the rules of procedure provided that the Court of Justice might require the applicant to lodge security as a condition for enforcing the order, the Court of Justice rarely imposed such a requirement.

73 Under English law, the criteria to be applied for the grant of interim protection were laid down in (a) the judgments in the *De Falco* case [1980] QB 460 and the *Hammel* case [1989] QB 518 concerning the grant of interim relief against public bodies other than the Crown, such as local authorities, and (b) the judgment of the House of Lords in the *American Cyanamid* case [1975] AC 396 concerning the grant of interim relief in proceedings between private individuals. The Commission stated that, according to the latter judgment, the court must first be satisfied that the applicant's claim was neither frivolous nor vexatious. If that condition was fulfilled, the matter was to be determined on a balance of convenience. Finally, if the court decided to grant the interim relief sought, the applicant was required to give a cross-undertaking as to damages.

74 Next, the Commission pointed out that there was nothing to prevent the English courts from applying the criterion already established by their case law for the grant of interim relief against local authorities.

75 In any case, the Commission submitted that, in accordance with general principles, the following matters were to be weighed up by the national courts: (i) the apparent strength of the applicant's case: it was not for Community law to determine whether the applicant must show a serious issue to be tried (see the *American Cyanamid* case) or make out a prima facie case (Article 83(2) of the Court of Justice's Rules of Procedure) or make out a strong prima facie case (the *De Falco* and *Hammel* cases); (ii) the balance of convenience, which included considerations of urgency, the risk of irreparable damage and the public interest. Where, as in this case, the applicant was deprived or his right to carry on his economic activity until the outcome of the main proceedings, great weight must be given to that factor. That was all the more so where, as in this case, he was likely to go bankrupt as a result.

76 According to the Commission, the fact that a cross-undertaking could not be required in a particular case need not constitute an obstacle to the grant of interim relief.

77 Finally, the Commission emphasised that in no case could any of the circumstances which might militate against the grant of interim relief, whether taken alone or with other such circumstances, operate as an absolute bar to such relief, since the person concerned would then be denied an effective remedy. For instance, the fact that the impugned measure constituted the straightforward application of an Act of Parliament could not automatically preclude its suspension.

78 In conclusion, the Commission submitted that question 2 should be answered as follows: 'In deciding whether to grant interim relief national courts must weigh up the interests involved in each case, without considering any particular circumstance or set of circumstances as constituting generally an absolute bar to such relief. Moreover, the criteria to be applied by national courts may not be less favourable to the individual than those applying to similar cases relating to national law alone.'

Sir Nicholas Lyell QC, SG, Christopher Bellamy, QC, Christopher Vajda and *TJG Pratt*, agent, for the United Kingdom.
James O'Reilly SC and *Louis J Dockery*, Chief State Solicitor, agent, for the Republic of Ireland.
David Vaughan QC, Gerald Darling, David Anderson and *Stephen Swabey*, solicitor, for the first to 94th applicants.
Nicholas Forwood, QC the 95th applicant, Rawlings (Trawling) Ltd.
Götz zur Hausen and *Peter Oliver*, agents, for the Commission of the European Communities.

17 May: **Mr Advocate General Tesauro** delivered the following opinion.

1 The reply which the Court of Justice is called upon to give to two questions referred to it by the House of Lords for a preliminary ruling in *Regulation v The Secretary of State for Transport ex p Factortame Ltd* [1990] 2 AC 85 will rank amongst those which help to define the context of relations between national courts and Community law. And, I would add, on a point of unquestionable importance. The questions are clear. Pending a ruling by the Court of Justice on the interpretation of provisions of Community law having direct effect, and where United Kingdom law does not permit the national court to suspend, by way of interim relief, the application of the allegedly conflicting national measure and thus, provisionally, to acknowledge an individual's right claimed under Community law but denied by national law: (1) must (or may) the national court grant such relief on the basis of Community law? (2) if so, applying what criteria?

2 The dispute which gave rise to the reference for a preliminary ruling concerns a considerable number of companies operating in the fisheries sector, which are incorporated under the laws of the United Kingdom but represent Spanish interests. These undertakings contest the validity under Community law of a United Kingdom statute of 1988 (the Merchant Shipping Act 1988) which altered the requirements for registration in the register of fishing vessels, in particular as regards nationality and residence of the beneficial ownership, deliberately strengthening those

requirements in the case of foreign interests (including Community interests). Relying on certain provisions of the EEC Treaty having direct effect, Factortame Ltd and others instituted proceedings for judicial review of the Act in question, seeking a declaration that the Act should not apply to them on the ground that such application would be contrary to Community law, an order prohibiting the authorities from treating the registration of the vessels under the old Act (the Merchant Shipping Act 1894) as having ceased, and interim relief pending final judgment.

3   At first instance, the Divisional Court of the Queen's Bench Division made a reference to the Court of Justice for a preliminary ruling on the interpretation of the provisions of Community law raised and, as an interim measure, ordered the Secretary of State for Transport not to apply the new Act to the applicants pending final judgment or further order of the court.

4   The Secretary of State for Transport appealed against the order for interim relief which was set aside by the Court of Appeal on the ground that United Kingdom courts do not have the power to suspend, by way of interim relief, the application of statutes or to grant an injunction against the Crown.

5   The House of Lords, before which the matter was brought, confirmed that as a matter of English law the courts have no power to suspend the application of an Act of Parliament on the ground of its alleged, but unproved, incompatibility with Community law, and referred to the Court of Justice for a preliminary ruling the questions mentioned above, in order essentially to ascertain whether that which is not permitted by English law is required or permitted by Community law.

6   It should be stated by way of a preliminary observation that the House of Lords acknowledges that it has the power and the duty to give preference over the conflicting national statute to a provision of the EEC Treaty or a provision of secondary Community law having direct effect to the United Kingdom legal order, and that this is so when the conflict is immediately and readily discernible, either by virtue of an existing interpretation of the Community provision by the Court of Justice or by virtue of the fact that the provision itself is sufficiently 'clear' in its content. The problem arose, however, because there was no certainty as to the interpretation of the Community provisions relevant to the circumstances, but rather there were 'serious arguments both for and against the existence of the rights claimed,' which prompted the Divisional Court to ask the Court of Justice to give a preliminary ruling on the interpretation of those provisions. The questions raised form the subject matter of different proceedings (Case 221/89) which are separate from the present proceedings. Moreover, to complete the picture, I would recall that, as regards the alleged incompatibility with Community law of the same United Kingdom statute in point, the Commission of the European Communities brought proceedings under Article 169 of the EEC Treaty against the United Kingdom, but solely on the nationality aspects, likewise seeking, by way of an interim measure, the suspension of application of the Act. The Court of Justice has already made an order granting such a measure in *Commission of the European Communities v United Kingdom* (Case 246/89R) (1989) *The Times*, 28 October, and the Act has also been amended in that respect.

7   As a further preliminary matter, I think it is appropriate to point out that the problem has arisen in the context of the special proceedings by way of application for judicial review provided for by English law which were brought by the parties concerned even before the new Act on the register of shipping entered into force. On this point both the House of Lords in its order for reference and the United Kingdom in its written observations have stressed that, had the question of a conflict with Community law arisen in the course of criminal or administrative proceedings brought against those same parties for contravention of the Act on the register of shipping, the national court could well have stayed the proceedings (and even any forfeiture proceedings in respect of vessels) pending the outcome of the request for a preliminary ruling by the Court of Justice on the interpretation of the relevant Community provisions. The consequences of the Court of Justice's ruling, whether favourable or unfavourable as regards the claim made by the parties concerned, would then have been applied to them retroactively. The House of Lords infers therefrom that, in such a case, 'the prosecution or forfeiture proceedings would not be frustrated but suspended': see the order for reference.

It is not wholly clear in what perspective attention was drawn to the difference between the situation in this case (proceedings for judicial review) and that which might have arisen in ordinary proceedings of a criminal or other type instituted following the contravention of the Act. What is true, it seems to me, is that, for present purposes, the difference is not of any great importance. The mere stay of proceedings as a result of a reference to the Court of Justice pursuant to Article 177 of the EEC Treaty is not an interim measure and does not satisfy any requirements of interim protection of the rights claimed. On the contrary, it unquestionably poses in more acute terms the very problem which necessitates interim protection: whether, if stayed, the proceedings may, precisely, be 'frustrated' by the delay in giving final judgment.

Thus the question raised by the House of Lords is of importance in the same way and in the same terms with regard to both the procedural situations indicated to the Court of Justice. It would only be otherwise if, whatever the type of proceedings, the national court were entitled, where proceedings are stayed and a reference is made to the Court of Justice under Article 177, also to grant an interim measure of the type requested by the applicants in this case and if, accordingly, it had the power provisionally to allow the ships to be registered on the basis of the old Act pending final judgment; as became clear also at the hearing, this is plainly precluded whether in judicial review proceedings or any other type of proceeding.

8   On the other hand, I attach importance to the fact, stressed by the national court, that in a situation such as the one now before the Court of Justice, that is to say in the absence of interim measures, the economic damage suffered by the applicants in the course of the proceedings would remain irreparable, an action for damages being precluded by settled national case law: see the order for reference. It follows that, even were an interpretative ruling to be given by the Court of Justice, upholding the arguments of the applicants, the subsequent judgment by the national court could not award compensation for the damage suffered and the proceedings might in any event be 'frustrated'.

That is not to say that compensation for loss suffered is a decisive factor and constitutes a real alternative to interim protection, in view of the fact that, even were it provided for, it would not always and in any event be sufficient in itself to satisfy the requirement of interim protection, a requirement which arises precisely out of the inadequacy of monetary compensation from the point of view of the 'utility' of the future judgment: see, for example, the order of the Court of Justice in *Agricola Commerciale Olio Srl v Commission of the European Communities* (Case 232/81) [1981] ECR 2193, 2200, paragraph 9. Rather the fact that compensation for damages is precluded makes it by definition impossible to make good the losses suffered pending judgment in the proceedings

9   'The national court has specifically identified the principles of Community law whose interpretation by way of a preliminary ruling by the Court of Justice would enable it to resolve the problem, in one way or another: the direct effect of the Community provisions relied on, the obligation to provide direct and immediate protection of individual rights, the practical efficacy of judicial remedies, the obligation to refrain from applying national measures and/or practices which render the exercise of such rights and the protection afforded to them impossible.

Similarly, the formal obstacles to the exercise by the English courts of the power to grant interim protection in proceedings of the type in question have been made clear: the presumption of validity that attaches to a statute until a final determination is made, a process which may include a ruling by the Court of Justice, and the impossibility of granting an injunction against the Crown, an impossibility which moreover relates not only to interim measures but also to final determinations: see the observations by the United Kingdom.

10 The principles of Community law which the House of Lords has stated to be relevant and on whose interpretation its decision will depend are fundamental principles enshrined in numerous judgments of the Court of Justice. Those principles are, however, observed (and without difficulty) by the United Kingdom courts, with the sole reservation which constitutes at once the reason for and the subject of these proceedings. Are such principles also to be interpreted as meaning that the national court must (or may) grant an interim measure requiring the Crown to

refrain from applying, during the proceedings on the substance of the case, a 'measure' (in this case an Act of Parliament) in respect of which there is no certainty but merely a suspicion, however serious, that it is incompatible with Community law? In other words, do the obligations which Community law imposes on the national courts concerning the protection of rights conferred directly on individuals also include the requirement to order the suspension, by way of interim protection, of the application of a national law which is alleged to be in conflict with Community law?

11 In addition to a rapid survey of the relevant principles of Community law, which are well known to the national court, the reply to this question calls for an identification of the requirement which is at the origin and is also the raison d'être of interim protection, a concept long established in jurisprudence and in the legal systems of the Member States.

12 The starting point for the appraisal of the problem is that, as is accepted in this case, directly effective Community provisions are involved in the now uncontested sense of measures immediately conferring on individuals enforceable legal rights which, as such, may be relied upon before national courts. It is scarcely necessary to emphasise that it is on that assumption that the questions have been referred to the Court of Justice for a preliminary ruling, irrespective of which Community provisions are involved and the correct interpretation thereof. In fact, it is not the interpretation of the individual EEC Treaty provisions relied on by the applicants in the dispute before the national court which is requested in these proceedings (merely for the sake of clarity, I would remind the Court of Justice that Articles 7, 52, 58 and 221 of the EEC Treaty are involved), but rather the interpretation of the principles of Community law mentioned above. In other words, the Court of Justice is not requested to embark upon an examination of the substance of the provisions relied on by the applicants, which is the subject of other, and separate, proceedings for a preliminary ruling, which are, I repeat, also pending before the Court of Justice (Case 221/89), but rather to give a general reply with regard to the interim protection of rights claimed by individuals by virtue of directly effective Community provisions.

13 That being so, I would recall that provisions of Community law having direct effect 'must be fully and uniformly applied in all the Member States from the date of their entry into force and for so long as they continue in force' (among other authorities, see *Amministrazione delle Finanze dello Stato v Simmenthal SpA* (Case 106/77) [1978] ECR 629, 643, paragraph 14, and *Amministrazione delle Finanze dello Stato v Ariete SpA* (Case 811/79) [1980] ECR 2545, 2552–53, paragraph 5) and that 'this consequence also concerns any national court whose task it is as an organ of a Member State to protect, in a case within its jurisdiction, the rights conferred upon individuals by Community law': see the judgment in the *Simmenthal* case [1978] ECR 629, 643, paragraph 16. And again in that judgment the Court of Justice affirmed that, in view of the supremacy of Community law, the relevant provisions having direct effect 'not only by their entry into force render automatically inapplicable any conflicting provision of current national law', but also 'preclude the valid adoption of new national legislative measures to the extent to which they would be incompatible with Community provisions: see the judgment in the *Simmenthal* case, p 643, paragraph 17.

It is quite clear, therefore, that a Community provision having immediate effect within the Member States confers enforceable legal rights on the individual from its entry into force and for so long as it continues in force, irrespective and even in spite of a prior or subsequent national provisions which might negate those same rights. I do not consider it useful, and even less so in this context, to enter into a sterile dialectical discussion on the theoretical basis of such a firmly established principle. What matters, in so far as is relevant in this case, is that the national court is obliged to afford judicial protection to the rights conferred by a Community provision as from the entry into force of that provision and for so long as it continues in force.

14 Equally beyond dispute, and in harmony with the principle of collaboration enshrined in Article 5 of the EEC Treaty, which is the real key to the interpretation of the whole system, is the fact that the methods and the machinery for protecting rights conferred on individuals by provisions of Community law are and remain, in the absence of a harmonised system of procedure, those provided by the domestic legal systems of the Member States. That principle, which recurs

in the Court of Justice's case law, is nevertheless based on a fundamental pre-condition, which is also derived from the second paragraph of Article 5, namely that the methods and national procedures must be no less favourable than those applying to like remedies for the protection of rights founded on national provisions and must also not be such as to render impossible in practice 'the exercise of rights which the national courts are obliged to protect' see *Rewe-Zentralfinanz eG v Landwirtschaftskammer für Saarland* (Case 33/76) [1976] ECR 1989, 1997, paragraph 5; *Comet BV v Produktschap voor Siergewassen* (Case 45/76) [1976] ECR 2043, 2053, paragraphs 15, 16; the *Ariete* case [1980] ECR 2545, at p 2554, paragraph 12; *Express Dairy Foods Ltd v Intervention Board for Agricultural Produce* (Case 130/79) [1980] ECR 1887, at p 1900 paragraph 12. *Amministrazione delle Finanze delle Stato v Denkauf Italiana Srl* (Case 61/79) [1980] ECR 1205, 1226, paragraph 25; *Hans Just I/S v Danish Ministry for Fiscal Affairs* (Case 68/79) [1980] ECR 501, 522, paragraph 25: and *Amministrazione delle Finanze dello Stato v SpA San Giorgio* (Case 199/82) [1983] ECR 3595.

Moreover, in its judgment in the *Simmenthal* case [1978] ECR 629, the Court of Justice had affirmed, 644, paragraph 22:

> ... any provision of a national legal system and any legislative, administrative or judicial practice which might impair the effectiveness of Community law by withholding from the national court having jurisdiction to apply such law the power to do everything necessary at the moment of its application to set aside national legislative provisions which might prevent Community rules from having full force and effect are incompatible with those requirements which are the very essence of Community law.

(I would also cite *Commission of the European Communities v Hellenic Republic* (Case 68/88) (1990) *The Times*, 28 October, in which the Court of Justice reaffirms that 'Article 5 of the EEC Treaty required Member States to take all measures appropriate in order to guarantee the scope and effectiveness of Community law'.) In other words, the national court is to apply Community law either through the means provided for under the national legal system or, failing that, 'of its own motion': see the judgment in the *Simmenthal* case, p 644, paragraph 24.

15 It is therefore firmly established, in the light of the Court of Justice's well settled case law, which has moreover been pertinently cited by the House of Lords, that national courts are required to afford complete and effective judicial protection to individuals on whom enforceable rights are conferred under a directly effective Community provision, on condition that the Community provision governs the matter in question from the moment of its entry into force, and that from this it follows that any national provision or practice which precludes those courts from giving 'full effect' to the Community provision is incompatible with Community law.

The emphasis of this point should not appear superfluous merely because it recurs in the Court of Justice's case law, since it is precisely from this observation that I shall derive the reply which I propose that the Court of Justice should give in this case.

16 The problem which the national court has raised is a general one and is not new, even though, although it has been implicitly overcome by other courts (on more than one occasion on which a reference has been made to the Court of Justice in the context of an alleged conflict between a national provision (law or administrative act) and Community law, the national court without hesitation also granted interim measures, which in substance amounted to a provisional suspension of the application of the instrument in question: for example, a stay of execution of an expulsion order from the Netherlands was ordered in *Netherlands v Reed* (Case 59/85) [1986] ECR 1283; again, an employment relationship with the University of Venice was ordered to be maintained in *Alluè v Universitá degli Studi di Venezia* (Case 33/88) (1989) *The Times*, 16 June, and in another case a provisional residence permit was ordered to be issued in Belgium (Case 363/89, pending)), it is submitted for the first time for the judgment of the Court of Justice, perhaps not by chance in the context of the somewhat special situation represented by the procedure for judicial review of laws provided for in the United Kingdom. The question, therefore, does not concern solely the English legal system, nor does it relate solely to the relationship between a national law and a Community provision, but rather it relates to the requirement for, and the very existence of, the interim protection of a right which is not certain but whose existence is in the course of being determined in a situation where there is a conflict between legal rules of differing rank. This is a

conflict which, as regards the relationship between a national provision and a Community provision, quite apart from the theoretical or terminological choices and methods applied in the individual Member States, finds effective expression the concept of 'primauté,' that is to say the 'precedence' of the latter provision over the former.

The problem arises from the fact that in a structured and intricate context which a modern system of judicial protection demands there is a lack of contemporaneity between the two points in time which mark the course of the law, namely the point when the right comes into existence and the point (later on) when the existence of the right is (definitively) established.

17 To compensate for the fact that these two points in time do not coincide there is a first and general remedy. It is true that only the definitive establishment of the existence of the right confers on the right fullness and certainty of content in the sense of placing the right itself, and the means whereby it may be exercised, finally beyond dispute (res judicata in the substantive sense); but it is also true that that effect is carried back to the point in time when the right was invoked by initiating the procedure for judicial review. The effect of the establishment of the existence of the right, inappropriately but significantly described as retroactive effect, is merely the consequence of the function of the provision and of its nature and modus operandi which in fact gives rise to an enforceable legal right from the moment when the provision enters into force and for so long as it continues in force. The only possible delay is that which may occur before the right becomes fully effective and operational in cases where application to a court is needed in order to establish the existence of the right, and in particular in cases of prior review of the validity of the provision which is alleged to be applicable. And it is scarcely necessary to add that the situation would be no different if the question were examined from the opposite point of view and one were to consider the non-existence of the right and the finding to that effect.

What is important to stress is that at the time when an application is made the right already exists (or does not) and the provision which confers that right on (or denies it to) the individual is lawful or unlawful. The procedure for judicial review merely postpones the establishment of the existence of the right, that is to say its full and effective operation, to a later point in time and subject to the 'retroactivity' of the effects of the actual establishment of the right. That is plainly true both where the establishment of the right entails an appraisal of the link between the factual situation and the provision relied upon and where the national court is called upon to determine the provision applicable from between two or more provisions, which may even be in conflict. In the latter situation, too, where the existence of the right may also be established by means of a review of validity, the provision which will be determined as the one applicable (in place of another declared to be invalid or incompatible) was in reality so applicable at the time when the application was made, inasmuch as at that time what was lacking was only the establishment of the right's existence and not also its actual existence. That has been specifically emphasised also by the Court of Justice in *Amministrazione delle Finanze delle Stato v Mireco SaS* (Case 826/79) [1980] ECR 2559, when it held, p 2573, paragraph 7:

> The interpretation which, in the exercise of the jurisdiction conferred upon it by article 177, the Court of Justice gives to a rule of Community law clarifies and defines where necessary the meaning and scope of that rule as it must be or ought to have been understood and applied from the time of its coming into force.

18 The above-mentioned general remedy for the lack of contemporaneity between the establishment of the right's existence and its actual existence does not always succeed in achieving the main objective of judicial protection. Sometimes the right's existence is established too late for the right claimed to be fully and usefully exercised, which is the more likely to be the case the more structured and complex, and the more probably rich in safeguards, is the procedure culminating in the definitive establishment of the right. The result is that in such a case the utility as well as the effectiveness of judicial protection may be lost and there could be a betrayal of the principle, long established in jurisprudence, according to which the need to have recourse to legal proceedings to enforce a right should not occasion damage to the party in the right.

Interim protection has precisely that objective purpose, namely to ensure that the time needed to establish the existence of the right does not in the end have the effect of irremediably depriving the right of substance, by eliminating any possibility of exercising it; in brief, the purpose of interim protection is to achieve that fundamental objective of every legal system, the effectiveness of judicial protection. Interim protection is intended to prevent so far as possible the damage occasioned by the fact that the establishment and the existence of the right are not fully contemporaneous from prejudicing the effectiveness and the very purpose of establishing the right, which was also specifically affirmed by the Court of Justice when it linked interim protection to a requirement that, when delivered, the judgment will be fully effective (see, for example, the order in *Renckens v Commission of the European Communities* (Case 27/68) [1969] ECR 255, 274; and see also the opinion of Mr Advocate General Capotorti in *Commission of the European Communities v France* (Cases 24/80, 97/80 R) [1980] ECR 1319, 1337; further, the orders in *Gutmann v Commission of the European Communities* (Cases 18/65, 35/65) [1966] ECR 103, 135; in *Nederlandse Sigarenwinkeliers Organisatie v Commission of the European Atomic Energy Community* (Case 260/82 R) [1982] ECR 4371, 4377, 4378; in *Fabbro v Commission of the European Communities* (Case 269/84 R) [1984] ECR 4333; and in *De Compte v European Parliament* (Case 44/88 R) [1988] ECR 1669, 1670, are in substantially the same terms); or to the need to 'preserve the existing position pending a decision on the substance of the case': *CMC Cooperativa Muratori e Cementisti v Commission of the European Communities* (Case 118/83 R) [1983] ECR 2583, 2595, paragraph 37.

19 Now that the function of interim protection has been brought into focus, such protection can be seen to be a fundamental and indispensable instrument of any judicial system, which seeks to achieve, in the particular case and always in an effective manner, the objective of determining the existence of a right and more generally of giving effect to the relevant legal provision, whenever the duration of the proceedings is likely to prejudice the attainment of this objective and therefore to nullify the effectiveness of the judgment.

The requirement for interim protection, moreover, as has already been noted, arises in the 'same terms, both where the establishment of the right's existence involves the facts and consequently, the determination of the correct provision to be applied, that is to say where the uncertainty as to the outcome of the application involves (although the expression is not perhaps a happy one) 'the facts', and where it is a question of choosing between two or more provisions which may be applicable (for example, a classification problem), irrespective of whether both are presumed to be valid or whether one is presumed to be incompatible with the other, which is of a higher order or in any event has precedence.

In particular, where, as in the case now before the Court of Justice, the determination as to the existence of the right not only involves a choice between two or more provisions which may be applicable but also involves a prior review of the validity or compatibility of one provision vis à vis another of a higher order or in any event having precedence, the difference is merely one of appearance, particularly when that review is entrusted to a court on which special jurisdiction has been conferred for the purpose. This situation, too, is fully covered by the typical function of judicial proceedings, which seek to establish the existence of and hence to give effect to the right, so that the requirement that the individual's position be protected on a provisional basis remains the same, inasmuch as it is a question of determining, interpreting and applying to the case in question the relevant (and valid) legal rules.

20 It follows that what is commonly called the presumption of validity, which attaches to laws or administrative acts no less than it does to Community acts, until such time as it is established by judicial determination that the measure in question is incompatible with a rule of law of a higher order or in any event having precedence, to the extent that such a procedure is provided for, does not constitute a formal obstacle to the interim protection of enforceable legal rights. In fact, precisely because what is concerned is a presumption, which as such may be rebutted by the final determination, it remains necessary to provide a remedy to compensate for the fact that the final ruling establishing the existence of the right may come too late and therefore be of no use to the successful party.

In fact, it is certain and undeniable that a provision, whether it is contained in an Act of Parliament or a Community act, or in an administrative act, must be presumed to be valid. But that cannot and must not mean that the courts are precluded from temporarily paralysing its effects with regard to the concrete case before them where, pending a final determination on its validity or compatibility vis à vis a provision of a higher order or having precedence, one or other of the legal rights in question is likely to be irremediably impaired and there is a suspicion (the degree of which must be established) that the final determination may entail a finding that the statute or administrative act in question is invalid.

21 In brief, the presumption that a law or an administrative act is valid may not and must not mean that the very possibility of interim protection is precluded where the measure in question may form the subject of a final judicial review of its validity.

Far from running counter to the principle of the validity of laws or administrative acts, which finds expression in a presumption that may always be rebutted by a final determination, interim protection in fact removes the risk that that presumption may lead to the perverse result, certainly not desired by any legal system, negating the function of judicial review and, in particular, of the review of the validity of laws. To take a different view would amount to denying root and branch the possibility of interim protection, not only in relation to laws, but absolutely, given that any act of a public authority, whether it is a rule-making instrument properly so called or an individual decision, is presumed to be valid until the outcome of the judicial review of its validity.

22 In a procedural situation of the type with which we are concerned here, in which one provision is alleged to be incompatible with another of a higher order or having precedence, it is essential, as has already been stressed, to bear in mind the fact that both provisions hypothetically apply to the case in question from the moment when the application is made. That is especially so since the final determination, whose consequences are made to take effect from the time of the application, creates nothing new as regards the existence (or the non-existence) of the right claimed because the provisions in point are hypothetically valid and operative in the alternative (or invalid and inoperative) and to both is attached what is commonly called a presumption of validity, whilst what is postponed, owing to the time taken by the proceedings, is merely the point in time at which the final determination is made. In the meantime, a situation prevails which may be defined precisely in terms of 'apparent law' and which is the very reason for interim measures, neither of the provisions in point giving rise to rights which are more than putative. It is therefore not a case of there being certainty (with the corresponding presumption of validity) as to one provision and uncertainty as to the other but the putative existence of both provisions. It is for the courts to assess whether the putative nature of the right claimed is such that interim protection must be granted or refused, on the basis of substantive criteria linked to the greater or lesser extent to which provision at issue appears to be valid (prima facie case, fumus boni juris, however designated) and to the possibility or otherwise that one or other of the interests in question may be prejudiced pending the final outcome of the proceedings.

23 The foregoing observations are amply confirmed by the fact that in all the legal systems of the Member States (the Danish system constitutes a partial exception), however diverse may be the forms and requirements connected with the duration of the proceedings, there is provision for the interim protection of rights denied under a lower ranking provision but claimed on the basis of a provision of a higher order.

First of all, it is beyond dispute that the application of an administrative act, which however benefits from a presumption of validity in the same way as a law, so that the bringing of an action does not suspend its operation (except in certain rare cases), may be nevertheless suspended by way of interim relief pending a definitive ruling on validity.

The provisional disapplication of primary legislation, in legal systems in which judicial review of the validity thereof is provided for, is certainly rarer.

Often the problem of the constitutionality of primary legislation is raised in the context of proceedings brought against an administrative act adopted in pursuance of the legislation in question so that the question of disapplying the legislation as such does not arise; in some systems this is the only situation possible.

In other countries, on the other hand, and in particular in those where judicial review of the (constitutional) legality of primary legislation is not generally available but is confined to a specific judicial body, provision is made, or the practice is, for provisional suspension to be ordered. For example, in Germany, the Federal Constitutional Court may provisionally suspend the application of primary legislation in a context (*Verfassungsbeschwerden*) not dissimilar to that of the English procedure for judicial review (see *Bundesverfassungsgericht*, 16 October 1977, Schleyer, *Foro Italiano*, 1978, IV, p 222; *Bundesverfassungsgericht*, 19 June 1962, BVerfGE, Vol 14, p 153); so, too, may the ordinary courts, which must then refer the matter to the Constitutional Court: see *Bundesverfassungsgericht*, 5 October 1977, BVerfGE, Vol 46, p 43.

Of particular relevance, moreover, is the case in Italy, inasmuch as not only do the ordinary courts not have the power to determine the unconstitutionality of laws and must therefore refer the matter to the Constitutional Court, but no power is expressly conferred either on the Constitutional Court or on the ordinary courts (or administrative courts) to grant interim measures (by way of suspension of the application of a law) pending the outcome of review proceedings. Notwithstanding this, many ordinary courts (Pretore, Bari, order of 4 February 1978, *Foro Italiano*, 1978, 1, p 1807; Pretore, *La Spezia*, order of 29 March 1978, *Foro Italiano 1979*, I, p 285; Pretore, Pisa, order of 30 July 1977, *Foro Italiano, 1977*, I, p 2354; Pretore, Pavia, order of 14 March 1977, Riv Giur Lav 1977, II, p 640; Pretore, Voltri, order of 1 September 1977, Riv Giur Lav, 1977, II, p 639; Pretore, La Spezia, order of 23 November 1978, *Foro Italiano 1979*. I, p 1921 *et seq*), with the support of the majority view in academic literature (see Verde, 'Considerazioni sul Procedimento d'Urgenza'. Studi Andrioli, Naples 1979, pp 446 *et seq*; *Mortati, Istituzioni di Diritto Pubblico*, 1976, II, p 1391; Campanile, 'Procedimento d'Urgenza e Incidente di Legittimita Costituzionale', Riv Dir Proc 1985, pp 124 *et seq*; Zagrebelsky, '*La Tutela d'Urgenza,*' le Garanzie Giurisdizionali dei Diritti Fondamentali, Padua 1988, pp 27 *et seq*; Sandulli, *Manuale di Diritto Amministrativo*, Naples 1984, II, p 1408), have taken the view that it is possible to issue interim measures suspending the application of primary legislation (obviously with regard only to the parties to the proceedings) pending a ruling by the Constitutional Court. That court, although it has never decided the specific point which is before the Court of Justice (but see, with regard to the permissibility of interim protection pending settlement of jurisdictional questions, Corte Costituzionale No 73 of 6 June 1973, *Foro Italiano 1973*, I, p 1657; and see also Corte di Cassazione, Sezioni Unite, 1 December 1978, No 5678, *Foro Italiano 1978*, I, p 2704), has not failed to affirm, on the one hand, the essential role played by interim relief in ensuring the effectiveness of the system of judicial protection (see Corte Costituzionale 27 December 1974, No 284, *Foro Italiano* 1975, I, p 263) and, on the other hand, the existence of a general principle and of a 'rule of rationality' underlying the legal system according to which it is for the courts, where the necessary preconditions are fulfilled (that is, a prima facie case and *periculum in mora*), to adopt such urgent measures as are appropriate for ensuring, on a provisional basis, the effect, of the final decision on the merits: Corte Costituzionale 28 June 1985 No 190, *Foro Italiano1985*, I, 1881. See also, for some points of interest, Corte di Cassazione, Sezione Unite Civili, 1 December 1978, No 5678, *Foro Italiano 1978*, I, p 2704; Consiglio di Stato, 14 April 1972, No 5, *Foro Italiano 1972*, III, p 105; Consiglio di Stato, 8 October 1982, No 17, *Foro Italiano 1983*, II, p 41.

Albeit in a different context, it is also significant that the French Conseil Constitutionnel declared to be unconstitutional a law which did not empower the courts to suspend, by way of interim relief, the application of an administrative decision, and moreover described such suspension as a 'garantie essentielle des droits de la défense': see Decision No 8224 DC of 23 January 1987, JORF of 25 January 1987, p 925.

24 If attention is now turned to the relationship between national provisions and Community provisions, there is no doubt that, by means of preliminary rulings given by the Court of Justice and the 'direct' competence of national courts, machinery has been introduced which essentially consists of the review of the validity (or of compatibility, if this is preferred) of a national provision in relation to a Community provision, given that the national courts have jurisdiction to rule

definitively that the former is incompatible with the latter. And if therefore the national courts may, indeed must, disapply a national law which conflicts with a Community provision having direct effect, once a definitive finding has been made to that effect (or, at any rate, must achieve that substantive result), they must also be able to disapply that law provisionally, provided that the preconditions are satisfied, where the incompatibility is not entirely certain or 'established' but may call for a preliminary ruling by the Court of Justice. Otherwise, that judicial protection of the rights conferred on individuals by the Community provision which, as has been affirmed by the Court of Justice on numerous occasions and also specifically pointed out by the House of Lords, is the subject of a precise obligation on the part of the national courts, might be nullified.

25 This brings me back to the concrete case submitted for the consideration of the Court of Justice by way of the questions referred to it by the House of Lords. The right of the applicants in the main proceedings, which is denied by the national statute, is claimed on the basis of certain EEC Treaty provisions having direct effect, that is to say provisions which prevail over domestic law but whose interpretation in the sense contended for is not free from doubt and, consequently, requires a preliminary ruling by the Court of Justice. In the meantime, the national court finds a bar to interim protection of the rights claimed in the presumption of validity which attaches to the statute until a final determination is made.

Inasmuch as the English court, as is undisputed and as it has itself underlined, can and must give precedence, once the final determination is made, by virtue of the review which can be carried out of the compatibility of the English statute with Community law, to the 'certain' Community rule having direct effect, it must also be able, where the necessary preconditions are satisfied, to grant interim protection to the rights claimed on the basis of 'uncertain' Community rules and denied by the provisions of national law.

The problem is not one of form but of substance. The presumption of validity does not have preclusive effect in view of the fact that it may be rebutted by the final determination, as is the case in the English legal system also by virtue of the European Communities Act 1972, just as the presumption of the validity of any provision subordinate to a provision of a higher order does not preclude interim relief. And it is the national court itself which points this out in the order for reference in relation to the possibility of suspending the application of a subordinate measure which is suspected of being in conflict with a statute.

26 What I mean to say, therefore, is that this assessment must be carried out on the basis of substantive criteria and not, as suggested by the United Kingdom, on the basis of a formal criterion such as the presumption of the validity of statute.

To give priority to the national legislation merely because it has not yet been definitively established as incompatible with Community law (and thus to proceed on the basis merely of a putative compatibility) may amount to depriving the Community rules of the effective judicial protection which is to be afforded to them 'from the date of their entry into force and for so long as they continue in force.' Paradoxically, the right conferred (putatively) by the provision of Community law would as a general rule receive less, or less effective, protection than rights conferred (also putatively) by the provision of national law. That would be tantamount to saying that the right conferred by ordinary legislation may receive interim protection, whereas protection is denied to the right conferred by the Community, or in any event higher ranking, provision, on the basis of the presumption of validity in favour of that legislation; as if the same presumption, which after all is nothing other than 'putative', did not also avail the provision having precedence.

Let me be quite clear. I do not mean by this that the national court must always and in any event give priority to a right putatively conferred by Community law as opposed to a right putatively conferred by national law, but merely that it must have the power to do so where the factual and legal circumstances so require; in other words it may (and must) not find formal obstacles to any application for interim measures based on directly effective Community provisions.

27 Nor does it avail to put forward as a counter argument the presumption of validity which attaches to Community measures, a presumption stressed many times by the Court of Justice. That

is an argument which ends up by demonstrating the contrary. It is scarcely necessary to recall to mind Article 185 of the EEC Treaty which expressly provides that the Court of Justice may 'if it considers that circumstances so require, order that application of the contested act be suspended'.

But that is not all. Even in regard to a system for the review of the validity of Community measures which is rigorously centred on the Court of Justice (also as regards the preliminary rulings procedure under Article 177 of the EEC Treaty), the Court of Justice itself has not failed to stress that 'the rule that national courts may not themselves declare Community acts invalid may have to be qualified in certain circumstances in the case of proceedings relating to an application for interim measures': see *Foto-Frost v Hauptzollamt Lübeck-Ost* (Case 314/85) [1987] ECR 4199, 4232, paragraph 19.

28 Similarly, it is not at the formal but rather on the substantive level that it is necessary to assess the possibility that interim protection may be obtained (also) by way of an injunction against the Crown. By way of example, I would consider it unreasonable to think in terms of an injunction (to adopt a measure or enact primary legislation) which would amount to an interference with the discretionary powers enjoyed by the Crown or even by Parliament, whilst on the other hand I would regard it as being entirely reasonable and 'orthodox' order concrete non-discretionary action to be taken or, as in this case, the temporary suspension of application of the statute or administrative act, solely with regard to the parties to the proceedings, until such time as the court is in a position definitively to apply or to disapply one or the other.

29 In conclusion, the reply which I propose should be given by the Court of Justice to the first question put to it by the House of Lords is affirmative in the sense that, under Community law, the national court must be able to afford interim protection, where the pre-conditions are met, to rights claimed by an individual on the basis of provisions of Community law having direct effect, pending the final outcome of the proceedings, including proceedings on a reference to the Court of Justice for a preliminary ruling. And I also suggest that the Court of Justice should expressly link this power and duty of the national court to the requirement for effective judicial protection which applies in relation to provisions of Community law just as much as it does in relation to provisions of national law.

30 I need hardly add that such a reply does not amount to imposing remedies or judicial procedures different from those already provided for in the domestic law of the Member States but merely implies that such remedies or procedures must be used 'for the purpose of ensuring observance of Community provisions having direct effect, on the same conditions concerning admissibility and procedure as would apply were it a question of ensuring observance of national law': *Rewe-Handelsgesellschaft Nord mbH v Hauptzollampt Kiel* (Case 158/80) [1981] ECR 1805, 1838, paragraph 44. But I would recall once again that the principle in question, according to which the means of affording judicial protection to rights conferred by provisions of Community law remain exclusively those provided for by domestic law, does not apply if 'those rules and time limits made it impossible in practice to exercise rights which the national courts have a duty to protect': see the *Comet* case [1976] ECR 2043, 2053, paragraph 16; the *Rewe-Zentralfinanz* case [1976] ECR 1989, 1900 paragraph 15, the *Express Dairy* case [1980] ECR 1887, 1997–1998, paragraph 12, the *Denkavit* case [1980] ECR 1205, 1226, 6 paragraph 25; and the *Mireco* case [1980] ECR 2559, 2574, paragraph 13.

31 In fact, as is made clear also by the order for reference and the observations of the United Kingdom, provision is made in the United Kingdom procedural system for the interim protection of a right, pending the final determination, whenever a danger would be caused by delay (*periculum in mora*) and a prima facie case is made out (the Divisional Court granted the interim relief requested). Consequently, it is not a question here of a procedure which is not provided for by the national legal system, rather it is simply a question of using the existing procedure in order to protect a right claimed on the basis of a provision of Community law having direct effect. The same may be said of the impossibility, to which reference has been made, of obtaining an injunction against the Crown, when in reality it is merely a case or ordering the provisional suspension of the application of a statute to the parties concerned, it being clearly understood that it may be the latter who will bear the risk of a final determination unfavourable to them.

If that were not the case, on the other hand, there would in any event still be a specific obligation, where the appropriate preconditions are satisfied, to afford interim protection, since otherwise we would find ourselves confronted precisely with the situation (I would again mention the *Simmenthal* case [1978] ECR 629) of a procedural system which makes it impossible in practice 'to exercise rights which the national courts have a duty to protect'. That would be all the more serious if regard were had to the fact, also mentioned in the order for reference, that under the English legal system the definitive establishment of the right claimed never entails the recovery of losses suffered in the course of the proceedings by those claiming the legal right at issue. That is something which, let me be clear, is in itself a matter for concern in the light of the obligation of national courts to give full effect to the provisions of Community law.

32 Nor does there seem to me to be any justified basis for arguing *a contrario* (as in the observations of Ireland and the United Kingdom) that individuals are afforded sufficient protection by virtue of the right of the Commission, by infringement proceedings brought under Article 169 of the EEC Treaty, to apply to the Court of Justice for interim measures, a situation which in fact has occurred in this instance in regard to the nationality requirements of the United Kingdom legislation now before the Court of Justice, as I have already indicated. In this respect may it suffice to recall the judgment in *NV Algemene Transport en Expeditie Onderneming van Gend en Loos v Nederlandse Administratie der Belastingen* (Case 26/62) [1963] ECR I, in which the Court of Justice affirmed that a restriction of the guarantees against an infringement by Member States of a Community provision having direct effect to the procedures under Articles 169 and 170 'would remove all direct legal protection of the individual rights of their nationals'.

33 The reply to the first question raised by the House of Lords, therefore, can only be in the affirmative, in the sense that the national court's duty to afford effective judicial protection to rights conferred on the individual by Community law, where the relevant requirements are satisfied, cannot fail to include the provision of interim protection for the rights claimed, pending a final determination.

Moreover, the first question is whether Community law obliges the national court to grant such interim protection or gives it the power to grant such protection, so that the second question as to the criteria which the national court should apply is dependent on a negative reply as to the obligation and an affirmative reply as to the power.

Over and above the literal formulation of the questions and the corresponding replies to be given by the Court of Justice, I consider that it is necessary to be very clear as to the substance. In the first place, it does not seem to me that we are concerned with an alternative, in the proper sense of the term, between an 'obligation' and a 'power,' regard being had to the fact that what is involved is a judicial activity which the national court is called upon to carry out and which, by its very nature, is an activity involving an assessment of the factual and legal elements presented by the specific case before the national court at any given time. Consequently, it is possible to use the expression 'obligation', in accordance with the Court of Justice's case law, in the sense that the national court performs that obligation by means of an assessment on a case by case basis of the preconditions on which generally the adoption of an interim measure depends.

In this connection, I consider not only that it is for the national court, obviously, to determine whether the preconditions for interim protection are met, but also that, in the absence of Community harmonisation, those preconditions must be and must remain those provided for by the individual, national legal systems. Further, it does not seem to me that the subject matter allows much room for imagination or offers scope for revolutionary discoveries, since legal theory and positive law, including that of the United Kingdom, have long specified the prima facie case (however designated) and the periculum in mora as the two basic preconditions for interim protection. The accent may be placed on one or the other according to the legal system in question, or what is a prima facie case may or may not perfectly coincide with the not manifestly ill founded or the prima facie well founded nature of the claim and so on, or it may be that in the assessment of the periculum in mora, apart from the traditional and necessary balancing of the respective interests of the parties (ensuring that the interim measure does not in its turn cause irreparable damage to the other party), express consideration is also given to the public interest. All that forms part of the prudent appreciation by the national courts which, case by case, will carry out a just appraisal of the appropriateness or necessity of granting or refusing an interim measure for the interim protection of the rights claimed. And there is scarcely any need to point out that in considering whether there is a prima facie case the courts will take account of the possibility that the national provision may be declared incompatible with Community law.

In the result, as regards the second question in particular, I suggest that the Court of Justice should give a reply which is in conformity with the judgment in the *Comet* case [1976] ECR 2043 in the sense that 'the methods and time limits' of the interim protection are and remain, in the absence of harmonisation, those provided for by the national legal systems, provided that they are not such as to make it impossible in practice 'to exercise rights which the national courts have a duty to protect'.

Consequently, it is for the national court to draw from the above the necessary inferences as to the determination of the dispute before it on the basis of the factors set out in the statement of the grounds on which the questions are based; the Court of Justice clearly cannot make any assessment of the merits of those factors.

34 On the basis of the foregoing considerations, I therefore propose that the Court of Justice should reply as follows to the questions formulated by the House of Lords: (1) The obligation imposed by Community law on the national court to ensure the effective judicial protection of rights directly conferred on the individual by provisions of Community law includes the obligation, if the need arises and where the factual and legal preconditions are met, to afford interim and urgent protection to rights claimed on the basis of such provisions of Community law, pending a final determination and any interpretation by way of a preliminary ruling given by the Court of Justice. (2) In the absence of Community harmonisation, it is the legal system of each Member State which determines the procedural methods and the preconditions for the interim protection of rights vested in individuals by virtue of provisions of Community law having direct effect, on condition that those methods and preconditions do not make it impossible to exercise on an interim basis the rights claimed and are not less favourable than those provided to afford protection to rights founded on national provisions, any provision of national law or any national practice having such an effect being incompatible with Community law.

19 June: the following judgment was delivered in open court in Luxembourg.

1   By a judgment of 18 May 1989 in *Regulation v Secretary of State for Transport ex p Factortame Ltd* [1990] 2 AC 85, which was received at the Court Registry on 10 July 1989, the House of Lords referred to the European Court of Justice for a preliminary ruling under Article 177 of the EEC. Treaty two questions on the interpretation of Community law. Those questions concern the extent of the power of national courts to grant interim relief where rights claimed under Community law are at issue.

2   The questions were raised in proceedings brought against the Secretary of State for Transport by Factortame Ltd and other companies incorporated under the laws of the United Kingdom, and also the directors and shareholders of those companies, most of whom are Spanish nationals (hereinafter together referred to as 'the applicants').

3   The companies in question are the owners or operators of 95 fishing vessels which were registered in the register of British vessels under the Merchant Shipping Act 1894. Of those vessels, 53 were originally registered in Spain and flew the Spanish flag, but on various dates as from 1980 they were registered in the British register. The remaining 42 vessels have always been registered in the United Kingdom, but were purchased by the companies in question on various dates, mainly since 1983.

4   The statutory system governing the registration of British fishing vessels was radically altered by Part II of the Merchant Shipping Act 1988 and the Merchant Shipping (Registration of Fishing Vessels) Regulations 1988 (SI 1988/1926). It is common ground that the United Kingdom amended the previous legislation in order to put a stop to the practice known as 'quota hopping'

whereby, according to the United Kingdom, its fishing quotas were 'plundered' by vessels flying the British flag but lacking any genuine link with the United Kingdom.

5   The Act of 1988 provided for the establishment of a new register in which henceforth all British fishing vessels were to be registered, including those which were already registered in the old general register maintained under the Act of 1894. However, only fishing vessels fulfilling the conditions laid down in section 14 of the Act of 1988 could be registered in the new register.

6   Section 14(1) provides that, subject to dispensations to be determined by the Secretary of State for Transport, a fishing vessel is eligible to be registered in the new register only if:

> (a) the vessel is British-owned; (b) the vessel is managed, and its operations are directed and controlled, from within the United Kingdom; and (c) any charterer, manager or operator of the vessel is a qualified person or company.

According to section 14(2), a fishing vessel is deemed to be British-owned if the legal title to the vessel is vested wholly in one or more qualified persons or companies, and if the vessel is beneficially owned by one or more qualified companies or, as to not less than 75%, by one or more qualified persons. According to section 14(7) 'qualified person' means a person who is a British citizen resident and domiciled in the United Kingdom and 'qualified company' means a company incorporated in the United Kingdom and having its principal place of business there, at least 75% of its shares being owned by one or more qualified persons or companies and at least 75% of its directors being qualified persons.

7   The Act of 1988 and the Regulations of 1988 entered into force on 1 December 1988. However, under section 13 of the Act of 1988, the validity of registrations effected under the previous Act was extended for a transitional period until 31 March 1989.

8   On 4 August 1989 the Commission of the European Communities brought an action before the Court of Justice under Article 169 of the EEC Treaty for a declaration that, by imposing the nationality requirements laid down in section 14 of the Act of 1988, the United Kingdom had failed to fulfil its obligations under Articles 7, 52 and 221 of the EEC Treaty. That action is the subject of Case 246/89, now pending before the Court of Justice. In a separate document, lodged at the Court Registry on the same date, the Commission applied to the Court of Justice for an interim order requiring the United Kingdom to suspend the application of those nationality requirements as regards the nationals of the other Member States and in respect of fishing vessels which until 31 March 1989 had been carrying on a fishing activity under the British flag and under a British fishing licence. By an order of 10 October 1989 in *Commission of the European Communities v United Kingdom* (Case 246/89 R) (1989) *The Times*, 28 October, the President of the Court of Justice granted that application. Pursuant to that order, the United Kingdom made an Order in Council amending section 14 of the Act of 1988 with effect from 2 November 1989.

9   At the time of the institution of the proceedings in which the appeal arises, the 99 fishing vessels of the applicants failed to satisfy one or more of the conditions for registration under section 14 of the Act of 1988 and thus could not be registered in the new register.

10 Since those vessels were to be deprived of the right to engage in fishing as from 1 April 1989, the companies in question, by means of an application for judicial review, challenged the compatibility of Part II of the Act of 1988 with Community law. They also applied for the grant of interim relief until such time as final judgment was given on their application for judicial review.

11 In its judgment of 10 March 1989, the Divisional Court of the Queen's Bench Division (i) decided to stay the proceedings and to make a reference under article 177 of the EEC Treaty for a preliminary ruling on the issues of Community law raised in the proceedings; and (ii) ordered that, by way of interim relief, the application of Part II of the Act of 1988 and the Regulations of 1988 should be suspended as regards the applicants.

12 On 13 March 1989, the Secretary of State for Transport appealed against the Divisional Court's order granting interim relief. By judgment of 22 March 1989 the Court of Appeal held that under national law the courts had no power to suspend, by way of interim relief, the application of Acts of Parliament. It therefore set aside the order of the Divisional Court.

13 The House of Lords, before which the matter was brought, delivered its judgment on 18 May 1989. In its judgment it found in the first place that the claims by the applicants that they would suffer irreparable damage if the interim relief which they sought were not granted and they were successful in the main proceedings were well founded. However, it held that, under national law, the English courts had no power to grant interim relief in a case such as the one before it. More specifically, it held that the grant of such relief was precluded by the old common law rule that an interim injunction may not be granted against the Crown, that is to say against the government, in conjunction with the presumption that an Act of Parliament is in conformity with Community law until such time as a decision on its compatibility with that law has been given.

14 The House of Lords then turned to the question whether, notwithstanding that rule of national law, English courts had the power, under Community law, to grant an interim injunction against the Crown.

15 Consequently, taking the view that the dispute raised an issue concerning the interpretation of Community law, the House of Lords decided, pursuant to Article 177 of the EEC. Treaty, to stay the proceedings until the Court of Justice had given a preliminary ruling on the following questions:

> (1) Where: (i) a party before the national court claims to be entitled to rights under Community law having direct effect in national law ('the rights claimed'), (ii) a national measure in clear terms will, if applied, automatically deprive that party of the rights claimed, (iii) there are serious arguments both for and against the existence of the rights claimed and the national court has sought a preliminary ruling under Article 177 as to whether or not the rights claimed exist, (iv) the national law presumes the national measure in question to be compatible with Community law unless and until it is declared incompatible, (v) the national court has no power to give interim protection to the rights claimed by suspending the application of the national measure pending the preliminary ruling, (vi) if the preliminary ruling is in the event in favour of the rights claimed, the party entitled to those rights is likely to have suffered irremediable damage unless given such interim protection, does Community law either (a) oblige the national court to grant such interim protection of the rights claimed; or (b) give the court power to grant such interim protection of the rights claimed? (2) If question 1(a) is answered in the negative and question 1(b) in the affirmative, what are the criteria to be applied in deciding whether or not to grant such interim protection of the rights claimed?

16 Reference is made to the report for the hearing for a fuller account of the facts in the proceedings before the national court, the course of the procedure before and the observations submitted to the Court of Justice, which are mentioned or discussed hereinafter only in so far as is necessary for the reasoning of the Court of Justice.

17 It is clear from the information before the Court of Justice, and in particular from the judgment making the reference and, as described above, the course taken by the proceedings in the national courts before which the case came at first and second instance, that the preliminary question raised by the House of Lord's seeks essentially to ascertain whether a national court which, in a case before it concerning Community law, considers that the sole obstacle which precludes it from granting interim relief is a rule of national law, must disapply that rule.

18 For the purpose of replying to that question, it is necessary to point out that in *Amministrazione delle Finanze dello Stato v Simmenthal SpA* (Case 106/77) [1978] ECR 629 the Court of Justice held, at p 643, paragraph 14, that directly applicable rules of Community law 'must be fully and uniformly applied in all the Member States from the date of their entry into force and for so long as they continue in force' and that, p 643, paragraph 17:

> ... in accordance with the principle of the precedence of Community law, the relationship between provisions of the EEC Treaty and directly applicable measures of the institutions on the one hand and the national law of the Member States on the other is such that those provisions and measures ... by their entry into force render automatically inapplicable any conflicting provision of ... national law ...

19 In accordance with the case law of the Court of Justice, it is for the national courts, in application of the principle of co-operation laid down in Article 5 of the EEC Treaty, to ensure the legal protection which persons derive from the direct effect of provisions of Community law: see, most recently, *Amministrazione delle Finanze dello Stato v Ariete SpA* (Case 811/79) [1980] ECR 2545 and *Amministrazione delle Finanze dello Stato v MIRECO SaS* (Case 826/79)[1980] ECR 2559.

20 The Court of Justice has also held that any provision of a national legal system and any legislative, administrative or judicial practice which might impair the effectiveness of Community law by withholding from the national court having jurisdiction to apply such law the power to do everything necessary at the moment of its application to set aside national legislative provisions which might prevent, even temporarily, Community rules from having full force and effect are incompatible with those requirements. which are the very essence of Community law: see the judgment in the *Simmenthal* case [1978] ECR 629, 644, paragraphs 22 and 23.

21 It must be added that the full effectiveness of Community law would be just as much impaired if a rule of national law could prevent a court seised of a dispute governed by Community law from granting interim relief in order to ensure the full effectiveness of the judgment to be given on the existence of the rights claimed under Community law. It follows that a court which in those circumstances would grant interim relief, if it were not for a rule of national law, is obliged to set aside that rule.

22 That interpretation is reinforced by the system established by Article 177 of the EEC Treaty whose effectiveness would be impaired if a national court, having stayed proceedings pending the reply by the Court of Justice to the question referred to it for a preliminary ruling, were not able to grant interim relief until it delivered its judgment following the reply given by the Court of Justice.

23 Consequently, the reply to the question raised should be that Community law must be interpreted as meaning that a national court which, in a case before it concerning Community law, considers that the sole obstacle which precludes it from granting interim relief is a rule of national law must set aside that rule.

Costs

24 The costs incurred by the United Kingdom, Ireland and the Commission of the European Communities, which have submitted observations to the Court of Justice, are not recoverable. Since these proceedings are, in so far as the parties to the main proceedings are concerned, in the nature of a step in the proceedings pending before the national court, the decision on costs is a matter for that court.

On those grounds, the court in reply to the question referred to it for a preliminary ruling by the House of Lords, by judgment of 18 May 1989, hereby rules: Community law must be interpreted as meaning that a national court which, in a case before it concerning Community law, considers that the sole obstacle which precludes it from granting interim relief is a rule of national law must set aside that rule.

Solicitors: Chief State Solicitor, Republic of Ireland; Treasury Solicitor; Thomas Cooper & Stibbard.

[Reported by Paul H Niekirk Esq, Barrister at Law]

After the answers to the questions referred to the European Court of Justice had been received, the matter was reconsidered by the House of Lords.

On 9 July, their Lordships made an order for interim relief for reasons to be given later.

The facts are set out in the opinions of Lord Bridge of Harwich and Lord Goff of Chieveley.

David Vaughan QC, Gerald Barling and *David Anderson* for the first to 94th applicants.

Nicholas Forwood QC for the 95th applicant, Rawlings (Trawling) Ltd.

Sir Nicholas Lyell QC, SG, John Laws, Stephen Richards and *G Andrew Macnab* for the Secretary of State.

Their Lordships took time for consideration.

11 October: **Lord Bridge of Harwich**: My Lords, when this appeal first came before the House last year [1990] 2 AC 85, your Lordships held that, as a matter of English law, the courts had no

jurisdiction to grant interim relief in terms which would involve either overturning an English statute in advance of any decision by the European Court of Justice that the statute infringed Community law or granting an injunction against the Crown. It then became necessary to seek a preliminary ruling from the European Court of Justice as to whether Community law itself invested us with such jurisdiction. In the speech I delivered on that occasion, with which your Lordships agreed, I explained the reasons which led us to those conclusions. It will be remembered that, on that occasion, the House never directed its attention to the question how, if there were jurisdiction to grant the relief sought, discretion ought to be exercised in deciding whether or not relief should be granted.

In June of this year we received the judgment of the European Court of Justice (Case C213/89), p 852B *et seq*, replying to the questions we had posed and affirming that we had jurisdiction, in the circumstances postulated, to grant interim relief for the protection of directly enforceable rights under Community law and that no limitation on our jurisdiction imposed by any rule of national law could stand as the sole obstacle to preclude the grant of such relief. In the light of this judgment we were able to conclude the hearing of the appeal in July and unanimously decided that relief should be granted in terms of the orders which the House then made, indicating that we would give our reasons for the decision later.

My noble and learned friend, Lord Goff of Chieveley, whose speech I have had the advantage of reading in draft, has given a very full account of all the relevant circumstances arising since our decision last year in the light of which our final disposal of the appeal fell to be made. I gratefully adopt this account. I also agree with his exposition of the principles applicable in relation to the grant of interim injunctive relief where the dispute involves a conflict between private and public interests and where damages are not a remedy available to either party, leading, in the circumstances of this case, to the conclusion that it was appropriate to grant relief in terms of the orders made by the House. But I add some observations of my own in view of the importance of the subject matter.

Some public comments on the decision of the European Court of Justice, affirming the jurisdiction of the courts of Member States to override national legislation if necessary to enable interim relief to be granted in protection of rights under Community law, have suggested that this was a novel and dangerous invasion by a Community institution of the sovereignty of the United Kingdom Parliament. But such comments are based on a misconception. If the supremacy within the European Community of Community law over the national law of Member States was not always inherent in the EEC Treaty (Cmnd 5179-II) it was certainly well established in the jurisprudence of the European Court of Justice long before the United Kingdom joined the Community. Thus, whatever limitation of its sovereignty Parliament accepted when it enacted the European Communities Act 1972 was entirely voluntary. Under the terms of the Act of 1972 it has always been clear that it was the duty of a United Kingdom court, when delivering final judgment, to override any rule of national law found to be in conflict with any directly enforceable rule of Community law. Similarly, when decisions of the European Court of Justice have exposed areas of United Kingdom statute law which failed to implement Council directives, Parliament has always loyally accepted the obligation to make appropriate and prompt amendments. Thus there is nothing in any way novel in according supremacy to rules of Community law in those areas to which they apply and to insist that, in the protection of rights under Community law, national courts must not be inhibited by rules of national law from granting interim relief in appropriate cases is no more than a logical recognition of that supremacy.

Although affirming our jurisdiction, the judgment of the European Court of Justice does not fetter our discretion to determine whether an appropriate case for the grant of interim relief has been made out. While agreeing with Lord Goff's exposition of the general principles by which the discretion should be guided, I would wish to emphasise the salient features of the present case which, at the end of the argument, left me in no doubt that interim relief should be granted. A decision to grant or withhold interim relief in the protection of disputed rights at a time when the merits of the dispute cannot be finally resolved must always involve an element of risk. If, in the end, the claimant succeeds in a case where interim relief has been refused, he will have suffered an injustice. If, in the end, he fails in a case where interim relief has been granted, injustice will have been done to the other party. The objective which underlies the principles by which the discretion is to be guided must always be to ensure that the court shall choose the course which, in all the circumstances, appears to offer the best prospect that eventual injustice will be avoided or minimised. Questions as to the adequacy of an alternative remedy in damages to the party claiming injunctive relief and of a cross-undertaking in damages to the party against whom the relief is sought play a primary role in assisting the court to determine which course offers the best prospect that injustice may be avoided or minimised. But where, as here, no alternative remedy will be available to either party if the final decision does not accord with the interim decision, choosing the course which will minimise the risk presents exceptional difficulty.

If the applicants were to succeed after a refusal of interim relief, the irreparable damage they would have suffered would be very great. That is now beyond dispute. On the other hand, if they failed after a grant of interim relief, there would have been a substantial detriment to the public interest resulting from the diversion of a very significant part of the British quota of controlled stocks of fish from those who ought in law to enjoy it to others having no right to it. In either case, if the final decision did not accord with the interim decision, there would have been an undoubted injustice. But the injustices are so different in kind that I find it very difficult to weigh the one against the other.

If the matter rested there. I should be inclined to say, for the reasons indicated by Lord Goff of Chieveley, that the public interest should prevail and interim relief be refused. But the matter does not rest there. Unlike the ordinary case in which the court must decide whether or not to grant interlocutory relief at a time when disputed issues of fact remain unresolved, here the relevant facts are all ascertained and the only unresolved issues are issues of law, albeit of Community law. Now, although the final decision of such issues is the exclusive prerogative of the European Court of Justice, that does not mean that an English court may not reach an informed opinion as to how such issues are likely to be resolved. In this case we are now in a position to derive much assistance in that task from the decisions of the European Court of Justice in *Regulation v Minister of Agriculture, Fisheries and Food ex p Agegate Ltd* (Case C3/87) [1990] 2 QB 151 and *Regulation v Ministry of Agriculture, Fisheries and Food ex p Jaderow Ltd* (Case C216/87) [1990] 2 QB 193 and the interim decision of the President in the proceedings brought by the European Commission against the United Kingdom (*Commission of the European Communities v United Kingdom* (Case 246/89 R) (1989) *The Times*, 28 October) to which Lord Goff of Chieveley has referred. In the circumstances I believe that the most logical course in seeking a decision least likely to occasion injustice is to make the best prediction we can of the final outcome and to give to that prediction decisive weight in resolving the interlocutory issue.

It is now, I think, common ground that the quota system operated under the common fisheries policy, in order to be effective and to ensure that the quota of a member state enures to the benefit of its local fishing industry, entitles the member state to derogate from rights otherwise exercisable under Community law to the extent necessary to ensure that only fishing vessels having a genuine economic link with that industry may fish against its quota. The narrow ground on which the Secretary of State resists the applicants' claim is that the requirements of section 14 of the Merchant Shipping Act 1988 that at least 75% of the beneficial ownership of a British fishing vessel must be vested in persons resident and domiciled in the United Kingdom is necessary to ensure that the vessel has a genuine economic link with the British fishing industry. Before the decision of the European Court of Justice in *Agegate* that would have seemed to me a contention of some cogency. But in *Agegate* it was held that a licensing condition requiring 75% of the crew of a vessel fishing against the quota of a Member State to be resident within the member state could not be justified on the ground that it was 'irrelevant to the aim of the quota system': p 261. I confess that I find some difficulty in understanding the reasoning in the judgment which leads to this conclusion. But if a residence requirement relating to crew members cannot be justified as necessary to the maintenance of a genuine economic link with the local industry, it is difficult to see how residence or domicile requirements relating to beneficial owners could possibly fare any better.

The broader contention on behalf of the Secretary of State that Member States have an unfettered right to determine what ships may fly their flag raises more difficult issues. It would not be appropriate in the context of the present interlocutory decision to enter upon a detailed examination of the wide-ranging arguments bearing upon those issues. I believe the best indication that we have of the prospect of success of that contention is found in the interlocutory judgment of President Due in the case brought by the Commission against the United Kingdom. He concluded that the contention was of insufficient weight to preclude him from granting an interim order suspending the application of the nationality requirements of section 14 of the Act of 1988 to nationals of other Member States. His reasoning persuaded me that we should reach the same conclusion in relation to the residence and domicile requirements.

Lord Brandon of Oakbrook: My Lords, I have had the advantage of reading in draft the speech produced by my noble and learned friend, Lord Goff of Chieveley, and agree with it entirely.

Lord Oliver of Aylmerton: My Lords, I have had the advantage of reading in draft the speech of my noble and learned friend, Lord Goff of Chieveley. I agree with it and, for the reasons given by my noble friend, I, too, would allow this appeal.

Lord Goff of Chieveley: My Lords, this appeal was last before your Lordships' House in May 1989. The subject matter of the proceedings is an application by the applicants for judicial review, challenging the legality of certain provisions of the Merchant Shipping Act 1988, and the Merchant Shipping (Registration of Fishing Vessels) Regulations 1988 (SI 1988/1926), on the ground that they contravene provisions of European law. The matter came before a Divisional Court (Neill LJ and Hodgson J), who requested a preliminary ruling from the European Court of Justice under Article 177 of the EEC Treaty on the questions necessary to enable them finally to determine the application. They then made an order for interim relief in the form of an order that in the meanwhile Part II of the Act of 1988 and the Regulations be disapplied and the Secretary of State for Transport be restrained from enforcing the same in respect of any of the applicants and any vessel now owned (in whole or in part), managed, operated or chartered by any of them so as to enable registration of any such vessel under the Merchant Shipping Act 1894 and/or the Sea Fishing Boats (Scotland) Act 1886 to continue in being. The Court of Appeal [1989] 2 CMLR 353 allowed an appeal by the Secretary of State from the interim order of the Divisional Court [1989] 2 CMLR 353. On appeal by the applicants to your Lordships' House [1990] 2 AC 85, it was held by your Lordships that, as a matter of English law, the English courts had no power to make such an order as that made by the Divisional Court. My noble and learned friend, Lord Bridge of Harwich, said of the order for interim relief, pp 142–43:

> Any such order, unlike any form of order for interim relief known to the law, would irreversibly determine in the applicants' favour for a period of some two years rights which are necessarily uncertain until the preliminary ruling of the ECJ has been given. If the applicants fail to establish the rights they claim before the ECJ, the effect of the interim relief granted would be to have conferred upon them rights directly contrary to Parliament's sovereign will and correspondingly to have deprived British fishing vessels, as defined by Parliament, of the enjoyment of a substantial proportion of the United Kingdom quota of stocks of fish protected by the common fisheries policy. I am clearly of the opinion that, as a matter of English law, the court has no power to make an order which has these consequences.

Your Lordships' House further held that, in any event, there was no jurisdiction in English law to grant an interim injunction against the Crown; this provided an additional reason why the order made by the Divisional Court could not be supported. Your Lordships House however sought the guidance of the European Court of Justice on the question whether, in a case such as the present, European law overrides English law. Accordingly the following questions were referred to the court:

> (1) Where: (i) a party before the national court claims to be entitled to rights under Community law having direct effect in national law ('the rights claimed'), (ii) a national measure in clear terms will, if applied, automatically deprive that party of the rights claimed, (iii) there are serious arguments both for and against the existence of the rights claimed and the national court has sought a preliminary

ruling under Article 177 as to whether or not the rights claimed exist, (iv) the national law presumes the national measure in question to be compatible with Community law unless and until it is declared incompatible, (v) the national court has no power to give interim protection to the rights claimed by suspending the application of the national measure pending the preliminary ruling, (vi) if the preliminary ruling is in the event in favour of the rights claimed, the party entitled to those rights is likely to have suffered irremediable damage unless given such interim protection, does Community law either (a) oblige the national court to grant such interim protection of the rights claimed; or (b) give the court power to grant such interim protection of the rights claimed? (2) If question 1(a) is answered in the negative and question 1(b) in the affirmative, what are the criteria to be applied in deciding whether or not to grant such interim protection of the rights claimed?

On 19 June 1990, in answer to the questions so referred to it, the court ruled as follows, p 856B:

Community law must be interpreted as meaning that a national court which, in a case before it concerning Community law, considers the sole obstacle which precludes it from granting interim relief is a rule of national law must set aside that rule.

Following receipt of that ruling, the applicants returned to your Lordships' House on 2 July 1990 in order to pursue further their appeal from the decision of the Court of Appeal and to seek interim relief pending the determination by the European Court of Justice of the matters referred to it by the Divisional Court. However, for reasons which will appear, they sought interim relief in a form different from that ordered by the Divisional Court. On 9 July, shortly after the conclusion of the hearing, your Lordships announced the House's decision to grant interim relief, and an order was made by your Lordships for an interim injunction in the following terms:

Pending final judgment or further order herein the Secretary of State whether by himself his servants or agents or otherwise howsoever be restrained from withholding or withdrawing registration in the register of British fishing vessels maintained by him pursuant to the Merchant Shipping (Registration of Fishing Vessels) Regulations 1988 in respect of any of the vessels specified in the first column of the schedule hereto by reason only of the following: (a) legal title or beneficial ownership of such vessel is vested in whole or in part in the person or persons listed against its name in the second column of the said schedule; and (b)(i) in the case of any natural person 'so listed, that person is resident or domiciled in a member state of the European Economic Community other than the United Kingdom; or (ii) in the case of any company so listed, (aa) 25% or more of the shares or of any class of the shares of that company. or of any company owning shares in that company, are legally or beneficially owned by a person or persons resident or domiciled in a member state of the European Economic Community other than the United Kingdom or (bb) 25% or more of the directors of that company, or of any company holding shares in that company, are resident or domiciled in a member state of the European Economic Community other than the United Kingdom.

Provision was made for liberty to apply. It was indicated that your Lordships would publish at a later date your reasons for granting such interim relief. I now set out the reasons which caused me to agree that such relief should be granted.

When your Lordships decided to make the reference to the European Court of Justice in this matter in May 1989, my noble and learned friend, Lord Bridge of Harwich, delivered a speech with which the remainder of your Lordships, including myself, agreed. In his speech on that occasion, my noble and learned friend was concerned primarily with the jurisdiction of the English courts to grant an interim injunction in a case such as the present as a matter of English law. Even so, he gave a full account of the background to the present appeal (including a reference to, and extensive quotation from, the judgment of Neill LJ in the Divisional Court, and in particular his account of the common fisheries policy); and his consideration of the question whether, as a matter of English law the court had jurisdiction in the present case to grant interim relief inevitably touched upon the question which your Lordships now have to address in the light of the ruling of the European Court of Justice. In these circumstances, it would be repetitious if I once again set out the background to the present appeal: I shall only do so to the extent necessary to set in their context certain decisions of the European Court of Justice. Furthermore I wish to stress that, in expressing my reasons why in my opinion your Lordships should grant interim relief, I have no intention of departing from anything contained in the speech of my noble and learned friend, with which I have expressed my complete agreement.

The question which arose for consideration by your Lordships, following the ruling of the European Court of Justice, concerned the appropriateness of an order for an interim injunction in a case such as the present, which is concerned with a challenge to the lawfulness of an Act of Parliament as being incompatible with European law. This inevitably raised for consideration the principles to be applied in the case of an application for such an interim injunction, and in particular the extent to which the principles stated by your Lordships' House in *American Cyanamid Co v Ethicon Ltd* [1975] AC 396 are applicable in such a case, a matter upon which my noble and learned friend made some observations in his speech upon the first hearing of the appeal. I have however to say at once that your Lordships were not concerned with the simple question whether to interfere with the exercise of discretion by the Divisional Court in favour of granting an injunction. This is for three reasons. First, after the Divisional Court made its order, as I have already indicated, circumstances occurred which rendered an order in that form inappropriate. The purpose of the order was to continue in being the registration of the applicants' fishing vessels under the Act of 1894 and/or the Act of 1886. However, during the period which elapsed since the Divisional Court made its order, the register maintained under the Act of 1894 was closed. It was for this reason that the applicants sought an injunction in a different form, directed towards restraining the Secretary of State from withholding or withdrawing registration of their vessels in the register maintained under the Act of 1988 on certain grounds which, in the applicants' submission, were incompatible with European law – an injunction which your Lordships decided to grant. Second, important legal developments had taken place since the Divisional Court's order. Two judgments were delivered by the European Court of Justice concerning the validity of certain conditions imposed by the Secretary of State on the grant of licences to fishing vessels (*Regulation v Ministry of Agriculture, Fisheries and Food ex p Agegate Ltd* (Case C3/87) [1990] 2 QB 151 and *Regulation v Ministry of Agriculture, Fisheries and Food ex p Jaderow Ltd* (Case C216/87) [1990] 2 QB 193), and an interim order was made by the President of the European Court of Justice, on an application by the European Commission regarding certain nationality provisions in section 14 of the Act of 1988: *Commission of the European Communities v United Kingdom* (Case 246/89) (1989) *The Times*, 28 October. The latter order was of particular relevance to the applicants' application for an interim injunction in the present case. Third, there had been certain factual developments since the last hearing before your Lordships, which were the subject of evidence. In these circumstances, it was inevitable that your Lordships' House should consider the applicants' application *de novo*, and that it should, for that purpose, consider in some depth the applicable principles.

Before turning to those applicable principles, I shall briefly summarise the effect of the intervening decisions of the European Court and of its President. The present appeal is, of course, concerned with the question whether certain provisions of the Act of 1988 are compatible with European law. The same is true of the interim order of the President, but not of the two decisions of the court. Those decisions, which I shall refer to as the *Agegate* and *Jaderow* cases, were concerned with the validity of certain conditions imposed upon the grant of licences for British fishing vessels. They are not, therefore, of such direct relevance to the present appeal as the President's interim order. They have, however, some bearing upon the present appeal, and I think it desirable to refer to them; and I propose to set them in their context, even though this may involve some repetition of matters already recorded in the speech of my noble and learned friend, Lord Bridge of Harwich.

Under the Sea Fish (Conservation) Act 1967, as subsequently amended, fishing vessels registered in the United Kingdom are required to have a licence. That Act was supplemented by certain legislation in 1983 – the British Fishing Boats Act 1983, and the British Fishing Boats Order 1983 (SI 1983/482) and the Sea Fish Licensing Order 1983 (SI 1983/1206). This legislation was passed in an attempt to meet the situation created during the previous two or three years by the registration of Spanish fishing vessels as British fishing vessels, with a view to acquiring the same rights to fish in Community waters as those to which British fishing vessels beneficially owned by British nationals were entitled. Such registration was perceived as having the effect of circumventing restrictions imposed on Spanish registered vessels under the reciprocal fishing agreement concluded by the European Community with Spain in 1981) (following the Hague resolution of 1976 (Council Regulation of 3 November 1976; Official Journal 1981 No C105/I), whereby certain Member States of the Community extended their fishing limits in the Atlantic Ocean 200 miles from the coast); under the reciprocal fishing agreement of 1981, a limited number of Spanish fishing vessels were permitted to fish only for specified quantities of hake in specified waters of Member States. It seems that the Spanish fishing vessels saw this as a substantial exclusion from fishing grounds in deep waters previously fished by them, and sought to circumvent the restriction by registering their vessels as British. It was in response to that move that the legislation of 1983 was introduced, under which a British-registered fishing boat fishing within British fishing limits was required to have a crew consisting of at least 75% of European Community nationals.

In January 1983, the system of national fish quotas was introduced by Council Regulations (EEC) Nos 170/83 and 172/83. The British authorities experienced difficulty in monitoring the catches of ex-Spanish- registered vessels, and concern about their activities was being expressed by British fishermen, especially those based in the western parts of the United Kingdom. This concern was being expressed against a background of continued activity by British-registered fishing vessels with a largely Spanish beneficial ownership operating under British registration but mainly from Spain and with only tenuous links with the United Kingdom which were believed to be making substantial inroads into the fishing opportunities allocated to the United Kingdom under the common fisheries policy in the light of this country's traditional fishing activities. Accordingly, in December 1985, new licensing conditions for British fishing vessels were announced, taking effect as from 1 January 1986. These related to crewing, social security contributions and operations. The crewing conditions required that at least 75% of the crew must be British citizens, or EEC nationals (excluding, subject to certain limited exceptions, Greek nationals until 1 January 1988, and Spanish or Portuguese nationals until 1 January 1993) ordinarily resident in the United Kingdom, the Isle of Man or the Channel Islands. The social security conditions required the skipper and all the crew to make contributions to United Kingdom national insurance, or equivalent Isle of Man or Channel Islands schemes. The operating conditions provided as follows:

> The vessel must operate from the United Kingdom, Isle of Man or Channel Islands; without prejudice to the generality of this requirement a vessel will be deemed to have been so operating if, for each six-month period in each calendar year (that is, January to June and July to December), either: (a) at least 50% by weight of the vessel's landings or transshipment of stocks to which this or any other licence in force at the relevant time relates have been landed and sold in the United Kingdom, Isle of Man or the Channel Islands or transshipped by way of sale within British fishery limits; or (b) other evidence is provided of the vessel's presence in a United Kingdom, Isle of Man or Channel Islands port on at least four occasions at intervals of at least 15 days.

The validity of the crewing and social security conditions was challenged in the *Agegate* case [1990] 2 QB 151, and in addition the validity of the operating conditions was challenged in the *Jaderow* case [1990] 2 QB 193. The Advocate General's opinion in both cases was published in November 1988, and so was available at the time of the hearing before the Divisional Court: but the judgment of the European Court of Justice in the two cases was not delivered until 14 December 1989, and differed in certain important respects from the opinion of the Advocate-General. In the *Agegate* case, the court upheld the validity of the social security condition: but in respect of the crewing condition, while upholding the condition in so far as it required 75% of the crew to be nationals of Member States, the court held that Community law precluded a condition requiring 75 per cent of the crew to reside ashore in the United Kingdom. In the *Jaderow* case, the court held that Community law did not preclude a member state, in authorising one of its vessels to fish against national quotas, from laying down conditions designed to ensure that the vessel had a real economic link with that state if that link concerned only the relation between that vessel's fishing operations and the population dependent on fisheries and related industries; and, on that basis, the court broadly upheld the validity of the operating conditions imposed by the United Kingdom. These two decisions are significant in the context of the present appeal, in that they provide an indication of the nature of the economic link which the court is prepared to recognise for these purposes, a link which does not extend to include a residence requirement imposed upon 75% of the vessels crew.

Meanwhile the United Kingdom Government had come to the conclusion that there was substantial non-compliance with these conditions. Furthermore, the number of largely foreign beneficially owned vessels on the United Kingdom register continued to grow, mainly through the acquisition by Spanish interests of British fishing vessels; Spanish interests were also able to increase the number of licences held by them by acquiring vessel's already holding United Kingdom licences. As a result, the problem was considered at a more fundamental level, by looking at the arrangements for registration of United Kingdom fishing vessels; and it was decided to introduce fresh legislation which, it was thought, would bring United Kingdom fishing vessel registration requirements 'broadly into line with arrangements in a number of other Member States' (see the first affidavit of Mr Noble of the Ministry of Agriculture, Fisheries and Food) and to require fishing vessels on the United Kingdom register to be substantially owned by British interests. Hence the provisions of Part II of the Act of 1988.

The interim order of the President (Case 246/89 R) (1989) *The Times*, 28 October, related to certain provisions of section 14 of the Act of 1988. Other provisions of that section formed the basis of the applicants' application for interim relief before your Lordships' House, and I think it desirable that I should set out the relevant parts of the section. Section 14(1), (2) and (7) provide as follows:

> (1) Subject to subsections (3) and (4), a fishing vessel shall only be eligible to be registered as a British fishing vessel if – (a) the vessel is British-owned; (b) the vessel is managed, and its operations are directed and controlled, from within the United Kingdom; and (c) any charterer, manager or operator of the vessel is a qualified person or company. (2) For the purposes of subsection (1)(a) a fishing vessel is British owned if – (a) the legal title to the vessel is vested wholly in one or more qualified persons or companies; and (b) the vessel is beneficially owned – (i) as to not less than the relevant percentage of the property in the vessel, by one or more qualified persons, or (ii) wholly by a qualified company or companies, or (iii) by one or more qualified companies and, as to not less than the relevant percentage of the remainder of the property in the vessel, by one or more qualified persons ... (7) In this section 'qualified company' means a company which satisfies the following conditions, namely – (a) it is incorporated in the United Kingdom and has its principal place of business there; (b) at least the relevant percentage of its shares (taken as a whole), and of each class of its shares, is legally and beneficially owned by one or more qualified persons or Companies; and (c) at least the relevant percentage of its directors are qualified persons; 'qualified person' means – (a) a person who is a British citizen resident and domiciled in the United Kingdom or (b) a local authority in the United Kingdom; and 'the relevant percentage' means 75% or such greater percentage (which may be 100%) as may for the time being be prescribed.

The interim order of the President (Case 246/89R) (1989) *The Times*, 28 October, was made upon an application to him by the European Commission. The Commission brought an action under Article 169 of the Treaty for a declaration that, by imposing the nationality requirements enshrined in sections 13 and 14 of the Act of 1988, the United Kingdom had failed to fulfil its obligations under Articles 7, 52 and 221 of the Treaty. The Commission further applied under Article 186 of the Treaty and Article 83 of the Rules of Procedure for an order requiring the United Kingdom to suspend the application of the nationality requirements enshrined in section 14(1)(a) and (c) of the Act, read in conjunction with paragraphs (2) and (7) of the section, as regards the nationals of other Member States and in respect of fishing vessels which until 31 March 1989 were pursuing a fishing activity under the British flag and under a British fishing licence. Under Article 83(2) of the Rules of Procedure, interim measures such as those requested may not be ordered unless there are circumstances giving rise to urgency and factual and legal grounds establishing a prima facie case for the measures applied for.

The President granted the interim order asked for by the Commission. With regard to the issue whether a prima facie case had been established, he said:

> 25 The United Kingdom further considers that the nationality requirements introduced by the Act of 1988 are justified by the present Community legislation on fisheries; that legislation, although it establishes a common system, is based on a principle of nationality for the purposes of the distribution of fishing quotas. Under Article 5(2) of Council Regulation 170/83 it is for the Member States to determine the detailed rules for the utilisation of the quotas allocated to them and thus to lay down the conditions which the vessels authorised to fish from these quotas must satisfy.

26 It must be observed that the system of national quotas established by Council Regulation 170/83 constitutes, as the United Kingdom contends, a derogation from the principle of equal access for Community fishermen to fishing grounds and the exploitation thereof in waters coming within the jurisdiction of the Member States, which is itself a specific expression of the principle of non-discrimination laid down in Article 40(3) of the EEC Treaty.

27 That derogation is justified, according to the recitals in the preamble to Regulation No 170/83, by the need, in a situation where there is a dearth of fishery resources, to ensure a relative stability in regard to fishing activities in order to safeguard the particular need of regions where local populations are especially dependent on fisheries and related industries.

28 The possibility cannot therefore be excluded that in their legislation concerning in particular the registration of fishing vessels and access to fishing activities the Member States may be led to introduce requirements whose compatibility with Community law can be justified only by the necessity to attain the objectives of the Community system of fishing quotas. As the Commission itself has admitted in these proceedings, such requirements may be necessary in order to ensure that there is a genuine link with the fishing industry of the Member State against whose quota the vessel may fish.

29 However, there is nothing which would prima facie warrant the conclusion that such requirements may derogate from the prohibition of discrimination on grounds of nationality contained in Articles 52 and 221 of the EEC Treaty regarding, respectively, the right of establishment and the right to participate in the capital of companies or firms within the meaning of Article 58.

30 The rights deriving from the above mentioned provisions of the Treaty include not only the rights of establishment and of participation in the capital of companies or firms but also the right to pursue an economic activity, as the case may be through a company, under the conditions laid down by the legislation of the country of establishment for its own nationals.

31 These rights prima facie also include the right to incorporate and manage a company whose object is to operate a fishing vessel registered in the state of establishment under the same conditions as a company controlled by nationals of that state.

32 As regards the United Kingdom's first submission based on its obligations under international law, it is sufficient to note, at this stage, that in this respect nothing has been put forward which at first sight could necessitate any derogation from the above-mentioned rights under Community law in order to ensure the effective exercise of British jurisdiction and control over the vessels in question.

33 It must therefore be held that, at the stage of these proceedings for the grant of interim relief, the application of the main proceedings does not appear to be without foundation and that the requirement of a prima facie case is thus satisfied.

The President went on to hold that sufficient urgency had also been established; in particular, for fishing vessels hitherto flying the British flag, cessation of their activities could cause serious damage. As regards the balance of interests he had this to say:

39 Finally, as regards the balance of interests, it is not established that the interim measures applied for may jeopardise the objective pursued by the British legislation at issue, namely to ensure the existence of a genuine link between the vessels fishing against the British quotas and the British fishing industry.

40 It appears prima facie that the registration requirements laid down by the new legislation, other than those relating to nationality and the measures adopted by the United Kingdom authorities in 1983 and 1986 would be sufficient to ensure the existence of such a link. The United Kingdom itself considers that the Anglo-Spanish vessels, which do not have that link with the United Kingdom, will not be able to satisfy the aforesaid requirements.

Following the President's order, section 14 of the Act of 1988 was amended (by the Merchant Shipping Act 1988 (Amendment) Order 1989 (SI 1989/2006)) with effect from 2 November 1989 to give effect to his order until after the final determination of the issue which was the subject of the Commission's substantive application. In section 14(1)(a) and (2), the expression 'Community-owned' was substituted for 'British-owned'; in section 14(7)(a), the words 'or another state of the European Community' were added after the words 'United Kingdom,' and in (7)(c) the words 'or a citizen of a Community state' were added after the words 'British citizen.' These changes have the effect that the nationality issue ceases to be relevant for the purposes – of the present appeal, though the issue is, your Lordships were told, still being vigorously contested by the United Kingdom before the European Court of Justice on the substantive reference by the Divisional Court.

The applicants nevertheless pursued their application for an interim injunction before your Lordships' House, but their complaint was restricted to other matters in section 14. They did not object, for the purposes of the present application, to the requirement, in section 14(1)(b), that a vessel should be managed and its operations directed and controlled from within the United Kingdom, they stated that they were able to comply with these requirements. Their complaint was directed towards the requirements for domicile and residence in the United Kingdom contained in the definition of 'qualified person' in section 14(7), which apply both to beneficial owners of vessels and, in the case of vessels beneficially owned by companies, both to shareholders and to directors (under section 14(7)(b) and (c) respectively), with the effect that 75% of the relevant shareholders and directors are required to be resident and domiciled in the United Kingdom. This, they submitted, is contrary to the right of establishment under Article 52 of the Treaty, and the right to participate in capital under Article 221. In answer, the Secretary of State submitted that Articles 52 and 221 of the Treaty cannot be taken to apply in their full rigour to the fisheries sector. If these articles, and Article 7, were so to apply, it would be impossible to prevent fishing interests in one member state registering vessels in another member state in which event it would be impossible (inter alia) to prevent such vessels fishing against the quotas of the latter Member State, to the detriment of that Member State's fishing community and allied industries (who were intended to be protected by the quota system), and also to prevent Spanish vessels avoiding provisions of the Act of Accession of 1985 (Act of Accession of Spain and Portugal, Official Journal 1985 No L302).

It was further submitted by the applicants that the effect of the provisions relating to residence and domicile in section 14, whether or not coupled with the nationality provisions, was to render it impossible for many of the applicants' vessels to register as British fishing vessels on the register now maintained under the Act of 1988, with possibly catastrophic financial results for their owners. They relied upon the conclusion of Neill LJ in the Divisional Court that he was not persuaded on the evidence before him that there were identifiable persons or communities whose activities or livelihood were being so seriously damaged, or would be so seriously damaged, as to outweigh the very obvious and immediate damage which would be caused by these new provisions if no interim relief were granted to the applicants. They submitted fresh evidence to your Lordships as showing that such damage was already being suffered; and they referred to the fact that, on the law as it stands at present (*Bourgoin SA v Ministry of Agriculture, Fisheries and Food* [1986] QB 716), the applicants would have no remedy in damages for loss or damage suffered by them by reason of the enforcement against them of provisions of the Act of 1988 if subsequently held to be incompatible with European law. Finally, it was stated that the judgment of the European Court of Justice on the substantive reference from the Divisional Court was expected in about a year's time, and that it would therefore be for no longer than that period that interim relief was required.

I turn now to the applicable principles in cases in which an interim injunction is sought, with particular reference to a case such as the present, in which the public interest is involved.

The jurisdiction of courts to grant interim injunctions is to be found in section 37 of the Supreme Court Act 1981, under which the court has power to grant an injunction in all cases in which it appears to it to be just or convenient so to do, and has power to do so on such terms and conditions as it thinks fit. Guidelines for the exercise of the court's jurisdiction to grant interim injunctions were laid down by your Lordships' House in *American Cyanamid Co v Ethicon Ltd* [1975] AC 316, in the speech of Lord Diplock in that case, with which the remainder of their Lordships concurred. I use the word 'guidelines' advisedly, because I do not read Lord Diplock's speech as intended to fetter the broad discretion conferred on the courts by section 37 of the Supreme Court Act 1981; on the contrary, a prime purpose of the guidelines established in the *Cyanamid* case was to remove a fetter which appeared to have been imposed in certain previous cases, viz, that a party seeking an interlocutory injunction had to establish a prima facie case for substantive relief. It is now clear that it is enough if he can show that there is a serious case to be tried. If he can establish that, then he has, so to speak, crossed the threshold; and the court can then address itself to the question whether it is just or convenient to grant an injunction.

Nothing which I say is intended to qualify the guidelines laid down in Lord Diplock's speech. But, before I turn to the question of public interest, which lies at the heart of the rival submissions in the present case, I must advert to the fact that Lord Diplock approached the matter in two stages. First, he considered the relevance of the availability of an adequate remedy in damages, either to the plaintiff seeking the injunction, or to the defendant in the event that an injunction is granted against him. As far as the plaintiff is concerned, the availability to him of such a remedy will normally preclude the grant to him of an interim injunction. If that is not so, then the court should consider whether, if an injunction is granted against the defendant, there will be an adequate remedy in damages available to him under the plaintiffs undertaking in damages; if so, there will be no reason on this ground to refuse to grant the plaintiff an interim injunction.

At this stage of the court's consideration of the case (which I will for convenience call the first stage) many applications for interim injunctions can well be decided. But if there is doubt as to the adequacy of either or both of the respective remedies in damages, then the court proceeds to what is usually called the balance of convenience, and for that purpose will consider all the circumstances of the case. I will call this the second stage. Again, I stress that I do not wish to place any gloss upon what Lord Diplock said about this stage. I wish only to record his statement, p 408, that:

> ... It would be unwise to attempt even to list all the various matters which may need to be taken into consideration in deciding where the balance lies, let alone to suggest the relevant weight to be attached to them. These will vary from case to case.

and his further statement, at p 409 (after referring to particular factors) that 'there may be many other special factors to be taken into consideration in the particular circumstances of individual cases'.

I turn to consider the impact upon these guidelines of the public interest, with particular reference to cases in which a public authority is seeking to enforce the law against some person, and either the authority seeks an interim injunction to restrain that person from acting contrary to the law, and that person claims that no such injunction should be granted on the ground that the relevant law is, for some reason, invalid; or that other person seeks an interim injunction to restrain the action of the authority, on the same ground.

I take the first stage. This may be affected in a number of ways. For example, where the Crown is seeking to enforce the law, it may not be thought right to impose upon the Crown the usual undertaking in damages as a condition of the grant of an injunction: see *Hoffmann-La Roche & Co AG v Secretary of State for Trade and Industry* [1975] AC 295. Again, in this country there is no general right to indemnity by reason of damage suffered through invalid administrative action; in particular, on the law as it now stands, there would be no remedy in damages available to the applicants in the present case for loss suffered by them by reason of the enforcement of the Act of 1988 against them, if the relevant part of the Act should prove to be incompatible with European law: see *Bourgoin SA v Ministry of Agriculture, Fisheries and Food* [1986] QB 716. Conversely, an authority acting in the public interest cannot normally be protected by a remedy in damages because it will itself have suffered none. It follows that, as a general rule, in cases of this kind involving the public interest, the problem cannot be solved at the first stage, and it will be necessary for the court to proceed to the second stage, concerned with the balance of convenience.

Turning then to the balance of convenience it is necessary in cases in which a party is a public authority performing duties to the public that 'one must look at the balance of convenience more widely, and take into account the interests of the public in general to whom these duties are owed': see *Smith v Inner London Education Authority* [1978] 1 All ER 411, p 22, *per* Browne LJ, and see also *Sierbein v Westminster City Council* [1987] 86 LGR 431. Like Browne LJ, I incline to the opinion that this can be treated as one of the special factors referred to by Lord Diplock in the passage from his speech which I have quoted. In this context, particular stress should be placed upon the importance of upholding the law of the land, in the public interest, bearing in mind the need for stability in our society, and the duty placed upon certain authorities to enforce the law in the public interest. This is of itself an important factor to be weighed in the balance when assessing the balance of convenience. So if a public authority seeks to force what is on its face the law of the land, and the person against whom such action is taken challenges the validity of that law, matters of considerable weight have to be put into the balance to outweigh the desirability of enforcing, in the public interest, what is on its face the law, and so to justify the refusal of an interim injunction in favour of the authority, or to render it just or convenient to restrain the authority for the time being from enforcing the law. This was expressed in a number of different ways by members of the Appellate Committee in the *Hoffmann-La Roche* case [1975] AC 295. Lord Reid said, at p 341, that:

> ... it is for the person against whom the interim injunction is sought to show special reason why justice requires that the injunction should not be granted or should only be granted on terms.

Lord Morris of Borth-y-Gest, pp 352, 353, stressed that all considerations appertaining to the justice of the matter become within the purview of the court; but he also stated that, in a case where the defendant attacks the validity of what appears to be an authentic law, the measure of the strength of this attack must inevitably call for some consideration. Lord Diplock, p 367, asserted that prima facie the Crown is entitled as of right to an interim injunction to enforce obedience to the law; and that:

> To displace this right or to fetter it by the imposition of conditions it is for the defendant to show a strong prima facie case that the statutory instrument is ultra vires.

Lord Cross of Chelsea did not expressly address the point. Lord Wilberforce, in a dissenting speech, stressed, p 358, that, in the last resort, the matter is one for the discretion of the judge; in particular, he rejected a suggestion that the presumption of validity of subordinate legislation required the court to enforce such legislation, by an interlocutory injunction, against the party who was calling the validity of such legislation in question.

I myself am of the opinion that in these cases, as in others, the discretion conferred upon the court cannot be fettered by a rule; I respectfully doubt whether there is any rule that, in cases such as these, a party challenging the validity of a law must – to resist an application for an interim injunction against him, or to obtain an interim injunction restraining the enforcement of the law – show a strong prima facie case that the law is invalid. It is impossible to foresee what case; may yet come before the courts; I cannot dismiss from my mind the possibility (no doubt remote) that such a party may suffer such serious and irreparable harm in the event of the law being enforced against him that it may be just or convenient to restrain its enforcement by an interim injunction even though so heavy a burden has not been discharged by him. In the end, the matter is one for the discretion of the court, taking into account all the circumstances of the case. Even so, the court should not restrain a public authority by interim injunction from enforcing an apparently authentic law unless it is satisfied, having regard to all the circumstances, that the challenge to the validity of the law is, prima facie, so firmly based as to justify so exceptional a course being taken.

With these principles in mind, I come to the facts of the present case. There can be no question of the present application being decided at the first stage of Lord Diplock's approach, and it is necessary to proceed at once to the second stage.

Your Lordships heard submissions from both parties about the strength of the applicants' challenge to the relevant provisions of section 14 of the Act of 1988. It is plain that the United Kingdom will, before the European Court of Justice, be resisting most strongly arguments by the applicants that any provision in section 14 is incompatible with European law, whether in respect of nationality (despite the recent decision of the President to grant interim relief), or in respect of domicile and residence of beneficial owners, shareholders and directors. It is unnecessary, and perhaps undesirable, for your Lordships now to analyse these arguments. They are set out in detail in the written observations already submitted by the United Kingdom and by the applicants to the European Court of Justice on the substantive reference by the Divisional Court, copies of which have been made available to your Lordships. There are, however, certain reasons which persuaded me to conclude, for present purposes, that, prima facie, the applicants had strong grounds for challenging the validity of the provisions relating to residence and domicile. First, a central element in the argument of the United Kingdom, in seeking to uphold the validity of section 14, is that Articles 7, 52 and 221 of the Treaty should not be interpreted as affecting the nationality of vessels, or the grant of flags, in respect of which competence remains in principle with the Member States. It has to be said, however, that an argument on these lines does not appear to have found favour with the President on the Commission's application for interim relief: *Commission of the European Communities v United Kingdom* (Case 246/89 R) (1989) *The Times*, 28 October. Second, although in the *Jaderow* case [1990] 2 QB 193 the European Court accepted that a member state, in authorising a vessel to fish against national quotas, might lay down conditions designed to ensure that it had a real economic link with the state if that link concerned only the relation between that vessel's fishing operations and the populations dependent on fisheries and related industries, yet in the *Agegate* case [1990] 2 QB 151 the court rejected as invalid a condition requiring residence in the Member State of 75% of the vessel's crew. If such a residence qualification is rejected in respect of the crew, as a condition of the grant of a vessel's licence, it may well be difficult to persuade the court to adopt a residence qualification relating to beneficial owners, or to 75% of shareholders in or directors of a company which beneficially owns a vessel, as a condition of registration of a fishing vessel under the Act of 1988: *a fortiori* must the same be true of a condition relating to domicile. As to the final outcome on these issues after consideration by the Court, your Lordships can of course express no opinion; but these two points alone led me to conclude that the applicants' challenge is, prima facie, a strong one.

It is on that basis that I turn to consider the balance of convenience as a whole. I have already referred to the view formed by Neill LJ, when the matter was before the Divisional Court [1989] CMLR 353, that serious damage may be caused to the applicants if no interim relief is granted. Your Lordships were furnished with up to date evidence in the form of answers to a questionnaire sent to owners of 62 vessels during the recent hearing. None of the answers to the questionnaire was on oath; and it was not in the circumstances possible for the Secretary of State to test the answers. or indeed to check their accuracy. However, no objection was made to this material being placed before your Lordships.

The answers to the questionnaire were not complete. However, from the answers received it was possible to derive the following basic information. All 62 vessels ceased to be on the United Kingdom register after the lapse of the old register on 1 April 1989. Twenty four of the vessels have not fished since their registration lapsed; of the remainder, 33 have fished but only outside EEC waters, in some cases for very short periods and in most cases after being laid up for a considerable time. Twenty four vessels have succeeded in obtaining registration under the Act of 1988, but always for special reasons, 14 of them because shares in the owning company had been sold to qualified persons or companies. Thirty owners have tried to sell their vessels, but none of them has received an acceptable offer. Many owners claim to have suffered damages to date of well over £100,000; some fear imminent bankruptcy.

Your Lordships also had the benefit of a fourth affidavit sworn by Mr Noble of the Ministry of Agriculture, Fisheries and Food. Apart from specific comments on particular vessels in the ownership of the applicants, he placed evidence before your Lordships to the effect that, as a result of the introduction of the new register, a number of British fishing vessels other than those owned by Spanish interests had been able to take up the opportunities now available to them, taking increased catches, employing extra crew, investing in new vessels to take advantage of the new opportunities, and generating increased activity on shore. He considered that, if the applicants' vessels returned to the British fleet and resumed their previous activities, the owners of these British fishing vessels would suffer serious losses, and he anticipated that the re-introduction of stiff quota restrictions would be required. However, even taking this evidence fully into account, I have, on all the material available to your Lordships, formed the same opinion as that formed by Neill LJ in the Divisional Court on the material then before him, that there was not sufficient to outweigh the obvious and immediate damage which would continue to be caused if no interim relief were granted to the applicants.

It was for these reasons that, in agreement with the remainder of your Lordships, I concluded that the appeal should be allowed and interim relief granted in the terms of the order made.

Lord Jauncey of Tullichettle: My Lords, I have had the advantage or reading in draft the speech to be delivered by my noble and learned friend Lord Goff of Chieveley. I agree with the conclusion at which he has arrived and I gratefully adopt his detailed account of the circumstances giving rise to the present appeal. It is only because of the importance and novelty of the principal question to be considered that I venture to add a few observations thereanent.

The European Court of Justice has ruled, p 856B, that:

> Community law must be interpreted as meaning that a national court which, in a case before it concerning Community law, considers that the sole obstacle which precludes it from granting interim relief is a rule of national law must set aside that rule.

This House is accordingly now faced with the wholly novel situation of determining whether in the circumstances of this appeal interim relief against the application of primary legislation should be granted to the applicants, pending the decision of the European Court of Justice on the reference by the Divisional Court of 10 March 1989. In reaching a conclusion the following matters have to be addressed, namely: (1) the threshold which must be crossed by the applicants before this House will consider intervening, (2) whether they have crossed that threshold, and (3) if they have, whether the balance of convenience favours the granting of interim relief.

(1) The threshold

When this appeal was last before your Lordships' House [1990] 2 AC 85 my noble and learned friend, Lord Bridge of Harwich, referred to the familiar situation in which a plaintiff seeks an interim injunction to protect a right when the material facts are in dispute and continued, p 139:

> In this situation the court has a discretion to grant or withhold interim relief which it exercises in accordance with the principles laid down by your Lordships' House in *American Cyanamid Co v Ethicon Ltd* [1975] AC 396. In deciding on a balance of convenience whether or not to make an interim injunction the court is essentially engaged in an exercise of holding the ring.

American Cyanamid concerned a claim for alleged infringement of patent and an application for interim injunction was made upon contested facts. Lord Diplock referred, p 407, to:

> the supposed rule that the court is not entitled to take any account of the balance of convenience unless it has first been satisfied that if the case went to trial upon no other evidence than is before the court at the hearing of the application the plaintiff would be entitled to judgment for a permanent injunction in the same terms as the interlocutory injunction sought ...

and continued:

> Your Lordships should in my view take this opportunity of declaring that there is no such rule. The use of such expressions as 'a probability', 'a prima facie case', or 'a strong prima facie case' in the context of the exercise of a discretionary power to grant an interlocutory injunction leads to confusion as to the object' sought to be achieved by this form of temporary relief. The court no doubt must be satisfied that the claim is not frivolous or vexatious; in other words, that there is a serious question to be tried. It is no part of the court's function at this stage of the litigation to try to resolve conflicts of evidence on affidavit as to facts on which the claims of either party may ultimately depend nor to decide difficult questions of law which call for detailed argument and mature considerations. These are matters to be dealt with at the trial.

As I understand it Lord Diplock in that passage was saying that the court must be satisfied that there is a serious question to be tried before it considers the balance of convenience. Indeed, this must be so since it would be quite wrong that a plaintiff should obtain interim relief on the basis of a claim which was groundless. I agree that it is not the function of the court to try to resolve conflicts of evidence at an interlocutory stage but I would demur to any suggestion that in no circumstances would it be appropriate to decide questions of law. If the only question at issue between the parties is one of law it may be possible in many cases to decide this at the stage of a contested application for an interim injunction. For example. where an employer seeks to enforce a restrictive covenant in a former employee's contract of employment and the only defence is that the covenant by reason of its wide terms is unenforceable, it would be wholly illogical to grant to the employer an interim injunction on the basis that there was a serious question to be tried when the question could at the same time be resolved as matter of law in favour of the employee.

However, while the test of a serious question to be tried is appropriate to proceedings between private parties where no presumption favours the position of one party as against the other it does not follow that the same considerations apply when primary legislation and the public interest are involved. Indeed, my noble and learned friend, Lord Bridge of Harwich (*Regulation v Secretary of State for Transport ex p Factortame Ltd* [1990] 2 AC 85, p 140). remarked upon the fundamental distinction between the familiar situation and that which arises in this appeal. In *Hoffmann-La Roche & Co AC v Secretary of State for Trade and Industry* [1975] AC 299, the Secretary of State having sought by interim injunction to enforce a statutory instrument approved by both Houses of Parliament the defenders maintained that the instrument was *ultra vires*. Lord Reid said, p 341, that:

> ... it is for the person against whom the interim injunction is sought to show special reason why justice requires that the injunction should not be granted or should only be granted on terms

and Lord Morris of Borth-y-Gest, p 353, pointed out that the measure of the strength of the attack upon the statutory instrument must inevitably call for some consideration. Lord Diplock said, p 366:

> All that can usefully be said is that the presumption that subordinate legislation is *intra vires* prevails in the absence of rebuttal, and that it cannot be rebutted except by a party to legal proceedings in a court of competent jurisdiction who has *locus standi* to challenge the validity of the subordinate legislation in question.

He said, p 367:

> So in this type of law enforcement action it the only defence is an attack on the validity of the statutory instrument sought to be enforced the ordinary position of the parties as respects the grant of interim injunctions is reversed, the duty of the Crown to see that the law declared by the statutory instrument is obeyed is not suspended by the commencement of proceedings in which the validity of the instrument is challenged. Prima facie the Crown is entitled as of right to an interim injunction to enforce obedience to it. To displace this right or to fetter it by the imposition of conditions it is for the defendant to show a strong prima facie case that the statutory instrument is *ultra vires*.

These observations, in my view, apply not only where a defendant is seeking to resist an attempt by the Crown to enforce secondary legislation but also where a plaintiff is seeking to restrict the Crown in its operation of such legislation. They must be equally appropriate to a challenge to primary legislation as they are to a challenge to secondary legislation. Indeed, when this appeal was last before this House, Lord Bridge said, p 142:

> In this situation the difficulty which confronts the application is that the presumption that an Act of Parliament is compatible with Community law unless and until declared to be incompatible must be at least as strong as the presumption that delegated legislation is valid unless and until declared invalid.

Given this presumption it follows from the above observations of Lord Diplock that it is for the Crown to enforce the provisions of the Act of 1988 and that anyone, whether a plaintiff or defendant, who seeks to challenge the validity thereof must at least show a strong prima facie case of incompatibility with Community law. It is the presumption in favour of the legislation being challenged which in my view makes the *American Cyanamid* test of a serious question to be tried inappropriate in a case such as the present. In expressing this opinion I must emphasise that I am in no way criticising the appropriateness of the *American Cyanamid* test for cases where primary or secondary legislation is not being challenged nor am I suggesting that Lord Diplock's approach to the balance of convenience is not appropriate in this case.

My Lords, I have considered anxiously whether other factors such as relative hardship or injustice should play any part in determining the appropriate threshold which an applicant for relief in circumstances such as the present should cross. Given the wide discretion conferred upon the courts by section 37 of the Supreme Court Act 1981 I would not wish to lay down any rules which might unduly inhibit that discretion in unforeseen circumstances in the future. Suffice it to say that as at present advised it would only be in the most exceptional circumstances that I can foresee the threshold being lowered by factors not directly related to the invalidity of the legislation under challenge. In the normal case other factors would be considered in relation to the balance of convenience. If an applicant seeking an injunction against primary or secondary legislation cannot show a strong prima facie ground of challenge it will in the absence of quite exceptional circumstances avail him nought that a refusal of an injunction would result in greater injustice to him should he succeed at trial than would result to the other party if the injunction was granted and he failed at trial.

I therefore conclude that the applicants will only cross the threshold if they demonstrate that there is a strong prima facie case that section 14 of the Act of 1988 is incompatible with Community law, which failing that exceptional circumstances exist would justify lowering the threshold.

(2) Have the applicants crossed the threshold?

Section 14(1) provides that a fishing vessel shall only be eligible to be registered as a British fishing vessel if inter alia 'the vessel is British-owned'. Section 14(2) provides that a fishing vessel is British-owned if the legal title is vested wholly in one or more qualified persons or companies and section 14(7) provides that a qualified company is one which is incorporated in the United Kingdom with 75% of the shares held by and 75% of its directors being qualified persons. Qualified person is defined in section 14(7) as 'a person who is a British citizen resident and domiciled in the United Kingdom'. It is to this latter definition that Mr Vaughan confined his attack on the ground that such a restriction in ownership was incompatible with Community law.

Since the appeal was last before this House in 1989 certain important events have taken place in the European Court. On 4 August 1989 (*Commission of the European Communities v United Kingdom* (Case 246/89 R) (1989) *The Times*, 28 October), the Commission sought a declaration that the nationality requirements in section 14 of the Act of 1988 constituted a failure by the United Kingdom to fulfil certain of its Treaty obligations. On 10 October 1989 the President of the court made the following order:

> Pending delivery of the judgment in the main proceedings the United Kingdom shall suspend the application of the nationality requirements laid down in section 14(1)(a) and (c) of the Merchant Shipping Act 1988, read in conjunction with paragraphs (2) and (7) of that section, as regards the nationals of other Member States and in respect of fishing vessels which, until 31 March 1989, were pursuing a fishing activity under the British flag and under a British fishing licence.

Effect was given to this order by the Merchant Shipping Act 1988 (Amendment) Order 1989 which, in relation to the fishing vessels in question, amended section 14 by substituting 'Community-owned' for 'British owned' in subsection 1 and by amending the definition of the 'qualified person' to read 'a person who is a British citizen or a national of a member state other than the United Kingdom and is either resident 'and domiciled in the United Kingdom'.

It will be noted that the Commission did not seek to challenge the residence and domicile qualification which is now challenged by Mr Vaughan. On 14 December 1989 the European Court similarly constituted gave judgment in two cases which may for convenience be called *Agegate* [1990] 2 QB 151 and *Jaderow* [1991] 2 QB 193. Both cases concerned the grant to British-registered fishing vessels with strong Spanish connections of fishing licences which contained crewing conditions to the effect that: (1) at least 75% of the crew must be British citizens or EEC nationals (excluding until 1 January 1993 Spanish nationals), and (2) the skipper and all the crew must be making contributions to United Kingdom national insurance. In the course of the *Agegate* judgment the following observations on the quota system were made, [1991] 2 QB 151, 188:

> 24 It follows from the foregoing that the aim of the quotas is to assure to each member state a share of the Community's total allowable catch, determined essentially on the basis of the catches from which traditional fishing activities, the local populations dependent on fisheries and related industries of the member state benefited before the quota system was established.

> 25 In that context a residence requirement such as the one in point in this case is irrelevant to the aim of the quota system and cannot therefore be justified by that aim.

And the court ruled, inter alia, at p 192:

> 2 Community law precludes a member state from requiring, as a condition for authorising one of its vessels to fish against its quotas, That 5% of the crew of the vessel in question must reside ashore in that member state.

3   Save in those cases where Council Regulation (EEC) No 1408/71 otherwise provides, Community law does not preclude a Member State from requiring, as a condition for authorising one of its vessels to fish against its quotas, that the skipper and all the crew of the vessel must be making contributions to the social security scheme of that Member State.

In the *Jaderow* judgment [1990] 2 QB 193 the court recognised that the aim of national quotas derived from the common fisheries policy might justify conditions designed to ensure that there was a real economic link between the vessel and the Member State in question if the purpose of such conditions was that the populations dependent on fisheries and related industries should benefit from them. The court ruled, inter alia, p 226, that Community law as it now stands:

(1) does not preclude a member state, in authorising one of its vessels to fish against national quotas, from laying down conditions designed to ensure that the vessel has a real economic link with that state if that link concerns only the relations between that vessel's fishing operations and the populations dependent on fisheries and related industries; (2) does not preclude a Member State, in authorising one of its vessels to fish against national quotas from laying down the condition, in order to ensure that there is a real economic link as defined above, that the vessel is to operate from national ports, if that condition does not involve an obligation for the vessel to depart from a national port on all its fishing trips ...

It is to my mind implicit in these two decisions that the court did not consider that residence and domicile of a specified percentage of the crew was justified as a condition designed to ensure the existence of a real economic link between the vessel and the Member State.

Had the court so considered *Agegate* [1990] 2 QB 151 must have been decided differently. If residence of the crew is not relevant to ensure the existent of a real economic link between vessel and member state what is the position in relation to the residence of shareholders and directors of an owning company? The role of this House is not to give an answer to that question but rather to assess the prospects of the European Court giving an answer which is favourable to the applicants. Directors and shareholders are further removed from any link between a vessel and a member state than are members of the crew and the European Court having decided that residence of the latter is not relevant to ensure the existence of a real economic link there must at least be a strong probability that the court will take a similar view in relation to the former. Upon that assumption it would appear that the applicants can show a strong prima facie ground of challenge to the relevant statutory provision. However, there remains for consideration the argument of the Crown that Community law does not affect the sovereign right of a member state to lay down the conditions for the grant of its flag to ships. Customary international law, as expressed in Article 5(1) of the Geneva Convention on the High Seas, requires that there should be a genuine link between a vessel and the state of her flag. Article 94 of the 1982 Convention of the Law on the Sea sets out the important legal and international obligations incurred by a state in relation to a vessel to whom the flag of the state has been granted. In the absence of any express provision it should not be presumed that the Treaty interferes with the exercise by a member state of its sovereign powers. I was initially attracted by these submissions and in some doubt as to whether they should not be given effect to. However, on further consideration of the President's ruling of 10 October 1989, I have come to the conclusion that the applicants can show that they are very likely to be rejected by the European Court. In the context of legislative requirements introduced by Member States to obtain the objective of the Community system of fishing quotas the President said:

29 However there is nothing which would prima facie warrant the conclusion that such requirements may derogate from the prohibition of discrimination on grounds of nationality contained in Articles 52 and 221 of the EEC Treaty regarding, respectively, the right of establishment and the right to participate in the capital of companies or firms within the meaning of Article 58.

30 The rights deriving from the above mentioned provisions of the Treaty include not only the rights of establishment and of participation in the capital of companies or firms but also the right to pursue an economic activity, as the case may be through a company, under the conditions laid down by the legislation of the country of establishment for its own nationals.

31 These rights prima facie also include the right to incorporate and manage a company whose object is to operate a fishing vessel registered in the state of establishment under the same conditions as a company controlled by nationals of that state.

32 As regards the United Kingdom's first submission based on its obligations under international law, it is sufficient to note, at this stage, that in this respect nothing has been put forward which at first sight could necessitate any derogation from the above-mentioned rights under Community law in order to ensure the effective exercise of British jurisdiction and control over the vessels in question.

33 It must therefore be held that, at the stage of these proceedings for the grant of interim relief, the application of the main proceedings does not appear to be without foundation and that the requirement of a prima facie case is thus satisfied.

Given the foregoing observations of the President it would appear that the applicants have a strong chance of successfully arguing before the European Court that international law does not justify derogation from the prohibition of discrimination on grounds of nationality contained in Articles 52 and 221 of the Treaty.

In all these circumstances I consider that the applicants have crossed the threshold in relation to section 14 of the Act of 1988. It is therefore unnecessary to consider whether such exceptional circumstances exist as will justify lowering that threshold.

(3) Balance of convenience

In *Films Rover International Ltd v Cannon Film Sales Ltd* [1987] 1 WLR 670, Hoffman J in considering an application for an interlocutory mandatory injunction implicitly acknowledged that there was a serious question to be tried and said, p 680:

> The principal dilemma about the grant of interlocutory injunctions, whether prohibitory or mandatory, is that there is by definition a risk that the court may make the 'wrong' decision, in the sense of granting an injunction to a party who succeeds (or would succeed) at trial. A fundamental principle is therefore that the court should take whichever course appears to carry the lower risk of injustice if it should turn out to have been 'wrong' in the sense I have described. The guidelines for the grant of both kinds of interlocutory injunctions are derived from this principle.

I find this approach of assistance in the present case.

If the applicants are successful in the end of the day but are afforded no interim relief they will, standing the law as laid down in *Bourgoin SA v Ministry of Agriculture, Fisheries and Food* [1986] QB 716, suffer very severe and irrecoverable damage. If they are ultimately unsuccessful but are afforded interim relief, the loss suffered by the British fishing industry as a whole and by individual members thereof during the period of interim relief will be relatively minor. Beyond this I cannot usefully add anything to what has already been said on the matter by my noble and learned friend Lord Goff of Chieveley. It follows that, the applicants having crossed the threshold, the balance of convenience favours the granting to them of interim relief.

Order accordingly.

Solicitors: Thomas Cooper & Stibbard; Treasury Solicitor.

Tillotson, J, *European Community Law: Text, Cases and Materials*, 2nd edn, 1996, London: Cavendish Publishing, pp 56–59; 78–87; 479–82

TRANSFERS OF SOVEREIGNTY AND PARLIAMENTARY SOVEREIGNTY

Sovereignty is a word of many meanings. In the United Kingdom, the expression *parliamentary* sovereignty refers to the constitutional doctrine that there are no legal limits to the legislative power of Parliament except that Parliament cannot limit its own powers for the future. Thus, in national law there is nothing that a statute properly enacted cannot do and therefore no act is irreversible. Now, as Collins points out:

> It is only in the sense last mentioned that the word has any useful meaning in relation to the national law of the United Kingdom. In the international sphere and in the political sphere there may have been a limitation of sovereignty but there is no reason to believe that there has yet been any limitation on the sovereignty of the United Kingdom Parliament [Collins, *European Community Law in the United Kingdom*, 1990].

... Therefore, as regards transfers of *national* sovereignty ... it is agreed that whereas this involves the removal of legislative powers from the United Kingdom Parliament by limiting its authority, such transfers do not amount (at least in theory) to an encroachment upon the doctrine of parliamentary sovereignty:

> The stage has now been reached where the current legal and political reality is that there has been a transfer of powers to the Community. It has already been suggested that the traditional rule that Parliament may not bind its successors is not necessarily irreconcilable with the concept of a transfer of powers to another authority. It may further be suggested that whilst the political reality remains membership of the Community, such powers are unlikely in practice to be recovered, and at least to that extent the transfer can be regarded as irreversible [Usher, 1981].

For an international treaty to be binding and enforceable at the domestic level, UK law, which regards international law and domestic law as separate systems of law, requires the treaty to be incorporated into the national legal system by means of an enabling act. The European Communities Act 1972, which provides for the incorporation of Community law into the law of the UK, whilst recognising in ss 2 and 3 the supremacy of Community law (as established by the European Court of Justice), also lays down a rule of interpretation to the effect that Parliament is to be presumed not to intend any statute to override Community law. Community law will therefore always prevail over national law unless Parliament expressly states in a future Act that it is to override Community law.

In this way, the remote possibility that Parliament might some day wish to repeal the 1972 Act is not excluded and the ultimate sovereignty of Parliament is upheld:

> We have all been brought up to believe that, in legal theory, one Parliament cannot bind another and that no Act is irreversible. But legal theory does not always march alongside political reality ... What are the realities here? If Her Majesty's Ministers sign this Treaty and Parliament enacts provisions to implement it [the 1972 Act], I do not envisage that Parliament would afterwards go back on it and try to withdraw from it. But if Parliament should do so, then I say we will consider that event when it happens [Lord Denning in *Blackburn v Attorney General* (1971)].

Lord Denning is here referring to the unlikely eventuality of this country withdrawing from the Community. (The Treaty contains no provisions for withdrawal.)

The reality, therefore, is that while the United Kingdom is a member of the Community, the constitutional doctrine of Parliamentary sovereignty cannot be relied upon in the face of directly enforceable rules of Community law. Although in 1983, Sir Robert Megarry VC stated in *Manuel v Attorney General* that 'once an instrument is recognised as being an Act of Parliament, no English court can refuse to obey it or question its validity', this statement must certainly now be modified to read '... once an instrument is recognised as being an Act of Parliament and is compatible with enforceable Community law, no English court can refuse to obey it or question its validity'. That this is the present state of the law in this country was expressed in the clearest terms and on the highest judicial authority by Lord Bridge in the *Factortame (No 2)* case …:

> Some public comments on the decision of the European Court of Justice, affirming the jurisdiction of the courts of Member States to override national legislation if necessary to enable interim relief to be granted in protection of rights under Community law, have suggested that this was a novel and dangerous invasion by a Community institution of the sovereignty of the United Kingdom Parliament. But such comments are based on a misconception. If the supremacy within the European Community of Community law over the national law of Member States was not always inherent in the EEC Treaty it was certainly well-established in the jurisprudence of the European Court of Justice long before the United Kingdom joined the Community. Thus, whatever limitation of its sovereignty Parliament accepted when it enacted the European Communities Act 1972 was entirely voluntary. Under the terms of the Act of 1972 it has always been clear that it was the duty of a United Kingdom court, when delivering final judgment, to override any rule of national law found to be in conflict with any directly enforceable rule of Community law … Thus, there is nothing in any way novel in according supremacy to rules of Community law in those areas to which they apply and to insist that, in the protection of rights under Community law, national courts must not be inhibited by rules of national law from granting interim relief in appropriate cases is no more than a logical recognition of that supremacy.

The *Factortame* litigation involved the disapplication of certain provisions of an Act of Parliament pending a decision by the Court of Justice on the question of whether the legislation was in breach of Community law and the directly enforceable Treaty rights of a number of private parties. The Court later held that the statute did infringe Community law and the private parties concerned brought an action for damages against the government department responsible for the legislation on the basis of what is known as the Francovich principle of State liability … This case, one half of joined cases Case 46 and Case 48/93 *Brasserie du Pêcheur/Factortame*, has yet to be finally decided at national level but the following passages from the Advocate General's Opinion is of particular relevance in the context of the continuing developing relationship between Community law and national law:

> It is beyond argument that the State should not incur liability for legislative action except in exceptional circumstances. The freedom of the legislature must not be trammelled by the prospect of actions for damages … The 'power to express the sovereignty of the people' justifies the legislature's immunity in relation to the general rule of liability …

> State liability for breach of Community law and State liability in domestic law for legislative action do not have the same basis. The first type of liability is necessarily founded on illegality: breach of a higher ranking rule of law and therefore of the principle of primacy …

> Respect for primacy requires not only that legislation contrary to Community law should be disapplied. It requires also that damage resulting from its application in the past should be made good …

> Refuge can no longer be taken behind the supremacy or unchallengeability of legislation … the bringing of an action for damages against the State for the legislatures' failure to act is perfectly permissible where the State's liability is based on a breach of Community law, as *Francovich* shows, whereas refuge can no longer be taken behind the supremacy or unchallengeability of legislation … the bringing of an action for damages against the State for the legislatures' failure to act is perfectly permissible where the State's liability is based on a breach of Community law, as *Francovich* shows, whereas this is hardly conceivable in domestic law.

> As Lord Bridge explained in the judgment delivered after the Court had given its judgment in *Factortame (No 2)*, by ratifying the Treaty of Rome (or, in the United Kingdom's case, by adopting the 1972 European Communities Act), the Member States accepted that the legislative sovereignty of their Parliaments was limited by the principle of the primacy of Community law [pp 56–59].

Direct applicability, which strictly speaking only applies to Regulations, relates to *how* provisions of Community law enter the legal order of the Member States. The principle of *direct effect* on the other hand concerns the effectiveness of provisions of Community law once they enter the national legal systems. Although closely related, the two principles should be considered separately.

In *Costa v ENEL*, the Court of Justice stated that Community law binds both Member States and individuals and also that the national courts of the Member States are bound to apply Community law. As we have seen when examining the definitions of the binding Community acts in Art 189, such acts may well create rights for individuals which may be relied upon by them in national courts. And, if this is so as regards Community legislation (a secondary source), then, although the Treaty does not state as such, it must also be the case as regards Treaty provisions themselves (a primary source).

In the famous *Van Gend en Loos* case in 1963, the principle of direct effect, the clearest legal indicator of supranationality, was fully explained by the Court of Justice. In the course of answering questions regarding the nature and effect of one of the Treaty's customs union rules (Art 12), put to it by a Dutch court called upon to decide a case brought by a Dutch company against the national customs authorities, the Court ruled that this provision of Community law 'produces direct effects and creates individual rights which national courts must protect'. The Court stressed the constitutional nature of the Treaty – 'this Treaty is more than an agreement which merely creates mutual obligations between the contracting states' – and thus, a consequent need to provide 'direct legal protection of the individual rights of ... nationals'. These rights find their Community law corollary in *obligations* which rest upon others – in this case the Dutch State. Because the article in question was 'ideally adapted to produce direct effects in the legal relationship between Member States and their subjects', it enabled the plaintiff company, threatened by the breach of its Treaty obligations by the Dutch state, to assert its rights before the national court.

As Brown and Jacobs have explained:

> The notion of the direct effect of Community law, coupled with the jurisdiction of the Court to give preliminary rulings and so to determine the scope of the individual's rights and obligations, is a more powerful weapon than Arts 169 and 170. The individual has no direct remedy, before the Court, against the default of a State. The remedy lies with the national court, with the use of Art 177 where necessary. In this way the national courts enforce, if necessary against their own State, the rights conferred on the individual by the Treaty.

Van Gend en Loos Case 26/62

In September 1960, VG imported into the Netherlands from West Germany a quantity of a chemical product known as ureaformaldehyde.

In December 1959, a Dutch statute had been passed which brought into force modifications of the Benelux tariff system as a result of acceptance of the Brussels Nomenclature, a measure designed to secure international unification of the classification of goods for customs purposes. Regrouping of goods under the nomenclature resulted in an increase in the amount of duty payable on ureaformaldehyde to 8% on an *ad valorem* basis.

However, Art 12, EEC had come into force as regards intra-Community trade on January 1958.

Article 12: Member States shall refrain from introducing between themselves any new customs duties on imports or exports or any charges having equivalent effect, and from increasing those which they already apply in their trade with each other.

VG contended that on 1 January 1958 the duty payable under Dutch law on the product in question was 3% and they objected to paying the additional 5%.

The Customs Inspector having rejected their claim, VG appealed to the Dutch Tariefcommissie (Customs Court) in Amsterdam. Under Art 177, the Tariefcommissie certified two questions to the Court of Justice in Luxembourg regarding the nature of Art 12:

1   Does Art 12 have the effect of national law as claimed by VG, and may individuals derive rights from it which a national court must protect?

2   If the answer is affirmative, has there been an unlawful increase in customs duties or merely a reasonable modification of the duties which, although bringing about an increase, is not prohibited by Art 12?

The Governments of Belgium, West Germany and the Netherlands, and the EC Commission filed additional memoranda with the Court. All three Governments argued that Art 12 merely created obligations for Member States and did not therefore create rights for individuals. A claim might be brought against a Member State which broke its Treaty obligations under EEC Art 169 or 170.

The Court ruled as follows:

The first question of the Tariefcommissie is whether Art 12 of the Treaty has direct application in national law in the sense that the nationals of Member States may on the bask of this Article lay claim to rights which the national court must protect.

To ascertain whether the provisions of an international treaty extend so far in their effects it is necessary to consider the spirit, the general scheme and the wording of those provisions.

The objective of the EEC Treaty, which is to establish a Common Market, the functioning of which is of direct concern to interested parties in the Community, implies that this Treaty is more than an agreement which merely creates mutual obligations between the contracting states. This view is confirmed by the preamble to the Treaty which refers not only to governments but to peoples. It is also confirmed more specifically by the establishment of institutions endowed with sovereign rights, the exercise of which affects Member States and also their citizens. Furthermore, it must be noted that the nationals of the states brought together in the Community are called upon to co-operate in the functioning of this Community through the intermediary of the European Parliament and the Economic and Social Committee.

In addition, the task assigned to the Court of Justice under Art 177, the object of which is to secure uniform interpretation of the Treaty by national courts and tribunals, confirms that the States have acknowledged that Community law has an authority which can be invoked by their nationals before those courts and tribunals.

The conclusion to be drawn from this is that the Community constitutes a new legal order of international law for the benefit of which the Sates have limited their sovereign rights, albeit within limited fields, and the subjects of which comprise not only Member States but also their nationals. Independently of the legislation of Member States, Community law therefore not only imposes obligations on individuals but is also intended to confer upon them rights which become part of their legal heritage. These rights arise not only where they are expressly granted by the Treaty, but also by reason of obligations which the Treaty imposes in a clearly defined way upon individuals as well as upon the Member States and upon the institutions of the Community.

With regard to the general scheme of the Treaty as it relates to customs duties and charges having equivalent effect it must be emphasised that Art 9, which bases the Community upon a customs union, includes as an essential provision the prohibition of customs duties and charges. This provision is found at the beginning of the part of the Treaty which defines the 'Foundations of the Community'. It is applied and explained by Art 12.

The wording of Art 12 contains a clear and unconditional prohibition which is not a positive but a negative obligation. This obligation, moreover, is not qualified by any reservation on the part of States which would make its implementation conditional upon a positive legislative measure enacted under national law. The very nature of this prohibition makes it ideally adapted to produce direct effects in the legal relationship between Member States and their subjects.

The implementation of Art 12 does not require any legislative intervention on the part of the States. The fact that under this article it is the Member States who are made the subject of the negative obligation does not imply that their nationals cannot benefit from this obligation.

In addition the argument based on Arts 169 and 170 of the Treaty put forward by the three Governments which have submitted observations to the Court in their statements of the case is misconceived. The fact that these Articles of the Treaty enable the Commission and the Member States to bring before the Court a State which has not fulfilled its obligations doff not mean that individuals cannot plead these obligations, should the occasion arise, before a national court, any more than the fact that the Treaty places at the disposal of the Commission ways of ensuring that obligations imposed upon those subject to the Treaty are observed, precludes the possibility, in actions between individuals before a national court, of pleading infringements of these obligations.

A restriction of the guarantees against an infringement of Art 12 by Member States to the procedures under Arts 169 and 170 would remove all direct legal protection of the individual rights of their nationals. There is the risk that recourse to the procedure under these articles would be ineffective if it were to occur after the implementation of a national decision taken contrary to the provisions of the Treaty.

The vigilance of individuals concerned to protect their rights amounts to an effective supervision in addition to the supervision entrusted by Arts 169 and 170 to the diligence of the Commission and of the Member States.

It follows from the foregoing considerations that, according to the spirit, the general scheme and the wording of the Treaty, Art 12 must be interpreted as producing direct effects and creating individual rights which national courts must protect.

It follows from the wording and the general scheme of Art 12 of the Treaty that, in order to ascertain whether customs duties or charges having equivalent effect have been increased contrary to the prohibition contained in the said article, regard must be had to the customs duties and charges actually applied at the date of the entry into force of the Treaty.

Further, with regard to the prohibition in Art 12 of the Treaty, such an illegal increase may arise from a re-arrangement of the tariff resulting in the classification of the product under a more highly taxed heading and from an actual increase in the rate of customs duty.

It is of little importance how the increase in customs duties occurred when, after the Treaty entered into force, the same product in the same Member State was subjected to a higher rate of duty.

The application of Art 12, in accordance with the interpretation given above, comes within the jurisdiction of the national court which must enquire whether the dutiable product, in this case ureaformaldehyde originating in the Federal Republic of Germany, is charged under the customs measures brought into force in the Netherlands with an import duty higher than that with which it was charged on 1 January 1958.

The Court has no jurisdiction to check the validity of the conflicting views on this subject which have been submitted to it during the proceedings but must leave them to be determined by the national courts ...

The costs incurred by the Commission of the EEC and the Member States which have submitted their observations to the Court are not recoverable, and as these proceedings are, in so far as the parties to the main action are concerned, a step in the action pending before the Tariefcommissie, the decision as to costs is a matter for that court.

On those grounds;

Upon reading the pleadings;

Upon hearing the report of the Judge-Rapporteur;

Upon hearing the opinion of the Advocate-General;

Having regard to Arts 9, 12, 14, 169, 170 and 177 of the Treaty establishing the European Economic Community;

Having regard to the Rules of Procedure of the Court of Justice of the European Communities;

The Court in answer to the questions referred to it for a preliminary ruling by the Tariefcommissie by decision of 16 August 1962, hereby rules:

1   Article 12 of the Treaty establishing the European Economic Community produces direct effects and creates individual rights which national courts must protect.

2   In order to ascertain whether customs duties or charges having equivalent effect have been increased contrary to the prohibition contained in Art 12 of the Treaty, regard must be had to the duties and charges actually applied by the Member State in question at the date of the entry into force of the Treaty.

    Such an increase can arise both from a re-arrangement of the tariff resulting in the classification of the product under a more highly taxed heading and from an increase in the rate of customs duty applied.

3   The decision as to costs in these proceedings is a matter for the Tariefcommissie.

The decision in *Van Gend en Loos* dramatically increased the impact of Community law in the Member States. It is a decision which ultimately rests on two related factors: first, on the Court's perception of the federal and constitutional (as opposed to international) nature of the Treaty, key provisions of which bear directly upon the individual and, secondly, on the Court's clear appreciation that the establishment of the customs union was a key element of negative integration within the Community – and that Community law must be fully effective in that respect. It is 'undoubtedly the richest and most creative of all Community cases, and one in which virtually every later development can – at least with hindsight – be seen to have its germ' (Rudden).

Thus, the case law of the Court of Justice clearly shows that a *directly effective* provision of Community law, whether of the Treaty or a legally binding secondary act, always prevails (takes precedence) over a conflicting provision of national law. In such cases, individual Community rights must be protected irrespective of whether the Community provision takes effect before, or after, the national provision. The case which follows concerns the impact of a Community Regulation within Italian national law. A Regulation, as we have seen, is directly applicable. The

Court of Justice assumes that it is therefore 'a direct source of rights and duties for all those affected thereby', that is, that direct effect is the norm for Regulations. (On this point and possible confusion between direct applicability and direct effect, see Chapter 8.)

AMMINISTRAZIONE DELLE FINANZE V SIMMENTHAL CASE 106/77

S imported a consignment of beef from France into Italy. In accordance with an Italian statute of 1970, the company was charged fees for veterinary and public health inspections made at the frontier. S sued for the return of their money in the Italian courts, pleading that the charges were contrary to EEC law. Following an Art 177 reference, the Court of Justice held that the inspections were contrary to Art 30, being measures having an equivalent effect to a quantitative restriction, and the fees were contrary to Art 12 being charges equivalent to customs duties. The Court also held that this question of animal and public health had been governed by EC Regulations since 1964 and 1968.

In consequence the national court ordered the Italian Finance Ministry to repay the fees charged. The Ministry, however, pleaded the national statute of 1970 and argued that, under the Italian Constitution, this bound them until such time as it was set aside by the Constitutional Court. Following a further reference, the Court held:

> The main purpose of the first question is to ascertain what consequences flow from the direct applicability of a provision of Community law in the event of incompatibility with a subsequent legislative provision of a Member State.

> Direct applicability in such circumstances means that rules of Community law must be fully and uniformly applied in all Member States from the date of their entry into force and for so long as they continue in force.

> These provisions are therefore a direct source of rights and duties for all those affected thereby, whether Member States or individuals, who are parties to legal relationships under Community law.

> This consequence also concerns any national court whose task it is as an organ of a Member State to protect, in a case within its jurisdiction, the rights conferred upon individuals by Community law.

> Furthermore, in accordance with the principle of the precedence of Community law, the relationship between provisions of the Treaty and directly applicable measures of the institutions on the one hand and the national law of the Member States on the other is such that those provisions and measures not only by their entry into force render automatically inapplicable any conflicting provision of current national law but – in so far as they are an integral part of, and take precedence in, the legal order applicable in the territory of each of the Member States – also preclude the valid adoption of new national legislative measures to the extent to which they would be incompatible with Community provisions.

> Indeed, any recognition that national legislative measures which encroach upon the field within which the Community exercises its legislative power or which are otherwise incompatible with the provisions of Community law had any legal effect would amount to a corresponding denial of the effectiveness of obligations undertaken unconditionally and irrevocably by Member States pursuant to the Treaty and would thus imperil the very foundations of the Community.

> The same conclusion emerges from the structure of Art 177 of the Treaty which provides that any court or tribunal of a Member State is enticed to make a reference to the Court whenever it considers that a preliminary ruling on a question of interpretation or validity relating to Community law is necessary to enable it to give judgment.

> The effectiveness of that provision would be impaired if the national court were prevented from forthwith applying Community law in accordance with the decision or the case law of the Court.

> It follows from the foregoing that every national court must, in a case within its jurisdiction, apply Community law in its entirety and protect rights which the latter confers on individuals and must accordingly set aside any provision of national law which may conflict with it, whether prior or subsequent to the Community rule.

> Accordingly any provision of a national legal system and any legislative, administrative, or judicial practice which might impair the effectiveness of Community law by withholding from the national court having jurisdiction to apply such law the power to do everything necessary at the moment of its application to set aside national legislative provisions which might prevent Community rules from having full force and effect are incompatible with those requirements which are the very essence of Community law.

> This would be the case in the event of a conflict between a provision of Community law and a

subsequent national law if the solution of the conflict were to be reserved for an authority with a discretion of its own, other than the court called upon to apply Community law, even if such an impediment to the full effectiveness of Community law were only temporary.

The first question should therefore be answered to the effect that a national court which is called upon, within the limits of its jurisdiction, to apply provisions of Community law is under a duty to give full effect to those provisions, if necessary refusing of its own motion to apply any conflicting provision of national legislation, even if adopted subsequently, and it is not necessary for the court to request or await the prior setting aside of such provision by legislation or other constitutional means ...

It follows from the answer to the first question that national courts must protect rights conferred by provisions of the Community legal order and chat it is not necessary for such courts to request or await the actual setting aside by the national authorities empowered so to act of any national measures which might impede the direct and immediate application of Community rules ...

On those grounds the court hereby rules:

A national court which is called upon, within the limits of its jurisdiction, to apply provisions of Community law is under a duty to give full effect to those provisions, if necessary refusing of its own motion to apply any conflicting provisions of national legislation, even if adopted subsequently, and it is not necessary for the court to request or await the prior seeing aside of such provisions by legislative or other constitutional means.

The need for national courts to set aside the law of their own country when it is found to conflict with directly effective Community law is a point which will be seen to arise in many of the cases which follow, for example, *Factortame (No 2)*, see Chapters 2 and 20. Such national law must be repealed by the national legislature and the failure to do so amounts to a breach of Art 5 of the Treaty.

Reaction in the Member States

As these cases illustrate, some Member States, at least initially, encountered difficulties in accepting the supremacy of directly effective Community law in their courts. That the Court of Justice would brook no interference with the requirement that Community rules be uniformly applied by national courts throughout the Member States is thrown into sharp relief in the following German case. It concerns the question of a possible conflict between a provision of a Regulation (secondary Community law) and fundamental human rights provisions of the West German Constitution. The case also illustrates the point that the validity of Community law may not be tested against provisions of national law.

INTERNATIONALE HANDELSGESELLSCHAFT CASE 11/70

In order to export certain agricultural products an export licence was required. If the products were not exported during the period of the licence's validity, the exporter forfeited a deposit. The company, having lost a deposit of DM 17,000, claimed that this Community system, based on two Community Regulations and operated through the West German National Cereals Intervention Agency, was contrary to the fundamental human rights provisions of the German Constitution. In particular it was in breach of the principle of proportionality: it imposed obligations (relating to deposits) on individuals that were not necessary for the attainment of the intended objective (the regulation of the cereals market).

The question of the validity of one of the Regulations was referred to the Court of Justice under Art 177(1)(b) by the Frankfurt Administrative Court. The Court stated that the validity of Community measures could not be judged according to the principles of national law; Community criteria only might be applied.

The Court continued:

Recourse to the legal rules or concepts of national law in order to judge the validity of measures adopted by the institutions of the Community would have an adverse effect on the uniformity and efficiency of Community law. The validity of such measures can only be judged in the light of Community law. In fact, the law stemming from the Treaty, an independent source of law, cannot because of its very nature be overridden by rules of national law, however framed, without being deprived of its character as Community law and without the legal basis of the Community itself being called in question. Therefore the validity of a Community measure or its effect within a

Member State cannot be affected by allegations that it runs counter to either fundamental rights as formulated by the constitution of that State or the principles of a national constitutional structure.

However, an examination should be made as to whether or not any analogous guarantee inherent in Community law has been disregarded. In fact, respect for fundamental rights forms an integral part of the general principles of law protected by the Court of Justice.

The protection of such rights, whilst inspired by the constitutional traditions common to the Member States, must be ensured within the framework of the structure and objectives of the Community. It must therefore be ascertained, in the light of the doubts expressed by the Verwaltungsgericht, whether the system of deposits has infringed rights of a fundamental nature, respect for which must be ensured in the Community legal system ...

It follows from all these considerations that the system of licences involving an undertaking, by those who apply for them, to import or export, guaranteed by a deposit, does not violate any right of a fundamental nature. The machinery of deposits constitutes an appropriate method, for the purposes of Art 40(3) of the Treaty, for carrying out the common organisation of the agricultural markets and also conforms to the requirements of Art 43.

However, the referring Frankfurt court *did not apply* the Court's ruling that the Regulation did not contravene the Community concept of human rights. Instead it made a reference to the West German Federal Constitutional Court which, drawing attention to the absence of a 'codified catalogue of human rights' at Community level, allowed the reference and held that Community measures were *subject to the fundamental rights provisions of the German Constitution*. Nevertheless, it ruled that the Community Regulation in issue was not contrary to the Constitution. Thus, although the Federal Constitutional Court refused to acknowledge the absolute supremacy of Community law, an open rift with the Court of Justice was averted.

By 1986, however, the Federal Constitutional Court felt sufficiently confident regarding the protection of human rights at Community level that in *Wünsche Handelsgesellschaft* it reversed its previous decision in the following terms:

Since 1974, the Community has advanced convincingly in the protection of human rights both in the adoption in a legally significant manner of texts whereby the institutions agree to be guided as a legal duty by respect for fundamental rights and by the development of case law by the European Court. The consequent connection of human rights guarantees in the national constitutions and European Convention on Human Rights on the one hand and the general principles of Community law on the other obviates the continuing need for a catalogue of fundamental rights. In view of these developments, it is now the position that, so long as the European Communities and particularly the case law of the European Court generally ensure an effective protection of fundamental rights as against the sovereign powers of the Community which is to be regarded as substantially similar to the protection required unconditionally by the German Constitution, and in so far as they generally safeguard the essential content of fundamental rights, the German Federal Constitutional Court will no longer exercise its jurisdiction to decide on the applicability of secondary Community law cited as the legal basis for any acts of German courts or authorities within the sovereign jurisdiction of the Federal Republic of Germany; and it will no longer review such legislation by the standard of the fundamental rights contained in the German Constitution. References to the Constitutional Court under Art 100(1) of the Constitution for that purpose are therefore inadmissible.

On the strength of this development, together with similar ones in other Member States, it is possible to say that the courts (if not some politicians) of the Member States have now accepted the doctrine of the supremacy of directly effective Community law. Following the *Factortame (No 2)* decision, the Master of the Rolls, Sir Thomas Bingham, stated that: '... The supremacy of Community law has been accepted by the English courts with a readiness, and applied with a loyalty, which, if equalled in one or two other Member States, has probably been exceeded in none'.

In the light of these (at one time) controversial cases on direct effect, it is important to consider the attention they direct towards the role of the Member States in the development of the Community and the duty of solidarity which rests on them by virtue of Art 5 of the Treaty.

The Community, principally through the exercise of its Treaty powers by the Commission, is concerned to achieve full and effective implementation of the policies within its competence. However, in many cases the Commission must, in order to achieve its aims, work with and through one of a variety of national authorities (government departments, customs authorities, agricultural intervention agencies, etc). Within this working relationship, Member States and their agencies are required to adopt certain courses of action or to refrain from doing so. This can involve an obligation to adopt new legislation (or secondary legislation), to revise existing legislation, or to repeal existing legislation.

Similarly, national courts, often in co-operation with the Court of Justice through the medium of the preliminary rulings procedure of Art 177, have a duty, based again on Art 5, to ensure the full effectiveness of Community law within the scope of their jurisdictions. Where there is a Community dimension to a case, national courts and tribunals are obliged to interpret Community law (or request an interpretation from the Court of Justice), to apply Community law and to enforce it.

Interpretations of Community law by the Court of Justice are definitive in the courts and tribunals of the Member States. It may also be called upon to assess the validity of the acts of the Community institutions. It may not exceed its powers as laid down in the Treaty but it does not look to a Parliament as supreme law-maker. It is not bound by its own decisions but frequently cites such decisions to indicate a consistent line of reasoning. Its crucial role in the development of the Community will become increasingly apparent in succeeding chapters.

At national level again, in Art 177(1)(b) cases, a court may grant interim relief against the application of a national measure based on a disputed Community act (*Zuckerfabrik Süderdithmarschen*) and, in similar circumstances and under the same conditions, grant interim relief which in effect suspends the disputed Community act itself (Atlanta): both cases discussed in the previous chapter.

In the next section, it will be seen that a national court also has the power to grant interim relief against the application of national law alleged to be in violation of Community rules: *R v Secretary of State for Transport ex p Factortame Ltd* Case 213/89. The aim of the Court of Justice is to achieve balance and coherence as regards enforcement and remedies.

SUPERVISION AT NATIONAL LEVEL: RIGHTS AND REMEDIES IN NATIONAL COURTS

The 'quota hopping' litigation (generally known as *Factortame*) not only involved the Commission's actions under Arts 169 and 186 but claims at the national level as well: see diagram ... The compatibility of the Merchant Shipping Act 1988 with Community law was the subject of challenge by Factortame Ltd and other members of the 'Anglo-Spanish' fishing fleet in the English courts. This challenge was similarly double-edged.

Factortame claimed that the Act's new registration requirements were in violation of their directly enforceable Community right not to be discriminated against on grounds of nationality under Art 7, in conjunction with their similar rights of establishment under Arts 52 and 58 of the Treaty. These claims became the subject of an Art 177 reference from the Divisional Court of the QBD for a interpretive ruling. However, before examining this claim, or the second aspect of the case, Factortame's application for the relevant parts of the 1988 Act to be suspended by the national court pending a determination of their compatibility with Community law by the Court of Justice, it is important to recall the relationship between the first, substantive issue (concerning directly effective rights) and an enforcement action brought by the Commission under Art 169.

As we have seen on numerous occasions, on the basis of the twin principles of supremacy and the direct effect of Community law, an infringement of Community law by a Member State may be challenged by private parties at national level. Returning to the Court's landmark decision in *Van Gend en Loos* Case 26/62 regarding the standstill on customs duties in Art 12, following a reference from the Dutch customs court under Art 177, the Court stated in clear terms that:

> A restriction of the guarantees against an infringement of Art 12 by Member States to the procedures under Arts 169 and 170 would remove all direct legal protection of the individual rights of their nationals ... The vigilance of individuals concerned to protect their rights amounts to an effective supervision in addition to the supervision entrusted by Arts 169 and 170 to the diligence of the Commission and of the Member States.

THE FACTORTAME 'ANGLO-SPANISH' FISHING FLEET LITIGATION

Was an amendment of United Kingdom national law, designed to counter 'quota hopping', in breach of the directly effective Community rights of Spanish business interests?

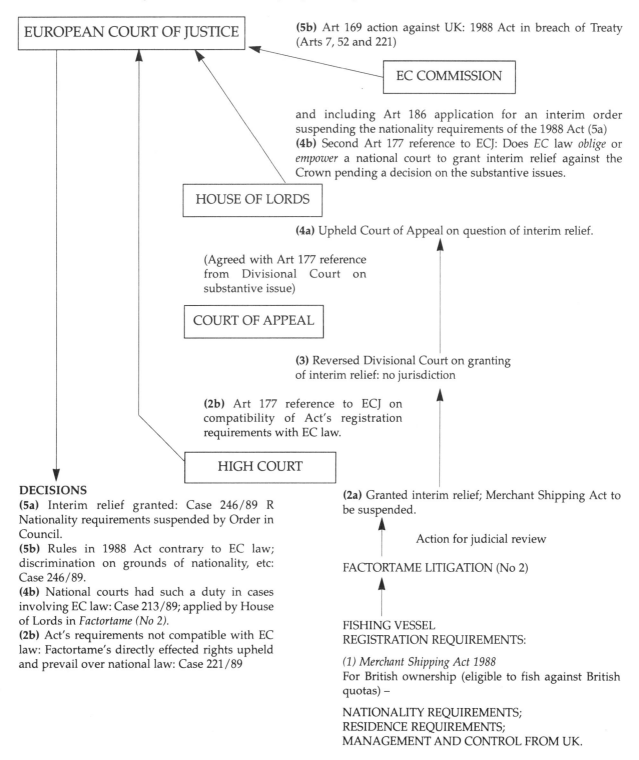

EUROPEAN COURT OF JUSTICE

(5b) Art 169 action against UK: 1988 Act in breach of Treaty (Arts 7, 52 and 221)

EC COMMISSION

and including Art 186 application for an interim order suspending the nationality requirements of the 1988 Act (5a)
(4b) Second Art 177 reference to ECJ: Does *EC law oblige* or *empower* a national court to grant interim relief against the Crown pending a decision on the substantive issues.

HOUSE OF LORDS

(4a) Upheld Court of Appeal on question of interim relief.

(Agreed with Art 177 reference from Divisional Court on substantive issue)

COURT OF APPEAL

(3) Reversed Divisional Court on granting of interim relief: no jurisdiction

(2b) Art 177 reference to ECJ on compatibility of Act's registration requirements with EC law.

HIGH COURT

DECISIONS
(5a) Interim relief granted: Case 246/89 R Nationality requirements suspended by Order in Council.
(5b) Rules in 1988 Act contrary to EC law; discrimination on grounds of nationality, etc: Case 246/89.
(4b) National courts had such a duty in cases involving EC law: Case 213/89; applied by House of Lords in *Factortame (No 2)*.
(2b) Act's requirements not compatible with EC law: Factortame's directly effected rights upheld and prevail over national law: Case 221/89

(2a) Granted interim relief; Merchant Shipping Act to be suspended.

Action for judicial review

FACTORTAME LITIGATION (No 2)

FISHING VESSEL
REGISTRATION REQUIREMENTS:

(1) Merchant Shipping Act 1988
For British ownership (eligible to fish against British quotas) –

NATIONALITY REQUIREMENTS;
RESIDENCE REQUIREMENTS;
MANAGEMENT AND CONTROL FROM UK.

It will be recalled that in this case the importer successfully argued that he could resist the application of national law (and a higher rate of duty) as it conflicted with his rights under the Treaty (to pay a lower rate). In another important decision, in the case of *Defrenne v Sabena (No 2)*, the effect of the Court's ruling was that compensation must be paid by any employer who discriminates against his employees in terms of pay. The equal treatment case of *Marshall* and *Van*

Colson each in their different ways established the plaintiff's right to compensation. In the latter, we have seen how national law was interpreted so as to provide damages beyond the merely nominal.

All these Art 177 rulings of the Court of Justice (and many others of course) were resumed to the originating national court or tribunal to be applied. An inquiry into the eventual outcome raises the important general question of the effectiveness of Community rights in national courts or tribunals in terms of the remedies available. For example, upon what terms did English law provide for compensation for Miss Marshall? What remedies were available for Factortame and the other members of the 'Anglo-Spanish' fishing fleet should their claims in the national courts succeed?

The general trend in the development of the law in this respect shows a gradual change of emphasis from the creation of Community law rights for private parties to the provision of effective remedies for such individuals in their national courts.

Community rights in national courts: national procedural rules and remedies

Although Community law has increasingly established substantive rights for individuals, as regards their vindication it has, until recently, and in the absence of any general Community rules, tended to leave the questions of the appropriate court, the *procedural rules* which apply and the *remedies* available to the national law of the Member States. As Steiner explained in 1987:

> The growing acceptance by national courts of the principle of directly effective Community law has brought in its wake a second problem. If EEC law may be invoked by individuals before their national courts, what remedies are available for its breach? It has long been clear that EEC law may be invoked as a shield, whether in civil or criminal proceedings, or to provide the basis for an action in restitution, for example, for money paid in breach of Community law It is less clear to what extent, and in what action, it may be invoked by an individual in order to prevent damage from occurring, or to seek compensation for damage already suffered. When, if at all, will a breach of EEC law give rise to a remedy in damages? When will an injunction be more appropriate? When a declaration? Where the defendant is a public body, should the plaintiff proceed by writ or by way of judicial review?

It might be asked why, in the pursuit of effective remedies, Bourgoin did not seek interim relief as soon as the embargo took effect in late 1981. The answer must be that it was accepted at the time that, despite a requirement that effective protection be afforded Community rights, interim relief was not available against the Crown: s 21 of the Crown Proceedings Act 1947 in relation to civil proceedings.

The non-availability (as a matter of domestic law) of an interlocutory injunction against the Crown or an officer of the Crown, together with serious doubts, following *Bourgoin*, as to any other than limited avenues to damages in tort against public authorities is the background against which to examine the claims at national level in the Factortame 'quota-hopping' affair, discussed earlier in this chapter in the section on the supervision of Member States at Community level: see *Commission v UK (Re Merchant Shipping Rules)* Case 246/89 R.

In the Divisional Court of the QBD (see the diagram on p 469), Factortame and the other members of the 'Anglo-Spanish' fishing fleet brought judicial review proceedings challenging the nationality (and other residence and domicile) requirements of the Merchant Shipping Act 1988 on the ground that, as in the case at Community level, they were in contravention of their directly effective Treaty rights, particularly their right of establishment under Art 52. This question was referred to the Court of Justice by the Divisional Court for a preliminary interpretive ruling under Art 177. As it would take perhaps two years for that ruling to be given and as in the meantime Factortame, not being able to fish against UK fishing quotas (or Spanish quotas either), claimed to be incurring heavy and irreparable financial loss, an application for interim relief pending final determination of the substantive issue was made to the court.

This application required the relevant section of the 1988 Act to be suspended to enable Factortame and the others to continue to operate their vessels as if duly registered as British ships. (It was also considered on the facts that in the light of Bourgoin no remedy in damages would be available.) On the basis of recent case law, the Divisional Court felt that it possessed the power in these circumstances to grant the application. This decision was reversed by the Court of Appeal, at which stage the Commission's application for interim relief under Art 186 with respect to the Act's nationality requirements was made and, as we have seen, was granted by the Court of Justice. Compliance was achieved by means of the Merchant Shipping Act 1988 (Amendment) Order 1989.

In the national courts, following a further appeal, the House of Lords held that, under *national* law, the English courts had no power to grant interim relief by way of an order suspending the operation of a statute pending a determination of its validity by the Court of Justice, nor had they the power to grant an interim injunction restraining the Secretary of State from enforcing the Act. Their Lordships, however, asked the Court for a preliminary ruling as to whether there was an overriding principle of Community law that a national court was under an obligation or had the power to provide an effective interlocutory remedy to protect directly effective rights where a seriously arguable claim to such rights had been advanced and irremediable loss was at stake.

Just over a year later, in June 1990, in response to this Art 177 reference, the Court, having drawn attention to the *Simmenthal* principle of the primacy of Community law and to the principle of co-operation in Art 5 of the Treaty, designed to ensure the legal protection which persons derived from the direct effect of Community law, ruled that: Community law was to be interpreted as meaning that a national court which, in a case before at concerning Community law, considers that the sole obstacle precluding it from granting interim relief is a rule of national law, must set aside that rule: *R v Secretary of State for Transport ex p Factortame Ltd* Case 213/89.

Amid considerable controversy regarding what was perceived by some in the UK as an unacceptable intrusion on UK sovereignty, the House of Lords just a month later applied the Court's ruling. This was on the basis of the facts before it and pending final judgment by the Court of Justice on the validity of the 1988 Act in the face of Factortame's putative rights under the Treaty.

R v Secretary of State for Transport ex p Factortame Ltd (No 2) (1991)

In July 1990, the House of Lords, using the powers established by the ruling of the Court of Justice, allowed Factortame's appeal and granted an interim injunction restraining the Government from withholding or withdrawing registration under the 1988 Act to named fishing vessels on grounds of residence or domicile abroad. (It will be recalled that the Act's nationality requirements had previously been suspended by an amendment to the Act following a ruling by the President of the Court of Justice, see above.) The position was summed up by Lord Bridge as follows:

> Some public comments on the decision of the European Court of Justice, affirming the jurisdiction of the courts of Member States to override national legislation if necessary to enable interim relief to be granted in protection of rights under Community law, have suggested that this was a novel and dangerous invasion by a Community institution of the sovereignty of the United Kingdom Parliament. But such comments are based on a misconception.

> If the supremacy within the European Community of Community law over the national law of Member States was not always inherent in the EEC Treaty it was certainly well-established in the jurisprudence of the European Court of Justice long before the UK joined the Community. Thus, whatever limitation of its sovereignty Parliament accepted when it enacted the European Communities Act 1972 it was entirely voluntary. Under the terms of the Act of 1972 it has always been clear that it was the duty of a UK court, when delivering final judgment, to override any rule of national law found to be in conflict with any directly enforceable rule of Community law.

> Similarly, when decisions of the European Court of Justice have exposed areas of United Kingdom statute law which failed to implement Community directive, Parliament has always loyally accepted the obligation to make appropriate and prompt amendments. Thus there is nothing in any way novel in according supremacy to rule of Community law in those areas to which they apply and to insist chat, in the protection of rights under Community law, national courts must not be inhibited by rule of national law from granting interim relief in appropriate cases is no more than a logical recognition of that supremacy.

When considering its decision, the House of Lords had available to it unsworn evidence indicating that many of the owners of the 95 vessels involved (the 'Anglo-Spanish' fleet) had already suffered losses well in excess of £100,000 and that some feared imminent bankruptcy.

In reaching their unanimous decision, their Lordships took account of the two-stage guidelines for the exercise of the court's discretionary jurisdiction to grant interim injunctions as laid down by the House in *American Cyanamid v Ethicon* in 1975. Such jurisdiction concerns the power to grant an injunction where it is just or convenient on such terms and conditions as the court thinks fit: s 37 of the Supreme Court Act 1981. Their Lordships also considered that on the basis of the decision in *Bourgoin*, the applicants would be unable to recover damages from the Crown if the Act were ultimately found to be contrary to the Treaty (their being unable to establish wrongful conduct on the part of the Secretary of State). It was therefore agreed that the application for an interim injunction against the Crown should go directly to the second stage of consideration, regarding the balance of convenience, and need not pass through the first stage, regarding whether damages were an adequate remedy.

On the question of the balance of convenience (the balance of interests in Community law), it was stressed that matters of considerable weight had to be put in the balance to outweigh the desirability of enforcing, in the public interest, what was on its face the law of the land. Each case was to be considered in the light of its circumstances. There was no rule that it was necessary to show a *prima facie* case that the law was invalid; it was enough if the applicant could show that there was a serious case to be tried.

In this respect, it is noteworthy that in *La Cinq v Commission* Case T-44/90 the Court of First Instance annulled a Commission refusal to order interim measures (see, also, *Camera Car* Case 792/79 R in Chapter 17), stating that the complainant company need not show a clear and flagrant breach of the competition rules by another party, merely a *prima facie* case. On the question of damage to La Cinq, if the interim measures were not ordered and the company had to await the outcome of the Commission's final decision, the Court stated that all the company's circumstances must be taken into account. Although the Court of Justice had held in *Cargill v Commission* Case 229/88 R that damage is not serious and irreparable (a necessary requirement for the ordering of interim measures) if it is purely financial and can, if the complainant is successful in the main action, be fully recovered, La Cinq's position was that it ran the risk of going out of business altogether in the interim (cf the position of Factortame and the others) and suffering serious and irreparable damage whatever the outcome of the final decision.

It is important to recognise that the granting of interim relief in *Factortame* meant that a new remedy had been created by the national court in order to ensure the effectiveness of Community law. This case therefore marks a significant development from previous rulings on supremacy and direct effect and a change of stance on the part of the Court of Justice which, in *Rewe v HZA* Case 158/80 (see above) had stated that 'it was not intended to create new remedies in the national courts to ensure the observance of Community law other then those already laid down by national law'. The House of Lords had stated that interim relief against the Crown was not available under national law. Nevertheless, this was a rule governing the grant of remedies which, according to other previous rulings of the Court, precluded the grant of an appropriate remedy. Accordingly, it was to be set aside. (Since *Factortame*, the House of Lords has changed its position concerning interim injunctions as a matter of English law irrespective of a Community dimension: see *M v Home Office* (1993), in which, in the Court of Appeal, Lord Donaldson MR stated that it would be 'anomalous and wrong in principle' if the courts' powers were limited in domestic law matters when the limitations had been removed by Community law in disputes concerning rights under that law. *M* is therefore authority for the availability of interim injunctions against ministers of the Crown as a matter of English law.)

That the applicant in *Factortame* had a serious case to be tried was later confirmed by the Court of Justice in response to the original Art 177 reference from the Divisional Court of the Queen's Bench Division. The Court ruled that the nationality, residence and domicile requirements of the 1988 Act were contrary to Community law, in particular Art 52 concerning the applicant's directly effective right of establishment: *R v Secretary of State for Transport ex p Factortame Ltd* Case C221/89. As in the case brought by the Commission, the Court stated that the system of national quotas under the Common Fisheries Policy did not affect the decision. However, although introduced on sound, conservational grounds, the national quota system does appear to lie at the heart of this problem. Nonetheless, as Lord Bridge had stated earlier in these proceedings:

> ... it is common ground, that in so far as the applicants succeed before the ECJ in obtaining a ruling in support of the Community rights which they claim, those rights will prevail over the restrictions imposed on registration of British fishing vessels by Part II of the Act of 1988 and the Divisional Court will, in the final determination of the application for judicial review be obliged to make appropriate declarations to give effect to those rights.

As regards a further action for damages brought by Factortame and the other members of the 'Anglo-Spanish' fishing fleet against the British government, see the final part of this chapter.

Further difficulties have arisen in the UK regarding remedies despite the fact that the situation in question involved loss suffered as the result of a breach of an individual's directly effective rights and that damages to compensate for losses of the type in question were provided for under the relevant provisions of national law.

THE EUROPEAN UNION BELONGS TO ITS CITIZENS: THREE IMMODEST PROPOSALS

JHH Weiler, Manley Hudson Professor of Law and Jean Monnet Chair, Harvard University; Co-Director, Academy of European Law, European University Institute, Florence

'Despite its rhetorical commitment to a Union ... which belongs to its citizens', the recent Irish Presidency IGC draft has precious little in the way of empowering individual citizens of the Union. This essay presents three suggestions from a broader study presented to the European Parliament which are designed to increase the democratic and deliberative processes of Community and Union governance. The first, the European Legislative Ballot, proposes a form of limited 'direct democracy' appropriate for the Union. The second, the 'Lexcalibur initiative', proposes placing Community and Union decision making on the Internet to enhance accessibility and transparency of Community decision making. The last proposes the creation of a Constitutional Council, modelled on its French namesake, to adjudicate, *ex ante*, challenges to the legislative competencies of the Community legislator

Introduction

Cast your mind back to the heady days of the Maastricht Treaty. The Mandarins heralded a remarkable diplomatic achievement: a new Treaty, new name, new pillars and above all a commitment to Economic and Monetary Union within the decade. Recall now the reaction in the European street ranging from fear and hostility through confusion and incomprehension to indifference and outright apathy. The Danes voted against that Treaty, the French approved it by a margin of barely 1% and most commentators agree that had it been put to public scrutiny in, say, Great Britain or even Germany the outcome would have been far from certain. Even those who supported it were motivated in large part by a 'what's-in-it-for-me' calculus – a shaky foundation for long term civic loyalty.

The reaction in the street did not relate only or even primarily to the content of the Treaty; it was the expression of a growing disillusionment with the European construct as a whole the moral and political legitimacy of which were in decline. The reasons for this are many but clearly, on any reading, as the Community has grown in size, in scope, in reach and despite a high rhetoric including the very creation of 'European Citizenship', there has been a distinct disempowerment of the individual European citizen, the specific gravity of whom continues to decline as the Union grows.

The roots of disempowerment are many but three stand out.

First, is the classic so called 'Democracy Deficit': the inability of the Community and Union to develop structures and processes which would adequately replicate at the Community level the habits of governmental control, parliamentary accountability and administrative responsibility which are practised with different modalities in the various Member States. Further, as more and more functions move to Brussels, the democratic balances within the Member States have been disrupted by a strengthening of the ministerial and executive branches of government. The value of each individual in the political process has inevitably declined including the ability to play a meaningful civic role in European governance.

The second root goes even deeper and concerns the ever increasing remoteness, opaqueness, and inaccessibility of European governance. An apocryphal statement usually attributed to Jacques Delors predicts that by the end of the decade 80% of social regulation will be issued from Brussels. We are on target. The drama lies in the fact that no accountable public authority has a handle on these regulatory processes. Not the European Parliament, not the Commission, not even the governments. The press and other media, a vital estate in our democracies are equally hampered. Consider that it is even impossible to get from any of the Community Institutions an authoritative and mutually agreed statement of the mere number of committees which inhabit that world of comitology. Once there were those who worried about the supranational features of European integration. It is time to worry about infranationalism – a complex network of middle level national administrators, Community administrators and an array of private bodies with unequal and unfair access to a process with huge social and economic consequences to everyday life – in matters of public safety, health, and all other dimensions of socio-economic regulation. Transparency and access to documents are often invoked as a possible remedy to this issue. But if you do not know what is going on, which documents will you ask to see? Neither strengthening the European Parliament nor national parliaments will do much to address this problem of post-modern governance which itself is but one manifestation of a general sense of political alienation in most western democracies.

The final issue relates to the competencies of the Union and Community. In one of its most celebrated cases in the early 1960s, the European Court of Justice described the Community as a '... new legal order for the benefit of which the States have limited their sovereign rights, albeit in limited fields' (*Van Gend en Loos* Case 26/62 [1963] ECR 1). There is a widespread anxiety that these fields are limited no more. Indeed, not long ago a prominent European scholar and judge wrote that there simply is no nucleus of sovereignty that the Member States can invoke, as such, against the Community'. (Lenaerts, 'Constitutionalism and the many faces of Federalism' (1990) 38 AJ Com L 205, 220. The Court, too, has modified its rhetoric; in its more recent Opinion 1/91 it refers to the Member States as having limited their sovereign rights '... in ever wider fields': Opinion 1/91 [1991] ECR I-6079, para 21.)

We should not, thus, be surprised by a continuing sense of alienation from the Union and its Institutions.

In the Dublin Summit the present thinking of the IGC has been revealed in a document entitled 'The European Union Today and Tomorrow'. The opening phrase of the document reads: 'The European Union belongs to its Citizens'. But don't hold your breath when it comes to the actual proposals. They are very modest. The second phrase of the new text reads: 'The Treaties establishing the Union should address their most direct concerns.' There is much rhetoric on a commitment to employment, there are a few significant proposals on free movement, elimination of gender discrimination and other rights. There are some meaningful proposals to increase the powers of the European Parliament and even to integrate formally, even if in limited fashion, national legislatures into the Community process. But overall, the net gainers are, again, the governments. At best, this is the ethos of benign paternalism. At worst, the proposals represent another symptom of the degradation of civic culture whereby the citizen is conceived as a consumer – a consumer who has lost faith in the Brand Name called Europe and who has to be bought off by all kind of social and economic goodies, a share holder who must be placated by a larger dividend. It is End-of-Millennium Bread and Circus governance.

What can be done? Here is a package of three proposals plucked from a recent study commissioned by the European Parliament which my collaborators and I believe can make a concrete and symbolic difference. (JHH Weiler, Alexander Ballmann, Ulrich Haltern, Herwig Hofmann, Franz Mayer, Sieglinde Schreiner-Linford, *Certain Rectangular Problems of European Integration, European Parliament*, 1996.) We also believe that they could be adopted without much political fuss. You decide.

Proposal 1: the European legislative ballot

The democratic tradition in most Member States is one of representative democracy. Our elected representatives legislate and govern in our name. If we are unsatisfied we can replace them at election time. Recourse to forms of direct democracy – such as referenda – are exceptional. Given the size of the Union, referenda are considered particularly inappropriate.

However, the basic condition of representative democracy is, indeed, that at election time the citizens '... can throw the scoundrels out' – that is replace the Government. This basic feature of representative democracy does not exist in the Community and Union. The form of European governance is – and will remain for considerable time – such that there is no 'Government' to throw out. Even dismissing the Commission by Parliament (or approving the appointment of the Commission President) is not the equivalent of throwing the Government out. There is no civic act of the European citizen where he or she can influence directly the outcome of any policy choice facing the Community and Union as citizens can when choosing between parties which offer sharply distinct programmes. Neither elections to the European Parliament nor elections to national Parliaments fulfil this function in Europe. This is among the reasons why turnout to European Parliamentary elections has been traditionally low and why these elections are most commonly seen as a mid-term judgment of the Member State Governments rather than a choice on European governance.

The proposal is to introduce some form of direct democracy at least until such time as one could speak of meaningful representative democracy at the European level. Our proposal is for a form of a Legislative Ballot Initiative coinciding with elections to the European Parliament. Our proposal is allow the possibility, when enough signatures are collected in, say, more than five Member States to introduce legislative initiatives to be voted on by citizens when European elections take place (and, after a period of experimentation possibly at other intervals too). In addition to voting for their MEPs, the electorate will be able to vote on these legislative initiatives. Results would be binding on the Community institutions and on Member States. Initiatives would be, naturally, confined to the sphere of application of Community law – that is, in areas where the Community Institutions could have legislated themselves. Such legislation could be overturned by a similar procedure or by a particularly onerous legislative Community process. The Commission, Council, Parliament or a national parliament could refer a proposed initiative to the European Court of Justice to determine – in an expedited procedure – whether the proposed ballot initiative is within the competencies of the Community or is in any other way contrary to the Treaty. In areas where the Treaty provides for majority voting the Ballot initiative will be considered as adopted when it wins a majority of votes in the Union as a whole as well as within a majority of Member States. (Other formulae could be explored.) Where the Treaty provides for unanimity a majority of voters in the Union would be required as well as winning in all Members States.

Apart from enhancing symbolically and tangibly the voice of individuals qua citizens, this proposal would encourage the formation of true European parties as well as transnational mobilisation of political forces. It would give a much higher European political significance to Elections to the European Parliament. It would represent a first important step, practical and symbolic, to the notion of European citizenship and civic responsibility.

Proposal 2: *Lexcalibur* – the European public square

This would be the single most important and far reaching proposal which would have the most dramatic impact on European governance. It does not require a Treaty amendment and can be adopted by an Inter-Institutional Agreement among Commission, Council and Parliament. It could be put in place in phases after a short period of study and experimentation and be fully operational within, we estimate, two to three years. We believe that if adopted and implemented it will, in the medium and long term, have a greater impact on the democratisation and transparency of European governance than any other single proposal currently under consideration by the IGC.

Even if it does not require a Treaty amendment we recommend that it be part of the eventual IGC package as a central feature of those aspects designed to empower the individual citizen.

We are proposing that – with few exceptions – the entire decision-making process of the Community, especially but not only Comitology – be placed on the internet.

For convenience we have baptised the proposal: Lexcalibur – the European public square.

We should immediately emphasise that what we have in mind is a lot more than simply making certain laws or documents such as the Official Journal more accessible through electronic data bases.

We should equally emphasise that this proposal is without prejudice to the question of confidentiality of process and secrecy of documents. As shall transpire, under our proposal documents or deliberations which are considered too sensitive to be made public at any given time could be shielded behind 'fire-walls' and made inaccessible to the general public. Whatever policy of access to documentation is adopted could be implemented on *Lexcalibur*.

The key organisational principle would be that each Community decision making project intended to result in the eventual adoption of a Community norm would have a 'decisional web site' on the Internet within the general *Lexcalibur* 'Home Page' which would identify the scope and purpose of the legislative or regulatory measure(s); the Community and Member States persons or administrative departments or divisions responsible for the process; the proposed and actual timetable of the decisional process so that one would know at any given moment the progress of the process, access and view all non-confidential documents which are part of the process and under carefully designed procedures directly submit input into the specific decisional process. But it is important to emphasise that our vision is *not* one of 'Virtual Government' which will henceforth proceed electronically. The *primary* locus and mode of governance would and should remain intact: Political Institutions, meetings of elected representative and officials, Parliamentary debates, media reporting – as vigorous and active a public square as it is possible to maintain, and a European Civic Society of real human beings. The huge potential importance of *Lexcalibur* would be in its *secondary effect*: It would enhance the potential of all actors to play a much more informed, critical and involved role in the Primary Public Square. The most immediate direct beneficiaries of Euro governance on the Internet would in fact be the media, interested pressure groups, NGOs and the like. Of course, also 'ordinary citizens' would have a much more direct mode to interact with their process of government. Providing a greatly improved system of information would, however, only be a first step of a larger project. It would serve as the basis for a system that allows widespread participation in policy-making processes so that European democracy becomes an altogether more deliberative process through the posting of comments and the opening of a dialogue between the Community Institutions and interested private actors. The Commission already now sometimes invites e-mail comments on its initiatives. (See, for example, its draft notice on co-operation with national authorities in handling cases falling within Arts 85 or 86 [1996] OJ C262/5.) Such a system obviously needs a clear structure in order to allow a meaningful and effective processing of incoming information for Community Institutions. Conceivable would be, for example, a two-tier system, consisting of a forum with limited access for an interactive exchange between Community Institutions and certain private actors and an open forum where all interested actors can participate and discuss Community policies with each other. This would open the unique opportunity for deliberations of citizens and interest groups beyond the traditional frontiers of the Nation State, without the burden of high entry costs for the individual actor.

Hugely important, in our view, will be the medium and long term impact on the young generation, our children. For this generation, the internet will be – in many cases already is – as natural a medium as to older generations were radio, television and the press. European Governance on the net will enable them to experience government at school and at home in ways which are barely imaginable to an older generation for whom this New Age 'stuff' is often threatening or, in itself, alien.

The idea of using the internet for improving the legitimacy of the European Union may seem to some revolutionary and in some respects it is. Therefore its introduction should be organic through a piecemeal process of experiment and re-evaluation but within an overall commitment towards more open and accessible government.

There are dimensions of the new Information Age which have all the scary aspects of a 'Brave New World' in which individual and group autonomy and privacy are lost, in which humanity is replaced by 'machinaty' and in which Government seems ever more remote and beyond comprehension and grasp the perfect setting for alienation captured most visibly by atomised individuals sitting in front of their screens and 'surfing the net'.

Ours is a vision which tries to enhance human sovereignty, demystify technology and place it firmly as servant and not master. The internet in our vision is to serve as the true starting point for the emergence of a functioning deliberative political community, in other words a European polity cum civic society.

For those who wish to see what this might look like we have prepared a simulation of Lexcalibur: http://www.iue.it/AEL/EP/Lex/index.html.

Proposal 3: limits to growth

The problem of competencies is, in our view, mostly one of perception. The perception has set in that the boundaries which were meant to circumscribe the areas in which the Community could operate have been irretrievably breached. Few perceptions have been more detrimental to the legitimacy of the Community in the eyes of its citizens. And not only its citizens. Governments and even courts, for example the German Constitutional Court, have rebelled against the Community constitutional order because, in part, of a profound dissatisfaction on this very issue. One can not afford to sweep this issue under the carpet. The crisis is already there. The main problem, then, is not one of moving the boundary lines but of restoring faith in the inviolability of the existing boundaries between Community and Member State competencies.

Any proposal which envisages the creation of a new Institution is doomed in the eyes of some. And yet we propose the creation of a Constitutional Council for the Community, modelled in some ways on its French namesake. The Constitutional Council would have jurisdiction only over issues of competencies (including subsidiarity) and would, like its French cousin, decide cases submitted to it after a law was adopted but before coming into force. It could be seized by the Commission, the Council, any Member State or by the European Parliament acting on a majority of its members. We think that serious consideration should be given to allowing Member State Parliaments to bring cases before the Constitutional Council.

The composition of the Council is the key to its legitimacy. Its President would be the President of the European Court of Justice and its members would be sitting members of the constitutional courts or their equivalents in the Member States. Within the European Constitutional Council no single Member State would have a veto power. All its decisions would be by majority.

The composition of the European Constitutional Council would, we believe, help restore confidence in the ability to have effective policing of the boundaries as well as underscore that the question of competencies is fundamentally also one of national constitutional norms but still subject to a binding and uniform solution by a Union Institution.

We know that this proposal might be taken as an assault on the integrity of the European Court of Justice. That attitude would, in our view, be mistaken. The question of competencies has become so politicised that the European Court of Justice should welcome having this hot potato removed from its plate by an *ex ante* decision of that other body with a jurisdiction limited to that preliminary issue. Yes, there is potential for conflict of jurisprudence and all the rest – nothing that competent drafting cannot deal with.

The IGC has proclaimed that the European Union belongs to its citizens. The proof of the pudding will be in the eating.

MANDLA AND ANOTHER (APPELLANTS/PLAINTIFFS) v LEE AND OTHERS (RESPONDENTS/DEFENDANTS) (1983)

THE JUDGMENT OF LORD FRASER OF TULLYBELTON IN THE HOUSE OF LORDS

Lord Fraser of Tullybelton: My Lords, the main question in this appeal is whether Sikhs are a racial group for the purposes of the Race Relations Act 1976 (the 1976 Act). For reasons that appear, the answer to this question depends on whether they are a group defined by reference to 'ethnic origins'.

The appellants are Sikhs. The first appellant is a solicitor in Birmingham and he is the father of the second appellant. The second appellant was, at the material date, a boy of school age. The first respondent (first defendant) is the headmaster of an independent school in Birmingham called Park Grove School. The second respondent is a company which owns the school, and in which the first respondent and his wife are principal shareholders. In what follows I shall refer to the first respondent as 'the respondent'. In July 1978 the first appellant wished to enter his son as a pupil at Park Grove School, and he brought the boy to an interview with the respondent. The first appellant explained that he wished his son to grow up as an orthodox Sikh, and that one of the rules which he had to observe was to wear a turban. That is because the turban is regarded by Sikhs as a sign of their communal identity. At the interview, the respondent said that wearing a turban would be against the school rules which required all pupils to wear school uniform, and he did not think he could allow it, but he promised to think the matter over. A few days later he wrote to the first appellant saying that he had decided he could not relax the school rules and thus, in effect, saying that he would not accept the boy if he insisted on wearing a turban. The second appellant was then sent to another school, where he was allowed to wear a turban, and, so far as the appellants as individuals are concerned, that is the end of the story.

The main purpose of the 1976 Act is to prohibit discrimination against people on racial grounds, and more generally, to make provision with respect to relations between people of different racial groups. So much appears from the long title. The scheme of the Act, so far as is relevant to this appeal, is to define in Part 1 what is meant by racial discrimination in various fields including employment, provision of goods, services and other things, and by s 17 in the field of education. There can be no doubt that, if there has been discrimination against the appellants in the present case, it was in the field of education, and was contrary to s 17(a) which makes it unlawful for the proprietor of an independent school to discriminate against a person in the terms on which the school offers to admit him as a pupil. The only question is whether any racial discrimination has occurred.

But the first appellant complained to the Commission for Racial Equality that the respondent had discriminated against him and his son on racial grounds. The Commission took up the case and they are the real appellants before your Lordships' House. The case clearly raises an important question of construction of the 1976 Act, on which the Commission wishes to have a decision, and they have undertaken, very properly, to pay the costs of the respondent in this House, whichever party succeeds in the appeal. In the county court Judge Gosling held that Sikhs were not a racial group, and therefore that there had been no discrimination contrary to the 1976 Act. The Court of Appeal (Lord Denning MR, Oliver and Kerr LJJ) agreed with that view. The Commission, using the name of the appellants, now appeals to this House.

The type of discrimination referred to in para (a) of that subsection is generally called 'direct' discrimination. When the present proceedings began in the county court, direct discrimination was alleged, but the learned judge held that there had been no direct discrimination, and his judgment on that point was not challenged in the Court of Appeal or before your Lordships' House. The appellant's case in this House was based entirely on 'indirect' discrimination, that is, discrimination contrary to para (b) of sub-s 1(1). When the proceedings began the appellants claimed damages, but that claim was pursued before this House. Having regard to s 57(3) of the 1976 Act, it would have been unlikely to succeed. They now seek only a declaration that there has been unlawful discrimination against them contrary to the Act.

Racial discrimination is defined in s 1(1) which provides as follows:

> A person discriminates against another in any circumstances relevant for the purposes of any provision of this Act if–
>
> (a) on racial grounds he treats that other less favourably than he treats or would treat other persons; or
>
> (b) he applies to that other a requirement or condition which he applies or would apply equally to persons not of the same racial group as that other but–
>
> (i) which is such that the proportion of persons of the same racial group as that other who can comply with it is considerably smaller than the proportion of persons not of that racial group who can comply with it; and
>
> (ii) which he cannot show to be justifiable irrespective of the colour, race, nationality or ethnic or national origins of the person to whom it applied; and
>
> (iii) which is to the detriment of that other because he cannot comply with it.

The case against the respondent under s 1(1)(b) is that he discriminated against the second appellant because he applied to him a requirement or condition (namely, the 'No turban' rule) which he applied equally to pupils not of the same racial group as the second respondent (that is, to pupils who were not Sikhs) but (i) which is such that the proportion of Sikhs who can comply with it is considerably smaller than in the proportion of non-Sikhs who can comply with it and (ii) which the respondent cannot show to be justifiable irrespective of the colour, etc of the second appellant, and (iii) which is to the detriment of the second appellant because he cannot comply with it. As I have already said, the first main question is whether the Sikhs are a racial group. If they are, then two further questions arise. Question two is what is the meaning of 'can' in para (i) of s (1)(b), and question three is, what is the meaning of 'justifiable' in para (iii) of that subsection?

'Ethnic origins'

Racial group is defined in s 3(1) of the Act which provides:

> 'racial group' means a group of persons defined by reference to colour, race, nationality or ethnic or national origins, and references to a person's racial group refer to any racial group into which he falls.

It is not suggested that Sikhs are a group defined by reference to colour, race, nationality or national origins. In none of these respects are they distinguishable from many other groups, especially those living, like most Sikhs, in the Punjab. The argument turns entirely upon whether they are a group defined by 'ethnic origins'. It is therefore necessary to ascertain the sense in which the work 'ethnic' is used in the Act of 1976. We were referred to various dictionary definitions. The *Oxford English Dictionary* (1897 edition) gives two meanings of 'ethnic'. The first is 'pertaining to nations not Christian or Jewish: gentile, heathen, pagan'. That clearly cannot be its meaning in the 1976 Act, because it is inconceivable that Parliament would have legislated against racial discrimination intending that the protection should not apply either to Christians or (above all) to Jews. Neither party contended that was the relevant meaning for the present purpose. The second meaning given in the *Oxford English Dictionary* (1897 edition) was 'pertaining to race: peculiar to a race or nation: ethnological'. A slighter shorter form of that meaning (omitting 'peculiar to a race or nation') was given by the *Concise Oxford Dictionary* in 1934 and was expressly accepted by Lord Denning MR as the correct meaning for the present purpose. Oliver and Kerr LJJ also accepted that meaning as being substantially correct, and Oliver LJ at [1983] IRLR 17 said that the word 'ethnic' in its popular meaning involved essentially a racial concept – the concept of something with which the members of the group are born; some fixed or inherited characteristic. The respondent, who appeared on his own behalf, submitted that that was the relevant meaning of 'ethnic' in the 1976 Act, and that it did not apply to Sikhs because they were essentially a religious group, and they shared their racial characteristics with other religious groups, including Hindus and Muslims, living in the Punjab.

For a group to constitute an ethnic group in the sense of the 1976 Act, it must, in my opinion, regard itself, and be regarded by others, as a distinct community by virtue of certain characteristics. Some of these characteristics are essential: others are not essential but one or more of them will commonly be found and will help to distinguish the group from the surrounding community. The conditions which appear to me to be essential are these: (1) a long shared history, of which the group is conscious as distinguishing it from other groups, and the memory of which it keeps alive; (2) a cultural tradition of its own, including family and social customs and manners, often but not necessarily associated with religious observance. In addition to those two essential characteristics, the following characteristics are, in my opinion, relevant: (3) either a common geographical origin, or descent from a small number of common ancestors; (4) a common language, not necessarily peculiar to the group; (5) a common literature peculiar to the group; (6) a common religion different from that of neighbouring groups or from the general community surrounding it; (7) being a minority or being an oppressed or a dominant group within a larger community, for example, a conquered people (say, the inhabitants of England shortly after the Norman conquest) and their conquerors might both be ethnic groups.

My Lords, I have attempted so far to explain the reasons why, in my opinion, the word 'ethnic' in the 1976 Act should be construed relatively widely, in what was referred to by Mr Irvine as a broad, cultural/historic sense. The conclusion at which I have arrived by construction of the Act itself is greatly strengthened by consideration of the decision of the Court of Appeal in New Zealand (Richmond P, Woodhouse and Richardson JJ) in *King-Ansell v Police* [1979] 2 NZLR 531.

In that case, the appellant had been convicted by a magistrate of an offence under the New Zealand Race Relations Act 1971, the offence consisting of publishing a pamphlet with intent to incite ill will against Jews, 'on the ground of their ethnic origins'. The question of law arising on the appeal concerned the meaning to be given to the words 'ethnic ... origins of that group of persons' in s 25(1) of the Act. The decision of the Court of Appeal was that Jews in New Zealand did form a group

with common ethnic origins within the meaning of the Act. The structure of the New Zealand Act differs considerably from that of the 1976 Act, but the offence created by s 25 of the New Zealand (viz inciting ill will against any group of persons on the ground of their colour, race, or ethnic or national origins) raises the same question of construction as the present appeal, in a context which is identical, except that the New Zealand Act does not mention 'nationality', and the 1976 Act does.

The reasoning of all members of the New Zealand court was substantially similar, and it can, I think, be sufficiently indicated by quoting the following short passages. The first is from the judgment of Woodhouse J, p 538, line 39 where, after referring to the meaning given by the 1972 Supplement to the *Oxford English Dictionary*, which I have already quoted, he says this:

> ... the distinguishing features of an ethnic group or of the ethnic origins of a group would usually depend upon a combination, present together, of characteristics of the kind indicated in the Supplement. In any case, it would be a mistake to regard this or any other dictionary meaning as though it had to be imported word for word into a statutory definition and construed accordingly. However, subject to those qualifications. I think that for the purposes of construing the expression 'ethnic origins' the 1972 Supplement is a helpful guide and I accept it.

Richardson J, p 542, line 51, said this:

> ... The real test is whether the individuals or the group regard themselves and are regarded by others in the community as having a particular historical identity in terms of their colour or their racial, national or ethnic origins. That must be based on a belief shared by the members of the group.

And at p 543, line 24, the same learned judge said this:

> ... a group is identifiable in terms of its ethnic origins if it is a segment of the population distinguished from others by a sufficient combination of shared customs, beliefs, traditions and characteristics derived from a common or presumed common past, even if not drawn from what in biological terms is a common racial stock. It is that combination which gives them a historically determined social identity in their own eyes and in the eyes of those outside the group. They have a distinct social identity based not simply on group cohesion and solidarity but also on their belief as to their historical antecedents.

My Lords, that last passage sums up in a way upon which I could not hope to improve the views which I have been endeavouring to express. It is important that courts in English speaking countries should, if possible, construe the words which we are considering in the same way where they occur in the same context, and I am happy to say that I find no difficulty at all in agreeing with the construction favoured by the New Zealand Court of Appeal.

The respondent admitted, rightly in my opinion, that if the proper construction of the word 'ethnic' in s 3 of the 1976 Act is a wide one, on lines such as I have suggested, the Sikhs would qualify as a group defined by ethnic origins for the purposes of the Act. It is, therefore, unnecessary to consider in any detail the relevant characteristics of the Sikhs. They were originally a religious community founded about the end of the fifteenth century in the Punjab by Guru Nanak, who was born in 1469. But the community is no longer purely religious in character. Their present position is summarised sufficiently for present purposes in the opinion of the learned county court judge in the following passage:

> The evidence in my judgment shows that Sikhs are a distinctive and self-conscious community. They have a history going back to the fifteenth century. They have a written language which a small proportion of Sikhs can read but which can be read by a much higher proportion of Sikhs than of Hindus. They were at one time politically supreme in the Punjab.

The result is, in my opinion, that Sikhs are a group defined by a reference to ethnic origins for the purpose of the 1976 Act, although they are not biologically distinguishable from the other peoples living in the Punjab. That is true whether one is considering the position before the partition of 1947, when the Sikhs lived mainly in that part of the Punjab which is now Pakistan, or after 1947, since when most of them have moved into India. It is, therefore, necessary to consider whether the respondent has indirectly discriminated against the appellants in the sense of s 1(1)(b) of the Act. That raises the two subsidiary questions I have already mentioned.

'Can comply'

It is obvious that Sikhs like anyone else, 'can' refrain from wearing a turban, if 'can' is construed literally. But if the broad cultural/historic meaning of ethnic is the appropriate meaning of the word in the 1976 Act, then a literal reading of the word 'can' would deprive Sikhs and members of other groups defined by reference to their ethnic origins of much of the protection which Parliament evidently intended the Act to afford to them. They 'can' comply with almost any requirement or condition if they are willing to give up their distinctive customs and cultural rules. On the other hand, if ethnic means inherited or unalterable, as the Court of Appeal thought it did, then 'can' ought logically to be read literally. The word 'can' is used with many shades of meaning. In the context of s 1(1)(b)(i) of the 1976 Act it must, in my opinion, have been intended by Parliament to be read not as meaning 'can physically', so as to indicate a theoretical possibility, but as meaning 'can in practice' or 'can consistently with the customs and cultural conditions of the racial group'. The latter meaning was attributed to the word by the Employment Appeal Tribunal in *Price v Civil Service Commission* [1977] IRLR 291, on a construction of the parallel provision in the Sex Discrimination Act 1975. I agree with their construction of the word in that context. Accordingly I am of opinion that the 'No turban' rule was not one with which the second appellant could, in the relevant sense, comply.

'Justifiable'

The word 'justifiable' occurs in s 1(1)(b)(ii). It raises a problem which is, in my opinion, more difficult than the problem of the word 'can'. But in the end I have reached a firm opinion that the respondent has not been able to show that the 'No turban' rule was justifiable in the relevant sense. Regarded purely from the point of view of the respondent, it was no doubt perfectly justifiable. He explained that he had no intention of discriminating against Sikhs. In 1978 the school has about 300 pupils (about 75% boys and 25% girls) of whom over 200 were English, five were Sikhs, 34 Hindus, 16 Persians, six Negroes, seven Chinese and 15 from European countries. The reasons for having a school uniform were largely reasons of practical convenience – to minimize external differences between races and social classes, to discourage the 'competitive fashions' which he said tend to exist in a teenage community, and to present a Christian image of the school to outsiders, including prospective parents. The respondent explained the difficulty for a headmaster of explaining to a non-Sikh pupil why the rules about wearing correct school uniform were enforced against him if they were relaxed in favour of a Sikh. In my view, these reasons could not, either individually or collectively, provide a sufficient justification for the respondent to apply a condition that is prima facie discriminatory under the Act.

An attempted justification of the 'No turban' rule, which requires more serious consideration, was that the respondent sought to run a Christian school, accepting pupils of all religions and races, and that he objected to the turban on the ground that it was an outward manifestation of a non-Christian faith. Indeed, he regarded it as amounting to a challenge to the faith. I have much sympathy with the respondent on this part of the case and I would have been glad to find that the rule was justifiable within the meaning of the statute, if I could have done so. But in my opinion that is impossible. The onus under para (ii) is on the respondent to show that the condition which he seeks to apply is not indeed a necessary condition, but that it is in all circumstances justifiable 'irrespective of the colour, race, nationality or ethnic or national origins of the person to whom it is applied': that is to say that it is justifiable without regard to the ethnic origins of that person. But in this case the principal justification on which the respondent relies is that the turban is objectionable just because it is a manifestation of the second appellant's ethnic origins.

That is not, in my view, a justification which is admissible under para (ii). That kind of justification that might fall within that provision would be one based on public health, as in *Panesar v The Nestles Company Ltd* [1980] IRLR 64, where the Court of Appeal held that a rule forbidding the wearing of beards in the respondent's chocolate factory was justifiable within the meaning of s 1(1)(b)(ii) on hygienic grounds, notwithstanding that the proportion of Sikhs who would [sc conscientiously] comply with it was considerably smaller than the proportion of non-Sikhs who could comply with it. Again, it might be possible for the school to show that a rule insisting upon a fixed diet, which included some dish (for example, port) which some racial groups could not

conscientiously eat was justifiable if the school proved that the cost of providing special meals for the particular group would be prohibitive. Questions of that sort would be questions of fact for the tribunal of fact, and if there was evidence on which it could find the condition to be justifiable its finding would not be liable to be disturbed on appeal.

But in the present case I am of opinion that the respondents have not been able to show that the 'No turban' rule was justifiable.

Before parting with the case I must refer to some observation by the Court of Appeal which suggest that the conduct of the Commission for Racial Equality in this case has been in some way unreasonable or oppressive. Lord Denning MR at p 21 merely expressed regret that the Commission had taken up the case. But Oliver LJ, p 23, used stronger language and suggested that the machinery of the Act had been operated against the respondent as 'an engine of oppression'. Kerr LJ, p 25, referred to notes of an interview between the respondent and an official of the Commission which he said read in part 'more like an inquisition than an interview' and which he regarded as harassment of the respondent.

My Lords, I must say that I regard these strictures on the Commission and its officials as entirely unjustified. The Commission has a difficult task, and no doubt its inquiries will be resented by some and are liable to be regarded as objectionable and inquisitive. But the respondent in this case, who conducted his appeal with restraint and skill, made no complaint of his treatment at the hands of the Commission. He was specifically asked by some of my noble and learned friends to point out any part of the notes of his interview with the Commission's official to which he objected, and he said there were none and that an objection of that sort formed no part of his case.

BIBLIOGRAPHY

Anderson, R, *The Power and the Word*, 1988, London: Paladin.

Anderson, T and Twining, W, *Analysis of Evidence*, 1991, London: Weidenfeld and Nicolson.

Bailey, SH and Gunn, M, *Smith and Bailey on the Modern English Legal System*, 1996, London: Sweet & Maxwell.

Barrass, R, *Students Must Write*, 1995, London: Routledge.

Berger, J, *Ways of Seeing*, 1982, London: BBC Pelican.

Clinch, P, *Using a Law Library*, 1992, London: Blackstone.

Coates, J, *Women, Men and Language*, 1991, London: Longman.

Costanzo, M, *Problem Solving*, 1995, London: Cavendish Publishing.

Cross, R and Harris, JW, *Precedent in English Law*, 1991, Oxford: Clarendon.

Fairclough, N, *Language and Power*, 1989, London: Longman.

French, D, *How to Cite Legal Authorities*, 1996, London: Blackstone.

Goodrich, P, *Languages of Law*, 1990, London: Weidenfeld and Nicolson.

Hargie, O, *A Handbook of Communication Skills*, 1986, London: Croom Helm.

Hartley, TC, *The Foundations of European Community Law*, 1994, Oxford: OUP.

Hawkins, L, Hudson, M and Cornall, R, *The Legal Negotiator*, 1990, London: Longman.

Holland, JA and Webb, J, *Learning Legal Rules*, 1991, London: Blackstone.

Honey, P, *Does Accent Matter?*, 1991, London: Faber & Faber.

Honey, P, *Improve Your People Skills*, 1989, Oxford: Blackwells.

Lee, S and Fox, M, *Learning Legal Skills*, 1991, London: Blackstone.

Maughan, C and Webb, J, *Lawyering Skills and the Legal Process*, 1995, London: Butterworths.

McGovern, D, *Reading*, 1994, Hemel Hempstead: Prentice Hall.

Nash, W, *Rhetoric: the Wit of Persuasion*, 1989, Oxford: Blackwells.

Northledge, A, *The Good Study Guide*, 1995, Milton Keynes: OU Press.

Riley, A, *English for Law*, 1991, London: Macmillan.

Russell, F and Locke, C, *English Law and Language*, 1995, Hemel Hempstead: Phoenix ELT.

Scherr, A, *Client Interviewing for Lawyers*, 1986, London: Sweet & Maxwell.

Tillotson, J, *European Community Law: Text, Cases and Materials*, 2nd edn, 1996, London: Cavendish Publishing.

Trzeciak, J and Mackey, SE, *Study Skills for Academic Writing*, 1994, Hemel Hempstead: Prentice Hall.

Twining, W and Miers, D, *How to do Things with Rules*, 1991, London: Weidenfeld and Nicolson.

White, R and McGovern, D, *Writing*, 1994, Hemel Hempstead: Prentice Hall.

Zander, M, *The Law Making Process*, 1992, London: Weidenfeld and Nicolson.

Zander, M, *Cases and Materials on the English Legal System*, 1992, London: Butterworths.

INDEX